The Political Economy
of Race and Class in
South Africa

The Political Economy of Race and Class in South Africa

Bernard Makhosezwe Magubane

Monthly Review Press
New York and London

Library of Congress Cataloging in Publication Data

Magubane, Bernard.
  The political economy of race and class in South Africa.
  Includes bibliographical references and index.
    1. South Africa—Race relations. 2. South Africa—Economic
conditions. 3. Blacks—South Africa—Employment. I. Title.
DT763.M315   301.45'1'0968   78-13917
ISBN 0-85345-463-9
ISBN 0-85345-506-6 pbk.

Manufactured in the United States of America

10 9 8 7 6 5 4 3 2

Dedicated to Grandma and Grandpa, whose fireside stories about the Zulu War of 1789 and the Bambatha Rebellion of 1906 made an indelible mark on my mind, and to Ma and Pa, who sacrificed every penny to put me through school.

Contents

Preface

The year 1974 was a turning point in the history of Southern Africa, and for the freedom struggle of its oppressed peoples. Events that had seemed only long-term possibilities at the start of 1974 brought fundamental changes to the balance of power in the area. Mozambique and Angola, after five hundred years of Portuguese rule, won independence. In Zimbabwe, the illegal white minority regime was pressured to release African leaders from ten years' detention and to begin serious negotiations for the transfer of power to African majority rule. South Africa's grip on Namibia was shaken by unexpected and unprecedented events, which had begun in 1971 with a strike of thirteen thousand workers that halted the vital copper-mining industry, paralyzed commerce, and crippled public services. Since the World Court's decision of 1971, South Africa has faced mounting pressure to move toward granting Namibia independence. Moreover, South Africa was suspended from the UN General Assembly for the 1974 session.

Inside South Africa, African workers and students rose in anger. The grim totals from the various uprisings of the past three years read like an indictment: according to official statistics, following the student uprising in Soweto there were 499 fatalities, with thousands injured and arrested. When Mozambique's independence was announced, the South African Student Organization (SASO) and the Black Peoples' Congress (BPC) immediately organized rallies to celebrate the new developments. And at the height of South Africa's intervention in Angola the BPC organized a conference and declared its solidarity with the Popular Movement for the Liberation of Angola (MPLA). All these events have crystallized the contradictions and conflicts that had developed in South Africa since the banning of the African National Congress (ANC) and the Pan-African Congress (PAC) in 1960.

Thus, ten years of tireless efforts by South Africa to contain the struggle north of the Zambezi have failed. The Portuguese colonies and Rhodesia—crutches on which white rule stood— have collapsed. Indeed, looking back at the past ten years, one may agree with Burrows Durham:

> It is interesting to observe, and I believe a moral can be drawn from it, that the whole of modern history (which we may date from Erasmus's youth, as being also the time of Columbus's discoveries) is a record of catastrophic defeats for right-wing politics. The popes lost, the peers lost, the kings lost, the emperors, Czars, and Kaiser lost, the führers and duces lost, the Asian Warlords lost, the imperialists are losing. Almost five hundred years of strikes— stubborn, constant, and decisive—proclaim the fact that, short of maiming or annihilation of our race, the members of it are to be supreme upon the planet, with none to molest them and none to rule.

This book is a glimpse both at some of the horrors inflicted upon South African peoples by white rule for the last three hundred years and the struggles the African people have waged that cumulatively brought the events of last year to pass. The intention is not to depict the horrors of white rule for the purpose of evoking pity, but to indicate the necessity for transforming the system of oppression so that we may help establish and create a society in which our children and our children's children will be free from exploitation, deprivation, and ignorance.

The present book is a sociohistorical account of the evolution of racial oppression in South Africa. The vastness of data means that I have had to be selective in presenting themes and facts. I focus more closely on the topic of the exploitation of African labor than upon the empirical features of that history; the object is to show why and how this labor was and is exploited, rather than to present an impeccably factual account. I am more interested in the relations between the facts of black exploitation as they influence the development of racism. The book neither disregards facts nor treats them lightly; but identifying causal relations is a key to the success or failure of an explanation of how racism developed to be what it is in South Africa today.

The present era is one of rapid change. The traditional forces of <u>imperialism</u> are collapsing. As South Africa's white supremacist state experiences political, economical, military, and ideological strains, contradictions are being intensified, and South Africa may well be left only one choice—to call on its imperialist allies to rescue it from its malaise. The racist state's epoch of unchallenged hegemony has given way to a period of doubt, uncertainty, and desperation. It is thus more evident now than ever before that South Africa's white supremacist state can neither regain the lost historical initiative nor reverse current developments.

With the development of the main social contradictions of white supremacist rule and the capitalist mode of production it serves, the oppressed of South Africa are increasingly showing they are the only force capable of overcoming the system that exploits them. The course of recent events and history testify to the tenacity and consistency of the African struggle.

The white settlers* today are the descendants and defenders of those who forcibly robbed the African people of their land three centuries ago. The lawlessness that prevailed then has not ceased, as is blatantly illustrated by the mass removal of Africans from the so-called black spots, or *urban areas*. Today, black and

---

* Throughout the book I refer to the whites as settlers and not as white South Africans; there is a philosophical reason for this. Before the Africans became "Kafirs," "Natives," "Bantus," and now "Blacks," they were citizens and owners of the land later usurped by their European conquerors. Both the statelessness and degradation of the African people emerged in one and the same historical process—in the act of conquest, the forcible robbery of their means of subsistence. Their indigence today is a result of the most cruel lawlessness known to human history. Having taken this into account, the whole meaning of being called Kafir, Native, Bantu, or Black, rather than being called African, changes the moral and legal status of the white settlers' claim to the South African state.

white have irreconcilable claims to the South African state. Only the restructuring of the entire economic and social system, as spelled out in the Freedom Charter adopted in 1956 by the ANC and its allies, could create the social climate in which a new start could be made to develop a truly South African society embracing all its peoples. The African people are struggling not only against the illegal forms of the white settlers' social practice, but also against the all-embracing, universal exploitation they experience under capitalism. They are challenging a history of violation that goes far beyond the juridical, into that which is economic and social as well.

Does this mean that the white settlers—some of whom have been in South Africa for more than ten generations—should be driven into the sea? Certainly not. But the system which has fed and sanctioned their inhumanity has to be destroyed root and branch. Progressive African nationalism is infused with a higher moral order—for its advocates have already been through the crucible of injustice—which enables progressives to realize that a good society must be based on truth rather than expediency. Their struggle has purged them of narrow opportunism; it has enhanced selflessness and dedication to justice.

This book was written as yet another installment in the growing list of books whose purpose is to help chart a clear ideological and analytical direction; it is based on the belief that the movement's strategy must be based on a correct historical understanding. I have focused on the past in order to give the movement a coherent developmental perspective. I have attempted to examine closely the myriad social, political, and economic changes and struggles that give meaning to the present. I have tried to show that the present is both a process and a system of definite historical developments, whose dynamics and mechanisms must be understood if the movement is to succeed. What social reality is mirrored in the conflicting ideas and sentiments of whites and Africans?

I am indebted to many friends who read, corrected, and made suggestions as I wrote. Professors H. J. and Ray Simons, with whom I taught at the University of Zambia between 1967 and 1970, were my initial inspiration. Then there are the members of the African National Congress and its allies, with whom I have had a long and close relationship. Among these were the first cadres of *Umkhonto We Sizwe* ("Spear of the Nation"), who crossed the Zambezi in the fateful July of 1967 and whose courage was a source of tremendous inspiration for me in undertaking this study. The acting president-general of the ANC, O. R. Tambo, gave me invaluable suggestions and encouragement. Friends of mine (too many to mention), including both students and faculty from the University of California in Los Angeles and the University of Connecticut at Storrs, have made immense contributions to my ideas. Let me take this opportunity to thank in particular James Faris and Martin Legassick; I benefited a great deal from discussions with them. Faris, above all, was instrumental in my coming to the University of Connecticut, and he has read and commented on several chapters in manuscript, in spite of his own work load.

I must express my gratitude to the Research Foundation of the University of Connecticut for a grant in 1972 and to Selma Wollman, to whom I am indebted for typing the several drafts of the manuscript.

Last but not least there is my wife, Thembie, and my daughters, Gugu, Bongie, Vukani, and Zine, who had to suffer through it all. Needless to say, these individuals are not in any way responsible for the errors—those are all mine. I feel very lonely just now, for my assumptions challenge authorities on South Africa, and my Marxist methodology is anathema to most liberal minds. This means a certain estrangement from popular wisdom and academic sanction. So be it! But the work is directed to those in struggle, and with those compatriots I feel no estrangement, but only kinship.

Amandla
Bernard Makhosezwe Magubane
September 1978

1

The Problem and Its Matrix: Theoretical and Methodological Issues

Our hypothesis is that racial exploitation and race prejudice developed among Europeans with the rise of capitalism, and that because of the worldwide ramifications of capitalism, all racial antagonisms can be traced back to the policies and attitudes of the leading capitalist people, the white people of Europe and North America.

Racism has its roots in Capitalism.

—Oliver C. Cox

The scientific study of racial inequality and oppression in the world in general and South Africa in particular has yet to transcend the state of idealist improvisation. To study the evolution of racially based inequalities is not exclusively of academic interest, for without a proper conception of the history of racism in the modern world, it is difficult to see how strategies can be devised that will solve this burning question. The plight of the black people of South Africa is intimately bound up with the history of white settlement in their lands, and the South African social formation itself represents a stage in the evolution of the world capitalist system. In order to undertake an analysis of racial inequality and exploitation in South Africa, we must know its historical roots.

In South Africa, a pyramid of wealth and social power exists as a fact of daily experience. Whites, who constitute less than 20 percent of the nation's population, consume more than 60 per-

1

health care —eg. infant mortality ↑

cent of its income, have legal occupancy rights to 87 percent of its land, and fill most of its skilled and semi-skilled occupations. Inequality of revenue and wealth is not only an economic fact; it implies inequality of life chances. Infant mortality statistics for Africans in South Africa have not been available since 1957, but it is estimated that the rate is five times that for whites and three times that for Asians. Estimates range from 200 to 450 infant deaths per 1000 live births.[1] A 1966 survey reported that "half the children born in a typical African reserve in South Africa died before reaching the age of five years." None of this is surprising given the distribution of physicians for the different "races": in 1972 there were 1:400 for Whites; 1:900 for Asians; 1:6,200 for Coloureds; and 1:44,000 for Africans.[2]

Every country is unique, but South Africa is so unique that it almost defies imagination. Despite the proclaimed policy of separate development, the African is everywhere: in the fields, in the factories, in the mines, in the shops, and in the offices. Every white person, no matter how poor he or she may be, keeps an African servant. The whites have reserved for Africans those hard and dirty tasks that they have refused to mechanize. South Africa's achievement in economic development, sports, or any other field of endeavor cannot be conceived of without the existence of the forced labor of Africans.

How, then, do we conceptualize inequality in South Africa? Racial inequality similar to that existing in South Africa has been the fate of other people in the so-called Third World. To understand the social inequality in South Africa, we must take into account the inequality between a small handful of advanced capitalist countries (considered thus from the point of view of capital accumulation and industrialization) and the so-called underdeveloped (colonial and semi-colonial) countries, where the majority of humanity lives. Not only are different economic functions assigned to different people within countries, but they are also assigned to the countries themselves within the world system. These inequalities are perpetuated by the principal social and legal institutions of the epoch.

Thus, although there are many ways to define and study racial inequality, in this book we shall conceptualize it as an aspect of imperialism and colonialism, concepts that will be used analytically to refer roughly to the same phenomena: the economic, political, and cultural domination of the African people by the white settlers. We will use the term imperialism to refer to the specific relation between a subjugated society and its alien rulers, and colonialism to refer to the social structures created within the colonized society by imperialist relationships.[3] While colonialism has an ancient history, the colonialism of the last five centuries is closely associated with the birth and maturation of the capitalist socioeconomic system. The pursuit and acquisition of colonies, their political and economic domination, accompanied the mercantile revolution and the founding of capitalism.[4] To study the development of capitalism is thus the best way to study race inequality, for to do so places socioeconomic relationships at the heart of the problem, and shows how underdevelopment and racial inequalities developed together. The economic, political, and ideological motives that have structured capitalist relations of production in the modern world cannot be separated. Capitalism required an expansionist policy of conquest and exploitation which set off a cumulative process that produced its own ideology: this ideology in turn became a force capable of orienting choices and determining decisions. The ideology of racism, called into life and fed by the expansionist and exploitative socioeconomic relations of capitalist imperialism, became a permanent stimulus for the ordering of unequal and exploitative relations of production along "racial" lines, and further demanded justification of these relations. The seemingly "autonomous" existence of racism today does not lessen the fact that it was initiated by the needs of capitalist development or that these needs remain the dominant factor in racist societies.

What is important, then, is to explain the phenomenon of racism, to clarify its manifestations in capitalist society, with all that this involves with regard to local variations. The essence of modern capitalism is the ruthless transfer of wealth from the colonized to the colonizer, from black to white, from worker to

capitalist. An economic system must not only produce and transfer wealth, however, but must produce political and ideological
systems that facilitate this transfer. As Louis Ruchames writes:

> During the Middle Ages and extending into the early modern
> period, racial thought was used to explain differences between
> economic and social classes, especially between the peasantry and
> the nobility. Some thinkers regarded the peasants as descended
> from Ham, the accursed son of Noah, and the knights from the
> Trojan Heroes, who had presumably settled in England, Germany,
> and France after their defeat. In the seventeenth century Count de
> Boulainvilliers, a spokesman for the French nobility, declared the
> nobles to be descended from their Germanic conquerers and the
> masses of the people from the subject Celts and Normans.[5]

As capitalism expanded, "racial" thought was applied to the
people in the colonies. To quote Ruchames again:

> With the increase in slavery and the slave trade, and more numer-
> ous encounters of Europeans with Indians and Negroes, European
> scholars began to give greater attention to race and racial differ-
> ence. It is interesting to note that it was only during the modern
> period that the term "race" came into use. The English term was
> first used at the beginning of the sixteenth century, the Italian
> *razza,* the Portuguese *raca,* and the French *race* were first used in
> the fifteenth century.[6]

The history of colonialism and imperialism is the history of
the development of cultural institutions and of ideas of class
and/or racial inequality in the newly created societies. Almost
without exception, the gross inequalities in white settler societies
came to be explained by the assertion that the colonized are
biologically and culturally inferior. *Everyman's Encyclopedia* describes this process as follows:

> The growth of modern racialist theories that hold that there are
> inherent differences between "superior" and "inferior" races is
> very recent. It seems to date from the days of slavery in America,
> when it was necessary to produce reasons for the continued subjec-
> tion of economically valuable slaves. Much the same is true of
> South Africa today, where Calvinist doctrines have given such
> scientifically false beliefs added support. It is noticeable that in
> many Catholic countries there has been little racialism, since their

doctrine has held to the inherent equality of all men. This fact adds support to the view that "race" relations are essentially economic and social, and that "race" as such has little to do with the real situation.[7]

Though the growth of ideas of racial inequality reflects a real process in capitalist society, it must not be understood as a simple or mechanical reflection. The structures of inequality acquire meaning only through human definition, and this can include a wide range of mediations and individual perceptions. The study of racial inequality therefore calls for the analysis of a multitude of processes, some historical, some psychological, others religious and philosophical; this in turn necessitates the use of concepts grounded in history and the rejection of those based on idealistic assumptions about human nature. Ruchames writes of the early stages of these beliefs:

> One of the important events in the history of racial thought took place in 1550 and 1551 at Valladolid, Spain, in a debate between Juan Genes de Sepulveda and Las Casas on the question of whether the Aristotelian theory, that some men are slaves by nature, could be applied to the Indians. Sepulveda argued that the Indians were rude and inferior beings by nature, with no capacity for political life, whose inferiority required that the superior Spaniards rule over them. Las Casas argued that the Indians were rational beings, superior to many ancient peoples, even the Greeks and Romans, and therefore worthy of freedom. Neither contestant gained a clear-cut victory. Although Lewis Hanke argues that Las Casas' publicly stated view strengthened those who believed "that all the people of the world are human beings" and represented "one more painful and faltering step . . . along the road of justice for all races," he admits that during the seventeenth century the Aristotelian view of race "reigned almost supreme in Europe and America."[8]

Translated, the Aristotelian theory states that society consists of people who differ not only in skin color but in ability. Members of certain races are masters because their achievements re-echo across the world; others are capable of nothing. They can serve, at best, as fertilizers for history, tilling the soil, digging the mines, and doing other chores for the European bourgeois civilization. W. E. B. DuBois, witness to the rise of imperialism, concluded in 1915:

> Most persons have accepted the tacit but clear modern philosophy which assigns to the white race alone the hegemony of the world and assumes that other races, and particularly the Negro race, will either be content to serve the interests of whites or die out before the all-conquering march. This philosophy is the child of the African slave trade and the expansion of Europe during the nineteenth century.[9]

Conceptually and theoretically, the meaning of this development is clear. The structures of racial inequality that developed during the nineteenth century were attempts to define relations between black and white in the era of capitalist hegemony. In *Black Reconstruction,* DuBois described the world order imperialism was creating and the role assigned to black, brown, and yellow labor:

> That dark and vast sea of human labor in China and India, the South Seas and all Africa; in the West Indies and Central America and in the United States—that great majority of mankind, on whose bent and broken backs rest today the founding stones of modern industry—shares a common destiny; it is despised and rejected by race and color; paid a wage below the level of decent living; driven, beaten, prisoned and enslaved in all but name; spawning the world's raw material and luxury—cotton, wool, coffee, tea, cocoa, palm oil, fibers, spices, rubber, silks, lumber, copper, gold, diamonds, leather—how shall we end the list and where? All these are gathered up at prices lowest of the low, manufactured, transformed and transported at fabulous gain; and the resultant wealth is distributed and displayed and made the basis of world power and universal dominion and armed arrogance in London and Paris, Berlin and Rome, New York and Rio de Janeiro.[10]

A theory of racially based inequality must first grasp the general character of the epoch opened by the so-called voyages of discovery during the mercantile order. But beyond this, each society so touched exhibits a particular blend of diverse "racial" groups, a particular mix of their activities, and a particular patterning of their socioeconomic relationships. The ideological instant of racism reflects the specificity of each society as an historical entity. The concrete differences between one country and another within the same political epoch must, therefore, be taken into account and explained. Instead of employing timeless categories to house social phenomena of different epochs, we must understand the dynamics of racism under specific conditions. The purpose of this book is thus to integrate sociological, economic, historical, and political approaches in an effort to comprehend the development of inequality and racism during South Africa's tragic and complex history. The approach is dictated by the belief that explanation is a statement of process and its historical determinations. "Every sociology worthy of the name," wrote C. Wright Mills, "is historical sociology."[11]

The South Africa Case

Given the complexity of South African history, the scope of this inquiry must be severely limited, and I will concentrate on what Perry Anderson has called the key events—those that appear to have the most explanatory value as far as the development of South Africa's socioeconomic order is concerned. These are: (1) the settlement by the Dutch in the seventeenth century and by the English in the nineteenth century; (2) the subsequent conquest and incorporation of the African into the evolving settler society, first into agriculture and then into mining; (3) the national struggles of the Africans, both before and after conquest; (4) the discovery of diamonds in 1867 and gold in 1886, and the role of the gold industry in the capitalist monetary system; (5) the reorganization of agriculture, which resulted in the depopulation of the countryside and the creation of the "poor whites"; (6) the growth of urban-based industry and the competition which ensued between the black and white proletariat; (7) Britain's granting of political power to the white settlers in 1910; and (8) the role assigned to South Africa in the imperialist division of labor. By examining the interaction among these events, I hope to demonstrate the coherence of South African economics, politics, religion, and culture.

The history of the white settler colonies in South Africa, as distinguished from their ideology, clearly illustrates the connection between the imperative of colonization—the desire to take land—and that of capitalism—the desire to exploit black labor. Because of its climate, South Africa, like the United States, Canada, Australia, and New Zealand, was to become a settler state. Africans were to be tolerated only if they would minister to the needs of whites; otherwise there was no need to spare their lives. The development of forced labor in South Africa could thus take place only after conquest. Karl Marx has explained what happens when a people is conquered:

> A conquering people divides the land among the conquerors, establishing thereby a certain division and form of landed property and determining the character of production, or it turns the conquered people into slaves and thus makes slave labour the basis of production. . . . Or legislation perpetuates land ownership in large families or distributes labour as a hereditory privilege and thus fixes it in castes.[12]

And just before the turn of the nineteenth century, J. A. Hobson, looking back at the history of the colonization movement, commented:

> Whenever superior races settle on lands where lower races can be profitably used for manual labour in agriculture, mining and domestic work, the latter do not tend to die out, but to form a servile class. This is the case, not only in tropical countries where white men cannot form real colonies, working and rearing families with safety and efficiency, and where hard manual work, if done at all, must be done by "coloured men," but even in countries where white men can settle, as in part of South Africa and of the southern portion of the United States.[13]

British imperialism developed a peculiar relationship to its colonies. The "white" dominions represented colonial settlements in the old Roman sense, a set of economies dependent on, and complementary to, that of Britain itself. Each colony was to exchange those primary products suitable to its geographical location: wool for Australia, meat and dairy products for New Zealand, wheat and beef for Canada, and gold and diamonds for South Africa.[14] Thus the South African economy of the last quarter of the nineteenth century was made to conform to the dictates of a world economy then dominated by Great Britain. Until recently, South Africa's development was largely conditioned by the objective circumstances of its dependence on gold mining, an industry controlled by British imperialist interests and described by one writer as a "state within a state." From an analytical point of view, one aim of this book is to determine the expression of this dependence on foreign capital in the internal organization of the country, and, more concretely, to analyze the articulation of the system of production and the resulting class relations.

As Britain gradually lost its hegemony, every major South African nonferrous-metal mining company, as well as those mining diamonds, came to be penetrated by foreign capital—if not British, then French or German. Most important, however, the mining industry sets the standard for the exploitation of African labor. This must be emphasized because the theory of South African race relations is cursed by a narrow focus on the character and experiences of the Afrikaner, rather than on those systemic aspects of imperialism that foster inequality and racism. Before Afrikaner racism acquired a structure and a consciousness of itself, the social processes that it would take advantage of were already in operation.

The first step in formulating a theory of inequality and racism in South Africa is thus to recover a sense of Britain's colonial legacy, against which to compare the thrust of contemporary development. Without knowing what British imperialism left behind, we lose sight of how the current system developed. Deliberately structured by racial laws and socioeconomic arrangements, and propelled by past and present exploitation, the system continues almost inexorably to reproduce racial inequality.

African labor was exploited in a constantly changing environment as the development of mines and farms, of secondary

industries and towns changed the methods by which the conquerors secured their surplus. The mountain of labor legislation,
beginning with the master and slave codes, is an indispensable
raw material for understanding the politics of racial inequality in these changing circumstances. But if explanation is
the goal, then a discussion of the statutes cannot be limited to
description and cataloguing: a particular piece of legislation can
only be understood in the light of changing forms of labor
appropriation, from the appropriation of surplus labor in
slave-owning societies, to the appropriation of the surplus product under feudalism, to the appropriation of surplus value
under capitalism. The nineteenth-century colonial wars in South
Africa were not intended to "clean the lands" of the original
inhabitants, as happened in the United States. Instead, they gave
the white settlers the best lands and a considerable measure of
control over African labor. Herein lies the origin of the historic
contradiction of South Africa today: caught between wanting to
exploit African labor, but not wanting the physical presence of
Africans, apartheid has emerged not merely as an ideology, but
as a myth that whites have a prior claim to parts of the land.

The practice of using Africans as cheap labor was openly
encouraged by the British prior to 1910. In the 1880s, Earl Grey,
secretary of state for war and colonies, told the mineowners
that the "natives" had to be induced to seek employment in the
mines, and to work willingly for long periods of more or less
continuous service.[15] This was not an isolated recommendation.
In a memo to General Smuts entitled "Notes on a Suggested
Policy Towards Coloured People and Natives," Lord Selborne,
high commissioner for South Africa and governor of the Transvaal and Orange River Colony from 1905 to 1910, discussed how
to establish a hierarchical structure that would ensure a cheap
labor supply:

> *Coloured people.* Our object should be to teach the Coloured people
> to give their loyal support to the white population. It seems to me
> sheer folly to classify them with Natives, and by treating them as
> Natives to force them away from their natural allegiance to the
> whites and into making common cause with the Natives. If they are
> so forced, in the time of trouble they will furnish exactly those

leaders which the Natives could not furnish for themselves. It is, therefore, in my opinion, unwise to think of treating them as Natives; and it would be as unjust as unwise. There are many Coloured people who are quite white inside, though they may be coloured outside. There are some, indeed, who are quite white outside also. The problem of the treatment of the Coloured people is, indeed, sadly complicated by the fact that they vary in every shade of character and colour from pure white inside and outside to pure black inside and outside.

I suggest that the wise policy is to give them the benefit of their white blood—not to lay the stress on the black blood, but to lay the stress on the white blood, and to make any differentiation of treatment between them and whites the exception and not the rule. A case for such differentiation would only arise when a Coloured man showed by his manner of living, e.g., by the practice of polygamy, that he had reverted to the tribal type.

Natives. The objects which the Government must have in their Native policy are: (i) to preserve the peace of the country, for nothing is so demoralizing or injurious to its true welfare as a native war; (ii) to ensure the gradual destruction of the tribal civilization among the Natives; (iii) to ensure the gradual destruction of the tribal system, which is incompatible with civilization. An important feature of this policy will be teaching the Natives to work. A large proportion of them do work now, but mostly in a desultory and inefficient manner. The object must be to teach them to work as continually and effectively as the whites are supposed to but do not always do.[16]

Once the exploitative capitalist structure had been installed, it continued to develop, accentuating its typical features. Perry Anderson has described the imperial political style:

Imperialism automatically sets a premium on a patrician political style: as a pure system of alien domination, it always, within the limits of safety, seeks to maximize the existential difference between the ruling and the ruled race, to create a magical and impossible gulf between two fixed essences. This need everywhere produces a distinctive colonial ceremonial and a colonial vice-regency. Domestic domination can be realized with a "popular" and "egalitarian" appearance, alien domination never.[17]

The ideological argument for the installation of a white supremacist state was admirably summed up by Lord Selborne at a degree-giving day at the University of Cape Town in 1908:

> It is impossible for us, who once sprung from races which were in contact with the Roman Civilization before the Christian Era, to look to the question from the same point of view as the Bantu races who are totally different. So far as we can form an opinion, our forefathers, 2,000 years ago . . . were distinctly less barbarous than were the Bantu races when they came into contact with white men less than 100 years ago. Nor has the Bantu hitherto evinced any capacity from their first contact with it. . . . Speaking generally so far as we can foresee, the Bantu can never catch up with the Europeans, whether in intellect or in strength of character. As a race, the white race has received a superior intellect and mental endowment. The white man is the racial adult, the black man is the racial child.[18]

The political history of South Africa in the decade prior to the formation of the Union demonstrates quite clearly that "race," while remaining a biological category, under exploitative conditions becomes a social category and an important element in the functioning of the socioeconomic formation. The structures of racial inequality in South Africa were the creation of people who systematically and deliberately fashioned conditions to separate blacks from whites in order to exploit the former. The architects of the Constitution of the Union of South Africa decided that political, economic, and social power was to be an exclusive European preserve, a decision that foreclosed the possibility of building a nonracial society based on cooperation between the races.

The creation of South Africa as a white dominion had another aspect: it provided a safety valve for growing class contradictions within England itself. Lenin quotes Cecil Rhodes as saying in 1895:

> I was in the East End of London [a working-class quarter] yesterday and attended a meeting of the unemployed. I listened to the wild speeches, which were just a cry for "bread, bread!" and on my way home, I pondered over the scene and I became more than ever convinced of the importance of imperialism. . . . My cherished idea is a solution for the social problem, i.e., in order to

save the 40,000,000 inhabitants of the United Kingdom from a
bloody civil war, we colonial statesmen must acquire new lands to
settle the surplus population, to provide new markets for the
goods produced in the factories and mines. The Empire, as I have
always said, is a bread and butter question. If you want to avoid
civil war, you must become imperialists.[19]

Although a surfeit of population and capital needed an
international outlet, and although South Africa provided such
an arena, the British were only able to establish their domination
because of historical and social circumstances. The Africans
were conquered by force and then faced with a formidable
battery of cultural symbols and weapons with which the conquerors justified their superiority and mystified their victims.
Karl Liebknecht discussed the role of the monopolization of
power by the colonizer:

The deciding factor in every social relation of power is, in the last
resort, the superiority of physical force, which, as a social phenomenon, does not appear in the form of the greater physical strength
of some individuals. . . . On an average, one human being equals
another, and a purely numerical proportion decides who is in the
majority. . . .

Economic superiority helps directly to displace and to confuse
the numerical proportion, because economic pressure not only
influences the height of the intellectual and moral stage and,
thereby, the recognition of class interest, but also produces a tendency to act in conformity with more or less well understood class
principles. *That the political machinery of the governing class lends its
increased power to "correct" the numerical proportion in favor of the ruling
group of interests is taught us by all the well-known institutions such as*:
the police, justice, schools, and the church which must also be
included here. These institutions are set up through the political
machinery and employed in an administrative capacity. The first
two work chiefly by threats, intimidation and violence; the
schools chiefly by blocking up all those channels by which class-
consciousness might reach the brain and the heart; the church
most effectively by blinding the people to present evils and awakening their desire for the joys of a future life, and by terrifying
them with threats of the torture chambers in hell.[20]

The inheritors of the colonial state used their power to deprive the Africans of those economic, political, and cultural attributes that whites provide for themselves. The oppressed "racial" groups and classes were denied the chance of development and then cursed for being backward and primitive. As Africans nonetheless made advances, the legislation of inequality assumed ever more dramatic, if ridiculous, dimensions. General Smuts described the situation facing whites in South Africa bluntly:

> Though the problem of mixed populations is not a new one in history, it nevertheless presents certain novel aspects in South Africa and the rest of the continent. Normally, it takes the form of a minority living in the midst of an overwhelming mass of other people, often under conditions of some disability. Here in South Africa, however, the small minority of whites lives not under the normal conditions of sufferance, but actually rule the majority with an iron hand. They have retained in their possession full initiative insofar as tactical power and intellectual advantage is concerned and they have clung aggressively to what they consider their rights in wealth and leadership.[21]

The white settlers never created a sense of "legitimacy," but only exercised dominance. The tendency of those who do this is to occupy an ever larger place in society, their insecurity propelling them to build their "security" upon a barrage of laws. Domination and coercion are the means whereby imperial capital violates those from whose labor it is derived. Racial laws are the means by which potentially violent class relations are contained and masked. Not only was a belief in racial inferiority indispensable to the superexploitation of black labor, but the social degradation embodied in the inequities of social, political, and economic impoverishment made racism imperative. Frantz Fanon showed that a colonial society functions because the colonists monopolize coercive violence to facilitate the exploitation and submission of the colonized. The use of violence aims to keep the "natives" enslaved and at arm's length; it seeks to dehumanize them.

The form of racial violence in South Africa was in part dictated by the fact that the white settlers formed a minority. The growth of the state's military apparatus is directly related to the escalating class and national struggles of the African people. How the war between two groups claiming the same territory and means of production, and bound together so intimately in the capitalist economy, will be resolved is a question of far-reaching theoretical and practical importance. To the extent that bourgeois theories of racial oppression neglect or minimize the role of force in general, and its structural and systemic implications for the exploitation and oppression of the African in particular, they must be judged inadequate.

South African society has posed a theoretical challenge to those social scientists interested in racial inequality. For some, the challenge has been to identify the key factor distinguishing race and class; for some, it has been to seek the underlying causes of racism, often seen as a "moral dilemma" that cries out for a solution, preferably one that does not apportion blame. Others have tried to show the sequence of events that has led to the present impasse, in correct order and sufficient, even exhausting, detail; often every "factor" becomes of equal importance. Still others prefer to find a suprahistorical category that will catch, in a snapshot, the structural relationships of South African society.

But racism is not an abstraction; nor is it its own justification. The racial structure of South African society arose from the severest exploitation and contempt, guaranteed by power. Anyone who wants to change the structure of racial oppression must understand its fundamental nature, its historical formation, and its manipulation by the rulers. Racial oppression and class exploitation are inextricably intertwined in the modern world; they cannot be neatly separated for the sake of theoretical purity. Kwame Nkrumah has described the dialectic between race and class with clarity and accuracy:

> Each historical situation develops its own dynamics. The close links between class and race developed in Africa alongside capitalist exploitation. Slavery, the master-servant relationship, and cheap labour were basic to it. The classic example is South Africa, where Africans experience a double exploitation—both on the ground of

colour and of class. Similar conditions exist in the U.S.A., the Caribbean, in Latin America, and in other parts of the world where the nature of the development of productive forces has resulted in a racist class structure. In these areas, even shades of colour count—the degree of blackness being a yardstick by which social status is measured.[22]

While a racist social structure is not inherent in the colonial situation, it is inseparable from capitalist economic development. In a racist-capitalist power structure, capitalist exploitation and race oppression are inextricably linked; the removal of one ensures the removal of the other.

We must thus seek the foundation of racism and not select those symptoms and phases of its manifestation that suit our ideological predisposition. The concept of class is useful not because it is "true," but because it correctly identifies the basis of exploitation in capitalist society; it directs our inquiry to the fundamentals of racism as an instrument for extracting surplus value from the laborer and of keeping the working people divided. The divisions in South Africa may appear racial in form, but their economic content is characteristic of all capitalist and settler societies—Ireland should suffice as an example. A class, or a coalition of classes with some common interest, stands in partial or complete antagonism to the nonpossessing classes. This is true in South Africa whether we look at ownership of land, industry, and commerce, or at the distribution of income between blacks and whites. The coalition of socially and politically dominant classes uses its power to preserve and extend the mode of production on which its income depends. And while for the white rulers Africans exist only as labor power, for the white workers Africans are considered (rightly or wrongly) a threat to their economic security, because it is in part derived from and guaranteed by the superexploitation of Africans. Racism as an ideological system had to be cultivated by the politically conscious classes to subvert class unity between black and white labor.

Such an analysis runs counter to that of the social and cultural pluralists, who see the economy not as a leading factor in the historical process but as one among many of its elements. The pluralist assumption inevitably leads to subjectivism, as social scientists arbitrarily select those factors which they believe to be pertinent to a given case.

South Africa is not a plural society; it is a society with a dual labor market: a primary (white) market of relatively secure, well-paid jobs, and a secondary (black) market of insecure, filthy, low-paid jobs. African workers are confined to a marginal, yet indispensable, role by fraud, violence, and a system of institutionalized racism that protects "the white masters of the world."[23] The evolution of racism in South Africa covers six qualitatively distinct phases, which can be distinguished even though they cannot be separated in fact. The first phase extended from 1652 to 1806, and was the period of rule by the Dutch East India Company. Cattle and land provided the only important resources for both white and black pastoralists, and racism expressed itself in genocidal struggle over their possession. The second period ran from 1806 to the discovery of gold in the Witwatersrand in 1884. It was characterized by the insatiable need of British capitalism for markets and raw materials, including mineral wealth. Britain subsidized white settlers on the plantations, and Africans were progressively dispossessed of their best lands and incorporated as instruments of labor for the settlers.

The third phase (the final colonial phase) was reached in the last quarter of the nineteenth century when, as the other capitalist nations caught up with Britain, the world began to be divided among the European powers. The era of modern imperialism was ushered in. To consolidate its rule, Britain was forced to launch a series of wars of conquest, ending with the constitution of South Africa as a British dominion in 1910. The fourth phase, which lasted until 1948, was the one in which the new dominion tried to find its identity. It was characterized not only by two world wars, but also by the consolidation of white supremacy and the ascendancy of Afrikaner political and economic power, the full-blown exploitation of the country's mineral wealth, and the development of secondary industries.

The fifth phase began with the coming to political power of the Afrikaner government in 1948, and saw it begin the process of shaping the capitalist economy in its favor. The emancipation of colonies elsewhere in Africa from alien rule aroused great fears among the white settlers and led them to adopt increasingly oppressive forms of rule. It was during this period that the armed struggle for national liberation began. Thus the character and content of Afrikaner rule was significantly influenced by the international climate and by the Africans' struggle for their own political emancipation.

(6)   The sixth phase takes us into the present; it began with the demise of Portuguese rule in Angola and Mozambique, the consequences of which are still unfolding.

The aim of this book is to begin the study of the economic, political, and social variables that have defined South African social history and that have been ignored or played down in most studies of South Africa's racism. It suffers from the shortcomings of work done with a sense of urgency and in not altogether favorable circumstances. It also suffers from a lack of first-hand documentary research on my part. Nevertheless, I am convinced that the kind of work that I have attempted is long overdue: we cannot wait until there is "enough" empirical research or until our circumstances improve. Further, in studying South Africa, one does not begin from nothing. There is a wealth of existing empirical knowledge and theoretical interpretation that must be examined from a different angle. The known facts can be interpreted with hitherto avoided theoretical tools.

The book is divided into seven sections: the first (chapters 2 and 3) deals in a synoptic way with the values and ideals of the societies that were in South Africa and with those that established their presence there in the seventeenth century, and with the social meaning of conquest and defeat; the second (chapters 4 and 5) deals with the political economy of the gold-mining industry, and with the migrant labor and "native reserve" systems; the third (chapters 5 and 6) discusses urbanization and the growth of manufacturing and commerce; the fourth (chapter 8) deals with the role of imperialism in the political economy of South Africa; the fifth (chapter 9) with apartheid and the class nature of Afrikaner nationalism; and the sixth (chapter 10) with African nationalism. The seventh (chapter 11) deals with the national and class struggles that characterize the period since 1948. At each point I concentrate on the <u>demand for African labor in the developing capitalist system of production.</u> The various sections are in a sense autonomous and there are thus inevitably some repeated arguments and restated assumptions, although in different contexts. The chapters, written polemically, are directed against the thoughtless apologists for South Africa whose interpretations are widespread in the works of liberal scholars.

2

The Impact of the Boer and British Societies on African Societies in the Eighteenth and Nineteenth Centuries: A Synopsis

In understanding the genesis of modern South African society it is of the greatest importance to know that the land beyond the Cape's borders was not the open land which lay before the Australian squatter. It was already an area of settlement, of settlement by a great Bantu population. Much of the energy and determination of the Boers was used more against the natives than against Nature. It is here that lies the true story of South African settlement in this period. Out of those raw materials of sun and grass, of white man, what new environment and what new community would be built?

—C. W. DeKiewiet

The Dutch occupation of the Cape of Good Hope in 1652 began a process that continued even after the takeover of the Cape Colony by Britain in 1806. Whereas Africans occupied their land in accordance with precapitalist traditions, the European settlers were determined to occupy the same land in accordance with the laws of capitalist property. The struggle for control of land and labor determined the political and economic status of the African in the settlers' scheme of things.

In this chapter, I discuss the Dutch and English colonists who arrived in South Africa in 1652 and 1806. What moral and material interests did these settlers represent? In particular, what determined the use of African labor in settler societies?

How did the imperatives of the mercantile-commercial and capitalist-imperialist systems operate to create the white-dominated society we know today? Discussing the role of overseas activity in the fifteenth and sixteenth centuries, Ernest Mandel writes:

> In the decisive formative period of the capitalist mode of production, extending from the sixteenth to the end of the eighteenth century, the creation of the world market was of crucial importance. . . . All through this period of the birth of capitalism the two forms of surplus-value appeared at each step. On the one hand, it was the outcome of the surplus labour of the wage workers hired by the capitalists; on the other, it was the outcome of values stolen, plundered, seized by tricks, pressure or violence from the overseas peoples with whom the western world had made contact. From the conquest and pillage of Mexico and Peru by the Spaniards to the sacking of Indonesia by the Portuguese and the Dutch and the ferocious exploitation of India by the British, the history of the sixteenth and eighteenth centuries is an unbroken chain of deeds of brigandage which were so many *acts of international concentration of values and capital in Western Europe,* the enrichment of which was paid for, in the literal sense of the word, by the impoverishment of the plundered areas.[1]

The socioeconomic and political-ideological factors which characterize the epoch of the decline of feudalism and the rise of capitalism constitute the background in which the historically rooted attitudes the European colonist had about other groups were shaped. Even more, these attitudes were buttressed by the military imperatives of the societies that came into contact. In the numerous conflicts that finally brought about the collapse of feudalism, Europe had produced a sophisticated war technology. This and a new body of social and economic institutions multiplied the capacity for European expansion and for the integration of the entire world into one mercantile capitalist system.

Given the European's technological and military superiority, what was achieved by arms was translated into a political and ideological conflict that assumed the intellectual and moral superiority of the conquerors. Inherently exploitative relations began to be explained as inevitable consequences of biological inequality between black and white peoples. To ensure the structures of inequality, Africans were treated as, and trained to become, unequal. Colonial imperialism necessitated that Africans be deprived of power, opportunity, and reward for their labor, and African societies fell into a condition of deliberately arrested development. The inherent imperatives of these processes affected relations between people of different "races" and constitute the background on which the legal and psychological supremacy of white over black was based.

To understand the social attitudes characteristic of Dutch and English settlers today, we need to understand something about the class structure of South African society in the eighteenth and nineteenth centuries, we need to know something about the transfer of political and economic practices from Europe, and we need to study the changes in the productive forces of capitalism in this period to understand their influence on the political system of the settler societies. First, a brief look at the African societies the Europeans found.

African Societies

It is impossible as well as unnecessary to offer a complete description of the various societies in South Africa in the seventeenth century. Prior to the advent of white people in South Africa, the indigenous inhabitants were organized into three basic modes of production consistent with the level of their material development. There were the hunters and herders who inhabited the western Cape. They spoke the click languages, and the white colonists pejoratively called them "Hottentots" and "Bushmen." The more correct designations, which will be used here, are *Khoikhoin* for the so-called Hottentots and *San* for the Bushmen.

The other major sociolinguistic groups are the Nguni, who comprise the Xhosa and Zulu speakers and who inhabited the eastern seaboard extending from the Mozambique coast to the

Eastern Cape, and, in the interior, the Sotho linguistic group, comprising the southern Sotho, the Pedi, and the Tswana. In the northeastern Transvaal there were other groups which, though distinct, have some affinity with the northern Sotho.

The Khoikhoin and the San

The Khoikhoin and the San inhabited the area around the Cape of Good Hope when the Dutch established a refreshment station there in 1652. The San were what is known anthropologically as "hunters and gatherers." They hunted the abundant game along the slopes of the Drankenstein, Cadaberg, Outeniqua, Camdebou, and other mountains in the area, and gathered roots, vegetables, and berries. From the seashores they harpooned fish and gathered shellfish.

The San were organized into bands that roamed the area in search of food. The optimal size of the band was ultimately a function of ecological conditions, such as the type and supply of fauna and flora. While in the drier regions bands of between twenty-five and fifty persons were common, in the wetter regions of the east, bands of two hundred to three hundred have been recorded.[2]

In contrast to the San, the Khoikhoin had domesticated animals, fat-tailed sheep, and great herds of long-horned cattle. They occupied the vast territory stretching from the Keiskanna River to the Cape Point, and northward along the Atlantic coast past the Olifants River. The social organization of the Khoikhoin was correspondingly larger in scale and more complex. Their pastoral economy offered more security. The units that made up Khoikhoin communities ranged from five hundred to two thousand persons.[3] These were grouped into clans and lived with their unrelated clients and servants. Each clan owned and grazed its own herds, but was subject to the political authority of the head of the horde. Insofar as their economy allowed accumulation of livestock, it could be concluded that there was status differentiation. Insofar as the head of the horde, with the

advice of the heads of clans, had both judicial and executive
authority over members of his horde, the Khoikhoin can be said
to have had chieftainships. The dispute about grazing rights and
livestock would be a serious bone of contention between the
Dutch settlers and the Khoikhoin.

The Nguni (Xhosa and Zulu)

In the seventeenth century the Nguni-speaking groups had
well-organized and highly developed states that were able to
maintain themselves in the face of all attempts at physical and
cultural genocide. The Nguni's mode of production was mixed:
it included cattle herding, agriculture, and hunting. However,
cattle constituted the backbone of the economy, and milk and
meat were the staple foods. Crops included sorghum, pumpkins,
melons, calabashes, beans, coco, yams, and ground nuts.

The practice of agriculture and cattle herding allowed the
Nguni a social organization that was very complex and differentiated. The social division of labor between men and women
was marked. The importance of the female's labor, and her
capacity to reproduce future labor power, was recognized;
through the *lobola* ("bride price") custom the parents of a bride
were compensated with cattle for the loss of labor power they
suffered.

The Nguni were divided into a number of kingdoms and
principalities. Each was independent, with a recognized king or
chief. The political system consisted of various levels of authority
organized in the form of a pyramid: at the bottom were heads of
families and lineages, then clan heads, regional chiefs, and
finally the kings.

In the late eighteenth and early nineteenth centuries the
casual tempo of life and politics among the Nguni changed. The
pressure of advancing Europeans, succession problems, civil
wars, the growth of certain states under skilled rulers and the
consequent loss of power for others—all these exacerbated
internal turmoil. The career of Shaka reflects the unsettled state
of the times. Born about 1787, Shaka was able in his forty-year

life span to unify the various Zulu principalities into a formidable state; at one point the Zulu empire was about to unite the whole of South Africa under one rule. It was a tribute to the organizational and agricultural capacity of the society as a whole that it could feed and maintain a standing army of thirty thousand men, reequip them with iron weapons, and issue each soldier a full-length shield made from cattle hide.[4]

The Sotho

The Sotho originally occupied the entire territory north of the Orange and Vaal rivers. Like the Nguni, the Sotho had a fully mixed economy, consisting of cattle herding as well as agriculture. Before the arrival of the Europeans, the Sotho mined and smelted iron, copper, and tin. The development of commerce and crafts among the Sotho raised new possibilities within their semipastoral economies. They fashioned tools and ornaments, which they traded with their neighbors. In many instances, the Sotho mode of production resembled that of the Nguni. In addition to their subsistence economies based, as we have seen, on agriculture and animal husbandry, these societies also practiced well-developed handicrafts using iron ore, clay, straw, ivory, and so on.

The preconquest peoples of South Africa did not exist in the timeless state of arrested development that Western anthropologists and imperialist apologists have too often depicted. Not only were they complex and differentiated but, like their European counterparts, they were also growing economically and demographically, and in conflict and cooperation among themselves.

The Dutch

The establishment of a refreshment station at the Cape in 1652 was a result of a decision, not by a government, but by a trading company, the Dutch East India Company, which was under the direction of seven rich merchants. The administration of the Cape station was not from Amsterdam but from Batavia, where the headquarters of the company was situated. The charter of the company, issued in 1602 by the Netherlands State-General, allowed the organization extensive political powers. It could negotiate treaties, declare wars, recruit military and administrative personnel, and establish colonial outposts. The sole object of the company's activities was business and profit. That is, the Dutch East India Company was a typical creation of mercantile capitalism—it was ferocious in its plundering; it was piracy on land, piracy reorganized and adapted to exploiting the natural and human resources of the peoples of the entire colonial world.[5]

The employees of the Dutch East India Company were selected from among the lower classes of Netherlands society. As one of them wrote when he enlisted in 1732: "Men who enlist as soldiers or sailors under the conditions offered by the Company are as a rule down at the heels and practically destitute."[6] Others were sent out as punishment for some offense. Many were completely illiterate, and few had more than a rudimentary education. After surveying the background of the Dutch settlers in South Africa, Leonard Thompson concluded:

> The South African fragment, therefore, was not a microcosm of seventeenth-century Dutch society. It was an inferior, partial selection from it. The cultural attainments and interests of Dutch society—the art, the literature, the spirit of scientific enquiry—were almost completely absent from the fragment. What were present were the toughness of the peasant and the unsuccessful townsman, their capacity to endure adverse circumstances, and their receptivity to a simplified version of the gloomy doctrines of primitive Calvinism.[7]

To obtain labor and to make the station serviceable, the representatives of the company took steps to dominate the local area. The Khoikhoin people of the Cape of Good Hope became fair game for these adventurers. They had two forms of wealth, land and cattle, and the Dutch settlers wished to rob them of both. The following extracts from the journal of the first Dutch governor of the Cape settlement illustrate the workings of a mentality of greed. In his entry of December 13, 1652, Governor Jan Van Riebeeck wrote:

Today the hottentots came with thousands of cattle and sheep close to our fort, so that their cattle nearly mixed with ours. We feel vexed to see so many fine head of cattle, and not to be able to buy to any considerable extent. If it had been indeed allowed, we had opportunity today to deprive them of 10,000 head, which, however, if we obtain orders to that effect can be done at any time, and even more conveniently, because they will have greater confidence in us. With 150 men, 10,000 or 11,000 head of black cattle might be obtained without danger of losing one man; and many savages might be taken without resistance, in order to be sent as slaves to India, as they still always come to us unarmed.[8]

A day or two later Van Riebeeck, characteristically blending piracy and piety, wonders at the ways of Providence, which permitted such noble animals to remain in the possession of heathens. It was not long before he thought it best to thwart the ways of Providence rather than wondering at them.[9]

The open practice of robbery could not be used if the people were strong enough to resist. On April 5 and 6, 1660, Van Riebeeck describes a meeting with the chief and overlord of the *Kaapmans,* or "Capemen," as the Dutch sometimes called the Khoikhoin, who had come to complain about the activities of the Dutch. The Kaapmans, according to Van Riebeeck's diary,

strongly insisted that we had been appropriating more and more of their land, which had been theirs all these centuries, and on which they had been accustomed to let their cattle graze, etc. *They asked if they would be allowed to do such a thing supposing they went to Holland and they added:* "It would be of little consequence if you people stayed here at the fort, but you come right into the interior and select the best land for yourselves, without even asking whether we mind or whether it will cause us an inconvenience."[10]

Van Riebeeck reports the reasons for refusing the Kaapmans' claims:

They said that they should at least be allowed to go and gather bitter almonds, which grow wild in abundance there, and to dig for roots as winterfood. This likewise could not be granted them for they would then have too many opportunities of doing harm to the colonists and furthermore we shall need the almonds ourselves this year to plant the proposed protective hedge or defensive barrier. These reasons were, of course, not mentioned to them, but when they persisted in their request, eventually they had to be told that they had now lost the land as the result of the war and had no alternative but to admit that it was no longer theirs, the more so because they could not be induced to restore the stolen cattle which they had unlawfully taken from us in a defensive war, won by the sword, as it were, and we intended to keep it.[11]

No chicanery was too dishonest for Van Riebeeck. After self-righteously blaming his victims, he writes at one point in his diary:

Against this they complained bitterly, saying that the colonists and others who lived in the country had done them much mischief, by sneaking off with either a sheep or a calf on occasion, by snatching off their beads and armlets from their ears and arms and giving them to their slaves, or by beating and striking them, without the Commander's knowledge—and there is some truth in this. Unable to bear this any longer, they had determined to take their revenge by stealing the cattle, and they roundly declared that they had had cause enough for this. In answer to this, they were reminded of the many exemplary punishments meted out by us to those against whom they had brought in charges of such molestation. If they were not satisfied with that, but preferred every time to take their revenge by means of robberies and thefts such as those mentioned, peace could never be maintained between us, and then by right of conquest we should take still more of their land from them, unless they were able to drive us off. In such a case they would, by virtue of the same right, become the owners of the fort and everything and would remain the owners for as long as they could retain it. If this alternative suited them, we would see what our course of action was to be.[12]

Once deprived of their rich lands and vast herds of cattle, the Khoikhoin were reduced into a state of indigency. Sir John Barrow, who visited the Cape at the end of the eighteenth and beginning of the nineteenth centuries, wrote:

There is not in fact in the whole extensive district of Graaff Reunet a single horde of independent Hottentots; and perhaps not a score of individuals who are not actually in the service of the Dutch. These weak people, the most helpless, and in their present condition perhaps the most wretched, of the human race, duped out of their possessions, their country and their liberty, have entailed upon their miserable offspring a state of existence to which that of slavery might bear the comparison of happiness. It is a condition, . . . not likely to continue to a very remote posterity. The same Hottentot will be forgotten or remembered only as that of a deceased person of little note.[13]

The Rev. Thomas Farrell Buxton of the London Missionary Society observed that the Khoikhoin had been subjected to the "heaviest labours, to every species of harassing annoyance, to every kind of revolting punishment. And beneath the grinding misery their numbers dwindled, their persons became dwarfed, and their minds brutalized till even slaves looked down on them as lower and baser drudges, far below the level of mankind."[14]

Van Riebeeck's tendency to apply the law of the jungle in dealing with the Khoikhoin peoples was not surprising. The Dutch settlers had come from developing capitalist states that had been forged after numberless wars, in which ferocious plunder was normal. The Europe from which the Dutch settlers came was very cruel to its subordinate classes, as Raymond Williams writes:

Even if we exclude the wars and brigandage to which it was commonly subject, the uncountable thousands who grew crops and reared beasts only to be looted and burned and led away with tied wrists, this economy, even at peace, was an order of exploitation of a most thoroughgoing kind: a property in men as well as in land; a reduction of most men to working animals, tied by forced tribute, forced labor, or "bought and sold like beasts"; "protected" by law and custom only as animals and streams are protected, to yield more labour, more food, more blood; an economy directed, in all its working relations, to a physical and economic domination of a significantly total kind. "The churl, like the willow, sprouts the better for being cropped." That bailiff's maxim is in all essential respects the principle of this "natural" and "moral" economy.[15]

When capitalism expanded overseas, European culture con-
doned any method, no matter how monstrous, to acquire wealth.
Sir John Barrow writes:

> There is scarcely an instance of cruelty, said to have been commit-
> ted against the slaves in the West-India islands, that could not find
> a parallel from the Dutch farmers of the remote districts of the
> colony towards the Hottentots in their service. Beating and cutting
> with thongs of the hide of the sea-cow or rhinoceros, are only
> gentle punishments, though these sort of whips, which they call
> *shambocs,* are most horrid instruments, being tough, pliant and
> heavy almost as lead. Firing small shot into the legs and thighs of a
> Hottentot is a punishment not unknown to some of the monsters
> who inhabit the neighbourhood of Camtoos river. And though
> death is not unfrequently the consequence of punishing these poor
> wretches in a moment of rage, yet this gives little concern to the
> farmer; for though they are to all intents and purposes his slaves,
> yet they are not transferable property. It is this circumstance
> which, in his mind, make their lives less valuable, and their treat-
> ment more inhuman.[16]

Within a few years the indigenous population near the Cape
settlement had become so impoverished that there were no more
cattle to be obtained and "battering" expeditions were organized
to go further afield. As the South African "frontier" moved
north and northeast, massacre and genocide became even more
clearly defined as methods of conquest. For those who escaped,
servitude, confinement, and cultural suppression were the price.
Their only chance of survival was in serving as menial labor for
those who now owned the land and cattle. A traveler named
Dampier wrote of this once independent people:

> Those of the Hottentots that live by the Dutch town have their
> greatest subsistence from the Dutch, for there is one or more of
> them belonging to every house. They do all sort of servile work.
> Three or four of their nearest relations sit at the doors or near the
> Dutch house, waiting for scraps and fragments that come from
> the table.[17]

The primary objective of settlement in the Cape of Good
Hope was the establishment of a victualing station, but in no
time an influx of white settlers came to make this new-found

territory their home. Between 1672 and 1679, the population not working for the Netherlands East India Company increased from 168 to 259, partly through the freeing of company employees, partly through an excess of births over deaths, and to a small degree through immigration. By 1752 the white population had grown to 5,419.[18]

After the revocation of the Edict of Nantes in 1685, large numbers of French Huguenot refugees in the Netherlands were encouraged to emigrate to the Cape. About two hundred arrived in 1688, and efforts were made to speed their incorporation into the society:

> To facilitate their rapid assimilation, the Cape government interspersed Huguenots among Dutch farmers, and made Dutch the only medium of instruction in public schools. The French language began to disappear and the Huguenots, who regarded the Cape as their permanent refuge, intermarried with other burghers. This helped to stabilize the free White population. By the end of the seventeenth century the crystallization of a distinction between "Afrikaner" burghers who regarded the Cape as a permanent home, and "Europeans," largely Company servants who were only temporary residents, was already under way.[19]

What is known as the Boer character began to crystallize as the settlers not directly employed by the company moved further inland. Lord Bryce, British ambassador to the United States for six years, visited South Africa and described the Boer society of the interior as follows:

> From the time when the settlers began to spread out from the coast into the dry lands of the interior a great change came upon them, and what we now call the distinctive South African type of character and habits began to appear. The first immigrants were not, like many of the English settlers in Virginia, men of good social position in their own country, attached to it by many ties, nor, like the English settlers in the New England colonies, men of good education and serious temper, seeking the freedom to worship God in their own way. They came from the humbler classes, and partly because they had few home ties, partly because the voyage to Holland was so long that communication with it was difficult, they maintained little connection with the mother country and soon lost

their feeling for it. The Huguenot immigrants were more cultivated, and socially superior to the rude adventurers who had
formed the bulk of the Dutch settlers, but they had of course no
home country to look to. France had cast them out; Holland was
alien in blood and speech. So it helped that the South African
whites were, of all the colonists that Europe had sent out since the
voyage of Columbus, those who soonest lost their bond with
Europe, and were the first set of colonists to feel themselves a new
people, whose true home lay in the new land they had adopted.
Thus early in South African annals were the foundations laid of
what we now call the Afrikaner sentiment—a sentiment which has
become one of the main factors in the recent history of the country.[20]

Here, then, we have a description of the development of the
Afrikaner, or Boer. They were mostly people who had lived very
near poverty in Holland. Except for the French Huguenots, they
had little religious piety. Their mode of production was simple.
They could not build industries; farming was for subsistence;
and they partook in only a very limited commerce. To build
their subsistence economy, they had to depend on slave labor,
and in this spirit they killed, dispossessed, and enslaved those
they found occupying the land they coveted. They found their
identity in the negation of those they conquered and exploited.

When the Boers were forced to migrate to the interior by the
threat of British occupation in the 1820s, they did so in order to
maintain, not to improve, their economy and standard of "civilization." The "Great Trek" of the 1830s (around which today's
Afrikaner has created so much mythology) is described thus by
C. W. DeKiewiet:

> The Boers moved inland not to found a new society and to win
> new wealth. Their society was rebellious, but it was not revolution-
> ary. Fundamental innovations in the use of land or in social prac-
> tice were not easily made in their minds. They trekked in spite of
> the Industrial Revolution, moving away before it reached them. In
> one sense, the Great Trek was the eighteenth century fleeing
> before its more material and more active and better organized
> successor.[21]

It is in the light of this process that racial nationalism must be understood. The Boers' espousal of a doctrine of African inferiority, justified on biblical grounds, was interconnected with their desire to justify peonage. And why not? These people had inherited from their settler forefathers feudal-like institutions with rigid hierarchical structures. For their ancestors, "race" had provided a suitable principle on which to create a servile population. Their religious leaders found in the Bible the "Curse of Canaan," which they adapted to justify their activities.

The English Settlers and the Conquest of African Societies

The British conquest of South Africa can be seen as an instance of what Darcy Ribeiro has described as "historical incorporation," which is characterized by the decimation of a population by wars of conquest, followed by the domination and enslavement of those who survive. The old methods of socioeconomic organization are exploited to facilitate the extraction of surplus value from the subject labor force, and the society as a whole is reorganized as part of an expanding world productive system and as a market for industrial goods.[22]

The arrival of the British in South Africa began a devil's dance between white settlers and African society seldom paralleled in human history. The British, backed by their navy, fought with frenzied determination until the Africans were either dead or reduced to the most degrading wage bondage in the modern world—all camouflaged with sweet-sounding professions of human rights and dignity.

The modern imperialist state cannot live by cynicism alone. The colonial rulers needed to feel that what they did was necessary. Thus, on the racial front, the era of British dominance was not only an era of "refined" white supremacist policies but of cultural activity as well. Everyone, including the Afrikaner, was subject to the "civilizing" process and was made to accept the British institutions, language, and culture as superior. The subjugated peoples thus had the traditions of their conquerors forced upon them.

In 1795 the Cape was temporarily annexed by the British as a spoil of the Napoleonic Wars. In 1803 it was returned to the Dutch in the Treaty of Amiens, only to be reoccupied again by the British in 1806. From then on it was the British who were in charge, whatever their temporary setbacks.

At the time it took possession of the Cape, Britain was engaged in a life or death struggle with its great rival, France. In 1776 Britain lost a large part of its American colonies. The center of the empire now lay firmly in the East; trade with the East increased more than threefold between 1760 and 1817.[23] It was the necessity of protecting these commercial routes and interests that determined British policy at the Cape in the first decades of the nineteenth century.

Although the Cape Colony was seized from the Dutch in 1806, it was not until 1820 that the British brought some 4,000 settlers to the district of Albany in the eastern part. Those who came between 1820 and 1850 were the latest victims of capitalist consolidation, displaced people willing to emigrate to escape their misery. But, as Marx pointed out, these were not only people who had been pauperized by the Industrial Revolution:

> The wheel of improvement [was] now seizing another class, the most stationary class in England. A startling emigration movement sprang up among the smaller English farmers, especially those holding heavy clay soil, who, with bad prospects for the coming harvest, and in want of sufficient capital to make improvements on their farms which would enable them to pay their old rents, have no alternative but to cross the sea in search of a new country and new lands.[24]

These arrivals brought with them a belief in private property and the acquisitive principles associated with capitalism. They came to lead a life similar to the kind they had always lived. To obtain labor, they adapted some of the methods that had been used to forcibly drive the English peasants from the soil. Thus, the treatment of the African subsistence producers by their English conquerors was the result of the transfer to Africa of traditional British institutions and practices for dealing with the poor. Oscar Handlin has described some of the structural relations between rich and poor that were adapted to relations between black and white in the colonies.

> The status that involved the most complete lack of freedom was villenage, a servile condition transmitted from father to son. The villein was limited in the right to hold property or make contracts; he could be bought and sold with the land he worked or without, and had "to do all that the Lord will him command"; while the Lord could "rob, beat, and chastise his villein at his will." It was true that the condition had almost ceased to exist in England itself. But it persisted in Scotland well into the eighteenth century. . . . Law and practice in the seventeenth century comprehended other forms of involuntary bondage. The essential attributes of villenage were fastened on many men not through heredity and ancient custom, as in the case of the villein, but through poverty, crime, or mischance. A debtor, in cases "where there is not sufficient distress of goods," could be "sold at an outcry." Conviction for vagrancy and vagabondage, even the mere absence of a fixed occupation, exposed the free-born Englishman, at home or in the colonies, to the danger that he might be bound over to the highest bidder, his labour sold for a term. Miscreants who could not pay their fines for a wide range of offenses were punished by servitude on "public works" or on the estates of individuals under conditions not far different from those of villenage. Such sentences, in the case of the graver felonies, sometimes were for life.[25]

The condition of the African in the English colonies must be viewed within the perspective of these practices, rather than as an expression of primordial sentiments on the part of the white settlers. It was in imitation of the English class structure and way of life that new colonial "aristocracies" emerged, and with them new classes of poor and oppressed. What the British settlers required in South Africa was that the African subsistence producers become the hirelings of capital and that their means of subsistence be transformed into capital. Race intruded and gave the class structure in the colonies a special justification and cruelty, but it did not constitute the essence of that structure.

Along with the impoverished British peasants and farmers came a group of mercenaries. During the wars at the close of the eighteenth and beginning of the nineteenth centuries, England had retained the services of considerable bodies of mercenaries, who, according to William and Lily Ries, "were almost necessarily lawless and violent characters, possessing the material for good soldiers, but likely to be very troublesome in English towns and villages."[26] These men came to be considered a security problem, and South Africa became a dumping ground.

The imposition of British rule in South Africa took the form of a many-dimensioned assault on traditional social organization and culture: (1) militarily and politically, the African population was subjugated; (2) economically, the displaced and defeated population was harnessed, first as a labor force in agriculture, and then in diamond and gold mining; (3) ideologically, Africans were systematically domesticated by being converted to the least utilizable aspect of European culture—Christianity; and (4) socially, a process of radical atomization shattered the fabric of traditional social structures. We will discuss the first two first because they helped set the environment within which the last two took place.

The Role of Force

From 1806 until 1906 South Africa was characterized by an uninterrupted series of wars. The consequences of victory and defeat were enormous and still plague South African society today, for they created a society of victors and vanquished.

From the perusal of the communications between the colonial office and the military governors who were sent to the Cape Colony after it became a British possession, one gets an idea of the British strategy. In 1846 Colonial Secretary Earl Grey concluded, after reading the dispatches from the frontier, that

> an enlightened regard for the real welfare of our uncivilised neighbours, not less than for the welfare of the Colonists, require that the Kaffir tribes should no longer be left in possession of the independence they have so long enjoyed and abused. Our past forbearance they have evidently been unable to appreciate; they have clearly been insensible to the obligations they have contracted by their treaties with us, and the cupidity or the violence of their young warriors has proved too strong for any restraint of authority

or law. Should we, on the successful termination of the present hostilities, brought on by unprovoked aggression on their part, be again content with imposing upon them terms of peace similar to those by which we have allowed former wars to be terminated, there would be no rational ground for expecting that the future history of our relations with those people would prove anything but a repetition of the past. It is therefore requisite that a new policy, more accurately and more carefully adapted to the necessities of the case, should now be adopted.[27]

The "new" policy, as formulated by Earl Grey, was that British authority must be established in what was called Kaffirland, that the chiefs and their people must acknowledge the Queen as their *protector*, that there must be a British officer resident in the country to whom all chiefs would be subordinate in civil, as well as in all military, matters, and that British authority was to be supreme. For all "injuries" which might be inflicted on the colonist by the Africans, reparation was to be exacted or due punishment inflicted by the resident officer, who was to be styled Commandant of Kaffraria. According to the historian George E. Cory,

> Earl Grey looked to a system of law and government guided, not only by justice and humanity, but by such methods as should, if possible, obtain the willing assent and cordial co-operation of the Kaffirs themselves, this co-operation to be connected with and sustained by a systematic endeavour to diffuse among them religious knowledge, moral instruction, and an acquaintance with the arts of civilized life.[28]

The man who was sent to put these policies into practice was Sir Harry Smith, who became governor of the Cape Colony in 1847. Sir Harry had already spent many years in South Africa before. He is said "to have known and loved the colonists, Dutch and English, and they him; he was a first-class soldier, 'the hero of Aliwal' fresh from his triumphs and bursting as ever with vigour and good intentions. He sprang ashore and sounded the double, and for twelve breathless months all South Africa doubled."[29]

In pursuance of his method of settling the affairs of the frontier, Sir Harry ordered a great meeting to be held at King

William's Town on January 7, 1848. Here the assembled chiefs, their counselors, and some thousands of their followers were told

> that conquest had deprived them of the land in which they were
> not permitted to build; that their political independence was at an
> end, that no more treaties would ever be made with them and that
> in future there would be no paramount chief, but the Inkosi
> Inkulu (himself or his successor). "No more Kreli," he shouted,
> "no more Sandilli, no more Umhala. Hear! I am your Inkosi
> Inkulu ["Great Chief"]." He held in his hand a decorated rod of
> some kind, which he called a "Stick of Office." Each chief had to go
> forward, touch it and swear to an oath which was recited to him.[30]

In the four so-called Kaffir Wars of 1835, 1847, 1851, and 1879 the British set out to reduce the Xhosa to impotence by systematic invasion and confiscation of their lands and cattle. These were not wars of genocide; they were scorched-earth campaigns that were meant to deprive the Africans of all means of independent livelihood. Cory reports that the English decided that the only really effective way to reduce the Xhosa to complete dependency was "to burn his huts and kraals, to drive off his cattle, to destroy his corn and other food, in short, to devastate his country."[31] The results of these ruthless tactics stand out starkly from Dr. George Theal's bold but unimaginative history, published in 1897. During the operations of 1851 and 1876 the "forests and jungles were scoured"—and scoured again, if only for cattle. In December 1851 two columns moved to the headquarters of King Krelie of the Gcaleka with the double object of punishing him and depriving the rebels of their sources of supply. When General Somerset, who led the British campaign against the Gcaleka kingdom, returned to King William's Town, he brought back 30,000 head of cattle, a few horses, and 14,000 goats; the second column brought back 7,000. The Fingos (the displaced Africans who supported the invading British troops) came back with 15,000 head of cattle, which they had seized from the Gcalekas, and which the British allowed them to retain. The Winter Campaign of 1851 began in earnest with the burning of Krelie's principal headquarters and the capture of another 10,000 head of cattle.[32]

These methods of depriving the Gcalekas of their livelihood proved most effective. The wretched fugitives, starved and destitute, had no choice but to submit. The so-called squatters now found on white South African farms are remnants of the deposed population, which was then left on its own ancestral land.[33] The British, in the course of these wars, thus began the creation of the African as a permanent class of proletarian.

Encouraged by missionaries, the Xhosa in 1856 and 1857 slaughtered their cattle wholesale in an attempt at redemption from the hated intruders, a tragedy that left them shorn of their principal economic base. In the area later known as British Kaffraria, some 200,000 cattle were destroyed, and 25,000 people—chiefly women, children, and the aged—died in a sacrifice aimed at exorcising the hated enemy. According to some estimates, the African population of British Kaffraria was reduced from 105,000 to 37,000. This mass self-destruction was welcomed by Sir George Grey, the first civilian governor and the high commissioner, who arrived in March 1854. For Grey, these sacrifices broke the Xhosa's military strength and enabled him to fill up their emptied and confiscated lands with European settlers. J. Rutherford, in a biography of Sir George Grey, writes:

> King William's Town was thrown open not merely to the thousand men of the German Legion planned for in 1856, together with their Irish wives, but to another 4,000 peasants obtained direct from Germany. Grey was at the same time for keeping the Bantus in check by planting Europeans and Griquas in the sub-mountainous no-man's land. He even hoped to carry the work of civilization by promoting European land settlement in the Transkei itself. . . .[34]

Sir George Grey's arrival marked the establishment of South Africa as a new settler society. The military campaigns he launched were mopping-up operations, and his main effort was directed at creating the structures that would enable permanent incorporation of the African as a cheap labor force for the settlers. The final military operations were carried out by Colonel Currie, who had been given a free hand to conduct forays against the remaining African chiefdoms. Colonel Currie's dispatches testify to the reckless violence and barbarism used in his so-called pacification campaigns:

> With little opposition, except the torrents of rain pouring down upon us day and night, we hunted this tribe of freebooters, numbering (from the best authority) about 900 fighting men, for three days, shooting down 40 of their number besides wounded, capturing 120 horses, 22 goats, and 8 head of cattle, and destroying by fire the whole of their kraals and huts. . . . This beautiful and valuable piece of country, in extent about 144 square miles, I would recommend the Government to keep in reserve until it can be filled up by a European population.[35]

This success was followed by the order to remove the Africans from their land and replace them with white settlers. Currie's next assignment was to capture Quesha, who had fought bravely in the war of 1850 and was regarded as "a most dangerous political character." He described the hunt for Quesha in these highly elated terms:

> This is perhaps the first Kaffir Chief that was ever fairly captured in his own country by white men—no humbugging but fairly run down with guns and assegais in their hands. The Tambookies are getting awfully frightened of us up here, and you have only to leave me alone with one hand and back me up with the other and everything shall be peace and quiet before the end of this month or a very short time after. . . . I hope all I have done is right and will be approved by His Excellency—half measures are no use, and leniency not understood by savages.[36]

And after accomplishing his task, Currie wrote:

> Never was a Cape Governor in such a noble and advantageous position, as Sir George Grey is at the present moment, with all Kaffirland under his feet; and with power to dictate any kind of system for their future Government which he may think suitable to their circumstances, and beneficial for the Colony at large—for in

the breaking up of Fadana's Confederacy, has expired the last ray of the Kaffir hope.[37]

Currie attributed his success to the considerable latitude Sir George Grey had given him:

> The success I have had is mainly owing to you in giving me such a wide margin in my orders, had I been cramped everything would have failed, but as it is everything has gone well. Kreli is as guilty as either Fadana or Quesha and God knows they are bad enough. You must never let those fellows back again, it is not so easy to catch them. . . . Now I hope if the Governor finds fault with me for going too far, you must soften it down, but I agree with you that silence gives consent and now that all is over as far as regards the Tambookies, why it does not much matter, but I am itching to go in at Kreli. We never had the Kaffirs as a nation under our thumb before, and it is our policy to keep them there.[38]

Fadanna and Quesha were tried for their resistance and found guilty; the former was sentenced to seven years at hard labor and the latter, because of his age, to one year. Currie was knighted.

Grey developed his strategy of creating a submissive African labor force along a number of lines, using both force and personal diplomacy to win over certain African rulers and creating in the process a class of educated Africans loyal to him. It was the timeworn policy of the carrot and the stick. Grey spelled out his aims in an address to the third session of the Colonial Parliament:

> The plan I propose to pursue with a view to the general adjustment of these questions is, to attempt to gain an influence over all the tribes included between the present north-eastern boundary of this colony and Natal, by employing them upon public works, which will tend to open up their country; by establishing institutions for the education of their children, and the relief of their sick; by introducing amongst them institutions of a civil character suited to their present condition; and by these and other like means to attempt gradually to win them to civilization and Christianity, and thus to change by degrees our at present unconquered and apparently irreclaimable foes into friends who may have common interests with ourselves.[39]

Africans employed in public works were paid in cash to enable them to buy goods produced by British industry, while their land was "opened up" to white settlers who then used them as cheap labor. In 1834 the number of Africans in the employ of white colonists was small, but by 1858 over thirty-three thousand Africans from the Transkei were already working in the colony—and depending on wage labor as a source of income.

Grey was casual in his underplaying of the destruction and devastation that he was forcing upon the African people. He created a false consciousness by describing Africans as savages with no moral concept of right and wrong. As he put it in a speech to the third session of the Colonial Parliament:

> Those well acquainted with barbarous tribes, as many of you are, must well know that unless those who are to rule them have at their disposal a force which is obviously sufficient to coerce and punish them if they break into revolt, it is almost hopeless to attempt to civilize them. For it is the nature of barbarians, in their ignorant pride, readily to attribute kindness to fear and to think generosity springs rather from timid apprehensions than from a desire to promote their interests.[40]

The advent of the British in South Africa had a lasting impact; they had a formidable army, organized into battalions of full-time professional soldiers with vast experience in regular warfare, to conquer, annex, and dominate their overseas territories.

From 1806 the boundary between the Africans and the intruding white colonists gradually shifted eastward and northward. According to the anthropologist Monica Wilson: "In 1806 the boundary was the Fish [river]. . . in 1811 Ndlambe, with 20,000 followers, was pushed across it. In 1819 the country between the Fish and the Keiskama was declared neutral; by 1824 it was partly occupied by Whites. In 1847 the boundary shifted to the Kei; in 1858 to Mbashe (Bashee); in 1878 to the Mthatha; and in 1894 Pondoland, between the Mthatha and Mtamuuma, was annexed."[41]

Together with the dispossesion and proletarianization of the African, British colonialism wrought far-reaching changes in the structure of African societies. In the next chapter I discuss the deculturation and enculturation of those Africans who became enrolled in British-sponsored Christian missions and their educational institutions.

The Great Trek, 1836–1854

Let me briefly retrace a few steps: the British presence made itself felt among the Boers as well. Prior to the British occupation of the Cape Colony, the northern and eastern expansion of the Boer farmers was largely a search for fresh pastureland. Quite different in character and magnitude were most of the migrations of 1836–1854; in the first ten years of that period an estimated 14,000 Boers, accompanied by their families, servants, and all their possessions, crossed the Orange River. The "Great Trek," as this exodus of the Boers from the Cape Colony is called, was not the extension of the frontier of the Cape Colony; rather the Boers' purpose was to escape British rule and to establish "free and independent states" beyond the borders of the British colony.[42]

The type of political economy the British created in the newly acquired colony produced many areas of friction with the Dutch-speaking colonists: the Boers resented the imposition of the English language, British officialdom, and, in particular, bourgeois-democratic liberalism. The British colonist found slavery, as practiced by the Boers, inhibiting to the full flowering of capitalist relations of production, which are based on an unlimited supply of workers "free" to sell their labor power. In 1833 slavery was abolished throughout the British Empire, which included the Cape Colony.

While the Boers stood for outdated slavery on a petty scale, the foundation of their patriarchal peasant economy, the British colonist represented large-scale capitalist exploitation of the land and Africans. The abolition of slavery and the trend it represented were seen as a threat by the Boers, whose pure peasant economy had depended on slave labor. During the eighteenth century, as we saw above, the Boers had killed off or driven out the Khoikhoin and the San in order to deprive them of their most valuable pastures and cattle.

A great deal of mythology now surrounds the Great Trek, but, as the historian De Kiewiet points out:

> "The Great Trek" [was] not simply the story of a people, oppressed and misunderstood, fleeing into the wilderness to escape from tyrannous imperial power. The trek movement was therefore a natural movement with an instinctive strategy of its own. It was stimulated by the knowledge that plenty of good land lay beyond the official boundary. But it was pricked also by a deep sense of grievance. In ways both great and small very many of the innovations of the British Government had been offensive to the Dutch population.[43]

Yet despite the areas of disagreement with Britain, the Boers enjoyed British support in their wars with the Africans. It was this support which gave them a critical advantage in arms.

In 1843 Great Britain made Natal a British colony in order to frustrate the Boer trekkers, who were attempting to establish a settlement there. Once again, the Boers were forced to pack up their wagons and depart for the interior. By the end of 1847 nearly all of them had left Natal. Their place was taken by large contingents of subsidized British immigrants, some five thousand of whom arrived between 1848 and 1854. The meaning of this new phase of British expansion is described by Lord Bryce:

> With the English annexation of Natal ended the first of the attempts which the immigrant Boers [had] made to obtain access to the sea. It was a turning-point in the history of South Africa, for it secured to Great Britain that command of the coast which has ever since been seen to be more and more vital to her predominance, and it established a new centre of English settlement in a region till then neglected, from whence large territories including Zululand, and recently Tongaland, have been acquired.[44]

Having been thwarted in Natal, the Boer trekkers crossed the Karroo and Drakensburg mountains, where the British allowed them to establish the South African and the Orange River republics in 1852 and 1854 respectively. In the process, the

Boers greedily carved up the country among themselves. Strictly speaking, the British were the masters of the situation, for the Boers did not have the material means to conquer, let alone unite, the country. The republics of the Transvaal and the Orange Free State were thus small enclaves superimposed on Africans whose lands had been appropriated.

In allowing the Afrikaners to establish these republics, the British made an adroit move, for they hoped that the Boer communities would unite in a common defense against the threat from the Africans. However, the British reserved the right to intervene. According to W. M. McMillan:

> Governor Cathcart's dispatches sufficiently show the underlying assumption that the *de facto* British supremacy, not to say suzerainty, remained unaffected, making it a simple matter to resume full sovereignty if and whenever that seemed necessary or convenient. The colonial self-government of that day conferred no such status as that conferred much later by the Statute of Westminster. It was thus in the spirit of the age that it was also assumed by British statesmen of all parties, then and much later, that recognition of two distant and land-locked republics could not and could never be allowed to affect the one British interest they all agreed was vital—to secure any exclusive control of the Cape sea-route. It certainly appeared to Lord Grey at the time to warrant the withdrawal from the distant interior that all such vital strategical interests would be served by retaining control of little more than the naval base at Simonstown.[45]

With the establishment of the Boer republics, South Africa became a series of enclaves engaged in continuous war: African chiefdoms against Boers, Boers against British, and the latter two against Africans. In the conflict with the Africans, the Boer republics found themselves increasingly dependent on Britain, which controlled all trade routes with Europe. Their very presence in the enclaves was due to the guns and ammunition they got from trade and commerce with the Cape Colony and Europe, all on British ships.

In 1867 and 1886 diamonds and gold were discovered at Kimberley, and in the Transvaal ridges of Witwatersrand. Once a liability and a burden, the interior of South Africa suddenly became a land of fabulous riches. Capital, adventurers, and entrepreneurs from all over the capitalist world descended on the diamond diggings and the gold fields. Within fifteen years, according to official statistics, $32 million in diamonds had been exported. By the 1880s the annual export of diamonds exceeded in value that of all exports from the two British colonies and the republics in the decade before.[46]

From 1870 to 1900 Great Britain instigated a wave of aggressive wars to make the entire subcontinent its possession. In the course of these three decades the political frontiers of South Africa were drawn, and the relations thus established among the various groups eventually became part of the routine of what in South Africa is called "custom and way of life," or native policy.

A brief chronology of the wars is given by A. Lerumo as follows:

> In 1873 a war was waged by Britain against the Hlubi people under Lengalibalele in Natal.
>
> In 1877—following a major defeat of the Commandos of the Transvaal (then the South African Republic) by the Pedi under Sekhukhune—British troops entered Pretoria without resistance and annexed the Transvaal.
>
> In 1879, following their shattering defeat by the Zulu at the Battle of Isandhlwana, the British moved into Zululand in force and imposed a peace which robbed the Zulu of most of their independence. (Zululand was annexed outright in 1877 and handed over to Natal in 1879.)
>
> In the same year, 1879, the Cape Colony annexed Fingoland, Idutywa, and the independent Coloured Republic of Griqualand East under Adam Kok. With British approval the Colony expanded to include all remaining African areas west of Natal, including Pondoland (1894).
>
> In 1884, the annexure of South-West Africa by Germany led Britain to annex southern Botswana outright as "British Bechuanaland." This was consolidated into the Cape Colony. Northern Bechuanaland (present-day Botswana) was declared a British Protectorate.
>
> In 1890 settlers of Rhodes' "British South Africa Company" invaded Mashonoland, followed by penetration into Matabeleland. Between 1896 and 1897, prolonged wars of resistance were waged by the peoples of present-day Zimbabwe.

Also in 1890 Great Britain and the Transvaal Republic imposed a joint administration over Swaziland.

The last area of independent African resistance was not overcome until 1898, a year before the Boer Wars, when, with the aid of African conscripts, the South African Republic defeated the Venda.

The Boer War broke out in October 1899. Following initial setbacks, British forces occupied Johannesburg in May 1900, the Boer President Kruger was exiled, and the annexation of the Transvaal Republics was proclaimed. But the Boers refused to accept defeat, and for two years carried out a guerrilla war. Peace was signed by the Treaty of Vereeniging on May 31, 1902.[47]

The British-Boer Alliance

The eighth anniversary of the Treaty of Vereeniging, May 31, 1910, was chosen by the delegates from the four white settler colonies—Cape, Natal, Orange Free State, and the Transvaal—for the inauguration of the Union of South Africa. On this fateful date, which symbolized the reconciliation of victor and vanquished, Britons and Boers were united under the British Crown. From thence forward, complete political equality between Boers and Britons was established in South African politics. The statement which British Foreign Secretary Lord Balfour delivered in the House of Commons on December 8, 1910, summed up the hopes of the British regarding the new society:

We have stated over and over again that what we look forward to is a condition of things in the two colonies in which the Dutchmen and Englishmen shall have equal privileges, in which the blessings associated with British colonial rule in all parts of the globe shall be shared by the inhabitants of the Transvaal and the Orange Free State as they are shared by others of Her Majesty's subjects. . . . The intention that the English colonial system in South Africa shall be what it is everywhere else, a free system, has never been disguised. It has been publicly and openly avowed by every reasonable Minister.[48]

Those Africans who had helped the English subdue the Boers,

according to Lieutenant-Governor Sir Arthur Lawly, had hoped that the old relation of master and servant would be altered. But this was not to be. For the British the stakes were African labor, African land, and the gold that had been found in the country's bowels. The Anglo-Boer War was a classic case of a "thieves' falling out," and the Treaty of Vereeniging and the Union of South Africa were a constitutional reconciliation between the intruders.

Britain had seven years of supreme authority after the Anglo-Boer War in which to give the African and colored people of South Africa a new deal. But, like their American offspring, instead of standing for democracy and the possibility of human brotherhood, the British rationalized human hatred and entrenched it in the constitution.

H. J. and Ray Simons, in their book *Class and Colour in South Africa, 1850-1950,* point out that after the Anglo-Boer War,

> African peasants were forced to give up their arms and return cattle seized during the war, but they never recovered their own stock seized by the British troops and republican commandos. Every adult African male was required to pay a labour tax of two pounds, with another two pounds for the second and each additional wife of a polygamist. The administration reshaped the laws on passes, labour contracts and liquor prohibition, authorized municipalities to segregate Africans in location, hired out African convicts to mining companies, and prohibited extra-marital intercourse between a white woman and any African, Asian or Coloured. Not surprisingly, some Africans wished "to call back the days of the Republic," since they had received better treatment and wages "when the Boers dominated."[49]

Africans and their welfare were, as ever, sacrificed to promote an abiding settlement for the whites. Let me make a brief digression here and look at the terms imposed on Cetshwayo, the Zulu king, after the defeat of the Zulus in the War of 1879. These terms are revealing when contrasted to those given the Boers in the Treaty of Vereeniging. Among other things, Cetshwayo was forced to agree to the following:

I will not permit the existence of the Zulu military system, or the existence of any military system within my territory, and I will proclaim and make it a rule that all men shall be allowed to marry whom they choose, and as they choose, according to good and ancient customs of my people, known and followed in the days preceding the establishment by Chaka of the system known as the military system, and I will allow and encourage all men living within my territory to go and come freely for peaceful purposes, and to work in Natal or the Transvaal or elsewhere for themselves or for hire.[50]

These are terms of utter subordination and dependence. They are very important in understanding the genesis of African exploitation. So long as people have economic, military, and political power, they can use it to defend themselves, and define their own ideology, culture, and sense of being. The decisive factor for the Africans in their conquest was that they lost power—the ultimate determinant in human society, being basic to the relations within any group and between groups. When the Africans found themselves forced to relinquish power entirely to the British colonizers, they suffered extreme deprivation.[51] This is what makes the treaty imposed on Cetshwayo so significant. The Zulus were made to renounce the one means by which they could defend their integrity. There was a cynical impudence in the agreement that the Zulu people could "go and come freely for peaceful purposes," but such is the arrogance of all conquerors.

The manifest inequity of the settlement of 1910, which gave the Boers political power so soon after their defeat and at the same time denied Africans any say, created a situation whose logic and drama are still being played out today. What greater claims had the Boers at the peace conference of Vereeniging than the Africans? The Boers had been conquered and colonized, and the lands they had laid claim to had been annexed in accordance with the rules of war. But to the English, they were part of the white "race," and as such they should share in the spoils of rape. Thus, according to the treaty, the "burghers" were asked to "lay down their arms and [to] desist from all further resistance to King's authority." All their "prisoners of war [were] to be restored to their houses on declaring themselves subjects of His Majesty King Edward VII." No burghers who surrendered were to be deprived of their liberty or property. Furthermore, no proceedings were to be taken for any "legitimate acts of war." Dutch was to be taught in schools and used in the courts whenever requested by the burghers. Burghers would be allowed to keep rifles if they took out licenses. And even more, "civil government" was to take the place of military administration as soon as possible, and representative institutions leading to self-government were to be introduced. No special war tax was to be levied on the Boers' landed property. A grant of £3 million was "to be given by His Majesty's Government to assist in the restoration of the people in their homes and farms, and to help them with food, seed, stock and implements." In addition to this, "the question of granting the franchise to the 'native' was NOT TO BE DECIDED UNTIL THE GRANT OF SELF-GOVERNMENT."[52]

The Treaty of Vereeniging thus allowed the Boers to retain their self-respect, and laid a secure foundation for the reconstruction of the Anglo-Boer class alliance—and thereby for the ultimate supremacy of white rule over Africans. At the Versailles Peace Conference in 1919, Louis Botha, one of the Boer generals who fought against the British, paid tribute to the Treaty of Vereeniging. Though the Boers, he said, had lost all they had fought for—independence, flag, and country—their conquerors had helped them in salvaging *their* country and saving *their* people:

> It was a generous peace that the British people made with us; and that is why we stand with them today side by side in the cause that has brought us all together. Remember, I say to you, there was no spirit or act of vengeance in that peace; we were helped to rise again, and were placed on equal terms.[53]

The Treaty of Vereeniging, though fundamentally racist in character, was first and foremost based on the interests of British finance capital, which was being invested in the mineral resources of South Africa. The British settled so generously with the Boers in order to obtain the gold mines and, having obtained a one-sided settlement, the Boers became the grudging vassals of British imperialism, to be repaid in the land and labor of Africans. Even earlier, as we have seen, the British refrained from using Africans as allies in their wars against the Boers, and they also tried to prevent guns from passing into the hands of Africans.

It is customary in liberal circles to see British actions toward the Afrikaners as a gesture of goodwill and to see the betrayal of the Africans as the unforeseen price that had to be paid for such magnanimity. But the ethical problem that faced Britain was less important than the political one, and far less so than the economic.

Marx discussed the fate that awaits the victims of conquest under different socioeconomic conditions:

> The conquering people may impose its own methods of production upon the conquered (e.g., the English in Ireland in the nineteenth century, partly also in India); or it may allow everything to remain as it was, contenting itself with tribute (e.g., the Turks and the Romans); or the two systems by mutually modifying each other may result in something new, a synthesis (which partly resulted from the Germanic conquests). In all these conquests, the method of production, or the one resulting from a combination of both, determines the nature of the new distribution which comes into play.[54]

Elsewhere Marx dealt with the question of land after conquest:

> A conquering people divides the land among the conquerors, establishing thereby a certain division and form of landed property and determining the character of production; or it turns the conquered people into slaves and thus makes slave labour the basis of production. Or a nation by revolution, breaks up large estates into small, imparts to production a new character. Or legislation perpetuates ownership in large families and thus fixes it in castes.[55]

The capitalist institutional structures and racist psychology which have developed in South Africa since the latter part of the nineteenth century function largely upon the infrastructure that resulted from conquest and the lingering colonial status to which the African people were subjected. General Jan Smuts's discussion of what he liked to call the "Native problem" was marked by a candor which the present-day apologist of the South African situation finds too brutal in its honesty. Smuts defined the policy of white settlers in South Africa as assuming

> that two peoples [black and white] cannot indefinitely go on living side by side without some major future explosion. For this day of reckoning we whites must prepare. We must see that we have in our power all those things which can ensure tactical and military superiority. We must prohibit non-Europeans from possessing firearms or the training in their use. Manufacturing, industry, wealth and education must be kept in white hands. All those add up to military strength. We must frown upon trade unionism among the Bantu or upon the formation of political bodies, for that leads to dangerous consolidation. The emotional fear complex is not to be confused with the military prerequisite.[56]

We can sum up the legacy and the consequences of the conquest of South Africa as follows: its major sociological legacy was the definitive consecration and consolidation of the whites as a ruling and hegemonic class. After a bitter defense of national territory and political sovereignty, both the Africans and the Boers were defeated, the former being transformed into a subject national class and the latter into a junior partner of the conquerors. The British, having usurped power, installed capitalism as the predominant socioeconomic system, under which the Africans were reduced to a secondary labor force without any influence over the political and economic processes of the evolving society. Undisturbed by Afrikaner nationalism but terrified by African numbers and resistance, the British were satisfied to control economic power and leave political power in the hands of the Afrikaners.

After the Anglo-Boer War, Britain felt impelled to create a rough working coalition between influential sectors of the Afrikaner community and the emerging mining interests. In arranging this coalition, Britain agreed to respect the fears and political prejudices of the Afrikaner as long as the new Union was safe for the British investor. The arrangement was very much like that described by Marx and Engels in their discussion

of the abortive 1848 revolution in Germany, in which the commercial and industrial class, finding itself too weak to rule in its
own right, threw itself into the arms of the landed aristocracy,
thus exchanging the right to rule for the right to make money.[57]

War and conquest influenced the process of the development
of classes. They produced a proletariat distinguished by race,
lack of skills, and lack of political power. This, however, will be
discussed later. But it should be stated here that the British
conquest and creation of the Union, whose constitution decreed
political servitude for the African, set up the conditions and
structures that made it possible for Afrikaner racial nationalism
to play its present role in South Africa.

Thus, the power structure of white supremacy is in the final
analysis a means of perpetuating class interests, and the racial
discriminatory legal structure is a means by which the class
relationship between the conqueror and the conquered is
mediated, to the advantage of the capitalist. Leonard
Thompson's summation of how the Africans were betrayed war-
rants quoting at some length:

> In 1910 British policy makers at last attained their primary goal in
> South Africa. The South Africa Act united the territories occupied
> by white people in a British dominion under a government which
> could claim to represent both white communities and which was
> led by men who were sincerely committed to a policy of Anglo-
> Afrikaner conciliation and cooperation with other members of the
> British Empire. H. H. Asquith and Lord Greme presided over the
> creative withdrawal that had eluded a long line of predecessors,
> stretching back to Sir George Grey. Greme expressed the cabinet's
> satisfaction in the House of Lords. The unification of South Africa,
> he said, would place the self-governing British Dominions in some-
> thing like their final form: "There is the great American group,
> and the great African group. There may be some rearrangement
> and some modification, but it is, I think, reasonable to say that for
> many years to come, longer than the life of any of us here, these
> three great divisions will form the main self-governing parts of the
> British Empire outside these islands."
>
> On the other hand, as Asquith was aware when he made his final
> speech on the South Africa Bill in the House of Commons, in
> attaining the primary goal of its South Africa policy, Britain had

sacrificed the secondary goal. That goal had been set out by Lord
Stabely, Colonial Secretary, in 1842, when he had instructed Sir
George Napier that in annexing Natal it was "absolutely essential . . . that there shall not be in the eye of the law any distinction
of colour, origin, race, or creed; but that the protection of the law,
in letter and in substance, shall be extended impartially to all
alike." Any final assessment of the achievement of an imperial
power must depend largely upon the sort of society it left behind
when it withdrew. In withdrawing from South Africa, Great Britain left behind a caste-like society, dominated by its white minority.
The price of unity and conciliation was the institutionalization of
white supremacy.[58]

Has the passage of time erased British crimes against the
African peoples of South Africa? A people that has a future to
look toward and a responsibility to its future progeny, and a
people that shares a humane and civilized historic experience, is
a people quite naturally preoccupied with what would constitute
equitable forms of government worthy of the present and future. But a people that is concerned with immediate material
gains has little regard for things of the mind. In South Africa,
then, racism appears, not as an incidental detail but as a substantial part of colonial conquest. It is the highest expression of the
colonial capitalist system and one of the most significant features
of the conqueror's ideology. Not only did it establish a fundamental discrimination between the conqueror and the conquered, a sine qua non of colonial life, but it also laid among the
conquered the foundation for a belief in the immutability of this
life.

3

Conquest and Cultural Domination

If we are stripped of experience, we are stripped of our deeds; and if our deeds are, so to speak, taken out of our hands like toys from the hands of children, we are bereft of our humanity. We cannot be deceived. Men can and do destroy the humanity of other men, and the condition of the possibility is that we are interdependent. We are not self-contained nomads producing no effects on each other except our reflections. We are both acted upon, changed for good or ill, by other men; and we are agents who act upon others to affect them in different ways.

—R. D. Laing

The conquest of the Africans was not a momentary act of violence which stunned their ancestors and then ended. The physical struggle against African societies was only the beginning of a process in which the initial act of conquest was buttressed and institutionalized by ideological activities. The supremacy of the whites, their values and civilization, was only won when the cultural and value system of the defeated African was reduced to nothing and when the Africans themselves loudly admitted the cultural hegemony of their conquerors.[1]

British hegemony, as it evolved in South Africa during the nineteenth century, was to be more than mere physical subjugation. It was to saturate the society with its values to the extent that they would become common sense for the people under its sway. It was to constitute a whole body of practice and expectation. It was to be enshrined in a set of meanings and values which would be confirmed by practice.

The architects of British colonial policy were old and wise, their heads full of centuries of practiced cunning. The most singular aspect of the British conquest, dominance, and exploitation of the African was the rationalization for it. Various agents of ideological and cultural diffusion were set to work: official and unofficial, conscious and unconscious, missionaries, explorers, and traders. The activities of the Dutch settlers, cruel and destructive as they may have been, did not go below the surface. The British, on the other hand, tried to break down the entire fabric of African society, and to substitute in its place a caricature of bourgeois culture. Dr. John Philips recounts in one of his dispatches a shrewd remark made by an old African man: "The Boers are like buffaloes; they have hard heads, but we see them before they attack us. But the English are like the tiger; they have too much here [pointing to his head]; they spring upon us before we see them."[2]

The missionaries, whether they were aware of it or not, were used by the colonists to justify their own position and to psychologically enslave the colonized peoples. They condemned African institutions and customs, and taught the social norms of a capitalist civilization as if they comprised a universal moral code. They instilled in their converts a belief in the virtues of work, private property, and respect for authority, and thus translated African peasant life in a methodical way to the life of industrial capitalism.

That the missionaries played such a prominent role in British colonial expansion should occasion no surprise. According to Louis Wright, "No better medium for propaganda existed in the sixteenth and seventeenth centuries. Lacking the facilities of a British Broadcasting Company and a highly developed press, the government and the stock companies utilized the next best thing to a loudspeaker: they induced the preacher to broadcast their information and commendations of their projects."[3]

In the mission schools, elements taken from the dominant and the subject cultures were fused into a body of common precepts that were indispensable to the maintenance of the new relations and for the direction of the labor force. Perry Anderson has explained the role of the missionary in conquest most aptly:

> The conversion of the native population represents, even if only symbolically, its incorporation into the mental and cultural universe of the white. It thus has the value, even to the most atheist and anti-clerical administration, of initiating the process of disciplined adaptation to European cultural norms. . . . Christianity in colonial areas is a domestication of the indigenous population: objectively, it breaks the Africans into European thought and mores; subjectively, it frees the European of his terrors of the African by including him within the same canon as himself. At the same time, it has a crucial additional merit for any colonizer. It represents an ideal arrested threshold of acculturation for the natives. A colonial system needs a subject population with a certain minimal level of Europeanization, for the purpose of order and exploitation. On the other hand, too great an assimilation of European culture and techniques would directly threaten the inequality on which religion offers almost the perfect device for securing the fruits of the first without incurring the dangers of the second.[4]

So money was invested in overseas missionary work to convert and to eradicate pernicious customs and to promote acceptance of the moral and political code of the conqueror. In time, knowledge about conditions on the frontier and about the attitude of the African toward the conqueror came from missionaries. Unlike the Boers, the British had to win the "hearts and minds" of their new subjects in order to incorporate them into the new economic order they were creating and to assert their right to act as rulers. Their moral authority was established through the implantation of evangelical Christianity.

The teaching of human brotherhood in a capitalist economy based on exploitation and racist class rule was Christianity's task in South Africa: guns might subdue without making a permanent impact, but a Christian God could touch the "natives'" hearts and minds and win their voluntary acceptance of a servile status. Unlike the Dutch, Englishmen of power understood clearly what missionary education could do to produce a class of "natives" who would help assure the stability of the new society.

Missionaries and traders thus undermined African societies

from within while military force overwhelmed them from without. The best expression of the political implications of planting missionaries among Africans in the frontier was made by Dr. John Philips of the London Missionary Society, who was sent to the Cape in 1819 and was the most far-sighted representative of British imperialism at the time. He wrote in the preface to his *Researches in South Africa:*

> While the missionaries have been employed in locating the savages among whom they labour, teaching them industrious habits, creating a demand for British manufactures, and increasing their dependence on the colony, there is not a single instance of a tribe thus enjoying the labour of a missionary making war against the colonists, either to injure their persons, or to deprive them of their property. Missionary stations are the most efficient agents which can be employed to promote the international strength of our colonies, and the cheapest and best military posts agreement can employ.[5]

A close bond thus developed between the missionary and the conqueror. The policies the missionaries advocated were those that legitimized colonial rule. The British colonial ruling class was well aware that to dominate successfully it needed to strengthen its position with associates recruited from among the ranks of the Africans. The mission schools were assigned the task of manufacturing that class, of bringing a spirit of harmony and cooperation to relations between the exploiters and exploited. The Christian missionaries who taught the Africans to accept their miserable lot on earth in return for post mortem rewards in heaven supplied the ideology that goes with absolute submission to conquest and colonial status.

The Christian church and the mission school were the most important institutions assuring a close personal contact between the European colonist and the indigenous population. In the mission school a great gulf was created between the colonized and their own traditions and systems of reference. Accepting bourgeois values was the price for acquiring formal education in the mission schools. As Fanon wrote: "The Church in the colonies is the white people's Church, the foreigner's Church. She does not call the Native to God's ways but to the ways of the white man, of the master, of the oppressor. And as we know, in this matter many are called but few chosen."[6] Fanon also noted how religion helped the colonial enterprise in its work of tranquilizing the African: "All those saints who have turned the other cheek, who have forgiven trespasses against them, and who have been spat on and insulted without shrinking [were] studied and held as examples."[7]

The London Missionary Society, which, beginning in 1799, provided the bulk of the missionaries to Southern Africa, was established by a group known as the Evangelicals. As early as 1776 it had found the Society for the Missions in Africa and the East. The Evangelicals was a congenial alliance between religion and commerce. Its leader, William Wilberforce, was the son of a rich merchant in Hull. Lord Teignmouth, a former governor-general of India, was also a member; another was the Reverend Thomas Farrell Buxton, who was a partner in a brewery concern and who, with Wilberforce, founded the Aborigines Protection Society and assisted Dr. Philips.

The triumph of the money economy was partly made possible by the activities of missionaries and traders. In converting the Africans and casting them adrift from their former culture and moral codes, the British missionaries were responding to the needs of capital to create laborers and consumers of British manufactures. The peasants, once deprived of their means of subsistence, were expected to work for wages from their new masters. The systematic and forcible deprivation of the African peasants of their wealth in land and cattle thus served the double purpose of ensuring the destruction of the economic basis of the old society and of providing the colonial social order with the means to dispense with the products of its own production. According to a missionary named Brownlee: "As the natives came under the influence of the teaching of missionaries, they at once abandoned red clay, and sought to cover themselves with European clothing, and thus, and in proportion to the spread of missionary influence the desire for articles of European manufacture grew and spread, and I think will well satisfy this meeting that to the missionary mainly we owe the great revenue now derived from native trade."[8] At the same time, traders

brought in cheaply produced goods, undermining traditional
industries and meshing African workers into the network of
British commerce. Sir George Yonge, governor of the Cape
Colony from 1799 to 1801, wrote a letter to the Right Honorable
Henry Dundas, acting governor of the Cape from 1801 to 1803,
complaining about the hypocrisy displayed by missionaries in
their relations with the Africans. He wrote:

> They are pushing themselves very much here. They deal largely in
> *European Goods,* which they supply their Proselytes with to *Good
> Profit.* Their Missionaries are most of them Merchanicks &
> Tradesmen, all *Reverend Men*; Blacksmiths, Shoemakers, Millers,
> and such like for the good of the Souls of their Congregations. I
> had it myself by accident from one of their Chief Missionaries that
> in this manner they dealt *largely* in *Wollen Goods* & c., and that they
> were possess'd of great Wealth and of *Funds* that were *equal to any
> Undertaking.*[9] [Emphasis in the original]

Even more direct methods were used to pressure African
peasants to become laborers and to cultivate their taste for
capitalist goods. For instance, an extensive program of road
building in the Eastern Cape embarked upon by Sir George
Grey facilitated both trade and warfare. The African labor force
was paid in cash and in such products as sugar and coffee, in
order to stimulate new wants. The wearing of British-produced
clothing was strongly encouraged as well: King William's Town
actually had a law requiring that European clothes be worn.

The pronouncements of British authorities make it quite clear
that two problems disturbed them: the nudity of the Africans
and their "idleness." After the war of 1835 Colonel Harry Smith
told the assembled chiefs, "I was highly pleased with Dudazi, he
came to me neatly dressed in clothes which he had purchased.
Why do you not all do so? This, England expects of her subjects."[10] At the close of the second campaign he stated: "It is an
important object to teach the Kaffirs the use of money and to
clothe themselves." To the defeated chiefs he said: "You shall
have traders and you must teach your people to bring gum,
hides, timber and so on to sell, that you may learn the art of
money and buy for yourselves. You must learn that it is money

which makes people rich."[11] A deliberate policy was thus embarked upon whose economic result was not in doubt.

The Natal "Kaffir Commission" of 1852–1853 stated that it was cheaper and infinitely preferable to train the "young Kaffir" in industry than to exterminate him, and "one or the other must be done." It then recommended:

> All Kaffirs should be ordered to go decently clothed. This measure would at once tend to increase the number of labourers, because many would be obliged to work to produce the means of buying clothing; it would also add to the general revenue of the colony through Customs duties.[12]

William Holden, a missionary in Natal at the time of the commission's report, paraphrased the English settlers' mentality: "Betwixt the barbarian Kaffir and the civilized Englishman, there is a great chasm, a mighty gulf. The cold, stern Englishman stands on the one bank crying, 'Civilise, civilise, civilise!!!' but lends no helping hand to convey the poor native across."

Because of the recommendations of the commission, all Africans in Durban and Pietermaritzburg were required by proclamation to wear European clothes. Shepstone, the secretary for native affairs in the Natal Colony, "proudly reported that on the stipulated day—only a month after the issue of the proclamation—every African appeared dressed as ordered. All men resorting to the towns carried trousers ready to be put on as soon as they entered the borough."[13]

The need to make Africans consumers of British manufactures was a recurring preoccupation. Sir George Grey's opening address to the Colonial Parliament in 1855 underlined the importance he attached to Africans becoming consumers of British goods. "The Natives were," he said, "to become a part of ourselves, with a common faith and common interests, useful servants, consumers of our goods, contributors to our revenue; in short a source of strength and wealth for this Colony, such as Providence designed them to be."[14] At the same time, the activities of the various missionary bodies in Natal illustrate the central role they played in the colonial enterprise. The Congregational,

Methodist, Anglican, and Catholic missionaries were lavishly financed and had easy access to influential officials in the early years of the Natal Colony. They received large grants of land, converted them into Mission Reserves, and groomed a privileged African Christian population which by 1880 was estimated to number 10,000. From these reserves the missionaries set about to effect an economic revolution. According to Norman Etherington,

> The clothing which missionaries recommended for the sake of modesty was for many of their converts an introduction to a new system of production and exchange. Whether a convert earned his new clothes by wage labor or fabricated them with European looms and needles, he was entering new kinds of economic relationships. The "upright houses" which rose in all mission stations embodied materials and demanded the use of tools unknown in the pre-colonial period. Indeed, on the assumption that the builders of such houses had become importers of durable goods, African Christians won exemptions from Natal's hut tax.[15]

The stress upon this purpose did not diminish. Lord Selborne, who was high commissioner for South Africa and governor of the Transvaal and Orange River Colony from 1905 to 1910, recommended:

> There will be no surer way of teaching them [Africans] to work than by increasing their wants, and especially the wants of the women. These wants can be engendered, and are engendered constantly, by contact with whites; but education, wisely directed, may do much to assist the movement.
> I lay particular stress on the women. If the women can be got out into domestic service, they would set free a large number of men for proper men's work, and the women, being themselves brought into contact with whites, would quickly develop their wants, which in turn would react upon the men.[16]

The economic role of the English missionaries is well exemplified by the activities of the Rev. Thomas Farrell Buxton, an abolitionist and a great friend of Dr. Philips. His desire to abolish slavery was only matched by his concern to advance British commerce. His policy is clear in the following quotations from his writings:

Legitimate commerce would put down the Slave Trade, by demonstrating the superior value of man as a labourer on the soil, to man as an object of merchandise; and if conducted on wise and equitable principles, might be the precursor, or rather the attendant, of civilization, peace, and Christianity, to the unenlightened, of warlike, and heathen tribes who now so fearfully prey on each other, to supply the slave-markets of the New World. In this view of the subject, the merchant, the philanthropist, the patriot, and the Christian, may unite; and should the Government of this country lend its powerful influence in organizing a commercial system of just, liberal, and comprehensive principles—guarding the rights of the native on the one hand, and securing protection to the honest trader on the other—a blow would be struck at the nefarious traffic in human beings, from which it could not recover; and the richest blessings would be conferred on Africa, so long desolated and degraded by its intercourse with the basest and most iniquitous part of mankind.

Central Africa possesses within itself everything from which commerce springs. No country in the world has nobler rivers, or more fertile soil; and it contains a population of fifty millions. This country, which ought to be amongst the chief of our customers, takes from us only to the value of 312,938 of our manufactures, 101,104 of which are made up of the value of arms and ammunition, and lead and shot.[17]

What seems to have excited Buxton's imagination more than the African's right to freedom was the right of the British to exploit Africans commercially; the abolition of slavery would merely facilitate commercial activities in Africa. Thus, in 1840, in disclaiming any desire to erect a new empire in Africa, Buxton asked:

> What is the value to Great Britain in the sovereignty of a few hundred miles in Benin or Eboe, as compared with that of bringing forward into the market of the world millions of customers, who may be taught to grow the raw materials which we require and who require the manufactured commodities which we produce? The one is a trivial and insignificant matter; the other is a subject worthy of the most anxious solicitude of the most accomplished statesmen.[18]

He explained the aims of the Society for the Extinction of the Slave Trade and the Civilization of Africa in a letter:

We determined to form two associations, perfectly distinct from each other, but having one common object in view, putting an end to the slave trade. One of these associations to be exclusively philanthropic in character, and designed mainly to diffuse among the African tribes the light of Christianity, and the blessing of civilization and free-labour—the other to have a commercial character, and to unite with the above objects the pursuit of private enterprise and profit.[19]

To complement his activities, a hamlet on the Kat River in the Eastern Cape was named Buxton. The Rev. James Read referred to the village of Buxton in the following report:

Buxton is one of our largest locations; we have a good school there—the school room, which is so large that it serves also for a chapel, has been proud of the name of their place; the situation is delightful, the soil very fertile, being watered by a small stream, which is tributary to the Kat River. It is furnished with forests and finest timber.[20]

In 1836 the Reverend Philips brought to England two men, named Tzatzoe and Andrew Stoffles, and referred to them respectively as Chief and Hottentot. These two specimens of missionary activity were invited to the Rev. Buxton's house for dinner. Here is how he describes their appearance that day:

Tzatzoe was dressed in fanciful English attire, with a gold-laced coat, something like a naval officer. He is rather a fine-looking, well-made man, but his hair is like a carpet. Both he and Stoffles behaved in a perfectly refined and gentlemanly manner. James Read acted as interpreter; he looks more like a Caffre than an Englishman; he is full of animation, and very clever and observing. He sat by Tzatzoe at dinner and kept up the conversation capitally. Tzatzoe was asked what struck them most in England. He said, "First, the peace, no fighting, all looking 'kind'; secondly, no beggars; everybody had their own business and wanted nothing of other men, but all looked comfortable and happy; thirdly, no drunkards, no fighting about the streets." He was then asked what he could mention to our discredit. He hesitated at first, but then boldly said we abused our Sabbaths: he was shocked to see the carriages about, and people selling in the streets; he admired the horses, but could not think what the donkeys had done to merit such different treatment: and as to the dogs, he thought it a most wicked thing "to make them work like Hottentots." He pleased my father very much by saying, that if it had not been for his labours in the committee, his nation must have been entirely extirpated.[21]

Tzatzoe was not, as some anthropologists and Western "civilization mongers" would have it, the product of "civilization" or "acculturation"; he was the victim of deculturation. As a concept, deculturation describes a situation in which the victims of subjugation are forced, under threat of liquidation, to abandon their own culture and to adapt to new behavior. Darcy Ribeiro, a Brazilian anthropologist, writes:

> We use the term "deculturation" to designate the process operating in situations where human contingents, torn from their society (and consequently from their cultural context) through enslavement or mass removal, and hired as unskilled labor for alien enterprises, find themselves obliged to learn new ways. In these cases the emphasis is on eradicating the original culture and on the traumas that result, rather than on cultural interaction. Deculturation, in this instance, is nearly always prerequisite to the process of enculturation. Enculturation crystallizes a new body of understanding between dominators and dominated that makes social coexistence and economic exploitation viable. It expands when the socialization of the new generations of the nascent society and the assimilation of the immigrants are brought about by incorporation into the body of customs, beliefs, and values of the ethnic protocol.[22]

Fanon also writes of this process of domination and cultural exploitation:

> The natives' challenge to the colonial world is not a rational confrontation of points of view. It is not a treatise on the universal, but the untidy affirmation of an original idea propounded as an absolute. The colonial world is a Manichean world. It is not enough for the settler to delimit physically, that is to say, with the help of the army and the police force, the place of the native. As if to show the totalitarian character of colonial exploitation the settler paints the native as a sort of quintessence of evil. Native society is not simply described as a society lacking in values. It is not enough for the colonist to affirm that those values have disappeared from, or still better never existed in, the colonial world. The native is declared insensible to ethics; he represents not only the absence of

values, but also the negation of values. He is, let us dare to admit, the enemy of values, and in this sense he is the absolute evil. He is the corrosive element, destroying all that comes near him; he is the deforming element, disfiguring all that has to do with beauty or morality; he is the depository of maleficent powers, the unconscious and irretrievable instrument of blind forces. All values, in fact, are irrevocably poisoned and diseased as soon as they are allowed in contact with the colonized race. The customs of the colonized people, their traditions, their myths—above all, their myths—are the very sign of that poverty of spirit and of their constitutional depravity. That is why we must put the DDT which destroys parasites, the bearers of disease, on the same level as the Christian religion which wages war on embryonic heresies and instincts, and on evil as yet unborn.[23]

Having been deprived of cultural, political, and economic autonomy, Tzatzoe and others like him likewise lacked the means to control their cultural creativity. Any possibility of assimilating the innovations imposed on them into their own cultural context was frustrated by the refusal of the conqueror to offer means for harmonious growth. As Ribeiro puts it: "In these circumstances, as they fed on undigested alien ideas not corresponding to their own experience but to the European efforts to justify rapine and to base colonial domination on moral grounds, their dependence and their alienation expanded."[24]

Jean-Paul Sartre has observed that colonization is not merely a matter of conquest:

> It is by its very nature an act of cultural genocide. Colonization cannot take place without systematically liquidating all the characteristics of the native society—and simultaneously refusing to integrate the natives with the mother country and denying their access to its advantages. Colonization is, after all, an economic system; the colony sells its raw materials and agricultural products at a reduced price to the colonizing power. The latter, in return, sells its manufactured goods to the colony at world market prices. This curious system of trade is only possible if there is a colonial subproletariat which can be forced to work for starvation wages. For the subject people this inevitably means the extinction of their character, culture, customs, sometimes even language. They live in their

underworld of misery like dark phantoms ceaselessly reminded of their sub-humanity.[25]

The subjection of the African to white colonial domination was at once total in its overall transformation of the context in reference to which African society was ordered, and yet partial and differentiated in its impact. The aim was a continued agony.

The chief instrument of ideological subversion was the colonial educational system assigned chiefly to mission schools. It is true that only a minority attended these schools; but it was on just this minority that the leading roles in the colonial relationship devolved. At the mission schools the Africans learned, together with the three R's, the ideological rationale of white rule over their communities, in particular the value judgments attached to the antonyms black and white. They were forced to use expressions, proverbs, and parables aimed at their own origin, and disparaging it.[26] The sense of agony which accompanied the African who was educated in mission schools is brought forward most succinctly in the themes found in African vernacular literature. Daniel Kunene, a professor of African literature, describes it thus:

> When we bear in mind that many indigenous African customs were declared by the missionaries to be incompatible with the Christian faith, and that the missionary would under no circumstances relax the rigid rules of that faith, then we can clearly see the beginnings, in respect of the Christianized African, of the process of deculturation. The African intellectual who came out of the missionary school was not only literate, but also he was a changed being. He looked about himself and saw nothing but evil. He saw his "heathen" brothers singing and dancing and drinking and loving in pursuit, as they thought, of the Good Life, and he shook his head in pity. For suddenly these things had become ugly and sinful. No wonder, for, in his school days, this Black intellectual was subjected to teaching materials chosen or prepared with an eye to making them effective instruments for the continuous absorption of the Christian religion. Not only that, but in reading lessons, for example, while the ways of life of the peoples of Western countries were praised in glowing terms, and suitable tribute paid to their national heroes, selections from the oral traditions of the Africans were mostly ones which painted their past black, and the moral, always strongly implied or even overtly

stated, was that they must be grateful for the coming of the White man who had led them out of their dark, dangerous, vile and sinful past. The process of alienation had begun, complex and divisive—Christian and non-Christian drifted apart; worse than that, they began to hate each other.[27]

The ideological and political intention of missionary education is obvious from this passage: it was to destroy the self-definition of the African people and to frustrate their creative impulse. As Kunene points out, in serving colonialism the church, through, for example, its schools, often became the arbiter of what was culturally correct and wrong with African culture.

F. Meli agrees with Kunene and points out that in the mission schools Africans were equipped with the knowledge that enabled them to read, even memorize (but not interpret), the Bible.

> The ideological and political intention was obvious: the church rather than the traditional institutions was to become the new centre of loyalty. In a sense, at the beginning of the twentieth century, one could speak of a "dual power" in the rural areas of South Africa. There was the power of the chief and that of the church (representing colonialism, above all, British). This factor more than anything else divided the loyalties of our people. The people were temporarily subdued but not conquered.[28]

Worse still, the Christian religion and the church-sponsored schools had developed in an altogether different historical context, and there was no effort to adequately adapt it to the experience of the African. The result was spiritual and cultural indigestion:

> Human beings are products of history not only in their bearing and their way of dressing, their stature as well as their mentality, but also in their manner of seeing and hearing, which cannot be dissociated from the process of social life as it has developed over the millennia. The facts presented to us by our senses are performed in two ways: on the one hand by the historical character of the object perceived, and on the other, by the historical character of the organ of perception.[29]

Thus, conquest and enculturation abruptly cut short the historical development of the African people and their civilization, which in several places had reached a highly advanced state. Having been subjugated, the African was declared a pagan and savage, a member of an inferior race, destined by the Christian God to slave to superior Europeans. This arrogance created serious tensions and divisions among previously unified groups. There was, as well, a loss of function and meaning by the traditional authorities, but the conqueror was determined to preserve and impose these disembodied institutions to legitimize his rule. The vaunted respect by the settlers of the traditions and the personality of the African people is, according to Fanon, inevitably tantamount to the most bitter contempt, and to the perpetration of a most elaborate sadism.[30] While any culture in the colonial situation is permeated by spontaneous, generous, fertile lines of growth, only a partial assimilation of European culture is allowed because the colonizer continues to maintain a truncated semblance of traditional society, but on nontraditional terms; placing "reliable men" in the chiefly positions to execute certain ceremonial gestures became the greatest deception of indirect colonial rule.

In South Africa there has grown in urban industrial areas a diffuse proletariat, a parasitic petty bourgeoisie of small traders, a professional elite, and an unstable stratum of "unemployed"—rogues, vagabonds, and beggars, who vegetate in the slums. Yet these groups are legally *temporary* sojourners to the cities and may be expelled to the reservations created for African occupancy after conquest. There, the Africans are supposed to develop along their "traditional" lines.

The white rulers have attempted through the creation of the reserve to have their cake and eat it too. The reserve system is meant to effectively arrest the African's development, while at the same time allowing whites to draw on Africans for exploitation in the urban industries. Thus, while the growth of industry and the accompanying process of urbanization changed the whole of South African society, for the African those changes were not supposed to lead to development; African "development" was to be along "tribal" lines, but as defined by the new rulers. The African societies in the reservations are deformed caricatures: they lack the economic and social means to develop independently.

The culture of the African people, once living and open to the future, became closed, fixed in the colonial status quo, and used as a yoke in their oppression. As Fanon said, "Both present and mummified, it testified against its members. It defines them in fact without appeal. The mummification leads to the mummification of individual thinking."[31]

In the next chapter I will discuss the evolution of the "native reserves" and their status today as bantustans. Suffice it to say here that in the process those individuals who, like Tzatzoe, were cut off from their disintegrating communities on the reservation found themselves in a classic situation of deprivation and rootlessness, while their reactions only confirmed the racism of the settler community. At the same time, the artificial constraints imposed on the original structures of African society completed their proletarianization and cultural pauperization.

The objective of the new white state was neither the total destruction nor the transformation of traditional societies, but the incorporation of individual members as laborers with the rest available as reserve labor and to provide a market. In South Africa the conquerors reconstituted the Africans as cheaper labor pools in specially designated reserves, incapable of any independent growth. The artificially preserved peasant structures became the most sinister inheritance of contemporary South Africa.

The imposition of settler rule and the capitalist mode of production thus interrupted the historical continuity of African societies. The African, estranged from the authentic possibilities of the new order, had no new alternatives for growth; their economy, technology, and culture became of marginal relevance. Indigenous customs lost their vitality and became instruments of oppression. Even the ideological elements which structure life—philosophy, art, literature, and the family—atrophied and became irrelevant. It is important, therefore, to see the present in terms of the past. Since the Africans have been subjected to settler rule, they have been born into a world where alienation awaits them. But present alienation is the result of the outrageous violence perpetrated by the agents of the settler state.

4

The "Native Reserves" (Bantustans) and the Role of the Migrant-Labor System

The Coloured people are generally looked upon by the whites as an inferior race, whose interests ought to be systematically disregarded when they come into competition with their own, and should be governed mainly with a view to the advantage of the superior race. For this advantage two things are considered to be especially necessary: first, that facilities should be afforded to the white colonists for obtaining the possession of land theretofore occupied by the Native tribes; secondly, that the Kaffir population should be made to furnish as large and as cheap a supply of labour as possible.

—Earl Grey, 1880

The above statement by an agent of British imperialism is particularly appropriate to introduce a description of the role of the reserve and the migrant system. It sums up the essence of what South Africa calls its "Native policy." If the capitalist mode of production was to develop, it was necessary to do more than deprive the immediate producers of the means of production and make them "free" paupers; wealth also had to be concentrated in the hands of the conquering settlers. The process of "imperialization" involved the restructuring of the African subsistence economy in such a way that peasants in the areas set aside for them after conquest could never again become economically self-sufficient. This is not unique. Marx wrote, in discussing Wakefield's discoveries regarding the colonies:

First of all he discovered that in the colonies the ownership of
money, the means of subsistence, machinery and other means of
production, do not suffice to stamp the owner as a capitalist unless
there exist, as a correlative, wage workers, other persons who are
compelled to sell themselves "voluntarily." He made the discovery
that capital is not a thing, but a social relation between persons,
and a relation determined by things. Mr. Peel, he says lamentingly,
took with him from England to Swan River, Western Australia,
means of subsistence and of production to the value of £50,000.
He had the foresight to take with him, in addition, 3,000 persons,
men, women and children, members of the working class. But, on
arrival at his destination, Mr. Peel was "left without a servant to
make his bed or fetch him water from the river." Poor Mr. Peel,
who had provided for everything, except for the export of the
English relations of production. He had forgotten to bring these
with him to Swan River![1]

When the British acquired the Cape Colony in 1814, they
brought settlers with capital who were expected to find workers
from among the indigenous population. Their problem was how
to avoid the fate of Mr. Peel. Behind the wars of conquest and
the "setting aside" of areas for African occupation lay a more
pervasive and sinister aspect of capitalist society—the need for
an exploitable class of laborers. Africans were not just to be
conquered and decimated: they were to be made dependent on
their conquerors for every aspect of their livelihood.

One of Marx's great achievements was to show that capitalism's attempt to create exploitative relations in the colonies encounters severe problems which have to be overcome by
extraeconomic means:

It is otherwise in the colonies. There the capitalist regime encounters on all hands the resistance of producers who own the means of
production with which they work, and who can gain wealth for
themselves by their own labour instead of working to enrich a
capitalist. The contradiction between these diametrically opposed
economic systems works itself out in practice as a struggle between
the two. When the capitalist is backed up by the power of the
mother country, he tries, by forcible means, to clear out of his way
the modes of production and appropriation that are based upon
the independent labour of the producers. Whereas in the mother

country, self-interest constrains the political economist, the sycophant of capital, to declare that the capitalist method of production is theoretically identical with its opposite; in the colonies, self-interest compels him to make a clean breast of it, and to acknowledge frankly that the two methods of production are antagonistic. To this end he shows that the development of the social productivity of labour, cooperation, and division of labour, the large-scale application of machinery, and the like, are impossible without the expropriation of the workers and a suitable transformation of their means of production into capital. In the interest of what is called "national wealth," he casts about for artificial means which will ensure the poverty of the common people. His apologetic armour, therefore, crumbles away bit by bit, like touchwood.[2]

One of the main determinants of the amount of land appropriated from the African was the size of the labor force that the white settlers needed. When the settler economy was agricultural, it was sufficient to clear excess Africans from fertile lands and deprive them of enough of their means of subsistence to force them to work part of the year for their new masters. But when the settlers began to establish sugarcane plantations, as they did in Natal, the need for a permanent class of proletarians unencumbered by the ownership of independent means of subsistence became more urgent.

Thus, the policies adopted in different places at different periods with regard to the maintenance, disposition, and size of the "locations" (as the areas "reserved" for African occupation were called then) were determined by the economy of the particular region. This explains the scattered, spotty nature of the reserves today. In rejecting the policy of "segregation," Earl Grey, for instance, suggested that natural and permanent locations be established with sufficient space between them to allow the spread of European settlements, in order that "each European emigrant would thus have it in his power to draw supplies of labour from the location in his more immediate proximity."[3] Sheila Van der Horst explains that

in embarking upon the policy of introducing European settlers into Victoria East and later into British Kaffraria, the administration was in fact creating what were to become in part pools of labour, even though at the time the predominant motive was to achieve security by breaking up the cohesion of the tribes and introducing European ideas and institutions.[4]

The policy of juxtaposing African locations and areas settled by whites had other consequences as well:

The effects of the intermingling of European and Native settlement and the imposition of European government were many-sided. The mode of living of the Natives, who had combined agricultural and pastoral subsistence farming, had to be modified. For one thing, it required more land than was now available. But, in the Cape Colony, the contact with Europeans tended for other reasons also to break their former self-sufficiency. New wants were awakened and new obligations, notably taxation, were imposed. All these developments necessitated change, the abandonment of that condition of self-sufficiency in which each household had produced the greater part of its own requirements.[5]

Before they were physically subdued, traditional African societies with plenty of land had posed difficult problems for the requirements of capitalism. The needs of an African living by subsistence agriculture and cultivating *mealies* ("corn") were confined to a *kaross* ("skin cloak") and some pieces of homemade cotton cloth. The prospects of leaving their families to work on other people's farms in order to earn wages to buy things they had no use for did not appeal to Africans.

In March 1851 a group of merchants, landowners, and inhabitants of Durban met to discuss their shortage of labor. In a resolution that was sent to the government of Natal by the Durban Corporation, it was stated:

Independently of measures for developing the labour of our own natives, we believe your Excellency will find occasion to sanction the introduction of a limited number of coolies, or other labourers from the East, in aid of the new enterprises on the coast lands, to the success of which sufficient and reliable labour is absolutely essential; for the fact cannot be too strongly borne in mind that on the success or failure of these rising enterprises depend the advancement of the Colony or its certain and rapid decline. Experimental cultivation has abundantly demonstrated that the issue depends solely on a constant supply of labour.[6]

In 1852 a commission of inquiry was appointed to investigate the past and present state of the Kaffirs in the District of Natal. According to the chairman of the commission, the membership embraced all the principal interest groups among whites in the district, including officials, newly arrived immigrants from Britain, "old" English colonists, and Dutch-speaking whites. Some of the evidence presented to the commission and the commission's conclusions are worth reflecting upon. They reveal the essence of the dilemma faced by colonists.

A farmer, Dewald Johannes Pretorious, when giving evidence before the commission stated that

> the locations are the cause of the inhabitants not being able to obtain labour, in as much as that I have asked Kaffirs in a Location to enter my service, and they have asked whether I was made to suppose that they would go and work for me at 5s. per month, when by the sale of wood and other articles they could obtain as much as they wanted, by which means they are afforded ample opportunity of roaming about the country and of stealing cattle when they see an opportunity without the owners being able to find out what has become of them.[7]

H. F. Flynn, assistant resident magistrate at Pietermaritzburg, made the following statement:

> The removal of natives from the vicinity of towns would, in my opinion seriously injure for a time the welfare of the white inhabitants of the district, if the views I have formed are well founded.
>
> I am aware that the natives generally raise double the quantity of corn required by them for the year's consumption, by which they are prepaired [sic] for a year of small production, or should this not occur, they are in a position to dispose of their surplus quantities to those who may be in want; and since a market has been opened by Europeans for a large quantity of corn, they have cultivated the land more extensively than formerly.
>
> I think that more than half the corn consumed in this district is raised by the natives. In addition to what they sell in the towns, many traders every year visit native kraals to purchase corn at an average rate of 4s. per muid, which is again sold at the stores to the consumer for 7s. 6d. per muid. A considerable quantity also is annually exported to the Mauritius and the Cape.[8]

The determination of the settlers to destroy the African mode of subsistence which stood in their way was very evident in the conclusions of the commission. First, the commissioners described what they called the African character as follows:

> When not effectually restrained and directed by the strong arm of power, the true and universal character of the Kaffirs, as framed by their education, habits and associations, is at once superstitious and warlike. Their estimate of the value of human life is very low; plunder and bloodshed are engagements with which their circumstances have rendered them familiar from their childhood; they are crafty and cunning; at once indolent and excitable; averse to labour; but bloodthirsty and cruel when their passions are inflamed. They pretend to no individual opinion of their own, but show the most servile compliance to the role of a despotic chief when it is characterized by vigour and efficiency. Cupidity is another strongly developed feature in the Kaffir character; their general habits, like those of other savages, debased and sensual to the last degree; possessing but a confused, indistinct idea of a future state, and of the existence of a Supreme Being, they cherish a belief in the most degrading system of witchcraft.[9]

The commission attacked the amount of land available to the African because it allowed them to follow idle, pastoral lives, instead of settling down to fixed industrial pursuits. It also attacked polygamy and the subordinate status of women, which enabled the men to live a life of ease:

> The Kaffirs are now much more insubordinate and impatient of control; they are rapidly becoming rich and independent, in a great degree owing to the polygamy and female slavery which prevails. They are better organised and consolidated, increasing in numbers by immigration, and more clearly aware of their real strength. If the wealth of the Kaffirs, above referred to, proceeded from the regular honest industry of the male population, the Commissioners would hail it as a certain sign of their improvement, but so long as it is drawn from the forced labour of females, it has no such signification, it is an index merely of the increasing numbers and exertions of the women, and can unfortunately only be taken as evidence of the increasing means of sensual indulgence available to the males.[10]

In 1855 the Natal Colony addressed a petition to the Queen praying for the introduction of convict labor, but it did not achieve the desired aim. In 1858 there was a movement to introduce Tongas from Portuguese East Africa, but the attempt failed because of the unwillingness of the Tongas to engage themselves for long periods of service.

With the discovery of diamonds in 1864 and gold in 1886, the shortage of labor became even more acute. As James Bryce, whose informed comments on South Africa have been referred to previously, observed:

> The white men, anxious to get to work on the goldreefs, are annoyed at what they call stupidity and laziness of the native, and usually clamour for legislation to compel the native to come to work, adding of course that regular labour would be the best thing in the world for natives. Some go as far as to wish to compel them to work at fixed rate of wages, sufficient to leave good profit for the employer.[11]

The British settlers in Natal eventually forced the British government to import indentured Indians, and 6,500 arrived between 1860 and 1866. Sir George Grey had seen the results of the use of indentured labor in the canefields of Mauritius, and when he visited Natal in 1855 he approved the importation of Indian laborers. He reported to the secretary of state that: "One measure which would greatly tend to promote wealth and security of that Colony [Natal], and render it of value and importance to Great Britain, would be to encourage the introduction of coolie labourers from India."[12] This scheme, however, was only a stop-gap measure. The diamond mines employed an average of 30,000 Africans in each of the first seven years of production. The discovery of gold only aggravated the shortage, and in 1876 Mr. John X. Merriman, prime minister of the Cape Colony, was under extreme pressure to bring in Chinese coolie labor. He wrote:

> In the Cape the government is called upon to survey mankind from China to Peru in the hope of creating and maintaining a class of cheap labourers who will thankfully accept the position of helots

and not be troubled with the inconvenient ambition of bettering this condition.[13]

But instead of looking to India and China, the 1893 Commission of Labour in the Cape Colony suggested that every male African should be taxed, with full remission if he could show he had been employed away from home during the year. In 1894 Cecil Rhodes, then prime minister of the Cape Colony, passed the Glen Grey Act. Its object was to encourage individual land tenure and to establish a simple system of local councils, thus making chiefs agents of the colonial power. It was hoped that limited individual land tenure would accelerate the dissolution of the traditional social structure. These two provisions, though praised by liberals as progressive, were intended to negate "tribal" communism and to encourage self-interest and egotistical calculation based on the cash nexus. Moving the second reading of the Glen Grey Bill and speaking in his other capacity as minister of native affairs, Rhodes explained that:

> If you are one who really likes the natives you must make them worthy of the country they live in, or else they are certain, by an inexorable law, to lose their country, you will certainly not make them worthy if you allow them to sit in idleness and if you do not train them in the arts of civilization.[14]

After the Boer War the mining industry again found itself desperately short of laborers. Despite pressure, Africans were still not coming forward in sufficient numbers, mainly because of low wages. In December 1903 a labor commission reported a shortage of 129,000 African laborers in the mines and estimated that by 1908 the shortage would grow to 365,000. The Chamber of Mines, created in 1889 with the objective of reducing mining labor costs, embarked, with the support of the press, upon an intensive campaign to win support for the importation of Chinese coolies. The Milner government (1902–1905), which saw the gold-mining industry as crucial not only to its own imperialist ambitions but also to the maintenance of British power in South Africa, agreed to introduce indentured Chinese labor. As H. J. and Ray Simons put it:

There was no time to spare, in the view of Milner and the owners; they wanted a ready-to-hand proletariat at the lowest possible cost who would restore the mines to full working capacity without delay, satisfy share holders, attract new capital, save Milner's reputation and the Transvaal from bankruptcy. They would not wait for taxation and land seizures to turn African peasants into work seekers.[15]

Now it was recognized, however, that indentured Chinese labor, like Indian labor, could not be a permanent substitute for local labor. Furthermore, the treatment of Chinese laborers became a major political issue in Britain. In the Transvaal, Louis Botha and Jan Smuts, elected to the government in 1906, pledged to repeal the Chinese Labour Ordinance and to refuse to admit more Chinese laborers. The repatriation of those Chinese whose contracts had expired began soon thereafter, and by 1910 all but a handful had left South Africa.

In March 1903 the South African Customs Conference had been convened to discuss the shortage of labor. It concluded, among other things, that the native population of Africa south of the Zambezi did not "comprise a sufficient number of adult males capable of work to satisfy the normal requirements of the several colonies, and at the same time furnish an adequate amount of labor for the large industrial mining centers."[16] In July 1903 the Transvaal Labour Commission had been created "to inquire what amount of labour is necessary for the requirements of the Agriculture, Mining and other Industries of the Transvaal, and to ascertain how far it is possible to obtain an adequate supply of labour to meet such requirements from central and south Africa."[17]

In 1909 Mozambique and the Transvaal Republic signed the Mozambique Convention, which provided for the annual exportation of 100,000 Africans from Mozambique to work in the Transvaal gold mines and the surrounding industrial complex the mines had spawned. Portugal was paid a fixed sum for each recruit, and a portion of each worker's wage was placed in a bank in Mozambique and given to the worker only on his return to one of the Portuguese colonies. In addition, when the Union of South Africa was formed in 1910 the government guaranteed

that 47.5 percent of the seaborne import traffic to the Johannesburg area would pass through Lourenço Marques. Formal arrangements for the procurement of cheap labor were not, of
course, limited to the Portuguese colonies, and the Tripartite
Agreement between Southern Rhodesia, Northern Rhodesia,
and Nyasaland had similar provisions for the repatriation of
workers after a certain period.

To avoid competition for labor and to reduce costs, the Native
Labour Association was organized in 1897. In 1901 it became
the Witwatersrand Native Labour Association (WINELA). It was
to be the sole recruiter for the mines from territories outside the
borders of Southern Africa—for East Africa, including the Portuguese and British High Commission territories. A similar organization, the Native Recruiting Organization (NRO), was
created in 1912 to coordinate African labor inside South Africa.
The extent of the base from which Africans were recruited is
described by Basil Davidson:

> The arms of this system reach far across the continent. Its fingers
> point into Northern Rhodesia, Nyasaland, far into Tanganyika,
> into all the High Commission territories; Bechuanaland, Basuto-
> land, and Swaziland; and they point, in so doing, a dreadful
> accusation at the whole concept and career of British colonial
> policy.[18]

Besides this external supply of labor, a "native policy" was laid
down by the South African Native Affairs Commission report of
1905. Its recommendations have been used by successive governments, sometimes with acknowledgment and sometimes
without, as a blueprint for the principle of territorial segregation. The commission report stated that "the time has arrived
when the lands dedicated and set apart, as locations, reserves, or
otherwise, should be defined, delimited, and reserved for natives by legislative enactment." It further recommended that this
should be done "with a view of finality" and that thereafter no
more land should be set aside for African occupation. As a slight
concession, it suggested that there should be no prohibition on
"deserving and progressive individuals among the natives acquiring land," but that this should be limited to areas defined by

legislation: tribal, collective, or communal possession should be prohibited.[19]

In 1910 a parliamentary select committee on native affairs published a preliminary bill which embodied the commission's conclusions. Although the bill itself did not become law at this point, the fundamental principle of territorial segregation was embodied in the interim Natives Land Act of 1913, while another commission was appointed to recommend the permanent lines of territorial segregation.

The act defined as "scheduled African areas" all existing African reserves and locations in the rural areas of the Union, as well as rural land privately owned by Africans—a total of 10.7 million morgen (one morgen equals 2.116 acres), but only a bare 7.3 percent of the total land area of the country. Africans could only acquire land or interest in land outside of the scheduled African areas from other Africans, unless they had the consent of the governor-general; concomitantly, only Africans could acquire any land or interest in any land within a scheduled African area, unless the owner had the approval of the governor-general.

A further 5.7 percent of the total land area was to constitute "released" land, where Africans were free from the general prohibition on buying land. But when the white farmers raised an outcry against such areas, on the ground that they would be prevented from obtaining farmland for themselves and that Africans settling there would cease to provide labor for the whites, politicians promised that the actual release of these areas would be contingent on the abolition of the voting rights held by Africans in the Cape. Although voting rights were not abolished—the Act of Union (1910) and the promise not to betray the Africans were too recent to abrogate—neither were the "released" areas released. The result was that Africans, already land-starved, were deprived of the right to purchase and acquire land.

The 1913 Land Act also abolished farming-on-the-half, a system whereby Africans who owned their own plows and oxen agreed to cultivate, graze stock, and live on a white landowner's property in return for giving him half the harvest. The abolition of this system uprooted thousands of Africans, forcing them to wander around the country without giving them any place to establish new homes. Sol Plaatje, secretary of the African National Congress in 1912, described their plight: "Awakening on Friday morning, June 20th, 1913, the South African Native found himself, not actually a slave, but a pariah in the land of his birth."[20] According to Francis Wilson, an economist at the University of Cape Town,

> few laws passed in South Africa can have been felt with such immediate harshness by so large a section of the population. The system of farming-on-the-half, which had flourished ever since whites gained control of the interior, was dealt a blow from which it never recovered. The next three decades were to see the almost total elimination of that class of rural Africans who, in the words of Sol Plaatje's policeman, had once been "fairly comfortable, if not rich and [who] enjoyed the possession" of their stock, living in many instances just like Dutchmen.

Wilson also discusses the long-range effects of the act:

> In the longer term, the Act served well to fuse those idealists, who felt that partition alone was a realistic means of protecting Africans from total domination by whites, with those more selfish and more numerous people who wanted economic integration, without the uncomfortable social and political consequences. For the new law set aside sufficient land to tantalize the idealist without providing enough to enable all Africans to make their living there and so to be able to exist without working for the white man on his terms. In later years much political dexterity was displayed in using the reserves to maintain a policy which simultaneously won the support of idealists . . . without alienating the confidence of those voters for whom Africans were primarily units of labour whose presence was essential but only tolerable so long as they ministered to the needs of the white man.[21]

After the passage of the 1913 Land Act, even more than before it, the areas set aside for Africans became reservoirs of labor for the mines, towns, and white farms. We pointed out above that the land wars of the nineteenth century were also labor wars. That is, Africans, having lost access to their lands, were permitted to draw sustenance from it as laborers, herdsmen, tenants, or renters. According to C. W. DeKiewiet, dispossession and collapse of the tribal system, erosion and drought, cattle diseases and taxes, new needs and old clothes—all these conspired to accelerate the change from independent tribesmen to a servile group. Because the nineteenth century created a great class of Black workers upon the farm and in industry, the impression was easily created that white society had won a special position for itself, elevating all of its members beyond the reach of the forces which govern the life of the natives.[22]

Here DeKiewiet formulates a view of the genesis of the structures that characterize the South African social formation. It is a complex social process, the internal developments of which were not predetermined. To exploit the diamond and gold mines, and to provide white farmers with their needs, the white conquerors developed strategies to *articulate* and make complementary antagonistic social formations and their modes of production.

African subsistence production, however, showed considerable resilience; hence the need for legislation to overcome this resistance. Legal land alienation transformed self-supporting peasants into squatters, tenant farmers, or laborers on settlers' farms or drove them into the mines and cities in search of work. After the 1913 act, the Chamber of Mines and the capitalist farmers had a regular flow of "temporary" labor.

Following this landmark law, a whole series of acts were enacted: in 1920 there was the Native Affairs Act, with its provision for Native Councils. This act contained hints of the eventual disenfranchisement of the Cape Africans. In 1922, to increase the economic pressure on the African peasants, the Native Taxation and Development Act (number 41 of 1922) forced all African males between the ages of eighteen and sixty-five to pay a poll tax of £1 per annum and every male occupant of a hut in the reserves to pay a local tax of ten shillings. Taxation authority at the same time passed from the provincial administration to the central government.

While the Native Taxation Act forced Africans into wage labor, the Urban Areas Act of 1923 abolished the rights that Africans had to freehold land in Johannesburg and other urban areas and declared that they could not be granted the same place in urban life and industry as whites. This act carried with it the plain implication that the future of the African population was primarily in the reserves. The Transvaal Local Government Commission of 1922 put it thus:

> If the Native is to be regarded as a permanent element in municipal areas, there can be no justification for basing his exclusion from the franchise on grounds of colour. The Native should be allowed to enter the urban areas . . . when he is willing to enter and minister to the needs of the white man, and should depart therefrom when he ceases so to minister.[23]

The Native Administration Act of 1927 put Africans outside the rule of law and thrust them under the discretionary authority of the governor-general and his retinue of white officials of the Native Affairs Department. The act also revived native law, declaring it valid when it did not conflict with "public policy and national justice." The chiefs were also restored to some authority, which in the nineteenth century had been violently wrested from them. Such customs as the *lobola,* or "bride-price," once reviled by the missionaries as the buying and selling of women and the mark of paganism, were restored in a caricatured form. The "tribe" and "tribalism" were now seen as the bulwark of African existence, as the structures which would prevent the spirit of individualism.

In 1927 Professor Edgar Brooks lamented what he called the "glorification of tribalism and all the old customs, precisely because these are old"; he calls this "a kind of twentieth century adaptation of the 'noble savage' theory" which he said "has had direct effects upon the Union Native Policy, for here what [he] called the 'Anthropological School' came into immediate contact with life. It [stood] behind many of the provisions of the Native Administration Act of 1927 by which the chief has been made an important part of the administrative machinery. One of the complaints made against the Act [was] that it tend[ed] to assimilate all Natives to the position of Tribal Natives in the reserves. Others may exist, they may even form the majority, but they are embarrassing phenomena. They do not live as the social anthropologist thinks they ought to live. They do not think on the lines which the Department considers suitable for natives. They obstinately refuse to develop 'on their own lines.' "[24] No matter! In the sacred name of policy, Africans were to be made to conform to the mockery of the tribal system.

In 1932 the Native Service Contract Act was passed, obliging landowners in the Transvaal and Natal to choose between turning their African squatters into wage-labor tenants, subject to the penal sanctions of the Master and Servant Laws, or sending them to a declared native area. Landowners who could not prove that all their tenants had rendered a minimum of 180 days of labor a year could be deprived of those considered surplus to their needs. The Native Service Contract Act thus complemented the Native Affairs Act of 1920, the Urban Areas Act of 1923, and the Native Taxation Act of 1922.

In 1936 Parliament passed the Hertzog Bills—the Representation of Natives Act and the Native Trust and Land Acts. The first took away the franchise that Africans in the Cape Province had been given by the Act of Union. Instead, the governor-general was made the supreme chief of all Africans, and they were given three white representatives to Parliament and a representative council to which to take their grievances. The second act extended the Native Service Contract to the Cape and the Orange Free State. It also provided machinery for the acquisition and development of the 5.7 percent of the "released" land promised in 1913 for African subsistence when not employed in the "white" economy. The principles of the Native Trust Act thus went far beyond those of the 1913 Land Act, which forbade sale or lease of land outside the scheduled areas to Africans. The 1936 act established once and for all that the conquered land could not be acquired by Africans either by commercial purchase or political means.

The struggle for land, which had lasted for three centuries, was now drawing to a close. The white settlers had won. The victims of conquest were dispossessed and reduced to permanent "hewers of wood and drawers of water." The three white representatives that Africans in the Cape Province could still elect to represent their interest were, according to the historian DeKiewiet, a concession which only imperfectly concealed the truth that the Cape native franchise had been destroyed, and that with it had disappeared all hope of an extension of the franchise to the rest of the population. The Act further established four electoral areas, the Province of Natal, the Transvaal and Orange Free State, the Transkei Territories and the Cape Colony, with an electoral college in each area to elect altogether four white senators. The electoral colleges were composed of chiefs, headmen, local councils, native reserve boards of management and other similar bodies. These bodies, which were only indirectly representative of the native population and frequently nominated by the Government itself, would each exercise votes in proportion to the number of native tax payers whom they represented.[25]

With no political power to defend themselves and not enough land to provide for an independent existence, Africans had no choice but to work as pure labor. Starvation became a relentless goad that pushed men out to earn money to support their families. The Afrikaans expression "Too little to live on, too much to die from" is an apt description of the conditions in the reserves, which are in effect dormitories for cheap labor: severe handicaps are imposed on the African people, which depress their earnings, deny them skills, and put a premium on instability. With only a paltry budget and no real political status, the reserves became rural slums whose rhythm of toil is at the mercy of what happens in the mines and urban areas of what is called "white" South Africa. This is truly what Marx described as the "martyrdom of the producer."

The great advantage of the reserves is that not only can Africans be reproduced cheaply there, but they can also be used as a dumping ground for the human waste discarded by the urban and mining industries. As a result, a "perfect" number of African laborers can be maintained in the so-called white areas, while the "African" areas are kept in a state of social and economic dependence, a state the capitalist sector maintains with all the political means at its disposal. This is the situation some social scientists label the "dual" or "plural" society, but the importance of the reserves for the development of South Africa lies precisely in their integration into the economy of the "white" state. This is a relationship based on a classic division between superior and subordinate, between those who own capital and the means of production and those with nothing but their labor power. What would it mean to the mining and agricultural industries to be without labor from the reserves? Black African labor means a difference between profitability and bankruptcy. Out of the exploitation of reserve labor comes the surplus value that is invested in urban-based industries.

The South African native reserves—now renamed Bantu homelands (see map)—are today concentrated areas of poverty, disease, and ignorance, where all activities or thoughts that the white rulers fear or dislike are repressed and extraeconomic coercions and controls can be swiftly applied. The reserve system represents the ultimate in deliberately conceived human retardation.

The Transkei Bunga, or council system, was a method of indirect rule conceived in accordance with traditional cultural patterns, but which granted the council only as much power as was correspondent with the white settlers' aims. In a previous chapter we referred briefly to the terms of the treaty Cetshwayo, the Zulu king, was made to sign by the British as a condition for retaining his throne. Having lost their authority, the traditional rulers were now being restored to power only to perform ceremonial gestures. The kings were reduced to the status of paramount chiefs and their subordinates to chiefs, becoming no more than cogs in the administrative machinery and often representing nothing "traditional" or "customary."

The political principle of the native reserves is domination of the African people through their disembodied traditions. By negating their history through conquest, the white settlers were able to usurp the operation of the Africans' precolonial social formations. The reserves were deliberately designed so that the people who reside in them have no choice but to seek employment in the capitalist sector.

In 1951 the Bantu Authorities Act was passed: this act changed the status of the reserves into "homelands," or "bantustans." In 1959 the Promotion of Bantu Self-Government Act was passed, laying the basis for the "independence" of the Transkei

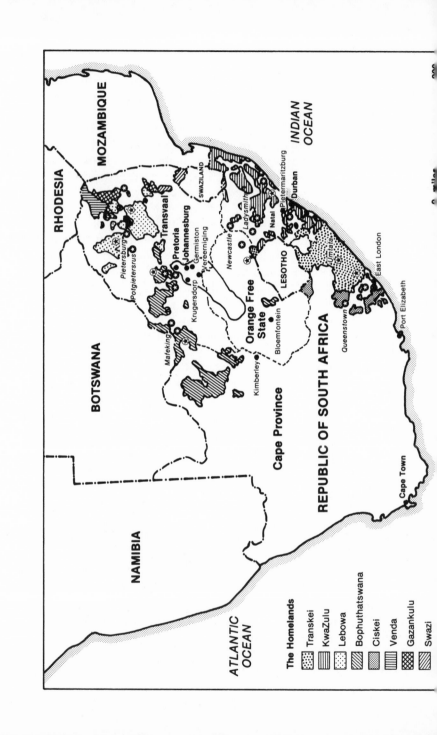

Homeland	People	Living in homelands (thousands)	Persons per square mile	Living in white areas (thousands)	Percent
Transkei†	Xhosa	1,730	124	1,320	45
KwaZulu	Zulu	2,100	174	1,900	49
Lebowa	Northern Sotho	1,080	132	890	44
Bophuthatswana	Tswana	880	62	1,110	64
Ciskei	Xhosa	520	114	400	44
Venda	Venda	260		110	33
Gazankulu	Shangaana	270	104	340	64
Swazi	Swazi	120	145	390	83
Basotho-Qwaqwa	Southern Sotho	30	140	1,310	98

The average density of "white" South Africa, including all races, is 34 persons per square mile.

Urban Areas with the Largest Populations* (in thousands)

Johannesburg, East and West Rand, Pretoria, OFS Goldfields, and Vaal Triangle
Total: 3,824 — Blacks 57%, Whites 36, Coloreds and Asians 7

Cape Town Total: 1,096 — 10, 56, 34

Durban Total: 843 — 27, 43, 30

Port Elizabeth Total: 469 — 43, 25, 32

Bloemfontein Total: 180 — 53, 6, 41

Pietermaritzburg Total: 159 — 44, 28, 28

East London Total: 123 — 42, 13, 45

Kimberley Total: 103 — 47, 25, 28

†Independent (October 1976) *1970 census

and other reserves. In 1963 the Transkei was granted "self-government" in terms of this act, and in 1976 it achieved "independence." Thus, the Nationalist Party government, which came to power in 1948, took over a ready-made system and renamed, extended, and systematized it with an entirely Teutonic thoroughness and determination.[26]

Hand in hand with the "change" of status of the reserves into bantustans, the government began a drastic program of population removal, uprooting three million rural Africans from what were called "black spots" between 1960 and 1970. Thus, the forcible removal of Africans from their ancestral lands that was begun during the wars of conquest and extended by the 1913 Land Act is being continued today on an even larger scale. In part, the process resembles the American solution to the "Indian problem" in the nineteenth century—the herding of an indigenous population into tiny pockets of rural obscurity, in areas which had been systematically underdeveloped by the development of the capitalist industry and agriculture elsewhere.[27]

Migrant Labor and Gold Mining

The creation of the reserves was only part of the process of using Africans as a cheap labor force; they also had to be incorporated into the industrial economy. The use of cheap migrant labor is neither new nor a purely South African phenomenon. As Stephen Castles and Godula Kosack, in a recent study of the use of migrant laborers in Europe, point out:

> The employment of immigrant workers in the capitalist production process is not a new phenomenon. The Irish played a vital part in British industrialisation. Not only did they provide a special form of labour for heavy work of a temporary nature on railways, canals and roads; their competition also forced down wages and conditions for other workers. Engels described Irish immigration as a "cause of abasement to which the English worker is exposed, a cause permanently active in forcing the whole class downwards."[28]

From the beginning, the South African mining industry searched for a method of combining two forms of labor: "skilled" and "unskilled," the levels marked as well by "race" and "color," and "victor" and "vanquished." Behind this dichotomy was to be developed a lasting strategy to make South Africa's gold mining profitable. What was to be the most profitable way of exploiting African labor? How were the disadvantages of expensive (white, skilled) labor to be corrected by the advantages of cheap (black, unskilled) labor? Given the political and class dynamics of South Africa in the late nineteenth and early twentieth centuries, employment of more whites, who had trade-union organizations, would mean less profit, while employing more Africans would mean more profit. Thus, even the most marginal mines could be worked at a profit, which also meant a longer lease on life for the mines.

Creating reserves from which labor could be drawn, through the migrant-labor system, became vital for the mining industry. The reserves and migrant labor satisfied not only the economics of gold mining but also the political and strategic considerations that were to constitute basic guidelines for national development throughout the twentieth century. The white national mission had become one with gold: to advance and become prosperous in the context of supplying the capitalist world with this rare metal. The impact was simply phenomenal, as is affirmed by the well-known South African economist Hobart Houghton:

> The Witwatersrand was proclaimed a gold-mining area in 1886, and the whole of South Africa was drawn into the mining boom which exceeded everything yet experienced. It soon became clear that the Witwatersrand was no mere flash in the pan, but was a huge auriferous formation, although few at the time would have believed that after eighty years, the mines would still have been in production, and the Witwatersrand would have yielded a total of over £6,000 million worth of gold.[29]

The reserves and migrant-labor system brought about the profitability of this prodigious industry. The abiding poverty and the breakdown of social life in the reserves due to migrant labor have been debated by earnest commissions, medical men, missionaries, social workers, and government officials. All these ills are intimately associated with the provision of cheap labor for the gold fields. Migratory labor has been several times condemned, but the Chamber of Mines laid great stress on the fact that it was the only way to make mines profitable.

The migrant-labor force in South Africa is almost entirely made up of "able-bodied" males, men who are single or are unaccompanied by wives and children and who are forced to live in compounds. R. W. Johnson describes the compounds thus:

> In fact the system finds its real apex and purest form in the urban compounds, and real home of thousands of black women and perhaps black men. The compounds range from the relatively small (30–50 men), run by schools, for example, to the great mine compounds, housing 10,000 men or more. It is to these latter that the migrant repairs from the bowels of the earth, to rooms usually unadorned by tables, chairs or electric light. They are the dormitories in which as many as 24 workers may sleep, in double-decker concrete bunks. Defecating is also normally a communal activity, with lavatories allowing place for as many as 20 men to sit side by side. Homosexuality is, perforce, the norm, though not a few of the migrants find solace with female prostitutes, and almost all find solace in drink. The system is richly productive of drunkenness, all forms of violence, venereal disease and, of course, the disintegration of the family relationships the men have left behind. It is on men such as these that the South African economy ultimately rests; it is they who dig the diamonds, uranium, copper and platinum.[30]

The period of employment ranges from six months to a year or two years, and the migration process is repeated again and again in an individual's lifetime—his career consisting of numerous short terms of employment, alternating with periods at home in his village or on the reserve. Migrants are recruited by agencies or are forced to seek work outside the reserves under threat of arrest for tax offenses or because of actual hunger, but they are paid as though they had no families to support. Following the recent changes in the status of the reserves, the government has now decided that migrant labor is to constitute the only basis for the employment of Africans in urban areas.

In *The Accumulation of Capital,* Rosa Luxemburg described the way the African labor force was incorporated into the diamond and gold mines in the nineteenth century:

> When Africans were first pressed to labour in the mines as wage earners, they were retained for six or nine months. In the rest of the year they were supposed to take part in their traditional subsistence, based on land. But the major portion of African lands, as we have seen, had been seized in the wars of conquest. The remaining land soon became overworked and "over"-populated. Thus with the opening of diamond and gold mining wage labor became a major source of subsistence and urban areas the main areas for earning a livelihood. The most striking sight at Kimberley, and one unique in the world, is furnished by the two so-called "compounds" in which the natives who work in the mines are housed and confined. They are huge enclosures, unroofed, but covered with a wire netting to prevent anything from being thrown out over the walls, and with subterranean entrance to the adjoining mine. The mine is worked on the system of three eight-hour shifts, so that the workman is never more than eight hours together underground. Round the interior of the wall are built sheds or huts in which the natives live and sleep when not working.[31]

Never in modern times has a country made such an extensive use of migrant labor as has South Africa, where more than 70 percent of the labor force is made up of migrants. What does this mean? We think of "modernizing" societies as those in which there is a permanent shift of population from agriculture to industry. What about South Africa? And, most particularly, what was the role of gold mining in this process?

The root and basis of the migrant-labor system and the reservations reaches deeply into the history of how African labor power has been exploited in South Africa. It stretches right back to the opening of the mines, and even before to the development of the Natal sugarcane plantations. To remember (or to remind one of) this context necessitates the delineation of comparative data from elsewhere that throws light on the true meaning of the use of Africans as migrant laborers who are forced for part of the time to eke out subsistence on the reserves.

Marx explains that in precapitalist economic formations

the process of dissolution which turns a mass of individuals in a nation, etc., into potential wage labourers . . . individuals obliged merely by their lack of property to labour and sell their labour . . . does *not* presuppose the disappearance of the previous sources of income or (in part) of the previous conditions of poverty of these individuals. On the contrary, it assumes that *only* their use has been altered, that their mode of existence has been transformed, that they have passed into other people's hands as a *free fund*, or perhaps that they have partly remained in the same hands.[32]

In Russia, Lenin spoke about the typical rural proletarian as the allotment-holding farm laborer who practiced insignificant farming on a patch of land, with a farm in a state of utter ruin. As such, the allotment-holding worker was unable to exist without the sale of his labor power.[33] Engels also speaks of rural domestic industry, carried on in conjunction with kitchen gardening, which formed the broad basis of Germany's new large-scale industry in the nineteenth century.[34] In England, according to Maurice Dobb, the use of forced labor in mining was not uncommon:

When the supply of labour for any new enterprise was insufficiently plentiful, for example in mining, it was not uncommon for the Crown to grant the right of impressment to the entrepreneur or to require that convicts be assigned to the work under penalty of hanging if they were refractory or if they absconded. This was done in the case of South Wales' lead mines leased to royal patentees in Stuart times, from which apparently numerous convicts ran away despite the threatened penalty, declaring that "they had better have been hanged than to be tied to that employment." Throughout this period compulsion to labour stood in the background of the labour market. Tudor legislation provided compulsory work for the unemployed as well as making unemployment an offense punishable with characteristic brutality.[35]

In this passage Dobb draws attention to two facts—the scarcity of labor in mining and the right of impressment granted by the crown to the entrepreneur. The Russian and English parallels are important because they point to the structural nature of forced labor in certain types of capitalist industries. In South Africa these earlier forms of forced labor were readjusted to meet the local conditions. The availability of peasants ready to be exploited has been central to the mining industry. The reserves offered cheap, hardened manual laborers eminently exploitable and with the expenses of their reproduction charged elsewhere. The so-called native reserves and the migratory labor system are not an aberration in the development of capitalism in South Africa. The reserves play an essential role in the service of the mining industry: the supplying of cheap labor.

Labor is cheap from an employer's point of view when the least possible is contributed to the subsistence and upkeep of the laborer and when the services of the laborer can be used long in excess of the labor time necessary for the laborer to earn an upkeep. Slavery provides the most extreme and straightforward example of this process of exploitation, for not only the means of production but also the workers are the property of the exploiting class. Everything created by the labor of slaves belongs to the slave owners, who supply the instruments and materials of production and distribute work and the means of subsistence as they wish.

Maurice Dobb's characterization of the meaning of plentiful labor is worth noting:

> It has always to be borne in mind that, when they spoke of plenty in connection with supply, both economists and factory-kings had in mind not only quantity but also price; and that they required the supply to be, not merely sufficient to fill a given number of available jobs, but in sufficient superabundance to cause labourers to compete pitilessly against one another for employment so as to restrain the price of this commodity from rising with its increased demand.[36]

Migrant labor, confined in the reserves, is not only plentiful but is also cheap. As practiced in South Africa, migrant labor is a variant of forced labor, and its resemblance to slavery is obvious. The fact that African migrant laborers are paid subsistence wages does not minimize the similarity, for they are paid at the minimal subsistence level for a single man, even when their families live with them in town.

The contribution of the migrant laborers to the prosperity of the gold-mining industry has been decisive. Brought in from the reserves in their youth and shipped back in their old age, the migrant laborers spare the mining industry a whole range of social costs, the burden of which is shifted to the poverty-stricken reserves. All that is produced over and above what is required to provide a bare living for the migrant workers goes to the mine owners as profit. The migrant laborers from the reserves provide the towns' labor power without having a right to the social benefits that are due them from the capital accumulated through their activity. The reserves fulfill the functions that capitalism prefers not to assume—those of social security for the migrant workers. The extreme destitution of the peasant in the reserves was brought about by this situation. The African migrants who are recruited to the gold mines are subjected to a kind of exploitation tantamount to slavery.

Take a typical white miner in South Africa: he is married, his wife may or may not be working, he has young children, he needs a house and other material things, and wants to be steadily employed from the time he enters the labor market until his retirement. When he retires, he expects government benefits, such as social security and insurance, which are partly made up of his employers' contributions and partly a redistribution via taxation of someone else's wages. From his total income he must sustain himself until he dies, and his children until they themselves enter the labor market.

Now let us take a typical African miner. He is a migrant, who is recruited only for a term of work. His wife and children are in the reserves (or bantustans). The social costs of reproduction—of caring for children, wife, and old age—are all borne by the household in the reserves. Thus, the typical income of an African miner is made up of what his employer pays him as a single man and what his wife ekes out from the subsistence sector. Unlike the white miner, the African is not able to claim from his employer a viable income to sustain him and his family during his productive years, much less throughout his life cycle.

Another advantage of the migrant-labor system that has been of inestimable importance to the white capitalist in South Africa is that it has kept the African working class in a state of permanent disorientation, unable to organize and confront white supremacy where it is weakest. As Hepple points out:

There is no doubt that the advantages of this kind of labour to employers are considerable. African mine workers are prevented from forming trade unions. Being compounded immigrants [sic], they are insulated from the influences of trade unionism among free workers. Attempts to establish unions are quickly scotched, and the organisers severely dealt with. The exclusion of trade unionism has created the extraordinary situation that the industry is organised only to the extent of its white employees, who comprise a mere ten percent of the workers employed.[37]

In addition, African labor can be rationed and moved from one employer to another, and from one branch of industry to another, as required by the developing economy, and capitalist accumulation can be subsidized in geographically selected areas.

The Landsdown Commission of 1944 fully recognized the importance of migrant labor for the economies of the gold-mining industry, and the country as a whole:

The gold mining industry of the Witwatersrand has indeed been fortunate in having secured, for its unskilled labour, native peasants who have been prepared to come to the Witwatersrand for periods of labour at comparatively low rates of pay. But for this fortunate circumstance, the industry could never have reached the present stage of development—some mines would never have opened up, many low-grade mines would have been unable to work with any prospect of profit; in the case of the richer mines, large bodies of ore, the milling of which has been brought within the limits of payability, could never have been worked, with the result that the lives of the miners would have been considerably reduced.

That the results accruing from this cheap native labour supply have had a profoundly beneficial influence on the general economic development of the Union is a matter that needs no demonstration. Not only has the earth yielded up a great body of wealth which would have remained unexploited, but vast amounts of money have been paid away in wages and put into circulation for the acquiring of equipment and stores necessary for the working of the mines and this, in turn, has had the beneficial effect upon the development of secondary industries.[38]

The history of the reserves demonstrates that capitalism can never totally eliminate the precapitalist modes of production nor, above all, the relations of exploitation which characterize these modes of production. On the contrary, and for as long as the gold mines need cheap labor, the political guardians of capitalism must reinforce these relations of exploitation. Charles Bettelheim, in discussing the articulation of modes of production in a social formation, puts it thus:

> Inside social formations in which the capitalist mode of production is dominant, this domination mainly tends to expanded reproduction of the capitalist mode of production, that is, to the dissolution of the other modes of production and subsumption of their agents to capitalist production relations. The qualification "mainly" indicates that this is the predominant tendency of the capitalist mode of production with the social formations under consideration. However, this predominant tendency is combined with another secondary tendency, that is, "conservation-dissolution." This means that within a capitalist social formation the non-capitalist forms of production, before they disappear are "restructured" (partly dissolved) and thus subordinated to the predominant capitalist relations (and so conserved).[39]

It is now easy to define South Africa's characteristics as a concrete capitalist social formation. True, South Africa has undergone a process of autonomous capitalist development which has been mainly concentrated in the cities, and thus development has been similar to that of other capitalist countries. However, it also continues to exhibit features common to the earlier forms of capitalist accumulation. This is because of the continued reliance on mining; and the dominance of the mining oligarchy over the ruling power bloc has generated the peculiarities of South Africa's capitalist development. The junior minister of Bantu Administration put the case for the continued use of migrant labor as follows:

> We are trying to introduce the migratory pattern as far as possible in every sphere. That is in fact the entire basis of our policy as far as the white economy is concerned, namely a system of migratory labour.[40]

The role of migrant labor in the economies of the Bantu homelands has increased dramatically in recent years; the accumulation of capital based on the mining model is the basis for entrenchment of the migratory-labor system. This fact is essential to an understanding of the border industries that are being developed on the peripheries of the homelands. The rationale of this new policy is described as follows by Stanley Trapido:

> The innovatory aspect of the new phase of labour repression consists in the creation of industrial centres—the border industries—to which capital and labour will be directed from older centres. Most border industries are located in areas where long-established Afrikaner communities exist and where African labour is close at hand (English-speaking East London is an exception). The most prominent border industries are located near Pretoria, Brintz, and Pietersburg in the northern Transvaal, and in the Ladysmith–Newcastle vicinity of northern Natal. These activities will ensure that Afrikaner areas acquire an increased share of the national income.
>
> Their effect upon the African worker will be to depress wages. Private capital, some of it redirected from the older industrial areas, estimated to be R314 million [R1 = $1.40], was invested in the border areas in the years 1965–1968. The Industrial Development Corporation has increased its contribution to the border areas from R21 million to R65 million in the years 1965–1968, while wage determinations for African workers in the border areas are lower than those in the older industrial centres. *Work which Africans are usually precluded from doing is permitted in the border industries at wage scales customary for Africans.*[41]

The bantustans are a key part of the present phase of capital accumulation. The Kwazulu homeland feeds the industrial complex centering on the Durban–Pinetown complex; the Transkei, besides feeding the mining industries, feeds its labor to the East London and Port Elizabeth areas. The proximity of industries to the homelands enables the government to keep the number of Africans in urban areas to the minimum required by the actual economic needs.

The changeover from the policy of segregation to apartheid also meant the development of a more carefully planned structure of exploitation of African labor power. In terms of the bantustan policy of the Nationalist government, there is no longer any black unemployment to worry about in the urban areas. "Migrant" black workers without jobs belong only in their "homelands." In 1964 government labor offices were established in each homeland at which all Africans seeking work must register. Black workers are not allowed to leave the homelands until the labor office has obtained labor contracts for them, and even then cannot work in white areas for longer than twelve months at a time. While working in the cities, the African lives in hostel complexes. Apartheid, then, is the distilled essence of the reservation theory.

An understanding of this new phase of the role of the reserves and the migrant-labor system can only come from an analysis of the needs of South Africa's capitalism in the present time. In the evolution of South Africa's so-called native policy, it is not difficult to discern the social and economic class interest which it serves. When the Afrikaner petty bourgeoisie came to power in 1948, one way it could make its interests prevail over those of other classes was to ensure that it could not be challenged politically. The very nature of its dominance made it introduce new structures of oppression; and to facilitate the process of capital accumulation by this class, the border industries were encouraged and the Group Areas Act was passed to destroy the thriving Indian merchant class and replace it with Afrikaners.

What type of theoretical conclusion can be made about the role of the reserves in the evolution of South African capitalism? The South African reserves have been conceptualized as internal colonialism. Does the concept of internal colonialism illuminate and explain the empirical data presented in this chapter? Above, references have been made over and over again to the various government commissions that have stated that the mining industry can only survive if it employs Africans as migrant laborers. And because of this, African mine workers' wages are calculated on the assumption that they supplement the produce of a subsistence economy.

Marx distinguished between constant capital and variable capital. The former denotes the raw materials and the fixed capital; the latter denotes that part of capital that is advanced as wages, i.e., for the purchase of labor power. This classification is closely related to Marx's labor theory of value, which, briefly stated, says that the value of a commodity is determined by the average amount of socially necessary labor required to produce it. Marx used this schema as the foundation for his analysis of the exploitation of the working class.

We have seen how critical gold export is for South Africa's political economy. The problem for the South African gold producers was that the price for gold was fixed by the consumer at $35 an ounce. Yet the absolute contribution to the economy of gold continued to grow: in 1946 gold output was worth R203 million; in 1960, R530 million; in 1967, R757 million (R1 = $1.40). This soaring production in the face of a static world price was achieved by a variety of means: by increasing capital investment in new equipment and techniques, by a system of averaging production costs, and by holding down wages of African miners to levels miserable even by the standards of other Africans. And the reserves and migrant labor played a crucial role in this emiseration of the African migrants.[42]

The reserves could not have existed into the present as just pools of cheap labor power. An elaboration of rationalization to justify their status was necessary. The colonial administrator and commissioner of native affairs had inherited from the military period not only despotism but also total control. This method, however, was considered too direct. An indirect method of control was devised, especially where potentially powerful individuals and traditions were still strong; they were kept in place, but now their prerogatives were mainly ceremonial. The chiefly institution, though it preserved the traditional appearance and utilized members from the ruling families, had a fundamentally new character. The traditional chiefdom gave way to the administrative chiefdom.[43]

5

The Political Economy of the
Gold-Mining Industry
and the Social Structure*

Modern society, which soon after its birth pulled Plutus by the
hair of his head from the bowels of the earth, greets gold as its
Holy Grail, as the glittering incarnation of the very principle of
its own life.

—Karl Marx, *Capital*

> Roar! and roar! machines of the mines,
> Roar from dawn till darkness falls;
> I shall wake, Oh, let me be!
> Roar, machines, and never stop
> For black men groaning as they labour,
> Tortured by their aching muscles,
> Gasping in the reeking air
> Poisoned by the dirt and sweat—
> (Shake, shake your haunches clammy wet!)
> —B. Wallet Vilakazi,
> *In the Gold Mines*

The discovery of diamonds in 1864, and more particularly gold
on the Witwatersrand in 1884, brought about economic changes
in South African life tantamount to a full-fledged revolution—
the gold industry gave a new complexion to almost every feature

---

* This chapter was completed before I had the opportunity to read a very
good study by Frederick A. Johnstone, *Class, Race, and Gold: A Study of Class and
Racial Discriminations in South Africa* (London: Routledge and Kegan Paul, 1976).
Since his conclusions correspond to and complement mine, I did not feel any
need to revise mine where our interpretations differed.

of South African life. As the mining industry expanded, it spawned an industrial economy in the heart of the country. The exploitation of gold brought into silent relief the intentions of British imperialism vis-à-vis the Afrikaner and the African.

From the 1890s until World War II, and to a lesser extent even today, gold mining has been the fulcrum of South Africa's political economy. Marx could have been thinking of an industry such as gold in South Africa when he wrote:

> There is in every social formation a particular branch of production which determines the position and importance of all others, and the relations of all other branches as well. It is as though light of a particular hue were cast upon everything, tinging all other colours and modifying their specific features; or as if ether determined the specific gravity of everything found in it.[1]

South Africa's capitalist development has revolved around gold mining, the industry most infiltrated by foreign capital in search of usurious returns. The industry quickly became the "heart" of the entire political economy; in time, the heart became independent of the body it controlled, able to rely on its own institutions and its worldwide network of interests. Through the poisonous nourishment provided by gold profits and dividends, the South African economy grew to be the deformed monster that it is today.

In 1910 gold made up 80 percent of South Africa's exports. The Dominions Royal Commission of 1914 estimated that 45 percent of South Africa's total income was attributable directly or indirectly to the gold-mining industry. Today gold and its by-product, uranium, account for almost half of South Africa's exports and are its major source of foreign exchange. In 1950 Sir Harry Oppenheimer, chairman of the giant Anglo-American Corporation, quoted figures to show that in 1946–1947 industrial raw materials valued at R208 million (R1 = $1.40) were imported, while exports of manufactured goods amounted to only R48 million. The export deficit of the manufacturing sector was therefore R160 million. Oppenheimer drew the following conclusion:

> Far, therefore, from secondary industry offering an alternative to

take the place of mining in our economy, the fact is that the
prosperity of gold mining and the other primary exporting industries is a prerequisite and a condition of our industrial development. . . . Manufacturing industry will only be able to serve as a
substitute for the wasting asset of our mining industry if it is able to
increase substantially its contribution to our export trade. This is
really another way of saying that, as a whole, industry in South
Africa, if it is to be able to stand on its own feet, must reduce costs.
And in order to reduce costs the principal requirements are
greater efficiency and a large internal market.[2]

In spite of the increasing importance of the manufacturing
sector, South Africa's mineral resources continue to provide the
foundation of its expanding economy and have subsidized much
of that growth. For instance, in 1969 there was a record gold
production of 31.3 million ounces and sales of $1.2 billion,
including uranium, sulphuric acid, pyrite, and the unofficial
uranium sales. Overall mineral sales (including premium gold
sales on the unofficial market) set a record of almost $2.1 billion,
an increase of 9.1 percent over 1968. Diamond production increased to seven million carats in 1969, with sales of $145 mil-
lion. In fact, mining still accounted for 58 percent of all exports
in 1968.[3]

Within the country, the gold industry spends $400 million a
year on supplies and equipment, quite apart from salaries and
wages, which amount to $300 million for over 400,000 people
(43,000 whites and 370,000 Africans). Gold profits have been
the motivating force behind the country's industrial expansion;
the prosperity of the rest of the economy has been a result of the
overspill from the gold industry.

Theodore Gregory, Sir Harry Oppenheimer's biographer,
writes that:

Without mining there would probably have been no explosives or
chemical industries in South Africa, nor a flourishing steel industry, nor an engineering industry on the present scale, since the
constantly growing technical demands of the mines constitute the
basic element in its growth. The very considerable afforestation
which is taking place over the years is a direct consequence of the
demand of timber by the mining industry.[4]

The gold industry enables the country to pay for machinery, electrical equipment, raw materials, foreign cars, clothing, and other imported goods, and provides for a large part of the state expenditure, including assistance to farmers. Recently the gold industry, especially that part of it which deals with explosives, has contributed the know-how to building South Africa's war machine.

British Imperialism and the Gold-Mining Industry

The central fact about the South African economy after the discovery of gold was its domination by British capital. Even after 1910, when the Boers were in control politically, the British owned the diamond and gold mines and the railways that transported these minerals. The country's basic industry, its "heart," was an appendage of Britain and the world economy.

The ownership and control of the Witwatersrand gold fields was from the start concentrated in the hands of a few capitalist monopolies. This was a legacy of a similar concentration in the diamond-mining industry. The Kimberley diamond mines, which had at first consisted of numerous individually owned small holdings, became progressively consolidated, until at the end of the century De Beers, a company created by Cecil Rhodes, gained control of all the diamond mines—and thus of 90 percent of the world's output. The planned structure of interlocking directorates in the gold-mining industry was facilitated by the formation in 1887 of the Chamber of Mines, a committee of representatives from each of the seven great mining houses, which came to represent and coordinate the interests of the mining groups and of the two African labor recruiting agencies—the Witwatersrand Native Labour Association (WINELA) and the Native Recruiting Corporation (NRC), created in 1896 and 1912, respectively.

The predominance of British finance-capitalist interests was guaranteed by the Chamber of Mines. The Chamber has been aptly described by Timothy Green as the inner sanctum of the industry: its deliberations are as secret as those of a cabinet. In its early years the Chamber was an extreme organ of British imperialism. "It was," said Harry Oppenheimer, "a highly Empire-minded body."[5] J. A. Hobson, writing in 1894, observed: "Nowhere in the world had there ever existed so concentrated a form of capitalism as that represented by the financial power of the mining houses in South Africa; nowhere else does that power so completely realize and enforce the need for controlled politics."[6]

We have already seen the various steps that were taken by the British government to ensure that gold production was not impeded after the Anglo-Boer War—including the importation of Chinese labor and the arrangement with Portugal for the recruitment of Africans for the gold mines. As a result of these measures, the Witwatersrand became the capital of an economic empire whose legislative capitals were in Cape Town, London, and Lisbon; labor legislation in all of them followed the dictates of South Africa's gold-mining needs.

After 1910 the use of the profits from the gold-mining industry became a major issue dividing the English-speaking mining magnates and the rising Afrikaans-speaking petty bourgeoisie. Gold is an exhaustible product, and the leaders of the gold-mining industry have been preoccupied, almost from the day the mines opened, with its possible exhaustion, and with the fear that the great industry and the urban complex it has spawned may be a transient phase in the mining history of the world.[7] In fact, some authorities in the capitalist world predict that by the close of the century gold, like silver, will be demonetized. To protect itself against this eventuality, South Africa had to industrialize, and when it did the initial capital was provided by taxation of the gold-mining profits.

A few weeks before the outbreak of the Anglo-Boer War, the *Standard,* the government gazette for the Transvaal, declared that it was the aim of the republic "to build up other industries on the back of the gold mines." The newspaper explained that by taxing the mines and giving encouragement to secondary industries, the government had introduced "other industries around which it had created a semi-protective wall." A note-worthy passage read:

> All men cannot be gold-miners, nor can the State live by gold-mining alone. Somehow or other . . . manufactures have to be encouraged if the ultimate condition of the State is to be sound. Monopolies (in the form of protective tariffs and monopoly concessions) have their weak points: but they come most conveniently to Pretoria's hand. Its idea, where it is at all protective, is to give the initial impetus to industry. . . . Besides the Transvaal is no exception in a matter of pursuing a protective policy and seeking to develop and reserve the home market. At one time or another most states and most countries have trod the highway of protection, and have passed through the stage of high tariffs and better things. . . . When protection and monopolies have served their end this State will get into line with other centres. . . . "Nations," it has been remarked by no less an authority than LIST, "can without inconsistency, and should, change their system in proportion as they advance. At first by free trade with nations of higher culture, they emerge from barbarism and improve their agriculture; then by means of restrictions they give an impulse to manufacture; then finally by a gradual return to the principle of free-trade they maintain the supremacy they have acquired." The Transvaal, it will be seen, is in the middle stage, and the Progressive need not be so impatient. He might spend the interval in getting information. He will find there is method, sound method, too, in Pretoria's policy.[8]

The struggle between those who favored the use of the taxes derived from the profits of the gold mines to industrialize the country and those who wanted to retain a primarily mining economy in South Africa reached a crisis after World War I. South Africa, as we shall see later, was faced by an immense problem in the number of poor whites. The post–World War I recession had caused a drop in mining profits. The mine owners' attempt to substitute black for white miners created a political crisis, which was resolved in 1924 with the election of the Pact government, made up of Afrikaner Nationalists and the Labour Party under General Hertzog and G. Creswell. This was a victory for those who favored industrialization as a precaution in case the gold was exhausted and also as a means to alleviate unemployment. Under the Pact government industrialization became more and more a function of the state. Using the threat of nationalizing the gold mines, the Pact government insisted that the strategic iron and steel industries be under state control. According to Ralph Horwitz,

> the political battle to make ISCOR, the Iron and Steel Corporation of South Africa, a state undertaking led to the first circumvention, by way of Senate manipulation, of the Act of Union of 1910. Though it was not always the governments of Afrikanerdom that initiated the legislation, it was Afrikanerdom that narrowed the vision and directed the subsequent motivation. It intensified direct and indirect state authority by way of public utilities, massive investment in the public sector, and through the chosen instruments of the Land Bank and the Industrial Development Corporation, the IDC.[9]

While the state was pushing its industrialization program from above, the owners of the mines and their representatives continued to lament the evils of protectionism, identifying it with corruption and inefficiency. The Economic and Wage Commission of 1925 wrote:

> Now protection in its early stages, whatever its ultimate effects, does nothing to increase the resources of total wealth of a nation. It may lead to the development of new industries, but it cannot create these out of nothing and, in fact, creates them by diverting to them labour, capital and enterprise, that, but for the protective policy, would have been applied elsewhere.[10]

The mining industry also called on the economist to bolster its case against state-financed and -directed industrialization and against protection of manufacturing or secondary industry. But those who favored state-directed industrialization argued that if protectionism was good enough for the advanced capitalist countries, then it was good enough for South Africa. The success of their policy was recognized in 1936 by the Tariff Commission: "It is clear that a great deal of the industrial development which took place after 1925, and of the employment resulting therefrom, is directly due to the stimulus given by the protectionist policy inaugurated in that year."[11]

It is not possible to trace in detail the contribution of gold mining to the industrial development sponsored by state agencies. In 1940 the Industrial Development Corporation was created, which has since built a very substantial industrial empire.

The Struggle for the Control of the Gold Mines

Until 1953 the gold-mining industry was, according to Basil Davidson, a pie into which the Afrikaner Nationalists had not managed to insert a thumb, nor pull out a single plum. Most of the profits of gold mining still went overseas, and most of the great mining corporations were based in London. The politics of gold mining were United Party politics, i.e., "English" politics. And, more important, many of the African miners were not South African natives, but British African natives.[12] After the Nationalist Party came to power in 1948, it launched an offensive against the domination of the gold industry by British capital.

We can get a glimpse of the kind of struggle that led to the inclusion of Afrikaner capital in the mining industry from an incident reported by the city editor of the London *Times* of May 2, 1957. The report stated, among other things:

> Any struggle that might have developed for control of the Central Mining and Investment Corporation, with its large holdings of liquid funds and its widespread mining interests, seems to have been prevented. A group of city bankers and mining finance houses, along with American interests, have acquired sufficient of the Ordinary and Preference shares in the corporation to forestall its acquisition by other parties. The group now holds, on behalf of a South African company about to be formed, some 80 percent of the corporation's Preference and a "substantial" amount of its Ordinary capital. . . . The new South African company, which is being incorporated with a share and loan capital of approximately £5m, will not only take over these Preference shares but also the substantial holding of Ordinary shares. The majority of the shares of this new company will be in British and South African hands. A

participation in it is expected to be offered to the Central Mining-Rand Mines group.

Those involved in this deal included, according to this report, C. W. Engelhard and Gordon Richdale of New York, the Anglo-American Corporation of South Africa, the Union Corporation, N. M. Rothschild and Sons, J. Henry Schroder and Company, and Robert Benson Lonsdale and Company of London. It was the combined efforts of these international corporations that saved Central Mining from being taken over by unnamed competitors.

The battle for Central Mining was important for two reasons. First, Central Mining (Corner House) is a huge international group, whose South African interests constituted the second largest holding in the South African mining industry. The liquid funds referred to by the London *Times* were dollars received from the sale of Trinidadian oil to the American interests. This sale of "Empire Oil" had been sufficiently important to lead to loud indignation in the British Parliament at the time. Through the Rio Tinto Mining Company, the Central Mining group also had a large share in the Canadian and Australian mining industries. The Central Mining takeover bid by the unnamed group combined, according to G. Fasulo, first-rate importance and drama with an element of mystery.[13]

Second, the political importance of the incident lies in the fact that the defeated but unnamed group was the central institution of Afrikaner Nationalist capital—the insurance company, SANLAM. With the formation of the Union in 1910, a powerful group of Afrikaner Nationalist capitalists came into being and grew rapidly. A. Dickson described the position of Afrikaner capital in 1955 as follows:

> The economic power of Afrikaner finance capital is concentrated in the great financial institutions, Volkskas and SANLAM, and in a number of investment companies all tied to a greater or lesser extent to these giants. The power of these investment companies is surprisingly extensive and the rate at which their assets have increased since the war can only be described as breath-taking. . . . The total capital assets of the SANLAM group are today well over £50 million, that is to say, of the same order as those of Anglo-

American. . . . The Volkskas bank itself has seen a truly meteoric rise in its fortunes in the last ten years. Between 1944 and 1953 it increased its assets from less than £7 million to about £45 million. Three most important features of the position of national capital in 1955 were also discussed: . . . the Small Mines and General Investment Company [is] an Afrikaner financial group which is actually trying to muscle in on that stronghold of British capital, the gold mining industry. . . . The big established financial institutions of the country have been forced to recognise Afrikaner capital's rise to a place in the sun. The latter's representatives now sit on the boards of the biggest financial institutions; for example, Havenga is now a director of Barclays Bank, and Sauer, the Nationalist minister, has for some time been a director of the Old Mutual. . . . And how well our financial groups have known to cash in on the nationalistic sentiments of the ordinary Afrikaner! They have induced him to insure only with Afrikaner banks, to build his home through an Afrikaner building society, to patronise Afrikaner shops, as far as possible.[14]

The Central Mining takeover bid was an attempt by Nationalist capitalists to restore the economic "heart" to its political body. The threat was so serious that British and American help had to be called in on a large scale to defeat the Nationalist bid.

The anomaly of 1910, in which Afrikaners were allowed to dominate the state, was gradually corrected but only after bitter struggles, during which the British capitalists made sure that the essential power and economic interests of British imperialism were not undermined. However, the need to preserve British capital interests resulted in the incorporation of prominent Afrikaner financiers into the Chamber of Mines. According to Timothy Green:

The character of the Chamber has changed to meet new conditions. It now has Afrikaner members, a very important step forward in bridging the long-standing gulf between the English and Afrikaners in South Africa. For generations the Afrikaners, engrossed in politics, looked with great suspicion on those "foreigners" who had established the gold mining industry in Johannesburg. At first they expected the industry to last only a few years, like other gold rushes. Even when it became clear that this was a permanent rush, the reconciliation between English and Afrikaners was a long time coming. Now that it has been achieved, gold is indeed a South African industry. The first tangible result of the reconciliation was a merger in 1963 between General Mining and Finance Corporation and a new Afrikaner mining group, Federele Mynbou.[15]

The Gold Connection in the International Monetary System

To get a picture of the gold connection, and the social relations involved in gold mining, imagine an African miner. He works long hours and is a migrant separated from his family—left behind in Malawi, Lesotho, or one of the South African reservations. He digs gold for a period ranging from six to eighteen months. In the process, he may contract silicosis. Then imagine a British squire's home, with green lawns, appropriate furnishings, and a retinue of well-trained servants. The wife is spending a summer vacation in France; her family is not wealthy, but it has sufficient "independent" means from investment in South African gold to enjoy life without work. Imagine also a Zurich banker. He buys and sells gold and foreign currencies for his customers, just as some brokers buy and sell wheat. Imagine an American investor. He likes a speculative fling now and then. He has just seen ads in the *New York Times* for gold stocks and for the gold Kruger Rands that are being marketed worldwide, and he makes a mental note to ask his broker if there is any chance of a quick killing. Imagine an Englishman who works for the Bank of England. He notices that many people are selling pounds for other currencies and wonders if today the central bank will have to step into the market to buy pounds in order to keep up their price. How are all these individuals related, or are they? How are they responsible for the plight of the African miner in the South African gold fields?

These people have never met one another. Their daily lives, their problems, and their hopes are probably quite different. Yet they are connected in the international monetary system. The one thing they have in common is an interest in money; they all are concerned with whether gold and the scraps of paper called currency have the same value. Will the franc, the dollar, or the pound depreciate, thus requiring more currency to buy the same goods? Will gold be assigned an ever higher value by most countries—or no value at all? What will this mean for the black mine worker? This is how R. W. Johnson describes the gold connection:

> The world gold market and thus, in part, the world's monetary system rest on the African miners, for it is they who dig the gold, as also the coal to provide electricity for the gold mines. They are the unsung (and poorly paid) heroes of every Anglo-American report, every De Beer balance sheet; it is the fruit of their labours which have, over the years, filled the vaults of Fort Knox, bought horses for the Oppenheimer family, endowed Rhodes scholarships, and provided Elizabeth Taylor with her jewelry.[16]

In 1815 the capitalist world agreed on an international financial structure. The rules of this system, simply put, state that if one country wishes to purchase the goods of another it can either barter one of its own products for them or can pay with gold. This relatively rare metal, long regarded as having great intrinsic value and beauty, was accepted as a medium of exchange by all countries. The coin, as marked and shaped by the currency standards of a particular national authority, had no significance for international trade; here it was the weight of the crude metal, the bullion, that counted. Bullion served as a means of payment for settling international balances.

South Africa is the main supplier of gold to the international monetary system. Some mining exports, such as copper and diamonds, are highly sensitive to variations in world demand; gold is not. In fact, falling world prices make gold mining *more* profitable without reducing the market. For the country that produces it, gold acts to stabilize national income and the balance of payments because it is capital par excellence—its value is determined by the quantity of labor incorporated in it and by the fact that it is an expression of the social character of wealth.

For almost a hundred years, South Africa's gold-mining industry has been in the enviable position of knowing that its entire output will be readily absorbed by the world monetary system at a guaranteed price and with no marketing problems. The international price of gold—$35 per troy ounce—remained unchanged from 1934 to 1971, when it was officially raised to $42 per ounce. The price was determined by the U.S. Treasury, which stood ready to buy and sell gold at the official price.

Since the 1880s more than 800 million ounces of gold worth over £20 billion, about one-third of all the gold ever mined anywhere, has been mined in South Africa. Therefore, South Africa occupies a unique position in the world economy—a position which cannot be ignored by international monetary authorities. Thus, according to Green:

> Nothing is more likely to send Bank of England or U.S. Treasury officials rushing for the first jet to South Africa than the thought that the South African Reserve Bank, which sells the Republic's gold, might be directing it to markets other than London, where the whole business is carefully monitored by the Bank of England. Indeed, when South Africa did mount a trial run in 1960 and 1961 of selling nearly one-quarter of her gold through the Zurich gold market, it was not long before British and American bankers were being ushered into the palatial office of the Governor of the South African Reserve Bank in Pretoria to argue for the full flow of gold to be channeled back through London.[17]

Obviously, South Africa's key role in the world capitalist monetary system is not lost to those who control its politics.

Gold Mining and the South African Political Economy

The gold-mining industry has been described as the golden duckling that laid the golden egg. How this duckling came to be such a precious bird is described by Hobart Houghton:

> At first the full import of the Witwatersrand was not appreciated, but as the extent and depth of gold bearing deposits came to be more accurately assessed, the best brains in the country were devoted to overcoming the enormous difficulties of their exploita-

tion. Difficulties of water disposals, of heat, of dust, of ventilation, of faulting of the rock formation, of gold recovery, and of the supply of power for such a vast industry were progressively solved by the application of the most modern scientific techniques to each problem as it arose. . . . Efficiency and economy were the foundation on which this industry was built. Mining at ever deeper levels might have been expected to raise working costs, but so efficient became the organization that average working costs between 1897 and 1937 actually fell from R2.95 to R1.90 per ton.[18]

Houghton, of course, ignores another aspect of the prosperity of the gold-mining industry; it was not just due to the efficient use of technology. The crucial factor of cost reduction was also assured by holding down the wages of African miners to levels miserable even by the standards of other African workers.

While industrialization has resulted in the increase of local capital supply and the reduction of dividends leaving the country, South Africa and the African workers have paid a heavy price for it. First, the imperialist interests which controlled the gold industry compelled South Africa to turn out gold at a fixed price, and for a long time this restricted the country's economic and political maneuverability. Further, as A. Bakaya points out:

From the most uneconomical ore in the world and from the greatest depths of the earth, South Africa is forced to increase the quantity of its gold output. The increased gold output has come from mechanisation which in turn adds to South Africa's balance of payments problem. The almost doubled value of imports in the last ten years is mainly made up of capital goods and it is these increased imports that had led to the balance of payments deficits. Gold mining, therefore, rather than being a blessing to the South African economy, is the millstone round its neck.[19]

Second, the dependence of industrial expansion on capital derived from taxing the profits from the gold mines has increased the burden borne by the African workers:

Indeed, the tendency has been to use legislative power to prevent African labourers from improving their economic lot, and the familiar spectacle has thus been reproduced of a small wealthy class living on the industry of a large class of poverty-stricken workers. The economic structure has become dangerously top-heavy, depending precariously on a waning asset and a continued supply of low-paid labour.[20]

From the above, it can now be generally recognized that the tyranny of the gold industry was to determine to a large extent the structure not only of the political economy, but of the social system as well. The gold-mining industry is thus the supreme expression of "a monstrous distortion of human society" to use Orlando Patterson's felicitous phrase.[21]

The necessity for an adequate supply of gold to provide capital to bridge the balance-of-payments gap has led to serious contradictions and aggravated the contradictions between workers and capitalists, since the demand for increases in wages to meet the need for life's necessities are always shifted to the poverty-stricken reserves.

The gold-mining industry has survived and prospered because it uses primitive methods to exploit African labor. It has been responsible for the growth of the worst poverty on the African reservations. Marx was quite correct when he said that the "working to death of people existed almost exclusively in the gold and silver mines, where value in exchange was produced in its independent form of existence: money." He goes on to explain why mining is so exploitative and destructive of human life:

> Whenever a nation whose production is carried on in the more rudimentary forms of slavery or serfage lives in the midst of a universal market dominated by capitalist production, and where therefore the role of its products forms its chief purpose—there to the barbarous infamies of slavery or serfdom are super-added the civilized infamies of overworking.[22]

In the gold mines the African suffers, first of all, the elementary form of robbery. That is the secret of extraordinary profitability of the most difficult mining ever undertaken anywhere in the world. James Gemmil, general manager of the mining industry's labor organization, recently stated that

> our case has always been that we want peasant farmers as labor. Our wage isn't sufficient to meet the needs of a man and his family unless it is augmented by earnings from a plot of land in the man's

homeland. A family man from Johannesburg, for instance, couldn't live on what we pay.[23]

From the very beginning, the mines became a "limbo of hell" that was efficiently ordered. The structure of apartheid has been built on the model established by the mines, as Francis Wilson points out: "In their labour policy in all sectors of the economy, the architects of apartheid have taken the gold-mining industry as their model."[24]

In the analysis of the impact of the gold-mining industry on Southern Africa, I have been concerned less with its economics as generally understood than with the structural determinations which this industry has built to ensure its privileged existence. Though the mining industry imposes certain technical limitations, it does not, let me point out, determine modes of productive relations. These always remain political acts and not inevitable results. In societies where labor had political and trade-union bargaining power, richer gold mines were found to be unprofitable and were abandoned. The South African gold-mining industry institutionalized its inhuman structures by shifting the burden of exploitation onto the backs of powerless Africans. This was done under the auspices of a white-settler state which had militarily overcome African resistance. Under these circumstances it was able, through duress, to install and preserve the most anachronistic economy.

One of the many illusions concerning the nature of capitalism is that it is "rational," "free" enterprise economy. However, its rationality is based neither on the maximum utilization of resources nor on the advocacy of progress, but on the maximization of profit. The historical specificity of the gold-mining industry was not the frustration of the economic factor by the political factor, but the creation by the latter of social relations of production that would ensure the most favorable conditions to realize super-profits by the former. Thus, the white-settler state introduced policies which integrated all sections of the population into a single national economy, but did not unify these nationalities into a homogeneous working class.

The imposing profits which gold mining derived from the institutionalization of racism would have been diminished and perhaps destroyed by the destruction of the racist structure. The white working class in the mines was assigned the role of defender of the "race" in the struggle to maintain and confirm the status quo. That is, structural racism, officially approved by Britain through its concession of political power to the Afrikaners in 1910, created a climate which legitimized racism among individuals. In the study of South Africa we must follow Marx and Engels and separate the ideas of those ruling for empirical reasons, as empirical individuals, from the ideas of the actual rulers. We must recognize the role of ideas or illusions in history.

As a final note, the actual and vital relationship of the mining capitalist to the system of racial oppression and exploitation has been ignored, if not misrepresented, by bourgeois social scientists. This results from the fact that the study of class and race relations is not anchored in the evolution of the South African economy as a concrete historical entity. Class and race relations are examined as if the capitalist class is above politics, only pursuing its rational economic interests. This, as has been shown, is a false assumption. The study of race relations in the gold-mining industry is essentially a microstudy of class relations in the society as a whole. Only by understanding the general and determining aspects of the gold industry can it be understood how relations first invoked there spread to other sectors of the economy.

Lenin realized the injustices that had been perpetuated by the seekers of gold when he proposed a new use for the metal:

> When we are victorious on the world scale, I think we shall use gold for the purpose of building public lavatories in the streets of some of the largest cities of the world. This would be the most "just" and most educational way of utilizing gold for the benefit of those generations which have not forgotten how, for the sake of gold, ten million men were killed and thirty million maimed in the "great war of freedom," the war of 1914–18, the war that was waged to decide the great question of which peace was the worst, that of Brest or that of Versailles; and how for the sake of gold, they certainly intend to maim sixty million in a war say, in 1925, or 1928, between, say Japan and the U.S.A., or between Britain and the U.S.A., or something like that.[25]

6

The Political Economy of the City in South Africa

> The city is forged upon the hearth of a given mode of production and is shaped with a given set of technological instruments. In a capitalist society, urbanization and the structure and functioning of cities is rooted in the production, reproduction, circulation and overall organization of the capital accumulation process. Since the process of capital accumulation unfolds in a spatially structured environment, urbanism may be viewed as the particular geographical form and spatial patterning of relationships taken by the process of capital accumulation.
>
> —Richard Child Hill

The intention of this chapter is not to give a detailed history of the growth of cities and the particular forms they assumed in South Africa. Rather, it is to argue that the phenomenon of urbanization cannot be understood without reference to the overall structure and functioning of the political economy (in this case, the capitalist mode of production) as it is articulated in the South African social formation. It is the laws and tendencies of the capitalist political economy that determine the ecological forms we see. In order to establish that determination, it is necessary to define theoretically the relationship between the city and the dominant mode of production, i.e., to sketch the evolution of the city not only in terms of its substantive social reality but also in terms of the political and cultural determinants that have influenced its growth.

As a sociohistorical process, capitalist industrial-urban growth

usually involves, in different degrees, the total destruction of the
rural economy and a demographic shift of the population to the
urban centers. Marx discussed the growth of cities, stressing the
implications of the separation between industrialization and
commercial agriculture:

> The division of labour inside a nation leads at first to the separa-
> tion of industrial and commercial from agricultural labour, and
> hence to the separation of *town* and *country* and to the conflict of
> their interests. Its further development leads to the separation of
> commercial from industrial labour. At the same time, through the
> division of labour inside these various branches there develop
> various divisions among the individuals co-operating in definite
> kinds of labour. The relative position of these individual groups is
> determined by the methods employed in agriculture, industry, and
> commerce (patriarchalism, slavery, estates, classes). These same
> conditions are to be seen (given a more developed intercourse) in
> the relations of different nations to one another.[1]

The first major impetus to urbanization in South Africa came
with the discovery of diamonds and gold. In contrast to the
earlier period of commercial capitalism, characterized by a predominance of small-scale, export-oriented agriculture, the development of mining necessitated the development of capital as
a social relation, and therefore the divorce of the laborer from
both the object and instruments of production.

The way in which townward migration developed was related
to the historic process of the separation of the producer from
the means of production—the concentration of land and its
capitalization in the hands of the capitalist—and led simultaneously to the appearance of a social class which had nothing to
sell but its labor power. This transition from precapitalist to
capitalist social relations of production affected both Africans
and whites, but each was affected differently. Since the Africans
lacked political power, their employment in the diamond and
gold mines led to the entrenchment of the migratory-labor system, the intensification of racial oppression, the shoring up of
disembodied "tribal" institutions, and a whole range of measures
designed to prevent complete proletarianization and to de-
politicize their struggle.

The towns spawned by the mines created a home market for agricultural produce and profoundly changed the economy of the Afrikaner subsistence farmer. Some Afrikaner farmers were transformed into large-scale agrarian capitalists, using wage labor and labor tenancy, while others were impoverished. According to A. Lerumo,

> the rapid development of capitalism in the Union was dividing the Afrikaners along class lines. The Land Act and other measures to proletarianize the Africans had benefitted a section of the farmers; they produced cash crops for the booming urban centres and became rich men. They had no reason for dissatisfaction with the deal which "Slim Jannie" Smuts had struck with imperialism. But the same process destroyed the semi-patriarchal, self-contained economy of Boer agriculture. The successful farmers bought out or squeezed out those less successful.[2]

But the several aspects of what was a single process were treated by the government with differing concern: while congestion, landlessness, and crop failure on the reserve were welcomed as stimulants to the labor supply, similar developments among whites were viewed as national calamities.

The Phases of Urban Growth

Driven from their land, the propertyless peasants, both black and white, moved into the growing cities to seek their living. But competition for jobs and other urban amenities prevented either group from making a decent living; they were compelled to lead miserable lives as slum proletarians.

By the first decade of the twentieth century, and in spite of "race," the beginnings of worker amalgamation could be observed not only among urban Africans from different societies but also among urban poor whites who were in the same economic position as Africans. This development caused some stir in the government. The 1907–1908 Natal Native Affairs Commission predicted that

national and tribal disintegration would be quickly followed by
racial amalgamation. There was evidence of this process and this
result in the towns. "Let us stem back [sic] and keep off the process
of disintegration, both in ours as well as the interests of the natives
themselves."[3]

The fear of this development was translated into racial segregation, and then into a policy of excluding Africans as "permanent" city dwellers.

The tendency toward amalgamation was not the result of the
"urbanism" of particular geographical areas, but of their
industrial-capitalist nature. The city is the concentration in space
both of productive forces, which confront the laborer as capital,
and of labor power, which the laborer neither owns nor controls.
The development of industrial capitalism breaks the bonds of
previous modes of production as it destroys the conditions for
their own reproduction, but in so doing it creates a class which
stands opposed to it. Thus, the concentration of newly proletarianized Africans in the urban space dominated by capital
created the conditions for the ensuing political struggles between capital and labor.

Insofar as the townward movements of Africans and Afrikaners were thought to be a threat to capital, the ruling class consciously attempted to produce different effects among each of
the socially defined racial groups. Natal's official policy (which
bore a close resemblance to that of the Orange Free State and
the Transvaal, and was later to be employed by the Union
government) was that Africans should be allowed to develop
along their own lines, but territorially segregated in space. The
city was the creation and abode of the white settler, and the rural
reserve was the abode of the African. This meant that Africans
would be allowed to participate in the urban economy only as
migrant laborers, and while in the cities they should be confined
to compounds. The development of segregation in the process
of urbanization in the last decades of the nineteenth and in the
early twentieth centuries is explained as follows by Martin
Legassick and David Hemson:

> Segregation was the means whereby the economic interests of the
> mining industry were constituted as state policy, in conditions

where other classes and strata had to be allowed some representation of their interests. Segregation was the result of a policy of the state to preserve separate spheres in which the African labour force could continue to engage in household peasant production (in ever declining amounts) which would subsidise its wages, but not be able to avoid wage labour nor compete as peasant producers on the market with aspirant white capitalist farmers. Segregation meant that migrant labour would be preserved and that Africans would be recruited for the mines directly from rural areas by recruiting organisations (the notorious WINELA and NRC) which would fix the wage rates and terms of the contract. Segregation preserved some form of household production in the reserves at the one end of the migrant cycle and perpetuated a compound system at the other. Segregation meant the division of the working class on a racial basis, in which whites would be treated as fully proletarianised, and Africans not, and in which whites in the mining industry would be protected in defined jobs.[4]

But do what they might, neither the laws nor lack of amenities in the towns stemmed African urbanization and proletarianization. So long as the mines and urban industries were in need of labor power, the industrial masters did nothing to prevent the increase of the African proletariat. In practice, the policy of segregation imposed institutional restrictions on African migrants, which made it impossible for them to create trade unions to defend their interests.

Historically the migrant-labor system has performed multiple functions within the South African social formation: ideological, economic, and political. The racial aberration embodied in South African cities is the result of specific ruling-class policies. The gold producers, as we have pointed out in the previous chapters, required labor at below-subsistence remuneration; therefore, African peasants had to have land to sustain their own reproduction. But with access to wage employment, in addition to farming subsistence, Africans might accumulate enough and be less inclined to labor in mine armies. The setting aside of the African reservations as communities unequally integrated into the South African social and economic life had to be done in such a way that Africans would be unable to satisfy their barest needs. This became a point of consensus for the most powerful political groups in South Africa and in fact was the reason for the formation of the Union in 1910.

The white proletarians had a different, higher status. Because they were citizens, they had the right to vote for members of the city councils, for provincial representatives, and for national members of Parliament. They could thus use their power to create job opportunities and to bargain for better social amenities. In addition, they could obtain aid from the state. From the time the Union was formed, white politicians endeavored to curry favor with the white proletariat by giving it preferential treatment at the expense of the African. But despite these favors, the white proletariat was restive, and became violent when they found jobs unavailable and when they were forced to compete with Africans. In 1911 the Mines and Works Act, giving white workers access to better jobs and pay, attempted to remedy this situation.

The second phase of urban growth begins with the end of World War I. The impetus given to secondary industries during the war persisted in the boom that followed. Of the 6,000 factories recorded under the 1917 Factories Act, 4,300 employed a working force of 30,000 white and 74,000 other persons. The number employed in all manufacturing establishments topped the 180,000 mark at the end of 1920. The unionization of the work force increased correspondingly. In 1915 there were 10,500 recorded trade unionists, and by 1920 the number had increased to 132,000.[5] During the war, struggles with a definite class content took place among black workers. J. X. Merriman, writing to Lord Bryce in 1917, commented:

> The [Natives] have had some unpleasant riots in Johannesburg, which were suppressed by police, into whose methods an inquiry is now being held. There is a sullen feeling of discontent among the Natives all through the Union. They have broken away from their old friends and advisers, and we are within a measurable distance of some very serious trouble.[6]

The postwar worldwide inflation was critical; the wholesale price index rose from 1,000 in 1914 to 2,318 in 1919 and 2,707 in 1920. The political impact was a resumption of prewar industrial strife among all the sections of the working class. The incidence of strikes rose from twelve in 1914 to forty-seven in 1919 and sixty-six in 1920. The majority took place on the Rand (the Johannesburg complex of towns) and in the port cities.[7]

Because of these disturbances, systematic regulation of the process of African employment in cities became necessary, and the Stallard Commission of 1921 laid down the principles that were to guide African urbanization for the next thirty years. It concluded that

> the Native should only be allowed to enter urban areas which are essentially the white man's creation when he is willing to enter and minister to the needs of the white man, and should depart therefrom when he ceases so to minister.[8]

There was a flurry of legislation during the decade of the 1920s. The 1923 Urban Areas Act legalized the principle of territorial segregation in urban areas: whereas in the past urban locations had been compulsory areas of residence for Africans (in the Transvaal, the Orange Free State, in parts of the Cape Province, and in Natal), now the number of towns and the number of Africans affected was extended, and the Africans' position was made increasingly tenuous. The Urban Areas Act not only made political resistance more difficult, but it also facilitated the exploitability of the African laborer by capital (a consideration intimately bound up with the fact of political powerlessness). Further stringent measures were enacted in the 1930s to prevent permanent urban settlement by Africans. For instance, special legislation restricted the access of African women to urban areas in an effort to curtail the movement of families to the city. In 1930 local authorities were empowered to prohibit African women not possessing certificates of approval from entering the area to live or work. Certificates were issued only to females who were the wives or unmarried daughters of men who had been employed in the area of destination for at least two years.[9]

Pressure to tighten the law limiting the entry of Africans into the towns induced the government to appoint, in 1935, a departmental committee to inquire into the residence of Africans in urban areas and to recommend legislation to: (1) enforce the principle of limiting the number of natives in urban areas to the labor requirements of such areas; (2) provide for controlling the entry of natives into urban areas; and (3) provide for the withdrawal of superfluous natives from urban areas.[10] The recommendations were incorporated into the Urban Areas Act by Amending Act No. 461 of 1937 and were later included in the consolidating measure of 1945. The 1937 amendment limited African entry into urban areas to workers going to the mines.

In spite of all such discriminatory measures, African workers continued to move to the cities during the interwar years, more pushed out of the countryside by the decomposition of rural society than pulled in by the dynamism of urban society. Between 1921 and 1936 the urban African population doubled. In 1937 General Jan Smuts addressed a conference of municipal representatives in Pretoria and expressed the alarm of the ruling class when he declared:

> There is no doubt, the proper way to deal with this influx [of Africans into towns] is to cut it off at its source and to say that our towns are full, the requirements met, we cannot accommodate more natives, and we are not going to accept any more except in limited numbers.[11]

In 1938 Dr. D. F. Malan (who ten years later became prime minister) made a speech on the theme of the cities and compared the struggles there to a second Great Trek:

> The battle with weapons is over. That was the Vootrekers'. But one, even more violent, more deadly than theirs is being decided now. The battlefield has shifted. Your Blood River is not here. Your Blood River lies in town at the new Blood River of our people. White and non-white meet each other in much closer contact and in a much tighter wrestling-hold than one hundred years ago when the circle of white-tented wagons protected the laagers and the shot-gun and assegai clashed against each other. . . . Where he must stand in the break for his people, the Afrikaner of the new Great Trek meets the non-white at his Blood River, half-armed or even completely unarmed, without barricade, without a river between, defenseless in the open plains of economic competition.[12]

Behind Malan's rhetoric and war imagery lie the real conflicts of an urban capitalist civilization: the conflict between classes for jobs, for freedom from the brutalizing impact of urban sweat shops, and for a place in the sun.

A third major period of capital accumulation, the industrial boom which began during World War II, provided the third stimulus for the flow of Africans to the towns. Now, however, the African labor force was needed to fill vacancies created by white males who had gone to the front. The development of urban-industrial capitalism during World War II would not have been possible without the accelerated incorporation of African labor within the urban-economic complex. Moreover, the movement to the towns was becoming an increasingly permanent process, particularly because African women began to join the labor force as well. The 1939–1940 report of the Native Affairs Commission estimated the number of permanently urbanized Africans to be 750,000. The Broome Commission found that in 1946 nearly one-quarter of Durban's African population could be regarded as permanently urbanized.

The influx of Africans to the cities was accompanied by a resurgence of militancy and an epidemic of strikes. During the 1943 bus boycotts, thousands of Africans and coloreds who lived in Alexandra township, about nine miles from the center of Johannesburg, walked eighteen miles a day to and from work rather than submit to an increase in bus fares from 4 pence to 5 pence. Elsewhere, thousands of homeless African families took possession of vacant land adjoining Johannesburg; built shelters out of split poles, packing cases, hessian canvas, paraffin tins, or corrugated iron; and adopted slogans like "We will die together." Squatters' camps sprang up in periurban areas throughout the country as Africans, hamstrung by law and neglected by housing authorities, found their own solution to the problems caused by overcrowding in segregated ghettos.[13]

The struggle for shelter was accompanied by an even more ominous struggle for capital—the working class's struggle for a living wage. In the 1941–1949 period, 1,685,915 African work hours were lost due to strike activity, nearly ten times those lost in the comparable period from 1930 to 1939:

Strike activity by Africans reached a new peak in the Second World War: 304 strikes involving 50,000 more non-Whites took place during 1939–45, even in the teeth of the notorious war measure 145 of 1942, outlawing all strikes by Africans, and imposing swingering [sic] penalties for participation by Blacks in any industrial stoppage. In 1946 Black South Africans staged their largest strike: 75,000 gold miners on the Reef came out. They were driven back down the shafts at the ends of clubs and rifles, sustaining some dozen deaths and over 1,200 injuries. Smuts (whose government managed this and other similar exercises in industrial arbitration) introduced a Bill making African trade unionism illegal, and decreeing strikes in certain sectors of the economy a criminal offense.[14]

Smuts' action indicates a crucial feature of the policies of the United Party government during the war years. Although the party was subject to blistering attacks by the Nationalist Party because it could not curb the continued influx of Africans to the towns, both political parties—and all others (hence, all of the different fractions of capital which the parties represented)—agreed that Africans should be prevented from organizing, and therefore that they should be kept as disunified as possible.

By 1945 the South African economy had emerged from its dependency on primary production into a fully fledged secondary manufacturing economy in its own right. As a result of unsettled conditions in Europe, South Africa had become an attractive area for the investment of foreign capital in the manufacturing sector. The textile industry, in particular, found conditions in South Africa appealing. The industrial infrastructure was sufficiently developed, taxes were relatively low, and there was a sufficient urban-industrial population to provide a market for the local manufactures.

These developments led to the increasing mechanization of the manufacturing sector. The growing employment of African women necessitated a thorough revision of the structure of occupations to conform to the requirements of mechanized mass production and a reversal of governmental policy regarding African residence in urban areas so as to permit the development of a securely settled African work force. Pressure for changes in this direction mounted in the 1940s among powerful interests and found public expression in reports of government-appointed commissions and committees as well as in popular, academic, and business publications. For example, in its 1946 report, *Native Reserves and Their Place in the South African Economy*, the Social and Economic Planning Council argued:

> If the migratory system prevents the Native from becoming a good farmer, it also makes him a poor industrial worker. The system is in fact wasteful of the country's greatest asset—its human resources. Industrial development will be retarded, and productivity and the national income will remain lost unless our labour resources are used more effectively.[15]

The government-appointed Board of Trade and Industries, noting in the first interim report of its investigation of manufacturing industries that the structure of labor remained ill-suited to the requirements of manufacturing, recommended that

> discussions be initiated by the Department of Labour in the various Industrial Councils with the object of reviewing the classification of labour categories in order to increase the scope of operative labour and to obtain a more efficient labour and industrial organization in the Union. . . . The extension of the manufacturing industry of the Union can be stimulated especially by a reduction of the high cost structure through increased and improved mechanisation so as to derive the full benefit of the large resources of comparatively lower paid non-European labour.[16]

The argument for a policy of facilitating the orderly development of a stable African industrial work force was most fully and finally expressed in the report of the Native Laws (Fagan) Commission, appointed in 1946 by the United Party to inquire into the operation of Union laws relating to Africans who congregated in or near urban areas for industrial purposes other than mining. After an exhaustive investigation, the Fagan report concluded, among other things:

> Despite all efforts of municipalities to utilise their powers, they have been unable to control the urban drift of Natives; nor provide adequately for them once they have arrived in the area. . . . The present situation, has . . . been accentuated by the great industrial

expansion, associated with the war, and the labour requirements of these industries attracting Natives to towns.[17]

The report discussed three possible approaches to the African question: First, that of apartheid, or total segregation, which would involve a complete territorial division between Europeans and Africans; second, that of discrimination either in law or in administration on other than a racial basis; and third, that of accepting the coexistence of European and African communities side by side, by recognizing their intrinsic differences in legislation and administration.[18]

The first alternative, the report stated, was economically impracticable. Just as South Africa's economy required European initiative and skill, so it was equally dependent on the availability of African labor; and this was recognized by European employers' refusal or unwillingness to dispense with African workers. "What would happen," the commission said rhetorically, "if one of these two pillars is knocked down or even weakened is pure speculation."[19] The report argued that (1) the idea of total segregation was completely impracticable; (2) the rural-urban movement was a natural economic phenomenon engendered by necessity, one which might be regulated but could not be reversed; and (3) the African population in urban areas consisted not only of African migrant workers but also of a settled permanent African population.[20] It was clear to the commissioners that the old cry of "Send them back to the reserves" was no longer a solution to the problem of industrial growth.[21] The commissioners also realized that legislation based on the precepts laid down by the Stallard Commission of 1922—that the African should be in town only to minister to the needs of the white settler—was no longer applicable to a situation altered by twenty-five years of economic development. The report concluded:

> The Natives have come to town and in many cases they have come to stay. Economic forces have proved stronger than legislation—Natives have been pushed out of the rural areas because the Reserves are over-populated, because conditions on European farms are not sufficiently attractive to offset the seemingly higher wages and educational opportunities in the towns, and because the territories outside the Union are economically backward; and they

have been pulled towards the urban areas because of the labour requirements of the expanding industrial centres. Nor has it been possible to keep the Natives in town as migratory workers only, for conditions in the rural areas have forced many hundreds of thousands of Natives to regard the towns as their permanent home.[22]

The Fagan report marked a decisive point in the direction of African urban settlement. By 1945 the contradictions in the South African economy were becoming clear to all. The old system, which relied on segregation, could not work efficiently because the African population had pressed into the cities during the war years. The growth of slums in the major cities in the years 1942–1945 was a clear sign of crisis. The old fabric of racial oppression, based on migrant labor in the mines, was no longer tenable, and the mythical demarcation between so-called white and African areas could no longer be held with any sincerity. The growth of manufacturing necessitated not only the mobilization of vast reserves of labor but also their "permanent" settlement near their places of work; Africans could not be in town as "temporary sojourners."

The position of the African in the cities was to lead to vicious party politics in the 1950s; but to understand the way in which the crisis was resolved, it is necessary to understand why the United Party was unable to resolve these contradictions. It was the Nationalist Party, elected in 1948, which was to restructure African exploitation in the post–World War II era.

The United Party's attitude toward African urban settlement was vacillating and uncertain. This ambivalence was obvious in a statement made by the United Party's minister of native affairs in 1947. While proclaiming that he was doing everything he could to stem the flow of Africans to the towns, he also asked:

> Can we develop our industries when we have the position that the native only works for a few months and then returns to the reserves for a couple of years? No, the native must be trained for his work in industry, and to become an efficient industrial worker, he must be a permanent industrial worker. On that account, he must live near his place of employment.[23]

This pragmatic attitude led to the defection of those elements

Apartheid

within the white electorate that saw this as a threat to their situation—the white workers, farmers, and mining interests. The Nationalist Party promised to rid the unions of those elements whose nationalism was suspect and to eradicate the communists, who were stirring up class war. It promised that the state would regulate wages and that the unions would be confined to the role of looking after domestic matters and the workers' spiritual welfare. Black and brown South Africans were seen as a valuable economic factor whose welfare would be considered, but only after effective steps had been taken to segregate them. Their destiny was to remain as wards under trusteeship, the essential instrument for the protection of the white settler's status and civilization.[24]

The election of the Nationalist Party thus marks the end of the epoch of laissez faire segregation and the beginning of the fourth phase, that of apartheid. As its leaders saw the situation, if African workers were allowed to become completely "integrated" into the urban economy, nothing would stop them from struggling to gain political power. And there would be no justification for discriminating against them. The growth of African political organization (independent of traditional elements), together with growing political and labor unrest, convinced the Afrikaner political class that the growth of a stable African working class would be a threat to their capital accumulation.

In power, the Nationalist Party was ruthless. It introduced a wide range of repressive and discriminatory measures designed not only to stem the tide of African urbanization and break working-class resistance, but also to protect the position of the white workers and their petty-bourgeois supporters. A basic aspect of apartheid policy was the attempt to control the flow and allocation of labor. One such control was the Population Registration Act (1949). Another, the Native Abolition of Passes and Coordination of Documents Act (1952), repealed the inefficient pass laws and required every African over the age of sixteen to carry a reference book (which included all the information previously contained in separate documents). The act also established labor bureaus to direct African workers to places where white employers needed them. A 1952 amendment to the

Urban Areas Act made all urban areas subject to influx controls. There was a significant but limited provision for the permanent residence of those Africans who had been born in the towns, those who had worked for an employer for ten years or more, and those who had lived lawfully in a town for fifteen years or more. This was to accommodate the needs of the growing industries which could not subsist on a steady diet of migrant labor, and was a concession made by agricultural and mining capital to urban-industrial capital. Mining and agriculture still used labor recruitment mechanisms, so that restricting the entry of workers into urban areas ensured these two branches of capitalist production sufficient labor to fill their needs. Farm labor was distinguished from industrial labor at the source. As A. H. Voslos, deputy minister of Bantu development, described it:

> A record of every registered Bantu farm labourer is kept in a central register at Pretoria, and the position is that the labourer cannot be employed in the urban areas because as soon as his service contract must be registered, it will be established that he is a farm labourer and then he cannot legally be taken into service. The whole control of Bantu farm labourers revolves therefore around the single cog of registration of each labourer in your service at your local Bantu Affairs Commissioner's office.[25]

The Pass System and the African Labor Force

The cornerstone and the most efficient coercive method to stabilize African labor are the pass laws, which are deeply rooted in the economic system. They were introduced in the Cape Colony in 1760 to control the movement of slaves. In 1809 Lord Calendon, British governor of the colony, introduced a proclamation requiring the Khoikhoin to carry passes when moving from one area to another. Since then the pass system has been extended to other regions of the country. According to Walter Sisulu:

> In this system today is found a method of regulating the economic relations between black and white, a method unique in its nature to

South Africa. The extension of the pass system to children, African women and other racial groups in this country is in fact a continuation of this slave and feudal measure started 200 years ago.[26]

One of their major purposes is to identify those Africans in the towns who are employed and those who are not, and thus are there "illegally." All unemployed Africans may be removed from an urban area and sent to the reserves or to a work colony under an order issued by a native commissioner that declares the person, after an administrative hearing, to be habitually unemployed or without honest means of livelihood, or to be leading an idle, disorderly, or dissolute life.[27] Those Africans who are arrested under the pass laws and are unable to pay the fines become part of a cheap manual labor force. In 1960, due to the administration of the pass laws, 1,400 long-sentence prisoners were supplied to the gold mines daily and another 20,000 yearly to the state-owned railway and harbor systems for quarrying and other such work. Prisoners were also supplied to other private and governmental industries, and a considerable number of those sentenced to less than five months were hired out to individual farmers. According to Alpheus Hunton:

> The prisoners received no pay; the Prisons Department gets 9d [10¢] a day from farmers for each prisoner taken and 2/s [28¢] a day from the mining companies and other industrial employers. The revenue received from those sources in 1952 amounted to $523,270, while the value of convict labor used by the various government agencies (railway, etc.) and departments, including the Prisons Department itself, was $1,184,546.[28]

Thus, various statutes regulating African life in the urban areas operate as nonmarket techniques for creating a vast floating labor pool from which the government can detach individual units as needed, much as in a slave-labor system. Whenever the farmers and miners are faced with a shortage of agricultural labor, their immediate reaction has been to call for restrictive legislation to prevent easy access of Africans to towns: life in the towns must not be allowed to become too "attractive"; industries and the public works department must not be allowed to employ farm laborers and must pay the "wages customary in the district" (which means the farm wage); and the government must recruit labor from outside the republic.[29] If such labor proves not to be forthcoming, the police simply tighten the enforcement of the pass system; if this does not work, emergency labor for the farms and mines can be met from prison rosters.

Nor is the need to distribute Africans in various industries the only reason for the imposition of pass laws. City councils that want to "control" the "unemployed, idle, and dissolute" Africans use the pass laws as dragnets, in the hope of pulling in suspected criminals. Like the English Poor Law Statutes of the eighteenth century, the system is used to limit the liability of rate payers for the maintenance of the poor. The other major aspect of apartheid is its use to prevent attempts at unity among the various urban groupings. By far the most important law in that area was the 1950 Group Areas Act, which intensified the residential segregation previously in effect under the Urban Areas Act. Provision was made for designating each urban area the exclusive preserve of a particular group—including Africans, Indians, and coloreds, thus creating a massive upset as large numbers of Indians were uprooted and "rezoned." At the same time, new opportunities were created for the Afrikaner commercial class, which took over Indian retail shops.

In 1954 the government attempted to institute compulsory residential segregation by language group. While on the face of it this measure does not seem so divisive, it does much to prevent the development of a common language on which to build political unity.

The government also attempted to change the geography of capitalist accumulation and thus to defuse the possibility of political resistance and minimize conflict between agricultural and industrial capital, which would otherwise be forced to pay inflated wages to white workers. It introduced the "border industries" scheme discussed in the previous chapter.

The Nationalist government considers the border industries scheme to be in keeping with its policy of territorial segregation; it is simply the newest form of the unequal integration of African communities. "Homelands" are attached to the border industries so that members depend upon industrial employment in "white areas" for their survival. It is the union of the "home-land" with its corresponding white community which represents the true boundary of the South African version of the urban system.

But the border industries scheme has not been sufficient to prevent conflict between the competing fractions of capital. Successive amendments to the Urban Areas Act made it increasingly difficult for Africans to obtain permanent town residence. In 1966 the government proposed to reduce the number of African laborers in urban-industrial complexes by 5 percent a year, but was bitterly opposed by industrialists concerned about the possibilities for expansion.

The various measures passed by the Nationalist Party government from 1948 on were intended to stabilize the "chaotic" situation that it had inherited from the United Party. In 1950 it had appointed a commission "to conduct an exhaustive inquiry into and to report on a comprehensive scheme for the rehabilitation of the Native Areas with a view to developing within them a social structure in keeping with the culture of the Native and based on effective socioeconomic planning." The commissioners stated that they found it necessary to give the widest interpretation to these terms of reference and, consequently, made a comprehensive study of the problem referred to them. "This was done because the Commission very soon realized that the problems relative to the development of Bantu Areas could only be thoroughly analysed and studied in the light of the wider economic, social and political framework of the Union of South Africa."[30]

The 1955 Commission for the Socio-Economic Development of the Bantu Areas Within the Union of South Africa (the Tomlinson Commission) reflects the Nationalist Party's thinking on the question of African urban settlement. In a section dealing with the urbanization of the Bantu, the report notes that:

> The integration and utilisation of the Bantu as labourers and their consequent urbanisation in non-Bantu areas has given rise to numerous problems, as e.g., (i) the social problem in urban areas;

(ii) the housing shortage in urban areas; (iii) the westernisation of
the Bantu; and (iv) the dependence upon Bantu labour.[31]

The report goes on to state that while it had become customary to
describe the migration of Africans to towns "as a natural economic phenomenon, comparable with the process of urbanisation in other countries" and "with the flow of Europeans to the
towns in our country during the 1930's," and while "in certain
respects the townward movement of the Bantu can well be regarded as normal features," there were other implications in the
case of Africans. That is:

> Problems of much wider scope are created than are usually con-
> nected with the process of urbanisation. As a result of these and
> other considerations, urbanisation of the Bantu cannot be re-
> garded in the same indifferent light as was, for example, the case
> with the poor whites. The position would, of course, have been
> quite different had the urbanisation occurred within Bantu
> areas.[32]

The commission admits the obvious, that the integration of
the African into the national economy "has not led to a relaxation of the over-all pattern of segregation; in fact the segregation
principle has been strengthened and extended to cover the new
contingencies arising out of the process of economic integration
and urbanisation."[33]

What are these contingencies? The commission states that as a
result of economic integration the two population groups have
become "more and more interwoven, especially in the cultural,
political and economic spheres." The commission then analyzes
the objective consequences of integration as a result of industrialization and urbanization and concludes:

> At whatever speed, and in whatever manner the evolutionary
> process of integration and equalisation between European and
> Bantu might take place, there can be no doubt as to the ultimate
> outcome in the political sphere, namely that the control of political
> power will pass into the hands of the Bantu.
>
> It is possible that European paramountcy might be maintained
> for some time, by manipulation of the franchise qualifications; but
> without a doubt the government of the country will eventually be
> exercised by those elected by the majority of voters. Theoretically,

it is possible that the non-Europeans who would then constitute the majority of voters, might prefer to have the country ruled by Europeans. Such a supposition appears highly doubtful, and certainly improbable. But, even if such were to be the case, the rulers of a democratic country would have to carry out the will of the majority of the people, which means to say, that the European orientation of our legislation and government will inevitably disappear.[34]

The fundamental question, according to the commission, is whether evolutionary development and integration is possible. But even if it is, the commission is convinced that there is little hope of evolutionary development occurring in South Africa along the lines indicated.

The responsibility and task laid upon the European to Christianise and civilise the indigenous peoples demand that the former should retain the direction of affairs in the foreseeable future. *Even more important is the consideration that over the past 300 years the European population of the Union has developed into an autonomous and complete national organism and furthermore preserved its character as a biological (racial) entity.* There are not the slightest grounds for believing that the European population, either now or in the future, would be willing to sacrifice its character as a national entity and as a European racial group. *The combination of these two factors makes the position and struggle of the European people in South Africa unique in the world.*[35]

Furthermore, the European people will not be prepared to sacrifice their right of existence as a separate national and racial entity, and this must be accepted as the dominant fact in the South African situation. In this connection, the commission points out that: "Where the continued existence of a people is at stake, purely rational consideration plays a relatively unimportant role."

According to the commission, the confrontation between races, and the dilemma that is therefore faced by South African society, is clearest in the urban-industrial sphere and is explained in these grim terms:

On the part of the European population, there is an unshakable resolve to maintain their right of self-determination as a national and racial entity; while on the part of the Bantu there is a growing conviction that they are entitled to, and there is increasing conviction and demand for, the fruits of integration, including an ever-greater share in the control of the country.[36]

What a fearful specter!

The question of what the commission calls the "unshakable resolve" of the white community to maintain its part of South Africa as a *white community* reveals what Louis Althusser has called the immutable structure in the operation of ideology as a set of mythical or illusory representations of reality, expressing the imaginary relationships of people to their real conditions of existence. The members of the Nationalist Party know that African demands for equality cannot be met within the limitations of capitalism as it now exists, for this system is inconceivable without the exploitation and oppression of a subclass—the African. If industrial capitalism has become an unquestioned and dominant force in the life of all South Africans, it has at the same time exacerbated the fears of the ruling class.

Consider what is really the same point from another angle. The economic, political, and social development of South Africa created conditions for its own transcendence in the classic Marxian sense. But one class wanted to stop this evolutionary process in its own interests. The Tomlinson Commission represents a partisan assessment of the events and forces of urbanization and economic growth. It shows an exceptional honesty in translating the most complicated problems into the language of party politics.

In the House of Assembly in April 1950, Senator Verwoerd compared the conditions on the farms and in the cities. The urban work situation, he said, was a threat to master and servant social relations:

> Conditions on the farms are totally different from those in the cities. Natives who live or work on farms are employed by the farmers. In the farms there is no question of equality. The relationship of master and servant is maintained on the farms and there is no danger that conditions will develop as in the cities, where they are working with Europeans on an equal footing which gives rise to all kinds of undesirable conditions.[37]

The fear of the urban situation on the part of the rulers is not, of course, a peculiarly South African phenomenon. In the early phase of the development of industrial capitalism, the English bourgeoisie also deplored urbanization, and for good reason. According to Engels, under the old conditions the bourgeoisie was comparatively secure against revolt on the part of their hands:

> He could tyrannise over his workers and plunder them to his heart's content, and yet receive obedience, gratitude, and assent from these stupid people by bestowing a trifle of patronising friendliness which cost him nothing, and perhaps some paltry present, all apparently out of pure, self-sacrificing, uncalled-for goodness of heart, but really not one-tenth part of his duty. As an individual bourgeois, placed under conditions which he had not himself created, he might do his duty at least in part; but, as a member of the ruling class, which, by the mere fact of its ruling, is responsible for the condition of the whole nation, he did nothing of what his position involved. On the contrary, he plundered the whole nation for his own individual advantage. In the patriarchal relation that hypocritically concealed the slavery of the worker, the latter must have remained an intellectual zero, totally ignorant of his own interest, a mere private individual. Only when estranged from his employer, when convinced that the sole bond between employer and employee is the bond of pecuniary profit, when the sentimental bond between them, which stood not the slightest test, had wholly fallen away, then only did the worker begin to recognise his own interests and develop independently; then only did he cease to be the slave of the bourgeoisie in his thoughts, feelings, and the expression of his will. And to this end manufacture on a grand scale and in great cities has most largely contributed.[38]

The role of racial legislation in fostering specific kinds of urban patterns is immense but confusing. It reminds one of the ancient Roman myth of Cacus, told by Luther and related by Marx. Cacus, a Roman mythical figure, stole oxen by dragging them backward into his den so that the footprints made it appear that they had been let out from the den.[39] This is an excellent tale and fits the South African rulers, who pretend that what they have taken from the Africans emanates from the rulers themselves. By legislation that excludes Africans from the cities and the wealth they have created, the ruling class walks the oxen backward, giving the impression that it alone created the affluence of the cities.

What stands out most clearly from the apartheid laws is that bourgeois ideology does not so much falsify the facts as misrepresent them so as to reverse what has taken place. The footprints are there for all to see, but if we limit ourselves to what is immediately apparent (the urban legislation, which forms the subject matter of "empirical" social science), we will never understand the meaning of apartheid. Only if we examine the various laws in the context of variant class demands on African labor can we fathom why and how apartheid makes sense.

Whether under the segregation policies of the United Party or the apartheid policies of the Nationalist government, there was usually an explicit exception made for labor going to the mines. Unemployed Africans, the aged, and women—the casualties of the destruction of the rural economy—were the explicit objects of exclusion from the cities. Yet the general changes taking place in the rural economy were of an order which made exclusion impossible. Indeed, as so often happens, the rulers wanted the labor power of Africans, but not the bearers of the labor power. Unfortunately, the labor power was inseparable from the individuals. The growth of slums and the lack of amenities for the African in cities was not a consequence simply of rapid expansion but also of attempts to suppress that expansion. It reflected the organized irresponsibility of the ruling class.

Whatever the ideological differences were between the United Party and the Nationalist Party, the approaches to African urbanization remained those of settlers whose so-called native policy was embedded in a conservative counterrevolutionary tangle of pious delusions of grandiose immobilization. Behind the grandiloquent, laboriously maintained façade of restrictions lay a selfish and crass obsession to accumulate capital. Africans were remorselessly channeled to the mines, farms, and factories as the need dictated. After their labor power had been chewed up, they were then spit out into the reserves. Indeed, the ruling classes normally want to have the best of as many worlds as possible at any given moment, and sacrifice only what they have to.

The state-created apparatuses not only maintained the domination of capital over labor but also reconciled the interests of various fractions at the cost of continuously reproducing the class struggle. Although it is the ruling class, the capitalist class cannot be assumed to be a unified whole, because within it various fractions can come into opposition with one another. Within South Africa, we have pointed to the competition among mine owners, white farmers, and urban-based industrialists for African labor as the locus of contradictions. The state is the instrument through which various fractions attempt to increase their economic position by political hegemony. State policy therefore depends not only upon which fraction is exercising such hegemony but also upon the relationship of that fraction to the other fraction(s) in the economic sphere. For instance, is the economic position of another fraction so strong that continued disregard of its demands constitutes a threat to the political hegemony of the one fraction? If so, the state may become an organ which neutralizes conflicts between the competing fractions of capital.

Looked at in this light, the Fagan Commission's report, issued by the United Party, and the Tomlinson report, issued by the Nationalist Party, reflect the fact that the power bloc was disorganized and uncertain regarding the position of urban Africans. In the broadest sense, the period from World War II to 1955 saw important contradictions develop in the structure of the relations of exploitation of South African capitalism. The interests of different fractions of capital required different and contradictory solutions. Thus, bitter disputes developed over labor policy and African urban settlement. In the long struggle around the position of the African in the urban industries, the Nationalist Party won. This meant that the relations of exploitation of the African labor force would continue to be based on the migrant-labor system. The protection of the Afrikaner workers in their urban occupations became the sine qua non of Nationalist power politics.

In essence, then, apartheid is primarily an attempt to restructure the distribution of African labor for more effective exploitation and to cope with the often conflicting demands of the agricultural and mining industries and white workers. The an-

tithesis between the interests of rural- and urban-based fractions
of capital was the amount of labor each would have for
exploitation—African labor being the indispensable condition
for capital accumulation.

But in the larger sense, capital was united. The acceptance of
apartheid as outlined in the 1955 Commission for the
Socioeconomic Development of the Bantu Areas (the Tomlinson
commission) makes this clear. From 1955 to 1976 efforts to
tighten up restrictions concerning African urban residence were
intensified. In 1959 the government passed the so-called Promotion of Bantu Self-Government Act already discussed in the
previous chapter. The following year a bill was introduced in
Parliament proposing, inter alia, to do away with any permanent
residence rights in the urban areas for Africans who had not
been born or resident in an urban area for at least fifteen years
or had not worked for the same employer for at least ten years.
This was the Bantu Labour Act of 1964, and its aim was to
entrench the migrant-labor system.[40]

As so often happened in the South African economy, the
situation was anomalous. Manufacturing industries enjoyed
enormous labor surpluses, while the mines and agriculture experienced acute labor shortages. The surplus labor thrown out
of the urban area was to be pushed back to the countryside, only
to be rerouted to the mines and the farms via labor bureaus in
the countryside whose expressed purpose was to "correlate labor
with demands." "Endorsing out" of urban African workers who
had been declared "redundant Bantu" became the practice, and
the courts could not cope with the volume of pass offenders,
which reached a record of 694,000 in 1968. By the end of the
1960s over two million Africans had been registered with various labor bureaus, and about half a million of those had been
designated "farm labor." In Cape Town, African migrant workers had been particularly hit because of the government's intention to convert the western Cape into a "preserved zone" for
colored labor.

By the end of the 1960s the employment of Africans in urban
areas as migrant laborers had become an absolute government
policy. The Transkei "bantustan" became particularly conven-

ient as the dumping ground for the mass African labor expulsion from Cape Town, because most of the African workers in the area are Xhosa-speaking, whose original home was the Transkei.

In a parallel legislation called the Bantu Laws Amendment Act of 1964, the government set up special Bantu Labour Boards with jurisdiction over all farm laborers, domestic workers, labor-tenants, and squatters, and with the right to determine the size and composition of the labor force on farms. The act also required that all squatters be registered, at the same time introducing measures to discourage the system by imposing progressively rising fees on farmers for every member of a squatter family on the land not employed full time. This is perfectly matched by the "redundancy" clauses in the Bantu Labour Act, whereby the government is opposed to any of the urban migrant labor being "burdened with superfluous appendages like wives and children and unmarried adults who are not economically active."

It should be noted here that in all these cases there is an intriguing duplicity on the part of the government. While on the one hand it justifies the expulsion of the African workers and their families by appealing to the doctrine of apartheid, on the other it justifies the admission of African workers to the "white areas" in crude economic terms. This has been seen by liberal critics as one of the "irrationalities" of the Afrikaner government. May they not in fact be expressions of the same dialectical forces that have served the South African economy so well over the years?

The culmination of the 1964 labor acts was not reached until the end of the 1960s and the beginning of the 1970s when even greater legal and constitutional changes were introduced. One of the government's most striking measures to regiment labor was the Bantu Labour Regulation (Bantu Areas) Proclamation, which extended the labor bureau system started in 1964 "to cover every Bantu territorial district, tribal or community authority. . . ." In other words, under the system the Africans were being called upon to assume responsibility for the same oppressive system that the white administration had devised against them. Although there are no bantustans in the urban areas, in 1971 the government saw fit to pass a special law, the Bantu Affairs Administration Act, which transferred control over Africans in the urban areas from white local authorities to Bantu Affairs Administration Boards, one of whose responsibilities is to ensure "an even distribution and better mobility of Bantu labour in its area, according to particular categories of employment."

In the previous year the Department of Bantu Administration had announced that labor shortages in the rural areas had been reduced to a minimum and that, significantly enough, the greatest contribution to the agricultural labor supply came from the urban areas and not from the African areas. There is obviously a great logic in the system, and the ideology of apartheid has been used, albeit inconsistently, to supersede the usual bourgeois laws of "supply and demand."

Since the passage of the Bantu Laws Amendment Act of 1964 and the establishment of Bantu Labour Boards, the government has started on a complicated exercise of redrawing the lines of demarcation between white and black settlements. This has involved mass removals from both urban and rural areas. We have seen how in the urban areas the technique of "endorsing out" unwanted Africans and their families was employed with great effect. We have also seen how the government, through the Bantu Labour Boards, prepared itself for the eventual elimination of labor-tenants and squatters on white farms. About half a million Africans were affected. They were given the simple choice either of registering themselves as full-time "farm labor"—which involved accepting wages pegged at the lower end of the usual scale of R12–R18 per month, as well as separation from unemployed members of their families, who would have to migrate to a bantustan—or of facing immediate eviction, which often entailed loss of property and livestock (African squatters collectively owned 1.2 million cattle, 214,000 wool sheep, 129,000 nonwool sheep, and 500,000 goats), for which the farmers deliberately refused to pay market prices.

Thus, the number of registered labor-tenants/squatters declined from 163,103 in 1964 to 27,585 by the end of 1970. Two and a half years later the government could boast that there were no longer any labor-tenants in the Cape, Transvaal, or the Orange Free State and that in Natal only 16,350 labor-tenants remained. Of course, these figures reveal only one side of the story. Because of labor shortages in some areas, farmers have avoided declaring their labor-tenants; hence, there is a big discrepancy between the 200,000 African labor-tenants registered in 1960 and the 163,103 for 1964. However, to all intents and purposes labor-tenancy, squatting, and kindred institutions had been abolished by government decree by 1970. To empower itself for more ruthless action, the government passed yet another demographically inspired law. This was the Bantu Laws (Amendment) Act of 1972, which covered all possible contingencies by ruling that "a Bantu tribe, community or individual could be removed from where they lived without any recourse to Parliament, even if there was some objection to the removal." The government must have feared, among other things, compensation claims by "black spot" residents and Bantu authorities in "poorly situated" scheduled areas.

In 1972 the government census revealed that there were about eight million Africans in "white areas": 53.33 percent in urban areas and the rest in rural areas. In dealing with these Africans, two major considerations concern the government— their possible claims as citizens and their serviceability as labor. If the former is not at issue, they are free to stay in the "white areas" as "economically active" individuals; but if citizenship is an issue, they may not lay claim to anything that might resemble a citizenship right in the economically active part of South Africa. Instead, like refuse, they must be got rid of. The bantustan has become a convenient dumping ground, as is shown by the recent mass removals.

According to reports by organizations such as the South African Institute of Race Relations, over three million Africans have been moved since 1970. But the general assumption that they have been "discarded" is misleading in that it takes apartheid at its face value. The more subtle point is that it is women, children, the old, and the disabled that are being discarded. Able-bodied men are being recycled, through the labor bureaus mentioned earlier, as "migrant" or "contract" labor for the mines and the farms. For years, the South African mines depended for more than 50 percent of their labor supply on migrants from the neighboring African territories. But in 1963, under the impact of the independence of African states north of latitude 22°S and the increasing problems of internal security, the government felt a sudden urge to reduce the number of non–South African blacks in the country. The result was the Froneman Commission of 1963, part of whose brief was to look into the problem of "foreign labor." It found that in 1960 there were 836,000 foreign Africans in the republic. It is this labor force which has to be replaced with local labor "as fast as possible." Damming up African labor in the "reserves" is an ingenious way of obliging reluctant black labor to go to the mines and the farms; and limiting labor contracts to only one year for each worker is the best way to combine a growing black industrial labor force with maximum security. Without the concept of bantustans, some of these goals might have proved impossible to achieve.

This elaborately created façade came crashing down with the Durban strike of 1973, which ushered in the period of urban black revolt and widespread internal opposition to the bantu-stans. This revolt reached a high point in the Soweto student rebellion of June 16, 1976 (discussed later). Faced with the total rejection of Urban Bantu Councils and other bodies based on apartheid assumptions, the government made an about-face, granting "indefinite leasehold" arrangements to urban Africans and instituting measures to improve social services and to nar-row the wage gap between the "races."

In the Transvaal, the Chamber of Industries, faced with labor unrest among Africans, handed to Prime Minister Vorster a thirty-eight-page memorandum which outlined "practical suggestions" for "eliminating grievances." The chamber, made up of most of the industrialists in the Johannesburg urban complex, the country's major business center, expressed "a deep and vested interest not only in the economy of the country but also in the work force without which our factories cannot operate. The concern of the industry is that the right path of future harmony between the races should be taken and followed at a steady, unfaltering, and balanced pace."

Among its recommendations were:

1. That the permanence of urban African residents be recognized, and that land ownership and municipal voter rights be granted them.

2. That there be an improvement in housing ("adequate finance for urban black housing should be second only to national defence needs") and township amenities (electricity, street lights, paved roads, sports and cultural facilities, shopping areas, and telephones).

3. That efficient transportation be provided.

4. That there be compulsory African education, with free school books and materials.

5. That influx control be streamlined but not eliminated.

6. That there be greater advancement opportunities for African workers.

The proposal also introduced the concept of developing a black middle class with "Western-type materialistic needs and ambitions," because "only by having this most responsible section of the urban black population on our side can the whites of South Africa be assured of containing on a long-term basis the irresponsible economic and political ambitions of those blacks who are influenced against their own real interests from within and without our borders." Anton Rupert, an Afrikaner financier who controls a worldwide tobacco empire and has other interests in South Africa, told the Transvaal Chamber of Industries that "a prerequisite of achieving our over-all objectives should be the adoption of free enterprise values by urban Blacks"; to pursue these goals, Rupert and Harry Oppenheimer, chairman of the Anglo-American Corporation, founded the Urban Foundation to promote community development and improve township conditions. The foundation planned to raise $30 million from the business community. In April 1977 Prime Minister Vorster announced that the government had agreed to work out, in consultation with the Urban Foundation, "an acceptable form of land tenure in the African townships."[41]

In spite of these concessions, urban Africans have refused to go along with the government-sponsored "representative" bodies like the Urban Bantu Councils. Furthermore, since Soweto there has been an increase in strike action by black workers. Officially, thirty-six strikes, involving thousands of workers, were recorded during 1977. Altogether, an official 130,000 work hours were lost in recognized industrial disputes involving African workers. Up to June 1978 ten major strikes had been reported, including the April gold mine strike when five hundred workers decided to break their contracts and go home rather than work in inhuman conditions.

As even this skeletal outline shows, the attitude of the ruling class toward African urban settlement has moved full circle since 1948, when the Nationalist Party came to power. The perverted logic of apartheid, which declared urban areas out of bounds for permanent residence by Africans, has run aground. In some government circles there is now talk of a "canton system" for the urban areas, in which Africans, as well as coloreds and Indians, would eventually participate in decision-making processes. There is reluctant recognition that in the urban-industrial areas blacks and whites have entered into social relations that are indispensable for the welfare of capitalism, albeit independent of the will of the ruling class. We can subdivide the urban economic structure into two parts: (1) the material productive forces, consisting of all the social and technological relations that go into creating the products that sustain modern capitalism; and (2) the existing relations of production, consisting of the legal property relations within which productive forces operate. The inevitable conflict and contradiction between these two dimensions of socioeconomic life generated the conflict that culminated in Soweto; within the urban areas there now exists a proletariat which demands its rightful place in the political economy and may be the force for a socialist transformation.

Apartheid is facing great difficulties in reconciling the specific needs of capitalist growth with the existing fragile racial equilibrium, based as it has been on African powerlessness. Ultimately, it is the indispensability of black labor as the source of surplus value that explains the crucial contradiction of apartheid urban labor legislation. As Marx put it, "The economic relations, however much they may be influenced by other—political and ideological—ones, are still ultimately the decisive ones, forming the red thread which runs them and alone leads to understanding."[42]

Table 1 shows the racial composition of the thirteen principal urban centers in South Africa in 1976 (almost thirty years after the Nationalist Party government began its apartheid legislation), and gives a picture of the distribution of the various "racial" groups in South African towns and industry. (It should be remembered that these figures do not include the number of Africans actually residing in the cities or in the country's urban industries.)

The lack of freedom of movement and residence for Africans in what are called "white" areas means that we should include a large part of the "rural" population as part of South Africa's industrial population—that part which obtains its livelihood in the industrial centers and spends most or part of the year there—as well as including those who are kept out of the urban areas by the influx control laws. While migrant labor diverts a large part of the population in the reserves from subsistence farming into commercial and industrial occupations, the influx laws transfer individuals back to the reserves. Neither is included as a part of the industrial and urbanized labor force.

Those peasants who work in towns but live in the reserves constitute what Marx called the *proletariat foncier,* or "rural proletariat," whose interests are identical with those of the full-time township wage-laborers. For these peasants, subsistence farming is nominal, and communal land ownership is not taken seriously. The competition for their labor by farmers and mine owners, the poll tax, and the influx control laws degrade them into a rural lumpenproletariat, a position comparable to that of the slum dweller in town.[43]

The Relative Quantitative Deployment of Africans, Whites, Coloreds, and Indians in the South African Urban Labor Market

It was gold (as we have seen) that sparked rapid economic development in South Africa, and, though no longer a leading

TABLE 1

Racial Composition of South African Urban Centers–1968

Urban Area	Africans	Whites	Coloreds	Asians
Johannesburg	1,441,366	496,042	85,597	40,021
Cape Town	1,107,763	381,775	606,075	11,086
East Rand	909,680	328,483	19,617	11,462
Durban	850,948	256,836	45,189	321,204
Pretoria	563,384	303,765	11,448	11,275
Port Elizabeth	475,869	150,710	114,879	5,225
West Rand	428,386	153,223	11,691	2,042
Vanderbijlpark and Vereeniging/Sasolburg	310,188	112,885	2,382	2,253
Orange Free State gold fields	210,629	50,774	1,533	—
Bloemfontein	182,329	75,290	10,291	—
Pietermaritzburg	160,855	45,437	8,898	37,283
East London	124,763	57,042	13,571	1,972
Witwatersrand	2,779,432	977,748	116,905	53,525

The extents of the areas named are as follows:

Johannesburg: Entire magisterial district and portions of Germiston, Kempton Park, and Roodeport magisterial districts.

Cape Town: The magisterial districts of Bellville, Cape, Simonstown, Wymberg, i.e., the entire Cape Peninsula.

East Rand: Magisterial districts of Alberton, Benoni, Boksburg, Brakpan, Germiston (portion), Springs, and certain urban areas in the Kempton Park magisterial district.

West Rand: Urban areas of Krugersdorp, Oberholzer, Randfontein, Roodeport, and Westonaria magisterial districts.

Port Elizabeth: Port Elizabeth, Uitenhage, and Dispatch municipalities.

Vanderbijlpark and Vereeniging/Sasolburg: Vanderkylpark municipal area, urban areas of Vereeniging magisterial district, Sasolburg municipal area, and Vaellpark.

Orange Free State gold fields: Urban areas of Odendaalsrus, Virginia, and Welkom districts.

Durban, Pretoria, Bloemfontein, Pietermaritzburg, East London: Metropolitan areas consisting of the municipalities of these towns and the adjoining suburban areas.

Witwatersrand: Urban areas of the magisterial districts of Alberton, Benoni, Boksburg, Brakpan, Springs, Germiston, Johannesburg, Kempton Park, Krugersdorp, Oberholzer, Randfontein, Roodeport, and Westonaria.

Source: South African Statistics, 1976, compiled by the Department of Statistics, Pretoria, p. 1.23.

TABLE 2

Employees in the Mining and Quarrying Industry

	1945		1975	
	Number	*Percent*	*Number*	*Percent*
African	419,005	88.6	568,100	88.8
White	51,564	10.9	63,249	9.9
Colored	1,814	0.4	7,484	1.2
Asian	647	0.1	640	0.1
	473,030	100.0	639,473	100.0

Note: The 1945 data reflect the average daily number of persons in service. The 1975 data give the employment average for June.

Sources: Statistical Yearbook, 1964, p. H-23; *South African Statistics, 1976,* p. 7.7

sector in terms of economic growth, it is still an important factor. Tables 2 through 5, showing the deployment of Africans in the various sectors of the economy, demonstrate, if any demonstration were needed, the crux of South Africa's socioeconomic reality. South Africa as a concrete totality is an entity whose diverse populations are bound together against their wills, in

TABLE 3

Employees in the Manufacturing Industry

	1945		1975	
	Number	*Percent*	*Number*	*Percent*
African	175,837	49.8	705,000	56.2
White	110,929	31.2	270,400	21.6
Colored	49,955	14.2	206,800	16.5
Asian	16,656	4.8	71,900	5.7
	353,377	100.0	1,254,100	100.0

Note: Because of revisions in the scope of the industrial census and in the industrial classification, the data for the two years are not precisely comparable. The data for 1945 represent the total employment in private manufacturing. Employees comprise all executive, administrative, clerical, technical, production, and related workers and laborers, including seasonal and occasional workers and working proprietors and unpaid family assistants. The data for 1975 refer to employment in private industry, including public corporations.

Sources: Statistical Yearbook, 1964, p. H-25; *South African Statistics, 1976,* p. 7.9

TABLE 4

Employees in the Construction Industry

	1945		1975	
	Number	*Percent*	*Number*	*Percent*
African	21,692	64.2	325,100	72.8
White	8,502	25.2	61,200	13.7
Colored	3,539	10.5	54,600	12.2
Asian	57	0.1	5,900	1.3
	33,790	100.0	446,800	100.0

Note: The 1945 data represent the total employment in private construction. The employees comprise all executive, administrative, clerical, technical, production, and related workers and laborers. Working proprietors and unpaid family assistants are not included. The data for 1975 represent total employment in private construction.

Sources: Statistical Yearbook, 1964, p. H-32; *South African Statistics, 1976,* p. 7.15

such a way that any one of them considered separately is an abstraction. It is not an aggregate sum of its parts. The urban-industrial areas provide an empirical confirmation of this assertion. The bourgeois concept of the plural society is wrong because it defines the society by its secondary characteristics and thus obscures its real character. It portrays the society as split into empirical entities that are isolated from each other by cultural differences. Nothing could be more absurd or more calculated to create confusion.

The South African political economy is dependent on a sullen and discontented black proletariat with no rights, no permanent status, and no control over the terms and conditions of its employment. The only way in which this precarious position can be maintained is by keeping the black proletariat in a state of destitution, permanent disarray, and fragmentation, with no chance of gaining class cohesion or a political identity. The dispersion of black workers geographically throughout all the so-called white areas and across all the major industries has led to the formation of an urban complex at the very heart of the capitalist process of production, a force that has a tremendous potential in the struggle for liberation. This is the structural

TABLE 5
Employment by Industry—1975

Industry	Number					Percentage				
	African	White	Colored	Asian	Total	African	White	Colored	Asian	Total
Food	100,300	21,900	25,700	8,800	156,700	64.0	14.0	16.4	5.6	100.0
Beverage	17,900	4,500	2,900	700	26,000	68.8	17.3	11.2	2.7	100.0
Tobacco	1,900	800	1,000	0	3,700	51.4	21.6	27.0	—	100.0
Textiles	70,800	9,700	22,900	6,600	110,000	64.4	8.8	20.8	6.0	100.0
Clothing	31,700	4,300	38,300	23,100	97,400	32.6	4.4	39.3	23.7	100.0
Leather	3,800	1,000	4,300	400	9,500	40.0	10.5	45.3	4.2	100.0
Footwear	3,300	1,000	9,000	7,700	21,000	15.7	4.8	42.8	36.7	100.0
Wood and cork	42,500	3,400	5,600	1,800	52,800	80.5	6.4	10.6	2.5	100.0
Furniture	11,700	2,400	9,000	2,500	25,600	45.7	9.4	35.1	9.8	100.0
Paper	18,000	6,700	5,700	3,900	34,300	52.5	19.5	16.6	11.4	100.0
Printing	7,300	18,600	7,000	2,300	35,200	20.7	52.8	19.9	6.5	100.0

Chemicals	38,600	26,200	7,000	2,700	74,500	51.8	35.2	9.4	3.6	100.0
Rubber	10,000	4,300	1,800	500	16,600	60.2	25.9	10.8	3.0	100.0
Plastics	11,000	2,800	5,600	100	19,500	56.4	14.4	28.7	0.5	100.0
Nonmetallic minerals	68,400	11,400	7,300	900	88,000	77.7	13.0	8.3	1.0	100.0
Basic metals	64,200	36,900	2,500	900	104,500	61.4	35.3	2.4	0.9	100.0
Metal production	79,500	27,500	13,900	2,500	123,400	64.4	22.3	11.3	2.0	100.0
Machinery	40,300	27,800	7,100	1,500	76,700	52.5	36.2	9.3	2.0	100.0
Electrical machinery	29,100	20,600	7,900	2,500	60,100	48.4	34.3	13.1	4.2	100.0
Transport equipment	42,000	32,100	15,300	1,900	91,300	46.0	35.2	16.7	2.1	100.0
Professional equipment	3,300	1,700	800	300	6,100	54.1	27.9	13.1	4.9	100.0
Other	9,400	4,800	6,200	800	21,200	44.3	22.6	29.2	3.8	99.9

Source: *South African Statistics, 1976*, pp. 7.9–7.15

possibility, the hidden dynamic, that apartheid policies have
tried to frustrate.

In the place of local exclusiveness and self-sufficiency, there
now exists in South Africa's urban-industrial areas a multifa-
ceted interdependence between the various groups. The old
order has been dissolved, and an industrial capitalist society has
emerged on its ruins. The African potential to destroy white rule
and capitalist exploitation was demonstrated by the students' uprising on June 16, 1976, and the events that followed. Apartheid
legislation, once a most cunning strategy for directing and controlling the details of the life of the African worker in the
cities—at the economic level, it helped to create and maintain a
great industrial reserve army and thus to ensure the economic
wealth of the capitalist system; at the political level, it was used to
divert Africans' political claims from the areas where Africans
earned their livelihood; and at the military level, it was aimed to
preempt the revolutionary potential of the African working
classes—has turned out to have been no more than the art of a
sorcerer's apprentice who tried temporarily to harness the spirit
of the forces that eventually overwhelmed him. Since 1973,
strikes by African workers in the face of the most oppressive
government machinery have been an impressive display of
working-class "solidarity." The Durban strike, which brought
many industries to a halt and some even to bankruptcy, brought
into focus once again the important role of the African working
class.

A summary of the wage structure of the various sectors of the
South African economy helps explain the Achilles' heel of the
apartheid political structure.

The figures in Table 6 demonstrate most succinctly that the
development of mining, railways, building and construction,
and secondary manufacturing have all added to the wretched-
ness of the African. Whereas the ratio of employed to unemployed Africans has increased during the period of industrialization, wages have remained stable—and thus progressively dis-
proportionate to profits and to rising white wages (as in
mining)—or have increased only slightly, remaining at a tiny

constant fraction of the profits and white wages (as in manufacturing and construction).

Table 6 shows that of the nine separate industries listed, the
work force is from 72 percent to 94 percent African, while only
one employs less than 50 percent Africans. The average wage of
all African labor is roughly half the average white wage; it is
obvious that the vaunted prosperity of the white South African
urban working class has been achieved only by crass exploitation
of its coworkers. The truth of the Marxist proposition that
surplus value is nothing but the difference between the value
created by the worker and the cost of maintaining him or her is
nowhere better demonstrated than in South Africa's wage structure.

The white labor force is a labor "aristocracy" that is by and
large engaged in occupations that do not produce surplus value.
In 1970, for instance, over 700,000 of the 1.27 million white
wage earners were employed in the tertiary sector, comprising
civil service, banks, commerce, finance, professions, and the
wholesale and retail trades. They were what is called "paper
pushers" and cannot be included among productive workers.
They belong to the sphere of circulation, while other white wage
earners do not produce surplus value but help to realize or
increase it.[44]

The reliance of so many industries on African laborers makes
it obvious that the equilibrium of racial segregation that had
stabilized around migrant labor and tenancy agriculture has
broken down. The need for capital accumulation has placed the
black working class in a strategic position in urban commerce
and industry and has thus caused new political fears and a
demand for new methods of political control. The policy of
apartheid provided the structure and rationale for these controls by denying in its institutions, behavioral patterns, and pre-
vailing ideology the realities of industrial capitalism.

In the following statement Prime Minister Vorster, on April
24, 1968, proclaimed with refreshing brutality the aims of his
government vis-à-vis African employment in urban areas:

TABLE 6

Average Monthly Cash Earnings by Racial Group

| | Rands (R1 = $1.40) | | Percent |
	1969	1970	increase
Mining:			
White	316	360.8	14
Colored	62	75.2	21
Asian	78	98.9	27
African	18	18.3	1
Manufacturing:			
White	278	307.2	10
Colored	65	73.6	14
Asian	67	77.4	15
African	48	52.3	8
Construction:			
White	294	325.3	11
Colored	107	109.6	3
Asian	143	150.4	5
African	48	49.9	4
Electricity:			
White	299	369.1	23
Colored	47	76.7	43
African	51	55.3	8
Banks and building societies:			
White	219	298.2	36
Colored	61	80.4	31
Asian	83	106.8	29
African	55	66.9	22
Central government:			
White	255	282.1	25
Colored	96	114.3	25
Asian	136	114.7	15
African	41	44.8	10
Provincial administration:			
White	221	224.3	
Colored	47	59.3	26
Asian	70	73.5	4
African	33	35.9	9

TABLE 6 (*Continued*)

	Rands (R1 = $1.40)		*Percent increase*
	1969	*1970*	
Local authorities:			
White	258	293.6	14
Colored	80	85.9	8
Asian	59	60.2	1
African	42	45.0	7
Railways:[1]			
White	—	295.3	—
Colored	—	70.6	—
Asian	—	53.8	—
African	—	52.3	—

[1]No figures are available for 1969, but the average cash earnings at the end of 1968 were: Whites, R241; Coloreds, R61; Asians, R47; Africans, R45.
Source: UNO Unit on Apartheid, Document No. 13/72, June 1972.

The fact of the matter is this: we need them [the Africans] because they work for us, but after all we pay them for their work—but the fact that they work for us can never entitle them to claim political rights. Not now, nor in the future—and in no circumstances can we grant them political rights in our territory, neither now nor ever.[45]

Apartheid, as a policy of naked exploitation allied with dishonesty, is permeated by hysterical irrationality. Such a statement reminds us that the policy of apartheid is a flight from reality into fabulously convoluted rationalizations to justify any act against the African proletariat. Were it not such a tragic subjectivism, it could simply be dismissed as an evasion or, in Edgar Brooks' felicitous phrase, as the "ultimate expression of a supreme irrelevancy." Within the present system the African is considered a pure form of labor, a commodity.

Marx dealt with the problems of reducing human labor power to a commodity in capitalist society:

In as much as labour power attaches to man as quality inseparable from the individual, since it cannot be isolated from him, or utilized apart from him, the man as a whole, having sold his labour power passes into the possession of the purchaser. Not, of course, with his stomach, his hunger and thirst, his need for rest, his individual wishes and claims, but only in respect of his labour power. For the purchaser, he is not a human being with a soul, feelings, individuality, happiness and unhappiness, he is not a God's image, or the crown of creation; he is not even of like kind with the purchaser. For the purchaser, the man who has sold his labour power is nothing but labour power, nothing but arms, hands, fingers, capable of work, nothing but muscles, eyes, voice, nothing but capacity for labour, faculty for production.[46]

But what happens if African labor becomes obsolete or threatens the exploitative system? Human labor is a strange commodity, for it is not a thing. Its use value resides in the human. But humans have their social and economic aspirations. Ultimately, the struggle between African labor and white capital is a life or death struggle (as was demonstrated in the ruthless massacre of students on June 16, 1976), not between black and white, but between forces of human oppression and human liberation. African labor can liberate itself only by abolishing the capitalist system and the oppressive superstructure of white rule. It is impossible to reduce human beings completely to instruments or to completely repress their aspirations. Despite supreme efforts to imbue the African people with a sense of unworthiness and despite all efforts to shackle their superior physical power, there persists in the African the mighty spirit of struggle and a resistance motivated by a thirst for freedom.

The government's attitude to African settlements in the cities, although explicable only in terms of its origins, must ultimately be judged on the basis of present class interests and relationships. Those classes concerned with maximizing the use of internal resources for socioeconomic growth clash with those whose policy is based on maintaining control over African labor for primary production directed for export. South Africa's urban policy is thus riddled with many conflicts, not between separate entities, but between class fractions, and the urban legislation reveals efforts to harmonize these class interests. The ambiguity and elasticity of apartheid result from the conflicting demands made on African labor by the different class fractions, not from any conflict between political and economic rationality.

It must never be forgotten that the delusions of those who frame South Africa's urban policies are the result of colonialist assumptions as well. The policy of apartheid and its variation of separate development are classic illustrations of the mentality described by Albert Memmi:

> In the case of the colonialist . . . the temptation to effect the disappearance of the usurped finds its self-regulation within itself. If he can vaguely desire—perhaps even revealing it—to eliminate the colonized from the roll of the living, it would be impossible for him to do so without eliminating himself. The colonialist's existence is so closely aligned with that of the colonized that he will never be able to overcome the argument which states that misfortune is good for something. *With all his power he must disown the colonized while their existence is indispensable to his own. Having chosen to maintain the colonial system, he must contribute more vigor to its defense than would have been needed to dissolve it completely. Having become aware of the unjust relationship which ties him to the colonized, he must continually attempt to absolve himself. He never forgets to make a public show of his own virtues, and will argue with vehemence to appear just as much from his glory as from degrading the colonized.* He will persist in degrading them, using the darkest colors to depict them. If need be, he will act to devalue them, annihilate them. But he can never escape from this circle.[47]

The question of African exploitation, therefore, is not simply a question of white versus black, of justice versus injustice, of humanity versus inhumanity; it is a question of the operation of the capitalist system and its specific laws. The capitalist as a settler is subject to the compulsion of the capitalist system. Africans constitute the only large reserves of labor available for profit and economic expansion. Yet even though their frustrations are being constrained by apartheid, the system cannot continue forever. And the framers of apartheid know it. The African urban proletariat possesses a revolutionary potential which makes the rulers wish they could expel it from the towns. The frustration of the African workers, which has from time to time burst out in formless violence, may any day find revolutionary and organizational expression.

The South African urban-industrial areas are the supreme expression of human suffering, a "martyrdom of man" monstrous beyond conception, to use Kenneth Cameron's phrase. All the cleverness that sees in this situation the clash of cultures is simply an attempt to find a way out, to find a solution which is not revolutionary. Only the revolutionary emancipation of African working men and women—a revolution which will mean the emancipation of society from the universal misery of capitalist rule and wage slavery—will solve the urban problem. That is, we must begin to see that in South Africa's urban areas it is the powers of the minority's capital, in all its possible forms, that is the most active enemy of a decent social order; and this power will have to be not just persuaded but defeated and superseded. The decision to create a decent life for all requires social powers and social resources which capitalism in any of its forms denies, opposes, and alienates.

7

The Development of
Urban-Based Afrikaner
Industry

The urban system is not external to the social structure; it spec-
ifies the social structure, it forms part of it. But in every concrete practice, account must be taken of its articulation with
other levels than those specified in the system. This articulation
comes about because the urban agents necessarily occupy a position in the system of economic, political and ideological places
of the social structure and also in the different relations between the places that define the systems in their internal structure.

—Manuel Castells

In chapter 5, I discussed the struggles between British imperialism and the Afrikaner petty-bourgeois nationalists for the
control of the mining industry. Even though in 1910 the inheritors of state power in South Africa accepted British economic suzerainty, they continued to pursue a variety of economic and constitutional avenues to secure and enhance their
own economic and political position. The nature of South Africa's
capitalism, and the various intraclass struggles, cannot be understood, let alone reconstructed, except in the context of the conflict
with British imperial capital's interest in South Africa.

As adviser to President Stephanus Kruger prior to the formation of the Union of South Africa, General Jan Smuts understood clearly the dominant role of British imperialism, then and
in the future. In a memorandum to a conference at Bloemfontein (the breakdown of which precipitated the Anglo-Boer War),

he stated that "the great practical issue in Transvaal politics, before which the racial issue has receded, is the distribution of political power as between mine owners and the permanent population of the land, English as well as Dutch."[1]

The compromise that was the basis for the Union was historically unique, creating two separate spheres within the confines of a single state. An almost autonomous foreign enclave economy, based on mineral extraction, was ruled by the Chamber of Mines, and a domestic economy, based on agriculture, was ruled by the Union government. The Afrikaner bourgeoisie then entered a struggle to control the state in order to use it both to preserve and strengthen the interests of capital and imperialism and to fulfill their own economic aspirations. The contest between the mine owners and the Afrikaner national bourgeoisie produced a precarious and contradictory political and economic alliance, one which has influenced both the means by which the English and Afrikaner bourgeois intraclass rivalry has been pursued and the form it has taken.

The role of the South African state since its capture in 1924 by the Afrikaner political class has been an unbroken effort to provide the Afrikaner petty bourgeoisie with the necessary means for its continued existence in the capitalist economic system. The state's function has been to mediate and tame the English dominance of the economy while advancing Afrikaners' influence in the same area. In its efforts, the state bureaucracy has balked at nothing. It imposed arbitrary wage limits on the African labor force to enable the Afrikaner bourgeoisie to extract greater profit, while at the same time creating avenues for poor whites in the state and manufacturing sector.

The extent to which the Afrikaner bourgeoisie uses the state apparatus to achieve its aims is without parallel in any other capitalist country and is closely linked to its weak position in the political economy and to the strong role of foreign capital. The state policies of the Afrikaner political class are an attempt to curb the predominant role of foreign capital and to advance Afrikaner economic interests.* However, the role of the Af-

* By political class I mean a power group organized for conflict. Although the

rikaner political class is limited, because it was determined within the matrix of a capitalist economy and not outside it. In time, the Afrikaner bourgeoisie fulfilled the task which imperialism designated for it: it accepted the capitalist state as a limiting frame for any projected "reforms" to advance its interests.

The entrenchment of imperial monopoly interests introduces a series of questions having to do with the interaction between local and foreign capital in the political economy of South Africa. What we need to understand is the nature of intrabourgeois conflicts and how they have affected the workers' struggles.

In this chapter I discuss the second ingredient in the growth of the new urban areas, which was not discussed fully in the previous chapter: the growth of urban-based commerce and industry controlled by the Afrikaner bourgeoisie.

Modern urban-based commerce and industry, and their associated skills, did not develop out of the local handicraft economy but entered the country from the outside, with the economic power of British finance capital behind them. According to H. J. and R. E. Simons:

> The British had many initial advantages. Backed by the imperial state and representing a worldwide culture, they behaved with the arrogant assurance of conquerors. They dominated mining, industry and commerce, controlled banks and finance houses, and supplied most technical skills. Their urban culture engulfed the Afrikaner, left a permanent imprint on his style of life, fostered class divisions, introduced a liberal and a socialist radicalism, and undermined the values of his traditional agrarian society.[3]

British control of mining and British capitalists' access to foreign capital meant that the aspirations of the Afrikaner business class were at a perpetual disadvantage. After World War I, and notwithstanding wartime expansion to meet local demand, the manufacturing sector in South Africa remained weak. For example, in 1920–1921 the metals/engineering industry was the

---

political class is ordinarily weighted with persons from a special sector of the social status gradient, it includes persons from every position: "[Un]like the social class, the political class seeks to attract members of itself, and group solidarity is highly valued."[2]

single largest area of employment, accounting for 21.7 percent
of total employment in this sector (38,998 individuals, of whom
18,826 were white males). Nevertheless, it was completely ancil-
lary to mining and had not developed local supplies of raw
materials or actual manufacturing capacity; its operations were
largely limited to assembly and repair. For instance, in that same
year imported materials accounted for 97 percent (£10,895,844)
of the value of the materials used, while £7,644,674 (or 76
percent) of the £10,045,020 worth of metal products, iron, and
steel came from Britain. The large investment required for the
development of domestic iron and steel production was only
begun with the granting of a government contract in 1922; and
then with the government-sponsored Iron and Steel Corporation in 1928.[4]

The situation in the clothing industry was not any better,
despite the availability of a large local supply of raw materials. In
1920–1921 the textile and clothing industries accounted for only
3.8 percent (6,908 individuals) of employment in secondary
industry, while a mere 4.4 percent (£78,670) of the total value of
materials used was South African. At the same time, 16.1 percent of the value of all South African exports, *including gold,*
consisted of wool, which comprised no less than 62.4 percent of
the value of all agricultural and pastoral exports. The customer
for one-third of the wool exported was Britain.[5]

Despite this, the demand for textiles and manufactures in
South Africa far exceeded local productive capacity. In 1920
almost one-third of the value of the Union's total imports of
£101,827,104 consisted of textile goods, wearing apparel (excluding footwear), and other textile manufactures, 72 percent of which came from Britain. Textile goods and manufactures, moreover, constituted 40.5 percent of the total value
amount of South African imports from Britain.[6]

The character of both the metal/engineering industry complex and of the textile and clothing industries in the 1920s shows
that the requirements of Britain—South Africa's chief trading
partner and principal source of investment capital—rather than
the needs of the South African economy accounted for the
shape of the secondary sector. The Pact government, which

came to power in 1924, attempted to alter this balance of forces by promoting local manufacturing. The anti-British sentiment which accompanied this effort flowed from the colonial relationship and from the fact that the white population that suffered from economic underdevelopment was Afrikaner.

The Afrikaner petty bourgeoisie recognized quite early that the only way to real economic power, and to a share in the superprofits of the monopolies, lay in the coordination of the limited resources of the Afrikaner capitalist class as a whole. H. Lawson underscores the weaknesses of Afrikaner capital and the importance of controlling state power:

> The overwhelming strength of the established capitalist groups made it impossible to force them by purely economic means to share the fruits of exploitation. Thus the further progress of Afrikaner capitalism had of necessity to depend on the use of political means for economic ends. The two political trump cards in this game were the numerical superiority of the Afrikaner and the corrosion of his political consciousness by the poison of racialism. Together, they could be used to give the Afrikaner capitalist a position of power in the country which its economic position alone never could give him.[7]

From 1910 on, the Afrikaner petty bourgeoisie directed its energies toward conquering political power. To achieve this, however, the petty bourgeoisie realized that it would need the support of the white working class, in part because the urban-ward movement of the Afrikaner poor was exposing them to the "corrupting" influence of the cities. To forestall the growth of radical class consciousness, the condition of the poor whites in the cities became a main preoccupation of the Afrikaner political class. It cultivated a narrow, petty-bourgeois nationalism based on race, language, and religion and exhorted the Afrikaners to support their people, to buy from Afrikaner shopkeepers, to invest in Afrikaner firms, to read Afrikaans, to attend Afrikaner churches, to join Afrikaner societies, and to participate in Afrikaans cultural activities. According to the Simonses:

> They were spurred into making a great national effort to catch up with the British in the business of making money, by contributing

to funds established to assist Afrikaner entrepreneurs. A few of
the latter were spectacularly successful, but the gap remained. Like
other underdeveloped communities, Afrikaners found that national sentiment and party loyalties were not enough for a successful assault on an entrenched capitalism. Collectively and individually, they made little headway against the accumulated weight of
British capital, technology, managerial experience and imperial
connexions. In the event, political power proved to be more effective than private enterprise.[8]

In the circumstances of the last decades of the nineteenth and
the beginning of the twentieth centuries Afrikaner workers
and poor whites saw in the petty-bourgeois program their
only salvation from poverty and despair. The experiences of the
Anglo-Boer War and the frontier conflicts with the Africans
over land were fresh in their minds. In the new urban institutions created by the petty bourgeoisie, such as churches and
social clubs, the interest, ideas, faith, and hope of the Afrikaner
political class and of parts of the working class and poor peasants
coincided, and nationalist unity was not difficult to achieve. Such
coincidence of class interests is not unique: during its rise to
power, the European bourgeoisie projected its aims to coincide
with those of the peasantry in the struggle against the feudal
order.

The roots of the Afrikaner petty bourgeoisie were implanted in
the Nationalist Party, which came into being in 1914. What
distinguished the Nationalist Party was that it was made up of a
stratum of petty-bourgeois professionals, who made up its core
even before it attained power. It seems unusual that a political
party could be the beginning of a new class. Parties are generally
the product of classes and strata which have become intellectu-
ally and economically viable. However, if one grasps the actual
conditions in South Africa after the Anglo-Boer War, it will be
clear that a party of this type was the product of specific opportunities, and that there is nothing unusual or accidental in it
being so. The Nationalist Party was the product of the unique
circumstances of the Afrikaner. The Afrikaners had been conquered and incorporated into the sphere of British imperialism.
Their rural economy had been disrupted. They were subject to
competition from all sides.

The 1910 constitution, which created the South African state, provided a framework in which the Afrikaners would develop their brand of politics. The Nationalist Party came into existence for objective reasons and pursued its interests within a political framework that facilitated the exploitation of narrow sectional interests. The unrepresentative character of the South African constitution enshrined and politicized racial differences. It left relations of domination and conflict in the new society festering, to infect the political process. Thus, the form of political intercourse created by the South African constitution played no insignificant part in the future coalition of the Afrikaner petty bourgeoisie and workers in their pursuit of economic goals.

Afrikaner petty-bourgeois ascendancy in politics came with the aid of the proletariat and the poor whites. The monopoly that the Afrikaner political class eventually established over the whole society in the name of the working class was in fact a monopoly over the working class itself, while the consolidation of the Afrikaners behind the Nationalist Party was the biggest ideological victory Afrikaner economic nationalism accomplished.

The method chosen by the Afrikaner political class to achieve its goals was not easy; there were many hurdles to be cleared. First, since the Act of Union allowed the coloreds and Africans in the Cape Province a qualified franchise, and since in certain constituencies this token franchise made the difference between the election of Afrikaners and liberal politicians, both these groups had to be excluded from "white politics." Furthermore, since Afrikaans speakers made up 60 percent of the white population, their consolidation into a single voting bloc regardless of class and status position meant that the Afrikaner Nationalist would dominate white politics—and therefore the whole society.

Dr. D. F. Malan, one of the architects of this strategy, reflected in 1938 on how the Afrikaners had been separated from the English institutions for the purpose of achieving sectional goals:

> In place of the original one-stream idea that Afrikaans and English-speaking children ought not to be separated in school, we had first the introduction of parallel classes and thereafter, in the face of great opposition, parallel schools. Thus also our universities and colleges, without state encouragement, as by an inherent

force, followed suit. . . . Thus also the original common teachers' associations in all the provinces split, and although they are in friendly cooperation with one another, Afrikaans and English-speaking teachers remain separately organised. The same thing happened with the originally common Art and Cultural Associations (Eisteddfords) and with the Child Welfare Associations and the Scout-movement, which found its Afrikaans parallel in the Voortrekkers. And finally, the same developments took place in the religious and student worlds, for example, in the Christian Endeavour Society and the Students' Christian Association, and again recently in the general student union. If the history of the last thirty years teaches us anything, it is that the one-stream ideal of the *Samesmelter* is impracticable. It has been weighed by the Afrikaner, found too light, and definitely been rejected. . . . The two-stream development of the Afrikaner has largely freed him of his inferiority feelings; has given him back his self-respect and self-confidence; has awakened in him a new and living concern in areas where he was previously dead; and has been unbelievably successful in helping him ahead in political, social, and cultural spheres.[9]

An issue that was exploited with consummate skill by Afrikaner Nationalist politicians was the Afrikaners' poverty—the poor-white problem. A number of studies on the poor-white problem—the Select Committee on the Poor Whites (1906), the Transvaal Indigency Commission (1906–1908), a Select Committee on European Employment and Labour Conditions (1913), the Economic Commission of 1916 (1911–1914), and the Relief and Grants-in-Aid Commission (1916)—provided background information for developing strategies.

All politicans, *predikants* ("preachers"), teachers, writers, journalists, and shopkeepers who made a living out of the Afrikaner community wished to preserve its cohesion. Any interracial or class-based organizations that attracted Afrikaners and exposed them to class-based ideas and experiences were attacked vigorously by the Afrikaner political class.[10] The measures adopted to protect white workers and the white poor from so-called African competitors were typical, and included splitting trade unions along racial lines. In this way the poor whites were taught that their own security depended on white supremacy. After World

War I "European" unions emerged that worked to create and maintain a privileged position for their white members by such exclusionary devices as insisting on rigid scales of minimum wages and limiting entry into the unions through apprenticeship regulations. The first and most successful of these efforts was the Spoorbond, a union of railway workers organized in 1934 with the backing of the Afrikaner Broederbond, the secret organization of the Nationalist Party.

The political history of H. J. Klopper, a railway official who joined the service in 1911 and the Nationalist Party in 1912, is typical of members of the Afrikaner political class. Klopper's political activity paralleled his rise from clerk to system manager until he resigned in 1942 to enter Parliament. A founding member of the influential Federasie van Afrikaanse Kulter-verenigings (FAK—Federation of Afrikaans Cultural Organizations), he formed its first railway branch in 1930 and led the great ox-wagon trek during the centenary celebrations of 1938, from which emerged the Ossewabrandwag (The Trail of the Ox Wagon). In 1939 he took part in promoting the Reddingsdaadbond (RDB—Society for Active Rehabilitation), ostensibly created to collect money to build Afrikaner capitalism, rescue poor whites, and prevent Afrikaners from developing into a separate class outside the mainstream of their national culture.[11] Or take Dr. Malan, a minister in the Dutch Reformed Church, who in 1915 was appointed editor of the first Nationalist daily paper, *Die Burger*. At its inaugural conference in Middleberg in September 1915, Dr. Malan also became the first chairman of the Cape Nationalist Party. Malan's preoccupation was with the position of the urban Afrikaners. In a pamphlet entitled *Die Grote Vlug* ("The Great Flood"), written in 1932, he expressed his concern about the poor whites:

> There is in South Africa no class that does not know how to draw public attention to its grievances . . . civil servants, farmers, traders, teachers, railwaymen, miners, industrial labourers, natives, Asiatics all have unions . . . and define their own interests. No such organisation exists for the poor whites. It is true that there is no class about which more is spoken and written; but he keeps his sorrows to himself and is silent.[12]

In 1938, as we saw in the previous chapter, Malan made an impassioned speech in which he said that the first struggle between blacks and whites was played at Blood River in 1838 and that the second was about to be played on the new frontier, the city, where his fellow Afrikaners were·perishing daily on a new battlefield, the labor market. In 1948 Malan, then leader of the Nationalist Party, which had wrested power from the United Party, became prime minister. And of the three prime ministers who succeeded Malan, Strijdom and Vorster were lawyers and Verwoerd an academic and journalist. Herbert Tingsten writes:

> The Nationalist Party is often regarded as the party of the land-owning farmers. This is simply not true. Most of the farmers, of course, are Boers and nationalistic. It is the shift of the population to the towns, industrialization and commercialization, which has formed the social class now constituting the stronghold of Boer nationalism, workers, shop assistants, clerks, lower-grade civil servants.[13]

Afrikaner Agricultural Development

Although the leadership reflected the changed class composition of the Afrikaner population, the Afrikaner capitalist farmer remained important to the Afrikaner political class. In no country in the world have such sacrifices been made in support of agrarian capital as in South Africa. The white capitalist farmer has been assisted in financing his operations by the Land Bank and by a whole system of state subsidies and outright grants. He gets his produce delivered on the railways at rates lower than those applicable to mining or industry. He is protected by tariffs from the competition of low-cost food imports from abroad. Special bonuses are paid for agricultural exports, and these are financed through additional surtaxes on all imports.[14] State expenditure on irrigation schemes helped the farmers increase production dramatically between 1927 and 1928. Above all, the farmer has benefited from the development of cooperatives and control boards, which supervise the production, distribution, and sale of agricultural products both in South

Africa and abroad, so ensuring the best possible return for the farmer.[15]

The first control board was the Kooperatiewe Wynbouwers Vereniging (KWV), set up in 1918 and eventually vested by an act of Parliament with complete control over production and distribution for the entire wine-growing industry. Production is allocated in advance to ensure against unwanted surpluses, while the producer gets a fixed price. Similar control boards were established for wheat and dairy products in 1930, for maize in 1931, for livestock in 1932, and for sugar in 1936. The premium on local wheat prices over international prices rose from 9 percent to 50 percent between 1929 and 1931.

Capital accumulation in farming not only is based on creating artificial scarcity and exploiting the consumer but also, of course, derives from the exploitation of the African farm labor. Approximately one-third of the total African population is at the disposal of the white farmers, and the conditions for farm workers are among the worst in the country. "Most farm owners," writes Brian Bunting, "behave as though they count their labourers among their personal possessions."[16]

Many writers are puzzled that South African farmers are able to retain such a decisive influence. Although the advantages enjoyed by the farmers with regard to African labor were detrimental to mining capital, which was often forced to recruit labor outside the country, those benefits would not have been possible had they been at variance with the mining interests. But the miners were more interested in preserving big agrarian capital. The alliance strengthened the political base from which both mining and agrarian capital could advance their interests after 1910. In an address to a congress of the Federation of Afrikaans Cultural Organizations (FAK), Dr. M. S. Louw, managing director of the SANLAM life insurance company, told the delegates that the model they should follow in the pursuit of capital accumulation was that of the mining industry:

> If we want to achieve success, we must make use of the technique of capitalism, as it is employed in the most important industry of our country which will function in commerce and industry like the so-called "finance houses" in Johannesburg.[17]

In its pursuit of economic hegemony, the Afrikaner political class was careful not to interfere with the production of
surplus value in the mines; they needed to appropriate part of
that surplus value to subsidize the development of Afrikaner
capital. Nor was it in their interests to provoke a generalized rise
in wage rates that might affect all sectors by increasing those of
the white workers in the mines. Afrikaner nationalists divided
black and white workers, the better to control both, and un-
hesitatingly used black workers to undermine the position of
white workers and to remind them of their precarious position.
Thus, the period of the Nationalist Party and the Labour Party
pact did not see massive wage increases for the white miners.
Average wage rates, which ranged between £259 and £327 per
annum between 1925 and 1932, were below the £419 average
that had prevailed before the 1922 strike. Nor did this period
see the restoration of the racial demarcation between jobs that
had existed before 1922. The total number of whites employed
in the mines remained below the record numbers employed in
the years immediately following World War I, while the ratio of
whites to blacks averaged between 1:9.3 and 1:9.4, compared
with 1:8.3 in 1921.[18]

The Growth of Urban-Based Afrikaner Industry

E. P. Thompson has made an important observation about
governments that give prominence to sectional class interests:

> Whenever government appears in clearly predatory forms, and
> when the institutions of state are employed to secure private or
> sectional advantage, the political process can only be explained in
> terms of the rivalry of different interest groups within the ruling
> caste itself. These may appear as rival aristocratic "connections," or
> even (but this takes us at once to a deeper level of socioeconomic
> analysis) as the rival interests of "land" and of great trading com-
> panies.[19]

The 1930s saw the first major shift of Afrikaner private capital
to other than agricultural pursuits. Prior to that, apart from

small retail shops, the only enterprise of any significance founded by the Afrikaners had been Die Nasionale Pers, the company that owned the Nationalist newspaper, *Die Burger.* This was followed by the establishment of two insurance companies, SANLAM and SANTAM, in 1918 and the burial society AVBOB in 1921. Despite appeals to Afrikaners to invest in "their own" institutions, progress was slow until the Nationalist Party came to power.

The first successes of the new Afrikaner capitalists were in the banking sphere, and included Boere Saamwerk, Volkskas, and Uniewiakels, all registered in the early 1930s. The Nationalist Party soon became a powerful guardian of Afrikaner petty-bourgeois interests in the jungle of capitalist competition. Apart from its role in national politics, the party built popular support among a growing and increasingly wretched Afrikaner working class, which had been thrust into a hostile urban environment with few resources to deal with a bewildering welter of problems. In 1930 the Broederbond raised £1,000 for the repatriation of Boers who had emigrated to Argentina, £3,000 for loan scholarships to send students to the Afrikaner medical faculty in Pretoria, and £3,000 for an Afrikaans engineering faculty at Stellenbosch.

The reason behind this community effort was spelled out by Professor Geoff Cronje at a meeting in Bloemfontein:

> The Boer culture must be carried into the English cosmopolitan life of the city. . . . It is an appalling struggle and more than one Boer has already been demolished in this difficult transition period in our ethnic life. But our hope is that the organised Afrikaner action in the city will day by day become more purposeful and more irresistible. . . . We must not allow the urbanisation of the Afrikaner to divide our People. We must not allow our city Afrikaner to become a different kind of Afrikaner from the fellow on the farm.[20]

The earliest and probably the most effective instrument to advance Afrikaners' capitalist aspirations was the Broederbond. It was conceived in 1918, constituted in 1920, and made into a secret society in 1922. Its greatest achievement was to hold the

Ekonomises Volkskongress (National Economic Conference) in 1939, at which the Reddingsdaadbond ("salvation deed") was formed to promote the economic independence of the Afrikaner. The conference decided on a number of measures to improve the economic position of the Afrikaner, including the provision of commercial and technical training for Afrikaner youngsters, the mobilization of Afrikaner capital and savings for investment, the creation of an Afrikaanse Handelsinstituut (Chamber of Commerce and Industries), the formation of an Economic Institute of the Federation of Afrikaans Cultural Organizations (FAK), which, among other things, would have control of the Reddingsdaad funds.

Following the conference, the Federale Volksbeleggings (FVB), the first Afrikaner investment company, was founded; it was to grow into one of the giants of the economy. The executive of the FVB spelled out the organization's principles at a meeting on September 27, 1940:

> Federale Volksbeleggings BPK operates on the principle that it is a people's institution [volksinrigting], established on the mandate of the Ekonomises Volkskongress of 1939, to serve as a means of furthering the Afrikaner's drive for economic independence. But the company is nevertheless a business undertaking which wishes to pay its shareholders in clinking silver [*klinkende munt*] and not just in sentiment.[21]

The Handelsinstituut was formed in 1942 with a £5,000 interest-free loan from the Reddingsdaadbond. It held its first congress on August 24, 1942, and its second in August 1943, by which time it claimed that the purchasing power of the Afrikaner, only £100 million a year in 1939, had risen to £120 million. In the ensuing years the Handelsinstituut's actions were to become the core of the Afrikaner's drive for economic parity with the English.[22]

Prior to World War II the Afrikaners controlled 1,200 factories, including building and construction works—3 percent of all factories. By 1949, according to the Afrikaanse Handelsinstituut, their share had more than doubled, with the number of institutions having increased to 3,385, employing 41,000 people. But 80 percent of these were one-person businesses, and only 2.5 percent were registered as public companies. None were in heavy industry.[23]

In commerce, there was a substantial improvement in the Afrikaner's position. Whereas before World War II almost all businesses in the country towns were in the hands of English speakers—Jews or Indians—by 1949 the Afrikaners controlled 25 percent of all commercial undertakings. Three-quarters of the 10,000 Afrikaner trading concerns were established or taken over after the Economic Conference. During the same decade, Afrikaner-owned financial houses increased from 5 percent to 7.5 percent of the total. Nevertheless, such advances were largely relative. In 1945, of the 116 companies on the Johannesburg Stock Exchange with a capitalization of one million rands or more, only one was Afrikaner.[24]

In October 1950 the Second Economic Conference was held in Bloemfontein under the auspices of the FAK, the RDB, and the Handelsinstituut. The economic advancement of the Afrikaner was summarized as follows:

Afrikaner Percentage of Ownership and Control[25]

	Commerce	Industry	Finance	Mining	Total in private economy
1938–1939	8	3	5	1	5
1948–1949	25	6	6	1	11

The net income of the Afrikaners was given as £350 million a year, out of a total national income of £800 million a year. Under the Nationalist Party the state took increasing initiatives in economic development. It encouraged the Industrial Development Corporation (IDC), which it had inherited from the previous government, and, reinforced by private capital, the IDC became a permanent shareholder in a host of industries, mining, finance (Palabora and Central Accepting Bank), aircraft manufacture (Atlas), oil (Soekor), textiles, chemicals (Sasol and Sentrachem), and shipping (Safmarine). With a total investment

in 1968 of R300 million (R1 = $1.40), the National Finance
Corporation was to provide short-term loans for development,
and the Fisheries Development Corporation was to build up a
modern fishing industry.[26]

Dr. Holsboer sums up the role of the IDC as follows:

> There is hardly a branch of industry in which the Industrial
> Development Corporation has not taken an interest, and I am
> satisfied that many industries would hardly have developed if the
> IDC had not given its support.[27]

The spectacular progress of Afrikaner capital since 1948 has
been due in part to the direct placing of government contracts
with Nationalist firms, and in part to the association of Nationalist
capital with state capital. In *Die Afrikaner in die Landsekonomie*,
Professor J. L. Sadie explains:

> With a party in power consisting of an overwhelming majority of
> Afrikaners we find further a willingness in undertakings to seek
> cooperation with Afrikaner businesses, partly apparently because
> it is believed that the latter have easier access to authority. In the
> final instance the contribution of the government to the economic
> life by the establishment of undertakings such as Iscor, Sasol,
> Foskor, Escom, and the Industrial Development Corporation has
> created opportunities by which the Afrikaner could obtain experi-
> ence in the function of management, opportunities which he
> would otherwise not have had.[28]

State contracts have often gone to private Nationalist firms.
For instance, a diamond-prospecting company formed in the
early 1960s with a share capital of £1,250,000 won, through the
Nationalist investment company of Bonuskor, an important
concession on the coast of South-West Africa (Namibia). The
company obtained the concession in the face of strong competition from DeBeers and allied American interests. The Afrikaner
bank Volkskas, founded in 1935, had assets in 1950 of about
R40 million; by 1958 these had risen to R140 million, and by
1968 to R538 million.

In an October 1962 article on Nationalist capital, G. Fasulo
wrote:

This Broederly assistance from public funds is made easier by a system of interlocking directorates which has been built up between Nationalist capital and state capital. For example, Dr. H. J. van Eck of the state firm IDC is a director of SANLAM. Dr. M. S. Louw of SANLAM has been appointed head of the government's new Coloured Development Corporation. . . . Mr. C. H. J. van Aswegen, general manager of SANTAM, has been appointed a director of the state-owned National Finance Corporation. . . . Mr. J. G. van der Merwe is a director of Vootrekkerpers and of Massey Ferguson, the big agricultural machinery firm, in which Federale Volksbeleggings has a large investment, and the state firms Iscor and Klipfontein Organic Products (KOP). In addition, the state capitalist firms and state departments are used as a training ground for Nationalist business managers.[29]

Unquestionably, the free movement of Afrikaner politicians between government and business has greatly boosted the process of Afrikaner capital accumulation.

Here are a series of similar examples given by Brian Bunting: the building society SAAMBOU, launched in 1942, had in 1943 a total capital of about R25,000 and registered a loss for the year of R1,200. By March 31, 1968, its assets had risen to R110,518,988, and its after-tax profit for the previous financial year was R4,138,607. By March 31, 1969, its assets had increased again to a total of R125 million (*Johannesburg Star,* May 29, 1968, and April 14, 1969).

The life insurance company SANLAM, formed in 1918, had assets of R34 million in 1949. By 1968 these had increased tenfold to R334,043,000 (*Johannesburg Star,* April 9, 1968).

The insurance company SANTAM, also formed in 1918, had assets of R25 million in 1962; by 1968 these had risen by R91 million (*Rand Daily Mail,* November 23, 1968).

The banking concern Trustbank, formed as recently as 1955, today has assets of over R300 million and is the fourth largest bank in South Africa, exceeded only by Barclays, the Standard Bank, and Volkskas (*Transvaler,* November 16, 1967).

The investment company Bonuskor, formed in 1946, increased its assets from R16 million to R25 million between 1962 and 1964. It is now involved with the government in the development of the Atlas Aircraft Corporation.

The investment company Federale Volksbeleggings, formed in 1940 after the first Ekonomises Volkskongress, today has assets under its direct control worth R84,385 million compared with a mere R15 million in 1962 (*Transvaler,* November 16, 1967).

The building society Nationale Bouvereniging, formed in 1959, had assets in 1963 totaling R21,496,280; by 1964 these had risen to R31 million. Agricultural cooperatives, the majority of which are under Afrikaner control, increased their turnover from R58 million in 1940 to R666 million in 1964. In the twenty years between 1936 and 1956 their assets increased from R14 million to R246 million.[30]

The biggest fight to conquer the commanding heights of the South African economy began in 1953 with the formation of the Federale Mynbou, the only Afrikaner-controlled mining company. The domination of the mining sector by English capital had always been a sore spot among Afrikaner Nationalists. As Dr. Hertzog articulated Nationalist sentiment in 1949:

> I am satisfied that for all those who look to the future of South Africa there is only one solution, and that is that, irrespective of any other key industries, the gold mining industry should be nationalized by the state Nationalist.[31]

In 1957, as we saw in chapter 5, Afrikaner capitalists had failed in their attempt to take over Central Mining. In 1963 Federale Mynbou joined with the giant Anglo-American Corporation to form a new company, Main Street Investment, capitalized at R22 million. This was followed by the appointment one month later of T. F. Muller, managing director of Federale Mynbou, as managing director of Anglo-American's General Mining and Finance Corporation and of W. B. Coetzer, chairman of Federale Mynbou, as a director of General Mining. A year later Federale Mynbou took over General Mining completely, and at a stroke Federale Mynbou, begun with a capital of R200,000 and with assets in 1963 of R60 million, was in possession of an empire whose assets were estimated at between R200 and R250 million, and had increased to R350 million by 1967. After that, according to Bunting,

> the stake of the Afrikaner in gold mining jumped from one to nine per cent. In addition, Federale Mynbou now controls thirty-seven per cent of South Africa's uranium production, twenty per cent of its coal, and thirty-two per cent of its asbestos. It also has extensive interests in sugar, diamonds, platinum, salt and chrome, and is spreading itself into the world's banking, engineering and chemicals.[32]

The takeover was described by the Johannesburg *Sunday Times* of August 30, 1964, "not only as a personal triumph for Mr. Harry Oppenheimer, Chairman of Anglo-American, but also as an important step forward in his proposals for closer business cooperation across the South African language barrier." T. F. Muller said that the takeover "would probably not have come about but for the integrity of Mr. Oppenheimer."[33]

Oppenheimer himself, in an interview published in the *Sunday Times* of the same date, disclosed that as early as 1957 Muller and Coetzer of Federale Mynbou had approached his father, Sir Ernest Oppenheimer, to arrange "an Afrikaans breakthrough into the mining field." He went on to say: "We thought then that if we could help, it would be the right thing to do, but there were no opportunities at that time. Then, last year, came the chance to do something constructive. . . ."[34]

The dyed-in-the-wool Nationalists were dismayed by this development, and the newspaper *Die Vaderland* expressed its misgivings on September 8, 1964:

> The original idea of Afrikaner participation in the mining industry is dead and buried in Hollard Street in a coffin of 24-carat gold. Mr. Oppenheimer's break-through only existed in that he saw the rising pressure of the Afrikaner mining enterprise; but instead of opposing it, he was more realistic and made a breach in the wall, so that the small but swelling stream could dissolve into his dam.[35]

Since then, Federale Mynbou has increased its links with English financial interests and now has a large stake in Stewart and Lloyds, Union Carriage and Wagon, and Hall and Longmore, as well as a 10 percent interest in the R100 million Highveld Steel and Vanadium development, one of Anglo-American's biggest recent undertakings. In 1968, to crown the marriage between Afrikaner capital and its English counterpart, T. F. Muller was elected president of the South African Chamber of Mines. These developments in the economic sphere were accompanied in the political sphere by the growing irrelevance of the United Party, whose main backers were English capital and Oppenheimer.

The Afrikaner Worker and Capital Accumulation

Capitalist development and urbanization in South Africa disrupted Afrikaner rural life and, as we have seen, affected individuals and groups from all walks of life. The capitalization of agriculture led to the rapid migration to towns of large numbers of Afrikaners and caused not only subsistence farmers but also teachers, small shopkeepers, and the rural clergy to lose their livelihoods. In the city the cosmopolitan atmosphere began to erode the Afrikaners' sense of community. The Afrikaner petty bourgeoisie also experienced severe difficulties. The economy was dominated by British interests that were supported by imperialism. In a sense, all the economic, social, and political pressures of capitalism on all Afrikaners were crystallized in the urban areas of South Africa, where large numbers lived in dire poverty. Various secret and cultural societies were organized to resist British domination, eventually resulting in 1914 in the emergence of the Nationalist Party, which soon became the authentic political expression of the rural bourgeoisie. However, the Nationalist Party was too weak to triumph politically on its own.[36] The Pact government of 1924 was therefore a logical development. Through the Pact government the interests of the local bourgeoisie and the white workers received political expression. The success of this experiment made the mobilization of all Afrikaners, in particular the workers, the sine qua non of Afrikaner petty-bourgeois politics, which was aimed first at capital accumulation and second at solving Afrikaner poverty.

Today this class alliance remains the key to understanding the Nationalist. How did it happen? Like industry, early South African trade unionism was British in origin. The Chamber of Mines, in order to exploit the diamond and gold mines, resorted to importing skilled miners from Britain, who brought with them to South Africa the prejudices of skilled artisans. "They grafted their beliefs and patterns of organization on the colonial stock," as one writer has put it.[37] The dominance of skilled workers from Britain impeded the growth of organized labor because the imported skilled workers limited trade-union membership to skilled artisans in order to prevent undercutting by unskilled workers.

It was not without struggle that white workers, especially Afrikaner, had legal recognition accorded their unions. Like the African, the proletarianized Afrikaner was almost without skills and lived in extreme poverty. In 1897 the Volksraad ("parliament") of the Orange Free State Republican government instituted special schemes, such as the Brickfields project, to provide employment for impoverished Afrikaners.[38]

The Transvaal Indigency Commission of 1890 had found it impossible to estimate the number of poor whites. After World War I, in particular during the period 1921–1936, an average of 12,000 whites left the rural areas for the cities each year. By 1931, the Carnegie Commission, "as a conservative estimate," classified one-sixth of the white population as poor. The bulk of these were Afrikaners. The fear that unless standards were raised the white poor would fall to the Africans' economic level seemed to be borne out by the condition of urban poor whites. "Living in tents without their families on 5s. a day and free rations, they were only slightly better off than migrant peasants. The unskilled white had to learn that he was not above doing 'Kaffir work' declared Afrikaner *Predikants* at a government conference in July 1930."[39]

But the poor whites had the vote. And the petty-bourgeois politicians knew it. Professor Grosskopf, an author of the Carnegie Commission report on the economic aspect of poverty among whites, put it thusly:

> Since 1910 party politics have brought about more and more harmful results. Practically all the White indigents have the vote, and in several constituencies they hold the balance. Public men, who do not realize their responsibility or only consider election chances, have increasingly created wrong ideas and foolish expectations in the minds of the poor. Men who are returned on the strength of election promises are obliged to use all their personal and political influence to obtain something.
>
> The dangers and temptations are greater in a country like ours where the constituencies are small (in 1929 on an average 3057 electors for each member of the Legislative assembly). Instead of a healthy sense of civic duty, a tendency seems to develop to make use of the vote for personal interests. Nearly every parliamentarian should be able to cite cases of men threatening to vote for his opponent, if he could not procure this or that for them.

And then, continues Grosskopf:

> A large portion of the poorer settlers on state land and in the northern Transvaal are firmly convinced that they owe their land to a definite political party, and therefore consistently vote for the party under whose rule the allotment took place. The Poor White Commission in almost every one of hundreds of interviews with the poor throughout the whole Union put the following question to the man after hearing his grievances: "Well, what in your opinion is the solution of your troubles?" And in almost every case the reply was "The Government must do this or that," until the matter became almost ludicrous. . . . So conspicuous is this habit of expecting too much from the State, that even visitors from other countries have been struck by it. A well-known sociologist from America after a visit of some months to our country expresses himself as follows: "With the possible exception of Russia, I know of no country where dependence on the Government is greater than in South Africa."[40]

In a special section entitled "The Influence of the Poor Man's Vote on the State's Policy," the Reverend Albertyn said:

> If it were the law that any indigent person receiving a certain measure of State relief, would automatically lose his vote, the

efforts for his rehabilitation would be less prejudiced. The fear of disenfranchisement would also act as a wholesome deterrent against the seeking of State aid and as incentive to self-help. At present, however, even the person who is totally dependent on the State for his existence, has the vote, and so at least one of the means of breaking down the spirit of dependency remains inoperative.[41]

This period saw many important developments. After consolidating its alliance with labor in the Pact government of 1924 and 1929, the Nationalist Party set itself the goal of organizing the white poor. The combined voting power of white workers and poor whites provided the Afrikaner petty bourgeoisie with unlimited prospects for power. However, the economic crisis of 1929 introduced new dimensions, worsening the plight of workers and increasing the number of unemployed. In 1930 the Communist Party took the initiative in organizing the poor. In May 1930 a huge demonstration of 1,000 white and 2,000 black unemployed, the first of its kind in Johannesburg, was held. Despite strenuous resistance, the efforts of the Communists were not in vain—the demonstrators for once submerged their superficial differences and displayed unusual interracial solidarity. These developments had a great repercussion on the nation's political life.[42] They ushered in important changes in the country's political climate. Hardly anyone could doubt that the economic depression and unemployment were national issues of far-reaching consequence.

The "gold-standard crisis" of 1933 produced by the depression caused profound changes in party political alliances as well. General Smuts agreed to serve under the premiership of Hertzog (whose earlier alliance with the Labour Party had formed the Pact government) in the Fusion government. The price of this political unity was paid by the African people. The new United Party of Hertzog-Smuts for the first time provided the "new" administration with more than the two-thirds parliamentary majority needed to abolish the African franchise.

To the degree that the franchise rights of the Cape Africans made a difference between the election of ultra-rightists and liberals, their disfranchisement was a green light to reactionary developments, which in 1948 culminated in the election of the purified Nationalist Party under Dr. Malan.

When the United Party government was formed in 1933, Dr. Malan refused to join. He attracted around himself a group that claimed to represent the mantle of Afrikanerdom—the purified Nationalist Party. Thereafter began the long struggle by the Afrikaner petty bourgeoisie to wean the Afrikaner away from "alien" ideas and radical trade unions. The first Christian-Nationalist trade union (Spoorbond) was formed in 1934. After 1936 the organization of Afrikaner workers on Christian-National lines became one of the three major policy thrusts of the secret Afrikaner Broederbond.

We saw previously that when the Pact government came to power in 1924 it intervened more forcefully into the economy, and through its "civilized labor" policy it carved out a relatively secure niche within the state apparatus for Afrikaner workers. From about 1930 onward the ideologists of the Broederbond began to raise the danger of class divisions within the Afrikaner urban communities. Particularly after the black/white marches for bread, the Afrikaner Broeders became obsessed with the danger of communism and the dangers of a class-based trade-union movement based on class consciousness. Dr. J. de W. Keyter worried that

> in the cities black and white live together. There is no chance of moral development. Where is our religion and our love for the nation? We reject our own people and they shy from our reli-gion. . . . The people are easily exploited. They have but one ideal, bread alone is necessary for life, they know not religion and ethnic feeling. They have no sense of duty. The feeling of depen-dence [on charity] has overcome them. . . . Youth is by nature interested in politics. They would rather follow heroes but we are driving our young people to communism. . . . The chase for profit, irresponsibility towards our neighbours and preference for native-labour is driving our young people away from us.[43]

These developments led to a reinforcement of the demand for a segregated pattern of industrial relations. This strategy has to do with the position of the petty bourgeoisie in the process of accumulation as well as with the altered class base of Afrikaner

Nationalism after the formation of the Fusion government in 1934. In the long struggle for the loyalty of the Afrikaner worker the Broederbond had specific aims. We have seen that the Afrikaner banking institutions that were established in 1934 were dependent on the savings of Afrikaner workers for an important source of capital. It was thus doubly important that Afrikaner workers be weaned from the ideological and organizational hold of class-based groupings.

In October 1936 a group of Afrikaners of petty-bourgeois origin and in search of a working-class base, including Piet Meyer (who had returned from Amsterdam after having completed his doctoral studies), N. Diederichs, Albert Hertzog, and the Afrikaner banker Frekkie de We, met in Johannesburg to found an organization which would provide financial backing for the Christian-National Afrikaner trade unions. The new organization was called Nationale Raad von Trustees (NRT) ("National Council of Trustees"). Because of the importance of gold mining in the political economy of South Africa, the NRT decided that its first major task was to organize the mine workers. Not only were a majority of white miners Afrikaans-speaking, but also their past experience had created a general dissatisfaction with the Mine Workers' Union because of its corruption and ineffectiveness. After many frustrating campaigns, the NRT got its candidates elected in 1948 to the General Council of the Mine Workers' Union. The methods which had been used successfully in the Mine Workers' Union were also adopted in the garment, building, and leather workers' unions, but with less success.

Afrikaner Nationalism, then, is a product of bourgeois society, which manifested itself as a means to advance sectional economic interests. When it developed, Afrikaner nationalism was characterized by a neurotic fear of class division and an obsession with communism. The petty bourgeoisie looked increasingly to the formation of a cultural cohesion among their poor. In its struggle to capture, transform, and adapt South African capitalism, the Afrikaner petty bourgeoisie led an assault on the trade unions like that characteristic of the Nazis in Germany. The same individuals—Malan, Diederichs, Hertzog, Meyer, Strijdom, Verwoerd—figure centrally both in the development of an Afrikaner economic base and in the Christian-National trade-union movement. After the Nationalist Party gained power in 1948, the same individuals became ministers of state.

A white working-class base was of central importance to the Afrikaner bourgeoisie because it was too weak to achieve its class interests on its own. This was true in a formal electoral sense in 1924, and again in 1948 and after. The alliance between the Afrikaner petty bourgeoisie and the Afrikaner worker is therefore of strategic importance. The Afrikaner bourgeoisie feels, and is, threatened from all sides. The victory of African nationalism would, of course, eliminate it. If it could have, international capitalism would have dumped the Afrikaner bourgeoisie long ago to enjoy the benefits of South Africa's riches for itself.[44] The mistake of the Afrikaner petty bourgeoisie is that it adopted a strategy of capital accumulation that depends on holding state power. Without it, the very basis of its economic power would be destroyed. The Nationalists' control of the state gave them the means to accumulate capital at the expense of other groups. Not only the African, the colored, and the Asian but also the white non-Afrikaner had to accept the consequences of Afrikaner hegemony.

The role of the Nationalist Party since 1948 does not represent an abstract or unique adherence to an ideological construct. The political economic system it created has been reasonably rational. The consolidation of the Afrikaner behind the Nationalist Party and the monopolization of state power is the key to the Afrikaners' success in capital accumulation. If the Nationalist Party loses state power, it loses all else as well, "for it is through the use of State power that, *inter alia,* the ownership of 87 percent of the land and most of the national resources is declared to be white, that black labour is kept cheap, and that white labour is kept dear."[45]

Such is the meaning of national class hegemony. Afrikaner racism is only a part of a larger system. Within this system the Afrikaner petty bourgeoisie, although seemingly in conflict and opposition with the English bourgeoisie, is also party to mutual support and assistance at a deeper level through devotion to the totality and to the particular role they have created for themselves inside the capitalist political economy.

Thus, the Nationalist Party encouraged the racism of the white laborers, who tended to blame their troubles not on the system of capitalism but on the black workers. The perpetual emphasis on the "national" peculiarities and the "national" traditions of the people of South Africa is the cornerstone of the hegemony of the Afrikaner political class. It is designed to fragment the various language and cultural groups into their component units, for it is only through a lack of unity among non-Afrikaners that Afrikaner supremacy can be assured. The disfranchisement of the Cape Africans in 1936–1937 was a milestone in the Afrikaners' road to political hegemony, just as the elimination of the colored vote in 1956 was to consolidate this hegemony "indefinitely."

The three dimensions of the Nationalist Party—those of advancing Afrikaner capital accumulation, protecting white workers' interests, and protecting the capitalist economy—must be clearly understood. The Nationalist Party does not embody contradictory modes of existence. Its policy consists rather in the subordination of class struggle. The Nationalist Party mediates class and nation, a reality that has had a distinct bearing upon its outlook. That is, it exploits nationalist aspirations to seduce working-class aspirations. The Nationalist Party's real basis may be a popular and proletarian mass; but as a political movement, the Nationalist Party transmutes the hopes of the masses to advance its petty-bourgeois aspirations, to spiritualize the party into a bargaining force for capital accumulation. Thus, it has allowed capital to maintain its hegemony over both black and white labor.

It should be clear from this brief review that the state-capitalist policies of the Nationalist governments since 1948 have altered the balance of power within the white ruling bloc. Afrikaner private capital is now able to collaborate with English-speaking capital on equal terms. The success of the Afrikaners' racial and economic nationalism was, however, in large measure due to the tolerance shown it by the English bourgeoisie, which realized that the Afrikaner nationalists wanted to share in capitalist ex-

ploitation rather than abolish the capitalist framework. While
the Nationalist Party's pseudo-anticapitalist rhetoric and sectional organizational structures might be considered inimical by
the English bourgeoisie, the party has been able to safeguard the
economic interests of the English bourgeoisie better than the
English could have themselves. Yet by playing on the English
fear of nationalization, the Afrikaner political class was able to
extract the concessions it wanted. This was not the first time in
South African history that this has happened, as the Simonses
point out:

> Afrikaners and British never allowed their antagonisms to disrupt
> the racial order. They manipulated Africans and Coloureds for
> party gain, and made common cause against them in defence of
> white supremacy. At the crucial constitutional stages—in 1902–7
> after the Anglo-Afrikaner war; in 1909–10, when the terms of
> unification were being decided; and again in 1936, the year in
> which Cape Africans were removed from the common role—the
> British agreed to the principle of exclusive white power. . . . The
> power of government passed to Afrikaner nationalism. The
> British had the satisfaction of continuing to possess the bulk of the
> country's industrial and commercial wealth.
>
> Economic conflicts between Afrikaans- and English-speaking
> whites are likewise settled where possible by introducing some kind
> of racial discrimination from which both stand to gain. Compet-
> ing shopkeepers or estate agents will unite in pressing for mea-
> sures to limit the business activities of Asians, prevent Africans
> from trading in the main shopping areas, or give whites an exclu-
> sive right to own land in selected suburbs. Competition for African
> workers, to take another example, has been a chronic cause of
> dissension between farmers and industrialists. The farmers have
> clamoured for land obtained through stringent pass laws to direct
> the flow of peasants away from industrial areas to the farms.[46]

The meaning of the apartheid urban legislation passed by the
Nationalist Party government since it came to power in 1948 can
now be better understood. In a period where the tempo of
African urbanization and integration into urban areas reached
an all-time high, there was a legislative-administrative attempt to

immobilize the African working class. All the previous efforts were streamlined and given formal codification. The laws were applied with a ruthlessness and vigilance unknown in the past.

The period of Nationalist Party rule was the period when "Klein apartheid"—the rigidities of separation in social life—was most refined and applied. Africans were prohibited from being spectators at "white" sporting events, they were prevented from riding on the same public transportation and from using the same entrances to government institutions; almost every structure of association that might imply equal status contact between black and white was proscribed. According to Ralph Horwitz: "It was as if the guilt-complex of the bureaucratic machine which turned a blinder and blinder eye to economic integration was driven to proclaim publicly and with maximum ostentation that social segregation was never to be breached."[47]

Urban area legislation fulfilled one cardinal goal for capital: it facilitated the process of capital accumulation. The extended controls, progressively limiting Africans' rights of entry to urban areas, to continued employment, and to continued residence, were a smokescreen. The essence of the urban legislation lay in those laws that excluded "Natives" from the definition of "employee" under the terms of the Industrial Conciliation Act of 1925 as amended. Africans thus defined in the cities could not belong to registered trade unions or take part in industrial council or conciliation board proceedings. The Native Labour (Settlement of Disputes) Act of 1953 prohibited Africans from any kind of strike action. Such denial of trade-union rights to African workers and the maintenance of low wages made Nationalist Party rule welcome to capitalists from everywhere.

The greatest illusion of liberals who confronted the Afrikaner legislation was that industrialization and urbanization were incompatible; that Africans and those who control the manufacturing sector had common interests; and that the dependence of the urban sector would undermine the racial rigidities.

The domination of Afrikaner capital in the industrial sector depends on the interrelation among foreign investment, control of the workers' movement, and state economic policies. Under the Nationalists a new system of repression—more subtle, more diffuse, and more effective as an exploitative device—has developed, one that has clearly been beneficial to all sectors of capital. Thus, the present state structures in South Africa can best be described as a functional alliance between international and settler capitalism, after a considerable period of nonantagonistic conflict between them.

8

Imperialism and the Political Economy of South Africa

The ring of distant primary producers was evidenced from North America and Russia, to tropical and subtropical lands and, beyond them to Australia and South African areas, and lines of commerce that had previously been self-contained dissolved into a single economy on a world scale.

—*The New Cambridge Modern History*

Whatever the outcome of the war, America has embarked on a career of imperialism in world affairs and in every other aspect of her life. . . . At best, England will become a junior partner in a new Anglo-Saxon imperialism, in which the economic resources and the military and naval strength of the United States will be the center of gravity. . . . The scepter passes to the United States.

—Virgil Jordan, president of the U.S. National Industrial Conference Board, in a speech to the Investment Bankers' Association, December 10, 1940

Over two-thirds of the globe, along the great arc stretching from Europe to Japan, no treaty can be signed, no alliance can be forged, no decision can be made without the approval and support of the United States Government. Only the great Communist bloc is impervious.

Times (London), August 29, 1951

The characteristic features of South Africa, as a social formation, reflect the interaction of internal developments, representing the historical process leading to the present structure of society and its classes plus the impact of the imperial factor, that is, the specific way in which the South African social formation relates to the world capitalist socioeconomic formation.

The imperial factor assumed great significance with the discovery of diamonds and gold. It influenced the shaping of South Africa's political economy. In the structure that characterized the British Empire in the late nineteenth century, the specific location of the various countries was determined by their resource potential. The British Empire was characterized by a configuration of states which in their internal developments were expected to complement the economy of Great Britain. Eric Hobsbawn has described a set of economies dependent on and complementary to the British, each exchanging the primary products fitted to its geographical situation:

> Cotton in the Southern states of the USA until the American Civil War, wool in Australia, nitrates and copper in Chile, guano in Peru, wine in Portugal, etc. After the 1870s the growth of a massive international trade in foodstuffs added various other countries to this economic empire, notably Argentina (wheat, beef), New Zealand (meat, dairy products), the agrarian sector of the Danish economy (dairy products, bacon) and others. Meanwhile South Africa developed a similar relationship on the basis of its gold and diamond exports, the world market being controlled from London.[1]

The integration of the South African political economy with the world imperialist system increased dramatically in 1886, when the Witwatersrand gold reef was found in the heart of the Transvaal. A speculative boom in the "Kiffers" (as the gold stocks are called) on the London money market followed in 1888–1889, and by 1894 the gold of Johannesburg was believed to be practically inexhaustible. By the end of the second gold boom of 1895–1896, £57 million had been invested in the Rand. Five years later it was producing a quarter of the world's gold supply.[2] South Africa had become an important part of the capitalist world economy, enmeshed in financial and diplomatic dependence.

In a sense, the Anglo-Boer War was a logical outcome of this: the Transvaal government had to be forced to recognize Britain's superior claim to the recently discovered gold mines. Just prior to the war the British colonial secretary wrote that if Britain were forced into a war, "I should try to seize and defend the gold-bearing district. This is the key of South Africa and if we could hold this we need not follow the Boers into the wilderness."[3]

Since the end of the Anglo-Boer War, South Africa has been integrated into the capitalist world economy by every social, economic, cultural, and geopolitical bond that history can bestow. The present rulers never tire of telling the world that they are a Western outpost in the dark continent. Thus, in the study of South Africa what we need to understand is the relation between the economics of imperialism and specific internal political developments. What has been, despite conventional wisdom, an ever increasing volume of foreign capital in South Africa has gone hand in hand with the growth of the worst form of political repression. Furthermore, South Africa's dependence upon foreign capital bears qualitatively upon its political economy and independence. In the process of development, and in the struggle with its internal contradictions, South Africa's capitalism turns increasingly to foreign capital, thereby becoming ever more integrated into the imperialist world economy.

In the international division of labor the imperialist interests decided that South Africa was to be the key supplier of the gold necessary for the worldwide exchange system. Between Southern Africa, Britain, the United States, West Germany, France, and Japan there exists a complex network of horizontal and vertical economic, political, diplomatic, and military relations of considerable and enduring importance. These networks change in form and character over time as the fortunes of particular imperialist countries fluctuate with wars, depressions, financial resources, and the contest for world supremacy between capitalism and socialism. When Britain was the leading imperialist nation, it was also the arbiter in the affairs of Southern Africa. Now, however, the United States seems more and more to be both arbiter and beneficiary in the affairs of South Africa.*

---

* Since the collapse of Portuguese colonialism in Angola and Mozambique, world imperialism is making a unified stand to arbitrate the conflict in Zimbabwe

Though British capital is still strongly entrenched, there is no
question that the decline of Britain as a world power has forced
the United States to fill the vacuum. After a modest beginning at
the beginning of the century, the United States has, for instance,
supplanted Britain as South Africa's number one supplier of
imported goods and is the number two investor in the economy.

The case of South Africa clearly illustrates not only the international division of labor among imperialist countries, but also
the penetration and a fusion of capital from the leading imperialist nations. It also demonstrates the ways in which imperialism adapts itself to changing circumstances. In the last
chapter I showed how the strength or weakness of the English,
as opposed to the Afrikaners, could not be analyzed solely in
terms of the position of each within their own country. Capitalist
development tends to create social relations of production at the
world level, so the position of a fraction of the national
bourgeoisie must be analyzed in relation to other national
bourgeoisies. In this sense, the relative strength of the two
bourgeois fractions in South Africa has always depended on
which outside group supported which fraction. The Afrikaner
bourgeoisie, weakly developed economically despite its political
power, has until recently been marginal in resource ownership
and manufacturing, and hardly better in finance and trade,
precisely because the British imperialist bourgeoisie favored its
kith and kin: the English-speaking sector of the South African
bourgeoisie.

Anglo-American Rivalries and Accommodations

During World War I, the South African economy began to be
penetrated by American capital. The war inaugurated a phase of

---

and Namibia. Britain, the United States, France, Germany, and Canada are
currently engaged in an effort to persuade South Africa to withdraw its troops
from Namibia so that elections can be held to decide the future government of
that disputed territory. In Zimbabwe, Britain and the United States have united
to work out a "peaceful" transfer of power from the white minority. These
efforts are being prompted by the common class interests of the capitalist world.

monetary instability. The international gold standard, which had provided an unlimited market at fixed prices for the output of the gold mines, was no longer working well. The problem for the mining industry was to acquire sufficient capital to open up new mines despite the unwillingness of investors to risk capital. The formation and history of the Anglo-American Corporation is illustrative of these problems. In 1917 Ernest Oppenheimer, in order to obtain the capital necessary to launch himself in South Africa, called on American financiers to contest the British domination of South African mining. Writing to Herbert Hoover, then president of Morgan Guaranty & Trust Company, Oppenheimer stated: "If American capital wishes to obtain a footing in South African mining business, the easiest course will be to acquire an interest in our company."[4] With the capital obtained from Morgan Guaranty, Oppenheimer formed the Anglo-American Corporation (AAC)* and was able to finance and open up the Far West Rand, the Klerksdorp fields, and the Orange Free State, all of which called for large supplies of capital.[6]

The investment of American capital was publicly welcomed in Britain. The announcement of the formation of the new company was hailed by the London *Times* of September 28, 1917, as marking "the beginning of a new epoch, for it is the first occasion on which a definite arrangement has been made for the employment of American capital on the Rand." The *New Statesman* of October 18, 1917, commented:

> One would think that with the ever increasing rise in the price of commodities, and the consequent fall in the purchasing power of gold, gold-mining would cease to be a paying proposition, except where the gold contents were of a high percentage; but one cannot

---

* An interesting aside to the formation of the company was the dispute over its name. Oppenheimer suggested "African-American," but W. L. Honnold, who had left South Africa for America and had become associated with Hoover, declined to accept this because, in his words, "African-American would suggest on this side our dark-skinned countrymen and possibly result in ridicule." On July 6, 1917, Oppenheimer replied: "After full discussion with Hull, consider it very necessary American identity should form part of Company's title. Suggest the Anglo-American Corporation of South Africa Limited."[5]

teach the Americans much about gold-mining and presumably the founders of the Anglo-American Corporation know what they are about. The matter is of interest, as it denotes a further stage in the development of the American financial exploitation of the world, which the war has made imminent. If American skill, industry, and inventiveness thereby penetrate into hitherto undeveloped, or only partially developed, areas of the world (and goodness knows there is room enough in Russia, Brazil, and South America generally), American financiers certainly—the inhabitants of the respective countries and the world at large, possibly—will benefit very considerably.

The Anglo-American Corporation was registered as a South African company, which gave it great tax advantages, which Oppenheimer spelled out in June 1923:

> One of the chief considerations which made it possible to found the Anglo-American Corporation as a South African house, and one of the strongest points I was able to urge in support of our proposal to purchase the South African assets of the Consolidated Selection Company, was the fact that here in South Africa the profits of the mines were taxable only by the Union Government at the source, and, further, that the Union Government taxed only income which was derived from a source within the Union. Share-holders living in countries outside of South Africa could, therefore, rest assured that there was nothing to hinder or prevent a company registered in South Africa from undertaking new business in any part of the world, and that any profits accruing from such ventures would not be subject to double taxation.[7]

Since its formation the AAC has developed into the backbone of mining life in both South Africa and the former British dependencies. Its interests have expanded into industry, often by absorbing local firms incapable of resisting the competition from the multinational corporations. On May 6, 1920, Oppenheimer intimated his future ambitions to his American associates, saying that he had a firm belief in a great industrial and agricultural future for South Africa and that he was "satisfied that the right policy for this corporation [AAC] to pursue is to investigate any attractive proposition that presents itself and not merely to confine its activities to the mining enterprises. The

Anglo-American Corporation should be, and is, ready and anxious to play its part in the industrial development of South Africa."[8]

In 1921, summing up his previous discussions with his American associates, Oppenheimer wrote:

> Further to this, from the very start, I expressed the hope that besides gold, we might create, step by step, a leading position in the diamond world, thus concentrating by degrees in the Corporation's hands the position which the pioneers of the diamond industry (the late Cecil Rhodes, Warner Beit, etc.) formerly occupied.[9]

In the 1920s the AAC moved into Zambia (then called Northern Rhodesia), where today it controls the majority of the copper belt concessions. In Southern Africa it controls not only gold and diamonds but also cobalt, uranium, vanadium, iron, copper, coal, platinum, and other metals and minerals; it is also involved in industrial activities of diverse kinds, in merchant banking, estate management, consultancies, and so on. American investment in the Anglo-American Corporation now amounts to more than $100 million.

World War I disorganized the world's currency circulation. The war once again demonstrated the correctness of Marx's understanding of gold's function as world money because only it preserves this function unchanged. The belligerent countries renounced the gold standard by refusing to exchange bank notes for gold in internal monetary circulation. With the abolition of the gold monetary standard, internal money circulation was divorced from the gold basis. After the war U.S. gold reserves exceeded those of Russia, France, Britain, Germany, and Italy combined. Britain's position in the capitalist world never recovered from the consequences of World War I. The United States became the principal creditor country after World War I. It was naturally interested in stability as the primary condition for normal credit relations. Such stability demanded a guarantee of the repayment of debts at a firm exchange rate of currencies or in gold. This demanded a gold cover, but that did not signify a return to the gold standard in its classical sense of the exchange of bank notes for gold. Such maintenance of currency rates with the help of gold and stable liquid assets came to be known as the gold exchange standard.[10]

The world economic crisis of 1929–1933 exerted a tremendous influence on the world monetary system. Nothing indicates the changes in the economic relations between South Africa, Britain, and the United States better than the relationship between the pound and the dollar on the one hand, and gold on the other. After the depression, South Africa went off the gold standard. This reinforced the leading international role of the dollar, which replaced sterling as international money, and from 1934 onward the price of gold was officially fixed at $35 per troy ounce. The Bretton Woods system of 1944 and the International Monetary Fund were devised in recognition of the supremacy of the dollar. The "rules of the game" were based on the belief that the dollar would always be as good as gold, and that therefore all nations would be as willing to accept it as they would be to take gold. The pound was designated a secondary reserve currency, to be backed by dollars.

Since 70 percent of the capitalist world's supply of gold came from South Africa, the changing fortunes of the dollar and the pound were echoed in the South African gold-mining industry. Gold production increased to 14,039,000 fine ounces in 1941, and then fell to 11,936,000 fine ounces by 1945, with the realized value of gold sales falling by £15 million. Increased costs, labor shortages, and tight capital controls made the prospects for gold mining in the immediate postwar years discouraging.

Then, in 1946 the merger of a New York banking group, which included Ladenburg, Thelman and Co., and Lazard Frères, with British–South African interests prepared the way for the acquisition of extensive mining properties and more than one hundred South African industrial companies—an operation that took place in 1947 and was hailed by *Time* magazine as "the first big beach-head of American capital in South Africa."[11]*

---

* An article in *Business Week* of November 29, 1947, after describing South Africa's gold mining as a magnet, stated that "U.S. money has been literally pouring into South African mining, especially gold." This, according to the article, was not surprising because when the world currencies were realigned at

In 1951 additional loans totaling $80 million were organized to exploit the new gold fields in the Orange Free State. Eight U.S. banks—including Bank of America, First National City, Central Hanover, Bankers Trust, Chemical Bank and Trust, New York Trust, and Chicago's First National—were organized under the auspices of Dillon, Read & Co. This loan was described by *Time* as "the first such cooperative venture in the banks' history."[12]

Sir Theodore Gregory, Sir Ernest Oppenheimer's biographer, writes that

> by 1955, the development of the Orange Free State field as a whole had involved the provision of some £200,000,000. For the seven mines of the Anglo-American Corporation Group alone, over £63 million had been found by 1954 and the Anglo-American Corporation also provided part of the funds for mines under the control of other groups. Of this amount, over £18 million had been put up by DeBeers Investment Trust (out of a total investment outside the diamond industry of over £28 million). London and the Continent had also contributed heavily. In sum, 40 per cent or more of the total investment was furnished by the Anglo-American Corporation Group alone, and nearly 10 per cent of this amount came from the profits of the diamond industry.[13]

The South African gold industry more than doubled its output between 1956 and 1966. By 1959 the United States held $19.5 billion worth of gold out of a total of $32.9 billion in the capitalist world.

The Anglo-American Corporation has served as the major conduit of imperial capital and is today a powerhouse among multinational corporations. The *Newsweek* of November 24, 1958 noted that Harry Oppenheimer, son of Sir Ernest,

> presides over an empire headed by DeBeers Consolidated Mines, Anglo-American Investment Trust, and Anglo-American Corporation of South Africa. Through these corporations and a subsidiary web of interlocking partnerships, the cartel has assets in the neighborhood of 2.5 billion dollars, reserves of 747 million dollars and a 100-million-dollars-a-year payroll of 20,000 Europeans and

---

Bretton Woods in 1944, a direct link was established between the U.S. dollar and gold.

136,000 Africans. The cartel controls almost all the free world's diamonds, most of its gold, at least one-third of Africa's copper, and one-fifth of its coal. DeBeers alone was able to turn a profit of 65 million dollars last year (1957).

In the mining sector several affiliates of British and U.S. multinational corporations have become integrally linked to the mining finance house, often with state and local private enterprise. For instance, Anglo-American Corporation is interlocked with Engelhard Minerals and Chemicals Corporations (Anglo-American owns 30 percent) and Charter Consolidated—the former is U.S.-based and the latter based in the United Kingdom. Forty-nine percent of the shares in the gold fields of South Africa are held by Consolidated Gold Fields, the second largest mining finance house, also a U.K.-based firm.[14]

The American interest in South African mining became potentially much greater at the end of July 1973, when the National Aeronautic and Space Administration and the United States Geological Survey undertook the mapping of South Africa's buried mineral wealth by means of an earth satellite. The satellite's remote sensors mapped the geological strata masked by layers of sand and lava. Stanley Dayton, executive editor of *Engineering and Mining Journal,* gave some sense of the importance of such mapping to investors looking for a safe place for their money:

> Mining corporations must now rate South Africa high on their list of countries in which to invest, because of its political stability as well as its wealth of minerals. I have been surprised at the number of foreign companies which have recently opened offices in Johannesburg. I can see further ventures in South Africa with overseas companies participating financially, while South African companies provide management and mining expertise as well as finance.[15]

The South African gold industry, once the backbone of South Africa's prosperity, has grown to be a component of the higher reality which is the world imperialist system. The close control exercised over the gold industry bears qualitatively on the country's present and future, as we found in chapter 5. The burden of physical production of gold was shifted onto South Africa because of the presence there of cheap black labor. The most important and consistent features of South Africa's development—consonant with its history over the past ninety years—is the ever growing importance of foreign capital in the gold industry, even as gold mining's share in the total income of the country continues to decline.

Foreign Capital and Industrialization

The development of the secondary manufacturing sector that was initiated during World War I had greatly accelerated by World War II. The unsettled situation in Europe made South Africa an attractive area for the investment of foreign capital in manufacturing. The development of an industrial infrastructure, relatively low taxes and tariffs, the presence of a large cheap labor force, and an internal market for textiles large enough to support local production on an economic scale combined to draw the capital, technology, and entrepreneurial resources of large British, French, and Italian firms. F. J. C. Cronje writes that during World War II,

> European manufacturers, particularly the United Kingdom manufacturers, found their expansion hampered by labour, power and material shortages. Taxation and political considerations too played an important part in persuading interests to develop factories in the Union. [Company taxation is, for instance, much lower.] The Union's textile market was also one of the largest low tariff markets left in the world, and in the experience of textile exporters such a market is sooner or later protected. The fear of further wars and revolutions in Europe was another consideration.[16]

After World War II American capital also spread from mining into such areas as automobiles, tires, textiles, hosiery, petroleum, refrigeration, and even shipping. The reasons for this expansion were spelled out in an article in *Business Week:*

(1) South Africa has a strong dollar exchange position (important for the transfer of profits and repatriation of capital) based on an annual gold output of $400 million.

(2) Local industries (many started since 1939) are available for subcontracting and supplying raw materials.

(3) The South African government helps American as well as British firms get started.

(4) Skilled workers are beginning to come in from Britain and the European continent.

(5) The market within the Union and the rest of southern Africa is growing. (Prospects in eastern Africa and the Middle East are also bright.)[17]

In addition, the increased investment in the gold-mining industry necessitated the development of an explosives and chemicals industry, which also came to be dominated by foreign capital and technology.

In 1950, World Bank Vice-President Robert Garner, after a fact-finding mission to investigate South Africa's economic and political climate, reported:

The Bank's mission to South Africa is satisfied that a loan would be perfectly sound and a highly desirable one for the Bank to make, since South Africa's development is regarded as highly important. The mission found South Africa a fine, strong country of fine people and the loan would be an excellent banking proposition. The mission has been impressed by a variety of South Africa's industrial developments. South Africa's credit standing is high and it has many other sources of capital.[18]

Since the bank's mission, American and Western European involvement has increased dramatically in scale and importance. Aside from the period of the Sharpeville massacre, during which a huge outflow of capital (reaching R12 million a month) took place, investments have increased dramatically. Tables 1 through 5 show the extent of foreign capital in various sectors of the South African economy.[19]*

---

* The stock of total foreign investment refers to all foreign liabilities which are the various capital assets in and claims against South Africa owned by foreign residents. Foreign interest in organizations in South Africa and investment by foreigners who have a controlling interest is recognized when one foreign resident

Between 1960 and 1970 the economy grew at an annual rate of 7 percent. This growth was partly due to the inflow of foreign capital: in the same period total foreign liabilities grew from R3,024 million to R5,818 million. Direct foreign investment grew faster, however, more than doubling from R1,819 million to R3,943 million, so that the proportion of total foreign investment grew from 60 percent in 1960 to 68 percent ten years later.[20] This development was reflected in the number of U.S. companies with affiliates in South Africa: 297 in 1940 and over 400 in 1974. In the same year the U.S. Commerce Department reported that American corporations in South Africa had total assets of almost $1.5 billion, while, according to the British Board of Trade, British assets in South Africa totaled $2.2 billion, or 10 percent of Britain's total foreign investment, excluding loans.[21]

British officials estimate Britain accounts for 50 percent of foreign-held assets in South Africa and the United States for 20 percent. Giant British concerns, such as Imperial Chemical Industries and Alcan, have important interests, while two government-controlled firms, British Petroleum and British Leyland, are among the most important investors. In the financial sector, Barclays and the British-owned Standard Bank of South Africa hold an estimated two-thirds of all commercial banking assets. (The International Monetary Fund reported that trade between Britain and South Africa totaled $2.3 billion in 1976, about evenly split between imports and exports.)

The South African motor vehicle industry, a most crucial sector for the accumulation of strategic technology, has been a stronghold for American corporations. In 1971, for instance, 60 percent of the automobiles manufactured in South Africa were produced by three U.S. manufacturers: General Motors, Ford, and Chrysler. According to Ralph Horwitz:

> Motor vehicle manufacture and assembly is the government's chosen instrument for achieving the crucial sophistication of indus-

---

or several affiliated foreign residents own at least 25 percent of the voting or ownership rights in an organization, or when various residents of one foreign country own at least 50 percent of the voting rights, or when foreigners participate in a partnership.

TABLE 1

Stock of Foreign Direct and Indirect Investment in South Africa by Source
(Rand millions)

Type and source	1956		1966		1972	
	Rands	Percent	Rands	Percent	Rands	Percent
Direct investment						
Sterling area	1,178	72.8	1,765	69.2	3,235	66.1
Dollar area	276	17.1	438	17.2	928	19.0
Western Europe	143	8.8	333	13.1	697	14.2
International organizations	—	—	—	—	—	—
Other areas	21	1.3	13	0.5	35	0.7
Total	1,618	100.0	2,549	100.0	4,895	100.0
Indirect investment						
Sterling area	693	59.1	674	52.8	1,108	38.3
Dollar area	93	7.9	151	11.8	287	9.9
Western Europe	243	20.7	290	22.7	1,208	41.8
International organizations	134	11.4	152	11.9	235	8.1
Other areas	9	0.8	9	0.7	53	1.8
Total	1,172	100.0	1,276	100.0	2,891	100.0

Total investment

	Rands	Percent	Rands	Percent	Rands	Percent
Sterling area	1,871	67.1	2,439	63.8	4,343	55.8
Dollar area	369	13.2	589	15.4	1,215	15.6
Western Europe	386	13.8	623	16.3	1,905	24.5
International organizations	134	4.8	152	4.0	235	3.0
Other areas	30	1.1	22	0.5	88	1.1
Total	2,790	100.0	3,825	100.0	7,786	100.0

Note: Totals may not add up to 100.0 because of rounding.

TABLE 2

South Africa: Stock of Foreign Direct and Indirect Investment by Source in 1974
(Rand millions)

Source	Direct investment		Indirect investment		Total	
	Rands	*Percent*	*Rands*	*Percent*	*Rands*	*Percent*
EEC countries	4,467	66.7	3,478	57.4	7,945	62.3
Rest of Europe	466	7.0	681	11.2	1,147	9.0
North and South America	1,524	22.8	1,033	17.0	2,557	20.0
Africa	107	1.6	340	5.6	447	3.5
Asia	57	0.9	222	3.7	279	2.2
Oceania	66	1.0	18	0.3	84	0.7
International organizations	—	—	205	3.4	205	1.6
Unallocated	7	0.1	86	1.4	93	0.7
Total	6,694	100.0	6,063	100.0	12,757	100.0

Note: Totals may not add up to 100.0 because of rounding.

TABLE 3

South Africa: Role of Foreign Capital in the Financing of
Gross Domestic Investment
(Rand millions)

Year	Gross domestic investment	Net capital inflow from rest of world	Percent
1965	2,198	255	11.6
1970	3,701	541	14.6
1971	4,201	764	18.2
1972	3,976	396	9.9
1973	5,025	−92	−1.8
1974	7,100	885	12.5
1975	8,282	1,897	22.9

trialization in South Africa, and in the next decade their gold-mining is expected to decline in significance. An important control technique was perfected to ensure that the great car-manufacturing companies of America, Britain and Europe either abandoned their existing investment in South Africa or made additional investment exceeding R1,100,000,000 [R1 = $1.40] in the immediate future in an expansionist program of increased local manufacture.[22]

According to the *U.S. News and World Report* of April 22, 1968:

The U.S. auto companies produce 60 percent of all cars made here, and South Africa has half of all the cars on the entire continent of Africa. And half the gasoline for South African cars is refined here by American companies.

The biggest-selling auto in South Africa is an American compact, and the company that makes it is gearing up a new 35-million-dollar plant outside Pretoria. Its old plant at Cape Town could not keep up with production demand.

Still another U.S. auto company is establishing a plant in one of South Africa's official "border industry" areas. *It is thus contributing directly to the potential success of something that is officially abhorrent to Washington. Border industries are part and parcel of the program for racial segregation.* [Emphasis added]

TABLE 4

South Africa: Direct Investment in the Private Sector by
Economic Activity and by Source, End of 1973*

(Rand millions)

Source	Total rands	Share of investment to total investment (percent)	Agriculture, forestry, and fishing		Mining and quarrying		Manufacturing		Construction		Wholesale and retail trade		Transport, storage, and communications		Finance, insurance, real estate, and business services		Other	
			Rands	%	Rands	%	Rands	%	Rands	%	Rands	%	Rands	%	Rands	%	Rands	%
EEC countries	3,685	67.6	25	59.5	256	60.9	1,590	64.7	48	78.7	477	59.8	75	68.8	1,173	78.8	41	55.4
Rest of Europe	357	6.5	2	4.8	6	1.4	213	8.7	11	18.0	68	8.5	—	—	51	3.4	6	8.1
North and South America	1,205	22.1	6	14.3	157	37.4	608	24.7	1	1.6	234	29.3	27	24.8	154	10.3	18	24.3
Africa	114	2.1	7	16.7	1	0.2	11	0.4	—	—	17	2.1	6	5.5	68	4.6	4	5.4
Asia	28	0.5	2	4.8	—	—	3	0.1	1	1.6	1	0.1	1	0.9	17	1.1	3	4.1
Oceania	60	1.1	—	—	—	—	31	1.3	—	—	1	0.1	—	—	26	1.7	2	2.7
Total	5,449	100.0	42	100.0	420	100.0	2,456	100.0	61	100.0	798	100.0	109	100.0	1,489	100.0	74	100.0

Note: Totals may not add up to 100.0 because of rounding.

*This table includes only that investment that can be attributed to a particular source. There are an additional R2,000 whose source is not known.

TABLE 5
South Africa: Distribution of Direct Investment in the Private Sector by Category of Economic Activity, End of 1973* (Percentage)

Source	Total rands (millions)	Agriculture, forestry, and fishing	Mining and quarrying	Manufacturing	Construction	Wholesale and retail trade	Transport, storage, and communications	Finance, insurance, real estate, and business services	Other	Total
EEC countries	3,685	0.7	6.9	43.1	1.3	12.9	2.0	31.8	1.1	100
Rest of Europe	357	0.6	1.7	59.7	3.1	19.0	—	14.3	1.4	100
North and South America	1,205	0.5	13.0	50.5	0.1	19.4	2.2	12.8	1.5	100
Africa	114	6.1	0.9	9.6	—	14.9	5.3	59.6	3.5	100
Asia	28	7.1	—	10.7	3.6	3.6	3.6	60.7	10.7	100
Oceania	60	—	—	51.7	—	1.7	—	43.3	3.3	100
Total	5,449									

Note: Totals may not add up to 100.0 because of rounding.
*This table includes only that investment that can be attributed to a particular source. There are an additional R2,000 whose source is not known.

Other major transnational auto producers include the Leyland Motor Corporation (United Kingdom), Volkswagen (West Germany), and Toyota-Rambler and Datsun-Nissan (Japan).

The increase in foreign corporate activity in South Africa has been paralleled by a change in investment direction. Since the end of World War II the manufacturing sector has acquired increasing importance, reducing the relative significance of mining. Whereas in 1960 one-third of all private foreign capital was invested in mining and only one-quarter in manufacturing, by the end of 1974 manufacturing accounted for almost 40 percent of total foreign investment, while finance (including insurance and real estate) represented 25 percent, and mining had dropped to 15 percent. Private foreign direct investment had become even more heavily concentrated in the manufacturing sector—45 percent—and less in mining—7 percent.[23]

The European Economic Community (EEC) countries are another source of foreign capital in the manufacturing sector, the largest part of which originates in the United Kingdom. At the end of 1973 the EEC accounted for about two-thirds (64.5 percent) of total foreign investment in South Africa. The United States was the second largest source of foreign capital, accounting for nearly one-fifth (17 percent) of total foreign investment.

Figures alone do not reveal the full importance of U.S. capital investment, for it is the strategic role that counts as much as volume. At each stage of South Africa's development since World War II, foreign investment has provided the capital equipment and technological know-how which have enabled the country to build up new sectors of its economy. In the 1940s and 1950s the key growth sector was engineering, and Britain, the United States, and the EEC countries exported the capital, machinery, patents, and knowledge which enabled South Africa to make a breakthrough in this sector. Like their American counterparts, the EEC's companies pledge to observe a code of conduct in South Africa, including encouraging trade unions among Africans, combating the South African government's restriction on blacks' freedom of movement, and refusing to discriminate in rates of pay. In the 1960s, faced with the possibility of an arms embargo, French, German, and Belgian companies helped South Africa to become self-sufficient in weaponry. Other firms went into partnership with the government to provide South Africa with a modern textile industry, while American firms played a major role in the production of motor vehicles and automobile accessories, oil prospecting, and refining. In their book, *The South African Connection,* Ruth First, Jonathan Steele, and Christabel Gurney wrote:

> Foreign capital has been crucial to South Africa's economic development because of the technology and skills which it has brought with it. In computers, electronics, chemical and even nuclear energy this technological "bridge building" is linking South Africa with the latest Western trends.[24]

Besides the British and American multinationals, corporations from other Western countries are also active in the South African economy. For instance, the direct and indirect investments of transnational corporations based in the Federal Republic of Germany totaled more than R1 billion in 1974, and about four hundred West German firms active in the motor vehicle, chemicals, and engineering sectors have branches in South Africa.[25] French firms are estimated to contribute about 5 percent of South Africa's oil, construction, and military equipment, while Swiss-based multinationals represent another 4 to 5 percent of total foreign investment, concentrated mainly in the manufacturing and service sectors.[26] No further comment is needed; the close interdependence between the economies of South Africa and those of Europe and America is clear.

The Political Implications of Capital Investment

The export of capital raises the question of the political control of the country in which the capital is invested. After the collapse of Portuguese colonialism in Guinea-Bissau, Angola, and Mozambique in 1974, Henry Kissinger, then U.S. secretary of state, testified before the Senate Foreign Relations Committee:

Events in Angola encouraged radicals to press for a military solution in Rhodesia. With radical influence on the rise, and with
immense outside military strength apparently behind the radicals,
even moderate and responsible African leaders—firm proponents
of peaceful change—began to conclude there was no alternative
but to embrace the cause of violence. . . . We were concerned
about a continent politically embittered and economically estranged from the West; and we saw ahead a process of radicalization which would place severe strains on our allies in Europe and
Japan.

Kissinger was quite explicit as to why the United States must stop
such "radicalization":

> The interdependence of America and its allies with Africa is increas-
> ingly obvious. Africa is a continent of vast resources. We depend
> on Africa for many key products: cobalt, chrome, oil, cocoa, man-
> ganese, platinum, diamonds, aluminum, and others. In the last two
> decades, American investments in black Africa have more than
> quadrupled, to over one and one-half billion dollars. Trade has
> grown at an even faster rate. The reliance of Europe and Japan on
> Africa for key raw materials is even greater than ours.[27]

The Western world's political strategy in Southern Africa
since the collapse of Portuguese colonialism has been to diffuse
the possibility of revolutionary change and to work out a
negotiated, neocolonial settlement. Prime Minister Vorster has
been made a key figure in this strategy, and governments in
Europe and America have been concerned to portray him as a
pragmatic leader who is moving away from his earlier intransigent position. On October 20, 1977, the South African government took a step which alarmed its Western supporters and
placed them in a severe dilemma: it banned eighteen African
organizations, suppressed two African newspapers, detained the
editors of the *World,* and banned those of the *East London
Dispatch.* Vorster rejected American criticism as irrelevant, proclaiming, "We are not governed from overseas." A *New York Times*
editorial expressed the Western quandary: after asking, "What
gives Americans the right to react with horror and threat to his
[Vorster's] suppression of all major black political leaders and

organization?," the paper replied, "because his economy, Europe's and ours are interlocked."[28]

This interlocking relationship was described by Nancy Cardwell, a staff reporter of the *Wall Street Journal:*

> The importance of southern Africa to U.S. commerce and industry far exceeds the measurements shown by simple economic yardsticks. Beneath the mountains and savannas of Rhodesia, Namibia (also known as South-West Africa) and the Republic of South Africa lie vast reserves of essential minerals. Their uses range from the making of sophisticated electronic communications equipment and weaponry to the production of steel.
>
> Disruptions of supplies, whether by deliberate national policy or by production failures, would send world market prices soaring and threaten the viability of many industries. The resulting losses would dwarf the approximately $1.6 billion of direct U.S. investment in the region.
>
> Chromium, which is the corrosion-resistant ingredient of stainless steel, is the best-known industrial mineral found in the area. Rhodesia has 67% of the world's reserves of metallurgical-grade chrome ore, and the Republic of South Africa has another 22%. The U.S. doesn't have any. "We would have to revert 40 or 50 years in our standard of living and our technology in order to do away with chrome completely," says E. F. Andrews, a vice president of Allegheny Ludlum Industries, Inc., a stainless steel producer.[29]

There are many other equally important minerals that South Africa produces and sells to Western countries. It seems clear that any threat to the stability of the status quo in South Africa could endanger the short- and long-range interests of foreign capital. The relation of the exporter of goods to the customer, for instance, is short term and only reasonable political stability is required, but the relation of creditor and debtor is long term and inevitably gives rise to the demand for security, if not outright political control—especially if the country where capital is invested shows signs of political instability.

After the Sharpeville massacre, there was a great deal of instability in South Africa, and international financial circles panicked. Shares on the South African stock exchange fell in value by $1.75 million. Gold and foreign exchange reserves dropped from $439.6 million to $238 million, while $271.6 million in foreign capital fled the country. International and national capitalist spokesmen, fearing that the Sharpeville crisis signaled the possibility of an organized African revolt, called for measures to redress the Africans' grievances. The chairman of Anglo-Vaal, the president of the Johannesburg Stock Exchange, Harry Oppenheimer, and Charles Engelhard all called for a relaxation of repressive laws. Some conservative ministers asked for changes, especially when Sharpeville and the follow-up strikes were compounded by an assassination attempt on Verwoerd.

The situation was restabilized through a combination of big-stick methods and American corporate financial aid. The government banned African organizations, arrested their leaders, and adopted repressive methods that virtually destroyed any overt resistance. But it was the American corporate effort that was to save the economy.

In December 1960 the International Monetary Fund allowed South Africa to draw $38 million in credits, and within six months had extended another short-term loan of $75 million. A year later South Africa received two loans from the World Bank, totaling between $25 million and $28 million, for railway and electric power development. The First National Bank of New York, which had two branches in the republic, extended a $5 million loan to the government's Industrial Development Corporation. Chase Manhattan contributed $10 million and, together with Dillon, Read, ensured that a revolving credit fund was extended for two years at the end of 1961, and further extensions have continued until the present. Charles Engelhard reaffirmed his personal commitment to apartheid in September 1961 when he raised $30 million in the United States for his Rand Selection Mining Group. International Harvester, Newmont Mining, Universal Laboratories, Owens Corning, Pfizer, Underwood, and others all announced expanded investments.[30]

By the end of 1962 U.S. investment, having fallen off in 1960, had topped the previous high point ($323 million in 1959) and amounted to $442 million. The 60 American corporations in pre-Sharpeville South Africa had become 175 by 1962, and today are in excess of 400. According to the National Council of Churches, U.S. firms now account for 75 percent of all U.S. assets in South Africa.

With the winds of change blowing at gale force throughout the continent, the South African government apparently felt that the greater the amount of foreign-held assets, the greater would be the interest of the foreign powers in restraining economic sanctions against it. This hope has been fulfilled on a number of occasions, as when the Western powers—the United States, Britain, and France—used their veto power to prevent mandatory sanctions from being imposed to force South Africa to relinquish its illegal occupation of Namibia.

The strategy of South Africa's industrialization in the 1960s was dictated not only by a desire to develop industry, but also by fiscal and military-technical considerations that demanded self-sufficiency in key areas in case of U.N. sanctions. Thus natural resources have been used to develop production of strategic materials, such as oil, explosives, and war materiel; and American and European investment has played a major role in these sectors. The key U.S. companies in each of these areas include: General Motors,* Ford, Chrysler, Kaiser Jeep Corporation (automobiles); Firestone, Goodyear Tire and Rubber (rubber); Union Carbide, U.S. Steel, Charles Engelhard (mining); Chase Manhattan Bank, First National City Bank (finance); Standard Oil of New Jersey (Esso) (oil); ITT, General Electric, 3M, IBM (computers). A quantitative analysis reveals that, although American investment is small compared with that of the EEC countries, it is highly concentrated in these critical areas.

A little-discussed area of British, American, German, and South African cooperation is in nuclear development. The first uranium plant in South Africa was formally opened on October

---

* According to the *New York Times* (May 19, 1978), officials of General Motors Corporation in South Africa drafted a secret contingency plan in the summer of 1977 to deal with potential race riots in South Africa. The plan indicated that the company's executives in South Africa expected the entire auto industry to be taken over by the South African Ministry of Defense if a national emergency were declared.

3, 1952. It was undertaken by joint British and American interests, with the cooperation of the Massachusetts Institute of Technology, the Chemical Research Laboratory of Great Britain, the Ottawa Bureau of Mines, and the South African government's Metallurgical Laboratory. A very considerable volume of American capital was put up for the plant, which had a capital investment of $110 million.[31] In 1965 the Johnson administration granted South Africa a reactor, and South Africa apparently now has a fully operational nuclear weapons program. In August 1978 it was revealed that South Africa was preparing to test its first nuclear weapon.

The timing of the nuclear test raises serious questions for those states that support guerrilla movements fighting against South Africa. Since the collapse of Portuguese colonialism in 1974 and the student rebellion in Soweto in 1976, South Africa has felt itself beleaguered. It would be difficult to escape the impression that the nuclear testing was carefully calculated, and it seems reasonable that the United States and its NATO allies have long known all about South African nuclear developments; that the alarm they expressed after being confronted by the Soviet Union with satellite pictures of the test was simply a smokescreen. Possession of nuclear capability, however crude the weapon and however humble the delivery system, must be regarded as South Africa's trump card to ensure the survival of its regime. The threat of a nuclear weapon could have far-reaching effects on the continuing African struggle.

South Africa's nuclear capability raises disturbing questions about the role of imperialism. Why did the imperialist countries help South Africa develop a nuclear weapons capability while pleading that such weapons must be kept out of the rest of Africa to avoid a costly arms race and localized wars? Dr. Peter Janke, a member of the London-based Institute for the Study of Conflict, holds that continued white rule in South Africa is in the strategic interests of the West, and that this can help the Afrikaner white minority:

> The continued existence of the white man in Southern Africa depends upon the Afrikaner, not the White English-speaking

South African. The Western strategic interest at present depends upon this too, for majority rule in South Africa, under whatever guise, cannot offer the same degree of immediate security to the West. It is upon the Republic, too, that Ian Smith's government depends, as does the hope and desperate need for controlled change and settlement there and in Namibia.[32]

After the Soweto rebellion of June 16, 1976, the economy suffered from inflationary pressure, debt, and a growing trade deficit. Despite the turmoil, major United States financial institutions repeated their post-Sharpeville pattern, arranging loans totaling more than $700 million to shore up the hard-pressed South African regime. Reed Kramer, of Africa News Service, writes:

> The biggest U.S. banks have organized and participated in a number of multimillion-dollar loans to the South African government, state-owned corporations, and private projects. As a result, U.S. indirect investment (mostly bank loans) in South Africa has for the first time in history surpassed the direct stake held there by some 300 American corporations. The latest major credit agreement was signed in late October—a $110 million loan to the government from a syndicate led by Citibank and co-managed by Morgan Guaranty Trust. Total lending to South Africa by American banks and their overseas subsidiaries has now surpassed $2 billion—nearly double what it was one year ago. By comparison, direct U.S. investment, which totals about $1.6 billion, has slowed its headlong rush of recent years, and may even show a decline for 1976.[33]

This indirect economic involvement is part of a new strategy that relies more heavily on financial capital than on covert agents to influence political developments. The $2 billion trust fund promised for Zimbabwe is part of this strategy, designed as it is to preserve the present economic infrastructure by encouraging the whites who control it to remain after independence.

J. A. Hobson once wrote with remarkable foresight that the "new imperialism" of South Africa would forge its own path in life. The absorbing aim of big business, politicians, financiers, and adventurers in South Africa, he wrote, will be to relegate British imperialism to what they conceive to be its proper place, that of an *ultima ratio* to stand far in the background while locally based capital charts its own path. A South African–based subimperialist system, supported and financed by American and EEC capital and having a political career of its own, has emerged. But at the same time the U.S. monopolies have become particularly aggressive as capital investment in Southern African industries and raw materials has become an increasingly important means of supplementing their dwindling foreign earnings and of penetrating the markets of the South African subsystem. A report in the Hartford *Courant* stated:

> The lure of South Africa for corporate planners stems in part from the unusually high profits on investment there. For the U.S. corporations, the average rate of return on investment in 1974 was 19.1 percent, compared with a world average of 11 percent for U.S. investment, according to the U.S. Commerce Department. The British reported their rate of return for 1974 . . . as 13 percent compared with 10 percent world wide.[34]

It follows that Britain, the United States, and the EEC countries have an important stake in South Africa. For if South Africa is the key to change in Southern Africa as a whole, it is also the key to the protection of investments which are of growing importance to the capitalist world economy. If political stability in South Africa is essential to the protection of Western interests in Southern Africa, then the Western powers must remain involved in the fate of South Africa.

Given the size of the imperialist stake in the South African economy, the events that have been unfolding in the entire region since 1974 have taken on international character. A whole host of geopolitical theories have been advanced to substantiate imperialist policies, ranging from those that maintain that imperialist investment in South Africa promotes peaceful change to those that emphasize the importance of the Cape sea route for Western shipping in the case of the closing of the Suez Canal. Nevertheless, the counterrevolutionary nature of imperialism, despite rhetorical declarations critical of apartheid, should by now be clear to anyone. At the minimum, multinational investment has increased the imperialist stakes in retaining the status quo or some form of white supremacy over the whole of Southern Africa, and, at the maximum, it has fostered South Africa's economic and military threat to the neighboring states. Encouraged by the impunity it has seemed to enjoy in the face of all attempts at sanctions, the South African government unleashed the current wave of repression.

The interests of the South African ruling class and those of imperialism coincide; both are primarily interested in maintaining the status quo, the inequitable system of apartheid, which provides such lucrative profits. This identity of interests between imperialism and the South African ruling class in maintaining a superexploitation of the African work force is also seen in the propaganda offensive launched by both South Africa and imperialist circles concerning the role of foreign companies based in South Africa in improving working conditions for black workers. It is a propaganda offensive that is self-serving.

9

Apartheid Dogmas—and Afrikaner Nationalism

> Oh, what a tangled web we weave,
> When first we practice to deceive.
> —Walter Scott

In the preceding chapters, whether analyzing South African society as a developing capitalist system or the laws passed by politicians to regulate the process of development, I have implicitly touched upon the problems of ideology and nationalism. That is important because those who lead the affairs of any social community must explain their actions. But ideology is also a specific sphere of social life, a special social arena in which the struggles between various classes are fought, which therefore needs to be studied in its own right if its role in the history and development of any society is to be understood. In particular, ideology needs to be studied to find out how it justifies and boosts the economic activities of particular classes; that is, the study of ideology enables us to study the intentions of the articulate classes and the spiritual character of a particular class's rule. As Raymond Williams has pointed out:

> Intention, the notion of intention, restores the key question, or rather the key emphasis. For while it is true that any society is a complex whole of such practises, it is also true that any society has a specific organisation, a specific structure, and that the principles of this organisation and structure can be seen as directly related to certain social intentions, intentions by which we define the society, intentions which in all our experience have been the rule of a

particular class. One of the unexpected consequences of the crudeness of the base/superstructure model has been the too easy acceptance of models which appear less crude—models of totality or of a complex whole—but which exclude *the facts of social intention, the class character of a particular society and so on. And this reminds us of how much we lose if we abandon the superstructural emphasis altogether.*[1]

Throughout history those classes that exploit and dominate others have tried to find theoretical and ideological weapons to supplement their physical domination. They propagate these ideologies in all the institutions of society in order to convince themselves and the oppressed classes that inequality is inevitable, the natural state of human society. Aristotle wrote in his *Politics* that, on the basis of natural laws, people are subdivided into those who govern and those who work: "It is thus clear that, just as some are by nature free, so others are by nature slaves, and for these latter the condition of slavery is both beneficial and just." In a sentence just prior to this, Aristotle wrote:

> Tame animals have a better nature than wild, and it is better for all such animals that they should be ruled by man because they then get the benefit of preservation. Again, the relation of male to female is naturally that of the superior to the inferior—of the ruling to the ruled. This general principle must similarly hold good of all human beings generally (and therefore of the relation of masters and slaves).[2]

What Aristotle claims to be a natural way of ordering society simply expresses the fact that the Greek polity was a system built solidly on oppression and slavery. Aristotle's theory of the state merely ratified the domination of the Greek ruling class.

In the era of feudalism there was a distinction between "legal" and "natural" social inequality, a distinction formalized in religious canons. As a social system, feudalism was built on a complicated hierarchy of secular and religious bodies that split society into estates. Christianity played a decisive role in providing the ideological underpinnings for an explanation of economic and social classes. Racial and ethnic differentiation were not then major factors—the Bible distinguishes between Jew and gentile, but no more. Early Christianity was emphatic on the question of brotherhood among those who professed the religion. According to Gibbon, "Such was the mild spirit of antiquity, that nations were less attentive to the differences than to the resemblance of their religious worship."[3]

During the rise of capitalism—in particular because of the African slave trade—certain classes reneged on the Christian concept of the brotherhood of humanity. With the rise of the African slave trade, questions of a racial nature began to interest Europeans, such as whether Africans could be regarded as humans whose souls could be saved by conversion to Christianity and whether Africans were inferior to Europeans. Racialism emerged as a new basis for stratification and rationalized the scandalous inhuman exploitation that had turned Africa "into a warren for the commercial hunting of black skins." In time, brazen "scientific treatises" appeared which supposedly "proved" the inferior nature of the African slave. The formalization of racist theories took place in the era of imperialism—the era when various parts of the world were apportioned to the various imperialist powers. Raymond Betts writes:

> Tragically, the closest and most enduring contacts between Europeans and non-Europeans in this first phase of overseas imperialism were made in the course of the African slave trade. To treat people as animals, to herd them into dingy and excessively crowded ships, the European slave trader had to be either calloused or self-deluding about the fate of these people. He tended to be both; first, considering only the cash nexus, the value of his cargo of ebony; and second, deeming the Negro to be inferior, given to cannibalism, and hence no worse off in chains—perhaps better—than in savage freedom in the jungles. In the African slave trade some of the deepest roots of racism grew, and in the African slave trade was provided one of the most outrageous examples of man's inhumanity to man.[4]

The predatory principle governing black/white relations is revealed most noticeably in America and South Africa, where the white population's status as a "superior" race was cultivated systematically and became a kind of psychological structure and a fetish. Only in that way could unrestricted despotic political

power and complete economic exploitation become the acceptable lot of the entire white population. By every dishonorable
expedient, the imperialists and their intellectual agents endeavored to convince humankind that white people were superior
and were entitled to usurp the land and labor of the so-called
inferior races.

The doctrine of apartheid in South Africa's ideology of racism
is the latest systematic falsification of the inhumanity suffered by
the African people at the hands of white settlers. But like other
imperial mystiques, it has become a real political and socioeconomic force. In the study of ideology, as C. L. R. James
points out, "it is important to remember at all times that those
who are administering in the spirit of the myth are not hypo-
crites or criminals, although the myth often drives them to com-
mit hypocritical or criminal actions."[5]

Racism, though it certainly falsifies reality, in its four hundred
years of systematic propagation has become a real force and the
"true" consciousness of a large majority of whites in capitalist
societies. Racism does not indicate only a "body of ideas," but
distorted and inverted structures in which such ideas operate
and become an active force.

In the history of human contact there are not only self-
deceptions. There are also, of course, conscious deceptions,
ideas which one class sets in circulation to deceive and misguide
other classes. Self-deception proceeds very easily into conscious
deception of others. Fantastic ideas about the superiority of one
group over another have been the expression of the definite
political and economic interests of conquering and exploiting
groups throughout history. And while a historical understanding of how the conquered are incorporated into the service of
the conquering and of how ideologies justifying various forms of
exploitation develop is instructive, an uncritical reliance on past
oppressive ideas is fraught with danger. There is always the
temptation to lull oneself with the idea that "something of the
sort" has happened before and thus to rest content with only
establishing analogies, overlooking the specific features of new
forms of oppression and their ideological rationalizations. A
thorough understanding of the concrete situation in which op-

pressive ideas manifest themselves is indispensable for success in transcending those structures which foster certain ideas.

Because whites established a permanent settlement in South Africa, they wished to deny that the indigenous population could ever attain to national status and citizenship. The settlers therefore needed a theoretical justification by which they could deny the national autonomy of the societies they had conquered—the doctrine that all nations had the right to independence left little room for imperial conquest or the "eternal" subordination of one group by another. So racial superiority became the theory justifying conquest and territorial expansion: it was the manifest destiny of the "civilized" world to control and guide "inferior" peoples for the good of all.[6] Racism was thus a distorted representation of social reality, especially of the unequal social relations of capitalist production and exploitation. Once racial ideologies were formulated, they were widely disseminated and tended to take on a life of their own.

Having enjoyed in the past four hundred years or so certain opportunities for getting wealth, for exercising power and authority, and for successfully claiming prestige and social differences, whites everywhere in the capitalist world developed the conviction that these benefits were theirs by right. The advantages came to be thought of as normal, proper, and sanctioned by time, precedent, and the natural order of things. Proposals to change the existing situation were reacted to with moral indignation. An examination of the dogma of apartheid, especially its total rejection of the equality and right to self-determination of the African, is a present-day elaboration of this tendency, just as the pseudogenetic "theories" of black inferiority in America are an attempt to rationalize black oppression and exploitation.

The Genesis of the Idea of Racial Discrimination

The great Frederick Douglass once commented:

Slavery has been fruitful in giving itself names. It has been called "the peculiar institution," "the social system," and the "impediment." . . . . It has been called by a great many names, and it will call itself by yet another name; and you and I and all of us had better wait and see what new form this old monster will assume, in what new skin this old snake will come forth next.[7]

Racial exploitation in South Africa has called itself by various names; apartheid is only a new name for an old process. (Because of the stigma attached to it, the word "apartheid" is no longer fashionable. The government now favors "plural democracy.") Ideology in general does not exist; what exists are the different world views of particular classes. To understand a particular ideology we need to know something about the class that expounds it at a specific time. Thus, apartheid as a form of racialism bears the stamp of the Afrikaners and their historic situation in the socioeconomic development of South Africa. The Afrikaner reveals a curious combination of nationalistic fanaticism and petty-bourgeois concerns which can be described as protoeconomic nationalism. The Afrikaner's perception of reality is partly faulty logic and partly an irrational mixture of mystical beliefs, aggressive romanticism, and traumatic fears, which cannot be upheld in today's world.

Marx observed that "legislation, whether political or civil, never does more than proclaim, claim in words the will of economic relations."[8] Yet explanations of the "native policies" followed by the various South African governments almost totally ignore the socioeconomic structure of South Africa and its classes. Psychology, attitudes, and the utterances of "personalities" replace the study of the concrete, objective material conditions that foster certain beliefs and that would help in assessing particular actions. In the writings of many liberal scholars, apartheid is presented as an ideological inheritance of the frontier environment experienced by the Afrikaner forefathers, rather than in terms of the interest groups, economic processes, and institutional structure of South Africa as a capitalist society.

In South Africa, more than anywhere else, one can trace the relationship between economic structure and ideological superstructure. The turns and twists in the history of native policy bear an evident relationship to the history of the class that was in power when a particular emphasis was placed on "race" as the crucial element. For instance, the fallacious idea of the biological inequality between blacks and whites was an accepted ideology when the Dutch colonists of the Cape Colony were engaged in wars of genocide against the Khoisan people and when they imported slaves into the Cape Colony in the seventeenth and early eighteenth centuries.

When slavery was abolished in 1832, the Boers who trekked into the interior of South Africa introduced slavery, but disguised it as apprenticeship. This exploitation of African labor found legal expression in the Afrikaner republic's constitution of 1856, which declared in its preamble that there shall be "no equality of whites and blacks in Church or State." The Boers considered Africans to be objects destined by God and nature to slave for them, and as such an indispensable foundation for their peasant economy. The doctrine of "no equality" was, therefore, expressive of a primitive exploitative relationship; it was vulgar racism, which by its proclamation of biological inequality could be used to justify the most crude forms of exploiting human arms and legs. The changes in the exploitation of black labor (which correspond to a perfecting of the means of production) inevitably camouflaged the techniques by which humans are exploited, hence the changes in the forms of racism we see today.[9]

The arrival of the British, with their superior modes of production, demanded a more systematic exploitation of the African and led to important changes in ideological rationalization. Unlike the Boers, the British emphasized cultural differences, a shift that created conflicts between the two white groups. In the English scheme of things, the brutality of enforced inequality gave way to a politically organized inequality based on class traditions and class institutions. The English promised the African the possibility of ascent from the racially enforced hopelessness promulgated by the Afrikaner. They encouraged individual mobility as long as it did not threaten their hegemony. This was based on a well-calculated strategy. According to Rosa Luxemburg:

> The ultimate purpose of the British government was clear: long in advance it was preparing for land robbery on a grand scale, using

the native chieftains themselves as tools. But in the beginning it was content with the "pacification" of the Negroes by extensive military actions. Up to 1879 were fought 9 bloody Kaffir wars to break the resistance of the Bantus.[10]

When the bourgeoisie is strong, Fanon tells us, and when it can arrange everything and everyone to serve its power, it does not hesitate to affirm certain democratic ideals, which it claims to be universally applicable. Cecil Rhodes's proclamation of "equality among all civilized men," and what is called in the South African history of political ideas the "spirit of Cape Liberalism," both expressed the aggressive self-confidence of British imperialism and capitalism. When discussing ideological questions it is important to note the role played by the politically conscious classes. The English-speaking intellectuals who write most of South Africa's history are unable to study the activities of their "racial" class. What is called the English spirit of liberalism is an idealized self-conception of this class rather than a reflection of the real historical activities of the English conquering class that imposed racist political institutions.

The English bourgeoisie was fundamentally racist, but because it needed allies in its struggle with the Boers it managed to mask its racism by a multiplicity of nuances, which in the absence of serious critical analyses allowed it to maintain intact its proclamation of humanity's outstanding dignity. When the Act of Union was finally drafted in 1908, the English tried to preserve the qualified franchise granted to Africans in the Cape Colony—but at the same time they made sure to prepare enough fences and railings so that those whom they exploited would not be able to use constitutional safeguards to upset the status quo. During peace negotiations with Lord Kitchener on February 28, 1901, General Louis Botha expressed fear that the British would extend the vote to all Africans. Kitchener assured Botha that "it is not the intention of Her Majesty's Government to give such a franchise before representative government is granted to the colonies, and if given, it will be so limited as to justify the just predominance of the White race."

The history of liberalism in South Africa reveals the inconsistency and opportunism of the British bourgeoisie, in particular its fear for its own future vis-à-vis the Afrikaner and the African. British liberalism was only useful in the era of conquest, when, in contrast to the crude methods of the Afrikaner rule, it could always appear progressive. After 1910, and because of its internal weakness, the English colonial bourgeoisie threw itself into the hands of the Afrikaner landed bourgeoisie, exchanging the right to rule for the right to make money. As Herbert Vilakazi points out:

> The easy success of white workers, poor whites, and all white women—nay, their hearty welcome into politics by the capitalist class and state personnel—was due to the fear of Black revolt. The Afrikaners now began to leave their imprint on politics and the state, and the nature of this imprint was determined by their poverty, bitterness towards the English and hatred of the Blacks.[11]

In discussions of the differences in outlook between the English and Boers, the emphasis tends always to be placed on the ideological heritages of the two groups rather than on their material circumstances. Thus, the Calvinist background of the Afrikaners and the hostile frontiers to which they were pushed by the arrival of the English are always given prominence, while in the case of the English the liberal spirit that pervaded Europe in the period of the ascendancy of the bourgeoisie to power is overdramatized.

Though beliefs and inherited ideas may be constant from generation to generation, the social environment within which individuals and groups function is in a continual process of change and affects the implementations of such inherited outlooks. Given South Africa's social environment, and the social and economic benefits that were associated with white skin, the differences between the English and Afrikaners have worn thin. Over the years a large part of the English-speaking community, comfortable with swimming pools, servants, and a high standard of living, has shown that it is as racially prejudiced and as conservative as the Afrikaner. The "liberal" and "humanitarian" ideas which the English are supposed to have brought with them to South Africa were not innate attributes, but represented the optimism of a rising bourgeoisie, while the conservative world view held by the Afrikaners corresponded to the social and economic order they were creating in South Africa, based on inherited but outmoded economic practices. Rosa Luxemburg points out:

> The Boer peasant economy and great capitalist colonial policy were here competing for the Hottentots and Kaffirs, that is to say for their land and their labour power. Both competitors had precisely the same aim: to subject, expel or destroy the coloured peoples, to appropriate their land and press them into service by the abolition of their social organisations. Only their methods of exploitation were fundamentally different. While the Boers stood for out-dated slavery on a petty scale, on which their patriarchal peasant economy was founded, the British bourgeoisie represented modern large-scale capitalist exploitation of the land and the natives.[12]

Thus, when the epoch of imperialism began to show contradictions between reality and theory, i.e., when the "white man's burden" became recognized in fact as the "black man's burden," some of the metaphysical assumptions of British liberalism degenerated into reactionary fantasies and accommodated themselves to the Afrikaner world view. Since 1910 the English bourgeoisie has made many compacts with the Afrikaners in order to save its skin, and now it has nothing to barter but its skin. It is therefore not surprising that most of the English-speaking whites in South Africa have turned away from their grey liberalism and faded Christianity and accepted the Afrikaners' racial conservatism.

Hannah Arendt writes:

> When the Boers lost the war, they lost no more than they had already deliberately abandoned, that is, their share in the riches, but they definitely won consent of all other European elements, including the British Government, to lawlessness of a race society—today all sections of the population, British, or Afrikaner, organized workers or capitalist, agree on the race question.[13]

The British bourgeoisie in South Africa has always been conscious that in Southern Africa the fundamental conflict was between blacks and the white settlers. As James Bryce wrote in

1897, "So far as the future of South Africa is dependent upon the race question, the difficulties between Englishman and Dutchman shrink into insignificance in comparison with those between White and Black."[14]

In the post–World War I era white supremacy and the ideas associated with it, such as the "white man's burden," had to be revised in the light of the war experience. The imperial world could not continue as before; its members had to establish a new code, or "morality," about the proper way of conducting their relations with the colonized, and the result was the doctrine of trusteeship. It is instructive that its greatest exponent was General J. C. Smuts, then minister of defense of the Union of South Africa. The League of Nations Charter embodied the ideology of trusteeship. It stated:

> To those colonies and territories which as a consequence of the late war had ceased to be under the sovereignty of the States which had formerly governed them and which are inhabited by peoples not yet able to stand by themselves under the strenuous conditions of the modern world, there should be applied the principles that the well-being and development of such peoples form a sacred trust of civilization and that securities for performance of this trust should be embodied in this covenant.[15]

This was a variation on the ideological justification given by the signatories of the General Act of the Berlin Conference in 1885, which regulated the carving-up of the African continent and which stated that the natives must be "protected," their moral and material well-being upheld, slavery and the slave trade suppressed, the education of the "natives" furthered, and missionaries, scientists, and explorers protected.[16] The trusteeship system was, in reality, a continuation of the old Berlin fraud, draped in the veil of "new" moral concerns.

Besides this obvious aspect of trusteeship, it had other more subtle ideological implications. It promised self-government, while at the same time building barriers to any African political advancement. It affected to open the doors of "civilization" to those Africans who had undergone a definite process of cultural and physical maturation, but only in the remote and indefinite future. The ideological advantage of the concept of trusteeship over previous racist theories was that the trustee pronounced it perfectly possible for those under guardianship to become civilized people. This could best be accomplished, of course, under the firm hand and wise tutelage of the European colonists, who were all too eager to test the exploitative possibilities of the new rationales. The history of Namibia (South-West Africa), a country that was given to South Africa by the League of Nations, is tragic testimony to the trusteeship system.

The test of the ideology of trusteeship came in 1935–1936, when the Africans were removed from the Cape's voters' roll; and it was buried during the war years, by which time large numbers of Africans had become a permanent part of the industrial urban civilization. General Smuts, the architect of trusteeship, recognized this fact when he said in 1942, "Isolation has gone and segregation has fallen on evil days."[17] Between, on the one hand, the promise of trusteeship and the removal of the African from the Cape voters' roll and, on the other, this declaration by Smuts, there seems to be an obvious contradiction. But what it actually means is that in every society that is split into classes, i.e., based on exploitation, the exploiting class is vitally interested in the preservation of the existing pattern of social relations, and in administering the affairs of society it will seek to admit only such change as will not endanger this pattern.

> The point is therefore unavoidably reached when the progress of reason . . . [is] impeded, when existing and maturing possibilities for society's further advancement, for further growth and development of all its members, are sacrificed in favor of the interest of the dominant class in the continuation of the established social order—when, in other words, the particular interest of the ruling class comes into conflict with the interests of society as a whole.[18]

The end of World War II was the unavoidable point: ideologies like trusteeship and segregation had lost their rationale. Smuts's famous declaration of 1942 must be understood in the context of the time. The experiences of the war, particularly those at the "darkest moment," dictated that concessions, even if only verbal, be made to prevent an African revolt, which would have greatly undermined South Africa's contribu-tion to the war effort. With the war over, Africans were again expected to revert to their places.

In 1948 capitalist economic growth had undermined the old structures of oppression, and new structures which would rigidly divide society into hierarchical orders enforced by law had to be created. Apartheid, then, is an ideology of a society in crisis. It was a logical development from the previous laissez faire segregation policies, which in 1910 had resulted in the franchise being limited to whites only.

Since 1910 South Africa had built a social system, and a "civilization," with a distinct class structure, political community, economy, and ideology, as well as a set of psychological patterns which internal developments in the country, the demise of col-onialism, and the advent of independent African states would subject to severe strains. That the ideology of apartheid is an attempt to cope with the demise of white supremacy and the independence wave is not in doubt. South Africa's difficulties at present are not only military or economic or political or moral or ideological: they are all these, and they constitute a fundamental antagonism created by the end of the epoch of white domination on a world scale. What was acceptable when colonialism and white hegemony dominated the world is now unacceptable. The rationale for apartheid is explained thusly by Leo Kuper:

> Apartheid, in theory, rests on difference, not on inferiority. It thus recognizes the liberal rejection of the dogma of racial inferiority, and the inability of scientists, no matter how adequately motivated, to establish racial inferiority. The adoption of differences as the basis of discrimination introduces, however, the dilemma of finding a satisfactory criterion of difference. Race differences are rela-tively permanent, or at any rate long enduring, but discrimination based on race invites world criticism. Cultural differences, again even if acceptable to outside critics, may be very transient, and therefore provide only a shifting foundation for the maintenance of the *status quo*. The dilemma is that of using the differences between the racial groups in a form acceptable to world opinion on the one hand, and in such a way as to permit the perpetuation of the *status quo* on the other—a challenging dilemma.[19]

The basis of apartheid appears to have been a determination on the part of the Afrikaner rulers of the country to so organize society both by political and economic action as to make it impregnable to any attempt to effect a constitutional change. For the architects of Afrikanerdom, white domination of South African society is something which the current world developments could not transcend. For the Afrikaners, the supremacy of their class is the final and absolute limitation of any change.

The Logic of Apartheid

The present South African system is an anachronism, a flagrant contradiction of the universal rejection, at least in theory, of racism as a way to order human relations. The white settlers in South Africa imagine that their role cannot be changed and ask the world to share their illusion. But if South Africa believed its own dogmas, why would it hide naked racism in the specious concept of separate development? Why look for salvation in hypocrisy and sophistry? The white settlers in South Africa are a remnant of a world order that is dead. "History," according to Marx,

> is thorough, and it goes through many stages when it conducts an ancient formation to its grave. The last stage of a world-historical formation is comedy. The Greek gods, already once mortally wounded in Aeschylus' tragedy *Prometheus Bound,* had to endure a second death, a comic death, in Lucian's dialogues. Why should history proceed in this way? So that mankind shall separate itself *gladly* from its past. We claim this joyful historical destiny for the political powers of Germany.[20]

So it can be proclaimed for the white settlers in South Africa. Apartheid was propounded after World War II, when there were serious challenges to white rule and the beginnings of colonial emancipation. The demise of the doctrine of trusteeship showed that no historical situation can be established once and for all. The doctrine of apartheid, when it was proclaimed as an election slogan, was a doctrine of naked racism. But ideologies have a feature which we can call "perfectibility." When an ideology encounters problems, the difficulties are at first not of a kind to shake it fundamentally and the ideology is adjusted; details are altered, but the essentials are left intact. Louis Althusser has put it thusly:

> Unlike a science, an ideology is both theoretically closed and politically supple and adaptable. It bends to the interests of the times, but without any apparent movement, being content to *reflect* the historical changes of which it is its mission to assimilate and muster by some imperceptible modification of its peculiar internal relations. . . . Ideology changes, therefore, but imperceptibly, conserving its ideological form; it moves, but with an immobile motion which remains *where it is,* in its place and its ideological role.[21]

The evolution of apartheid from a doctrine of naked white supremacy to one of "separate development" and recently to "plural democracy" involves such an immobile adjustment. Keith Gottscholk explains:

> The Bantustan policy has simply assembled the already existing chiefs, with already increased powers of jurisdiction over their political opponents, into debating chambers graced with ceremonial mace symbolizing such properties (as the Minister reminded the Tsonga-Mashanganaland Territorial Assembly), as ORDER, OBEDIENCE AND INDUSTRIOUSNESS. These would seem to be less the attributes of constitutional sovereignty than the qualities which imperial rulers desire instilled in their subject race. These ethnic political institutions, "Legislative Assemblies," and "representative Councils," dominated by hereditary or appointed members, have had conferred upon them what in the United States or Britain would be considered only local government responsibilities—maintenance of public works and roads, education, some taxes, some part of the police.[22]

The evolution of apartheid shows that the most consummate expression of ideological beliefs tends to appear at the moment when the belief in question is no longer able to sway people's minds. We have seen how the belief in blacks' inferiority or "nonhumanity" lost its validity at the very time Smuts produced the most elaborate and sophisticated defense of the inferiority of the black man under the guise of trusteeship. And just when people awakened from that delusion of Hitler, the Nationalist Party under Verwoerd coined the ideology of apartheid—an ideology that has been more terrible in its consequences than any of its predecessors. Apartheid cannot eradicate the reality of oppression, even if it calls it "separate development" or "plural democracy."

If we are not to appear naive, we must look for the "true" reasons for apartheid, because the official ones are so patently false. That is, the logic of the theory is in the metaphysics of political economy. There seem, in fact, to be several grades and varieties of motives for apartheid, which overlie one another like so many geological strata, depending on who the speaker and his audience are at a particular time and place—the "idealistic" reasons for apartheid being for external consumption and the "practical" for home consumption. But since the two layers overlie one another, we must do some "strip mining," peeling away the top propaganda layer to expose the firmer underlying layers that give apartheid its base and purpose. In other words, there are the economic categories that are the foundation of society, but these are transmuted from time to time into a little-known language, which makes them look as if they have newly blossomed.[23]

There is in all living societies a continual movement of growth of productive forces, of destruction of archaic social relations, of formation of new social relations and new ideas. To understand the evolution of apartheid, we must move the analytic focal point to the substrata of apartheid which will explain its growth; it is in the development of the contradictions of capitalism where the less pious, and more honest, reasons for apartheid lie exposed. People, Lenin once observed, always have been the foolish victims of deception and self-deception in politics, and they always will be until they have learned to seek out the *interests* of some class or other behind all moral, religious, political, and social phrases, declarations, and promises.[24]

What, then, does the sociological analysis of apartheid yield for an understanding of its connection with practice and, correspondingly, for an understanding of its structure? It helps to analyze apartheid as an ideology expressing the aims of a particular ethno-class functioning within the framework of a definite socioeconomic system.

It is fruitless to argue with the advocates of apartheid in terms of what its exponents have to say. The apologetic view of South Africa sees two sides to apartheid, the one good and positive and the other bad and negative. It is a view which also accepts the paramountcy of white claims to the sole occupancy of the country. However, while the productive relations of capitalism in South Africa form a single and indivisible whole, in the ideology of apartheid the links of the society are converted into so many separate societies. This, of course, is politically advantageous to the Afrikaner. Almost all the advocates of apartheid admit that

> the white economy cannot survive the total removal of Bantu labour. For another thing, the Bantu in South Africa cannot exist without selling his labour to a very considerable extent to the white man. Whatever the position may be in time to come, this is the present position. For this reason total territorial separation has never been, and is not at this moment, the policy of the South African Government. It accepts total separation as an ideal worthy of achievement, and it is working for the maximum extent of geographical separation. But it also accepts the fact that total *apartheid* is at the moment, and will be for a very long time to come, economic nonsense.[25]

Thus, the doctrine of apartheid, though entrenched in the sphere of politics, involves no considerable interference with the fundamentals of economic reality. Its exponents are principally concerned with the removal of threats to their political supremacy, which is also a way to guarantee their economic supremacy. They have attacked the African's and colored's voting right, and they have banned African political organizations. They have denied African workers the right to organize into unions. The various aspects of apartheid as an ideological form differ; the political and juridical aspects have a direct relation to the economic bases. Thus, the labor laws reflect the relations of production more or less accurately, and in fact the laws regulating labor relations are shaped under the immediate influence of the economy and of class interests. They are what Engels calls ideologies of the "first order." The labor laws reflect social relations from the standpoint of the juridical regulation of the behavior and actions of the working class and other members of the society. As Engels puts it, "Economic fact must assume the form of juridical motives in order to revive legal sanction."[26]

Since the desire for more profit necessitated the continued exploitation of the Africans, the number of Africans increased in the urban industrial order. The political and ideological thrust of apartheid aimed to exorcise this reality—to frustrate the inevitable consequences of the contest between labor and capital. This has been the strategy of South Africa's ruling interests: the more their economic prosperity depended on the exploitation of African labor, the more barriers they built and the more desperately they attempted by means of legislation to arrest what all over the world is a normal process of economic emancipation. C. W. DeKiewiet, the economic historian, observes:

> A special theory is developed in which the economic life of society is [superficially] subordinated to its political objectives, so that non-European workers are not free to improve their standard of living, if thereby they seek also to gain added political opportunity or social advancement. The economy of South Africa is ruled by political and racial considerations to an extent that is unusual in most western democracies. The place and share which individuals and groups enjoyed in the economy are not the result of the services which they render but of their racial and political status.[27]

Because of the necessity for continued growth, apartheid is not fundamentally opposed to the presence of Africans in what are called "white" areas, but it is opposed to the African establishing there a wedge for social and political leverage. This creates the vicious circle in which the ruling interests find themselves today: the political economy from which their living standards are derived creates possibilities for their destruction as a political force. It has also created a situation in which the whites' pride, sense of honor, and way of life are synonymous with the subordination and exploitation of Africans.

Jan Smuts, characteristically candid, posed the question of the status of the African in South Africa in these classic arguments:

> What then are the basic facts of this insoluble Native Problem?
> The problem may be viewed from three different angles. There

is firstly the ethnical approach which purports to show that all men are equal. It is the old philanthropic outlook of the Bible. Apart from displaying an honest though over-easy outlook it has little realism to commend it. This basis of reciprocity of goodwill is a fictitious one as far as the native is concerned, *and anthropologists are quick to point out that the native has no gratitude in his social code.* It is a weakness unknown to him. He will take all he can get quite gladly, and then blithely ask for more. There is no convincing argument based on sound fact so far as I can see, to back up this ethnical approach. It is simply a noble white urge to see fair play. The idea of equality is based upon shifting sands, and in fact the native is wise enough not to ask for it. All he asks for is unhampered opportunity.

The second approach is the scientific one in which are automatically visualised grades of evolutionary advancement. It is easy for us to do so in South Africa, for we have had before us that arrested type in anthropological development known as the Bushman, like the Australian aborigine, a freak survival from some primitive age. We have never accorded this small evolutionary enigma an equal status. Nor has the native.

It is therefore not difficult to imagine the Bantu as an intermediate form between the European and Bushman. In fact, from the scientific aspect it has much to commend it, for undoubtedly the Bantu has features in his bone structure that we associate with Stone Age races. His very skull, for example, is almost half as thick again as that of the European. Yet, so far, study of his brain size and convolutions has not shown an inferiority to the European. But certainly the massiveness of the facial bone structure suggests a connection with the old Neanderthaloid group of men.

Thirdly there is the tactical approach. It takes into account that the white man in the Union is outnumbered by four to one. It takes into account the fact that the black man is increasing in numbers more rapidly than the white man.[28]

This is an imaginary charade overlaid with quack science. Christopher Caudwell once wrote that, "Man thinks fine things and does hateful ones. He is 'sinful,' base and degenerate, at the very time when his notions are most high-faluting."[29] A historical fatalism underlies the doctrine of racism and apartheid in South Africa. The protagonists of racism and its apartheid form lose almost all interest in social life as it is, concentrating all their attention on social life as it ought to be in keeping with what they consider to be "the natural order of the universe." The following statement by Smuts confirms this:

> Colour queers my poor pitch everywhere. But South Africans cannot understand. Colour bars are to them part of the divine order of things. But I sometimes wonder what our position in years to come will be when the whole world will be against us. And yet there is so much to be said for the South African point of view who fear getting submerged in Black Africa. I can watch the feeling in my own family which is as good as the purest gold. It is a sound instinct of self preservation where the self is so good and not mere selfishness. What can one do about it, when (as Isie says) the Lord himself made the mistake of creating colour.[30]

We stated above that racism was originally based on faith, and science, it was hoped, would confirm the political facts of imperialism. From its inception the social anthropology that Smuts refers to reflected the interests of the colonial bourgeoisie. This is the guilt of colonial anthropology. It suffered from a peculiar blindness, its practitioners conceived its task as that of providing answers to the imperial order of things in order to make colonial rule enduring. But in science, as in politics, nothing is more dangerous than to mistake what we wish for what is possible. DeKiewiet points out that apartheid

> in its various forms is a transfer of the responsibilities of the living world to the dream world of solved problems. It is the substitution of a wishful simplicity for a real complexity. The basic promise of *apartheid* is that the natives can seek no remedies and gain no citizenship within society, but only within their own segregated society. It is at this critical point that the remarkably well written documents issued by the South African Bureau of Racial Affairs step from fact into make-believe, using a dexterous logic to brush aside history and economics.[31]

Apartheid marks the last stage in the white settler's neurotic flight from reality. And because apartheid is situationally transcendent, i.e., it can never realize its projected content when attempts are made to put it into practice, it becomes the most brutal weapon in the white rulers' struggle against African emancipation and even against the process of change that has been going on in South Africa since the whites settled there. By identifying white rule with righteousness and permanence, it makes those opposed to it seem to be waging a struggle which is both wrong and impossible—hence its brutality. It presents itself as immortal in its embattlement. The attempt to assert that whites arrived in South Africa before or simultaneously with the African is indicative of the demented mental state of present-day rulers in South Africa. As we shall see, the theoretical and practical consequences of their assertion are not innocent.

At one level apartheid is an attempt to belie history; at another level it is an attempt to cope with the process of decolonization. As colonial freedom swept the African continent from north to south, South Africa found itself unable to escape the winds of change. The ruling interests could either resist the changes or feign to be in step with the times. Apartheid is a reactionary attempt to do both: it is at once a gesture and an attempt to bend to the interests of the times and a method of resisting and destroying African claims to a common citizenship with whites. Just as the political state in the period of enlightened absolutism had attempted to weaken and assimilate Protestantism itself through attempting to replace an objective interpretation of the world guaranteed by the church with one guaranteed by the state, apartheid attempts to destroy African nationalism by:

1. Diverting extra-ethnic African nationalism away from the global South African society to the remnants of traditional society. It aims at turning away Africans from their claims to rule in the general society by saying they can rule in the now defunct "tribal institutions."

2. Suppressing, intimidating, dividing, and beheading the new leadership produced by modern urban and industrial conditions by banishment and imprisonment, while building up traditional leadership as the "true" leadership of the African people.

In the apartheid scheme of things the decayed traditional institutions are exhumed and given artificial respiration, and their deformed state serves only one purpose—to perpetuate the agony of the African people. The culture of the African people is closed to the future and is fixed in the service of oppression. It is used to isolate and fragment the African opposition. Justifying the bantustan policy, Dr. Verwoerd once commented:

What is happening here in respect of the system of government is that a system which has developed over the centuries amongst the Bantu, a system which is known to them, indeed a system *which is engraved in their souls* and which is incorporated in their own Native laws, is being taken as the starting point for development. Just as in the White man's civilization development began with relatively simple systems of government but then developed to the highest levels that we have today, their system too will start with what the Bantu knows and will be developed from that point, but at an increased tempo, into what it is capable of becoming, in the light of their experience of the progressive modern White society in which they have already obtained a measure of learning and will continue to obtain learning. After all, that is the basis of all development. . . .

If the Leader of the Opposition reads the speeches of the Black leaders of Central African states, to which his followers frequently refer as something remarkable, he will see that what is demanded by people like Dr. Nkrumah is that the Black nation must not be expected servilely to take over systems which have developed in Europe up to the present time, but that they should be allowed to start with what is their own and that they should be able to adapt what they learn from the outside world to their own system. Not even the British parliamentary system has been taken over slavishly in the civilized countries. We find a great variety of adaptations because each nation has taken into account its own circumstances, its own character and requirements.

It must be realized once and for all that the developments in the Bantu areas, as well as the emancipation of those national groups, start with the system which is known to them and which is their own, and that their form of government and freedom will grow and be adapted in accordance with the demands of modern civilization. It will be adapted by the Bantu themselves with the assistance that we can give them. That is the position as far as the system of governments is concerned.[32]

At one and the same time the educated African, who is a spearhead of African opposition to the government, is dismissed in a backhanded manner by Dr. Eiselen "as a class of évolués who claim that they have relinquished their Bantu loyalties, and that they are building up a new comprehensive African community, which is no longer South African in character but claims the whole continent as his heritage. It is clear, I think, that there is no place in our South African policy for the program envisaged by this group, which has in common with natives of many other parts of Africa, adopted the name 'African.' " Elsewhere Eiselen referred to the urban Africans as "an unattached mass of Bantu individuals," and went on to state that the present system of having an unattached mass of Bantu individuals living in cities, not subject to any traditional authority or sanctions, has proved to be a dismal failure.[33]

In these two passages we have the contradictions and the illusory nature of apartheid exemplified in all its nakedness. When faced with new realities, the exponent of apartheid conceives of the changes as passing phenomena. S. Pienar, another supporter of apartheid, in a debate with a correspondent for a British newspaper, stated the government's attitude to the African National Congress as follows:

> It follows that it is not the urbanized African National Congress movement that will be the basis of Bantu political development, but the Bantu authorities in the Bantu areas, based on the traditional system of tribal chiefs, adapted to modern circumstances, in which process those Bantu who have acquired the Western know-how will have a vital part to play. Not the *denationalized* African but the civilized Bantu will be entrusted with the task of developing Bantu nations. One does not expect the African National Congress to share this view but it can be stated as a fact that in the Bantu areas themselves the Government finds impressive support.[34] [Emphasis added]

Another feature of ideological illusions is the process of inversion, by which social relations are represented as the realization of abstract ideas. According to an inverted way of looking at things, people create their social relationships in obedience to their abstract ideas, and not the other way around. As a result of ideological inversion the Afrikaner nationalists in particular, and South African whites in general, share the illusion that their institutions and public activities are expressions of their abstract character and ideas, of their religion, philosophy, political principles, and so on.[35]

When ideas about things are formed and worked out in this

way, it means that people are approaching reality with certain
more or less fixed preconceptions, which are accepted as axioms,
as natural and obvious ways of thinking. Conclusions are arrived
at independent of practice and uncritically, not as a result of
critical investigations and practical verification of conclusions.
Since 1948, South African politics has not been merely a struggle
for power. Infused in its aims has been a kind of political philosophy and a political conception of the world. Just as the idea of
"no equality between black and white" was an illusion of the
stagnant pastoral society in which the African was to be tied to
the land as a permanent serf, apartheid is an illusion in which
Africans are to participate in the industrial-urban system as
workers, without political and other civic rights, which Africans
are to seek in what are called their "homelands." DeKiewiet
writes:

> In the light of Africa's crisis today it is clear that the concepts of
> segregation and separateness in all their forms and whatever their
> motivation encouraged the false illusion that white man and black
> man could live in separate spheres whose margins usefully touched
> one another, but only in a secondary manner. Race and colour
> were the primary visible signs of differences that were primary and
> permanent. It was this interpretation of race and colour which
> caused generations of Europeans throughout Africa to accept the
> view that the only proper environment for the African was the
> rural tribe.[36]

The notion of illusion is used here to mean a state of mind which
is incongruous with the state of reality within which it occurs. It
takes refuge in a hypocrisy which because it is less and less likely
to deceive becomes all the more odious. Aimé Cèsaire has said:

> A civilization that proves incapable of solving the problems it
> creates is a decadent civilization.
> A civilization that chooses to close its eyes to its most crucial
> problems is a stricken civilization.
> A civilization that uses its principles for trickery and deceit is a
> dying civilization.[37]

Apartheid is based on absurdities and paralyzes action toward
a better world. In fact, it stimulates action toward a political state

bordering on fascism. It makes those who believe in it both escapists and storm troopers.

Why should people who are obviously intelligent believe in such a false solution? Apartheid can only be understood if we substitute "for conflicting dogmas the conflicting facts of real antagonisms which form the hidden background" of any society.[38]

Afrikaner Nationalism and Apartheid

In order to understand correctly the peculiarities of apartheid ideology, one must understand its historical roots and the evolution of its content and forms as determined by the development of class struggles. Afrikaner nationalism, like class consciousness, is rooted in the economic structure of the society in which it developed. That is, nationalism is an extremely vital force in petty-bourgeois struggles for a place in the sun in capitalist societies: without the goals of national honor and greatness, the masses will lack the enthusiasm and willingness to sacrifice on behalf of their petty bourgeoisie. Victor Alba remarks:

> Nationalism does not issue forth by spontaneous generation. "Nation" is an abstraction; the sense of it must be taught. Nationalism always, in one way or another, is due to propaganda. . . . Nationalism, then, is a bourgeois product that manifests itself in industrial societies as a means to higher ends.[39]

The ideology of nationalism is a set of practices which are both determined by other social relations and which have a determining effect on them. Thus, the analysis of national ideology must begin with the analysis of the social relations in which the advocates of nationalism are involved. As Paul Hirst points out: "Ideologies are social relations, they are as real as the economy."[40]

Three points need to be further highlighted in any attempt to provide a concrete analysis of Afrikaner nationalism and the Afrikaners as a people. One is the relation of the Afrikaner to the English bourgeoisie, on the one hand, and to the Africans on the other. The Afrikaners, like the Africans, were the victims of British imperialism. The Anglo-Boer war of 1900–1902 was an imperialist war, which finally placed the Afrikaner under British hegemony. Second, we must understand something of the economic forces which found their practical expression in the Nationalist Party. Third, we must distinguish between a broad, humanistic nationalism that seeks to mobilize people against injustice and oppression and the narrow, exclusive kind of nationalism, also known as chauvinism, which seeks to advance the interest of one section of society at the expense of all others.

Afrikaner nationalism as a historic force has gone through the two phases. The struggle against British imperialism in the Anglo-Boer War was expressive of the humanistic tendency, while the nationalism of present-day Afrikaners is reactionary and chauvinistic. The architects of social and economic nationalism are the Afrikaner petty bourgeois, who want to advance their economic stakes. We have seen how the "poor white" problem provided grist for the mill of national chauvinism. Petty-bourgeois class interests are the substance of present-day Afrikaner nationalism. Harold Wolpe points out how Afrikaner nationalism functioned:

> The alternative for the Afrikaner working-class, resisting competition from African workers, and for the growing Afrikaner industrial and financial capitalist class, struggling against the dominance of English monopoly capital, and, perhaps, for a petit-bourgeoisie threatened with proletarianization by the advance of African workers (and the Indian petit-bourgeoisie), was to assert control over the African and other Non-white people by whatever means were necessary. For the Afrikaner capitalist class, African labour could be maintained as cheap labour by repression; for the White workers, this also guaranteed their own position as a "labour-aristocracy."[41]

Capitalist development in South Africa subjected the Afrikaner to serious social strains. The consolidation of farms and the exodus from the farms to the cities affected all classes of Afrikaner society. In a sense, all the economic, social, and political pressures imperialism exerted on all Afrikaners were synthe-sized in a brand of national chauvinism.

Here is a brief recapitulation of how the alliance between the Afrikaner working class and the petty bourgeoisie came about. Beginning in 1906 the Labour Party and the Afrikaner National-ist Party had begun a hesitant courtship, in which they tested each other's policies and assessed the advantages and disadvan-tages of a firmer alliance. F. H. P. Creswell, the leader of the small but active Labour Party, sought the support of those who saw a legal color bar in the mines and industry as the only means of maintaining "civilized standards." By 1913 the tenuous bonds between the Labour Party and the Afrikaner Nationalists had been cemented more firmly. The brutal suppression of the min-ers' strike in that year, followed by the deportation of the leaders of the 1914 general strike, signified clearly to Creswell and his tentative Nationalist ally, General J. B. M. Hertzog, that the South Africa Party of General Louis Botha and J. C. Smuts was an instrument of the mine owners. Creswell and Hertzog found a common cause in the support of workers and poor whites. Their strictly protectionist policies were ultimately implemented by the Pact government, elected in 1924. Labour's role in the Pact government was to detach the British working class from Smuts and his imperialist South Africa Party.[42]

The leaders of the Nationalist Party made the poor-white problem their cause célèbre; they sought to develop a strong feeling of national identity between the Afrikaner petty bourgeoisie and the poor whites. Working in close cooperation with the Dutch Reform Church, the party tried to mobilize the urban and rural poor within an active core of cultural and political programs that engendered nationalism and racist jealousies. The petty bourgeoisie hoped to capture political and economic power through the unity of Afrikaner workers and capitalists.

Afrikaner Nationalists took advantage of the parliamentary system that excluded Africans from the vote in three of the four provinces of the Union. This enabled Nationalist politicians to make white interests paramount. According to the Simonses, "If universal suffrage produces a welfare state under capitalism, white suffrage gives rise under colonialism to a colour-bar state. A political party that appeals to white voters invariably makes their claims the touchstone of policy, plays on their collective fears of black power, excites and reinforces their racial antagonisms, and consolidates them into a hegemonic bloc in opposition to the voteless majority."[43]

Afrikaner nationalism is national consciousness of a perverse kind. It is a distorted love of one's own people based on hatred, fear, and contempt for others. It misdirects the service to one's own people into the subjugation and exploitation of all other peoples. It is a nationalism that is opposed to a free and independent growth of other nationalities. It spiritualizes the national sentiment into crass economic gains.

There can be no doubt that the struggles of the Boers against British imperialism did have certain democratic features. But the compromise, which the Act of Union sealed, between British imperialism and the Afrikaner petty bourgeoisie channeled Afrikaner nationalism into racial hatred. In its subsequent development, Afrikaner nationalism rapidly lost whatever anti-imperialist content it had once possessed and grew into that monster of vicious racism and chauvinism we know today.

Stanley Trapido explains the dilemma that fed Afrikaner chauvinism:

> Afrikaners have always occupied a limited number of roles in the economy, and this has made comparatively easy the political leaders' task of creating homogeneity within the language group. The roles themselves, however, have tended to necessitate the holding of political power for their protection and advancement. The English language group with its far greater diversity of economic roles could, in the thirties and fifties, lose political power and still prosper. Presumably it might continue to prosper if that power was transferred to non-white groups. Not so for the Afrikaner. He had first to gain, and then to maintain, political power or be submerged as an economic group.[44]

In such a situation class antagonisms become abnormally diffused, and national and ethnic chauvinism gains in strength. It is characteristic of national chauvinism to borrow propositions from various doctrines, including working-class ideology, which are then reconciled with petty-bourgeois goals. The fear of the English and Africans and the economic threat the Afrikaners felt were reinforced by religion and in their educational institutions. The socialization and recruiting processes now ensured that the Afrikaans language group and the Nationalist Party's economic and political interests coincided. Dr. Diederichs expressed the relationship between business and "national" sentiment thus:

> As regards the relationship between business and sentiment it has been our standpoint that business could not be based purely on sentiment but that an Afrikaner business could in no way exist without sentiment.[45]

The classes from which the Nationalist Party derives its support are wedged between the two fundamental classes in the South African society—the white, mostly English bourgeoisie and the black proletariat. In this unstable position, the Afrikaner, whether petty bourgeois or working class, is extremely susceptible to grotesque ideological conceptions and appeals to racial passions.

Though occupying a privileged position in the labor structure, Afrikaners have always looked with suspicion on big industry, which placed them on potentially equal footing with Africans (as the mining industry tried to do on several occasions and as industry is doing now), whereas they wanted to maintain the race relations of the old Boer republics. They had been taught to regard the African as created to minister to their needs. The key to the Afrikaners' reactions lies not in their blood or religious inheritance, but in their intermediate position in society and in their history. The distinction between a white person and one of color for the Afrikaner supporter is fundamental. It is their all. In defense of it they would bring down the whole world. Their privileges depend on the enforcement of the color-bar laws. The Afrikaner political elite openly acknowledges its debt to the worker, whose fears they exploit. As Ben Schoeman, the minister of transport, once stated:

I want to say that if we reach the stage where the native can climb to the highest rung in our economic ladder and be appointed in a supervisory capacity over Europeans then the other equality, namely political equality, must inevitably follow, and that will mean the end of the European race.[46]

On another occasion Vorster commented:

We know one person only to whom we owe explanation and that is the white worker in South Africa, who has brought the Nationalist Party to the position it occupies today and will keep it in that position in future.[47]

The Afrikaner political elite is composed of men who rose to power in a capitalist country, and their power is based on the acceptance of the logic of capitalism. Notwithstanding that, they have been trying to impart to the capitalist system a social, economic, political, ideological, and psychological content relevant to their class position and fears.

Apartheid, therefore, is more than mere racial discrimination or casual exploitation of one group by another. It is a strict ideology of white supremacy, racial oppression, and exploitation, whose logical extremity—genocide—is tempered by the need for African labor. "If only there were some way," runs the white person's dream, "of having them here and yet not having them here."[48]

The rise of Afrikaner racism in South Africa took place after the upheavals caused by the industrial development which followed the exploitation of mining as an industry. White workers saw the chance of escaping the worst excesses of capitalist exploitation by climbing on the backs of Africans. The Afrikaner petty bourgeoisie hammered the concept of *baaskap*, a traditional compound of race prejudice and exploitation, into an articulate theory of Afrikaner economic power consonant with capitalism, and it swept the political boards. Then it consolidated behind a barrage of social and industrial legislation. In power the Nationalist Party attempted to make apartheid pervasive—in jobs, residence, education, travel, birth, and death—without jeopardizing capitalist profits and labor.

The apartheid dynamic is built upon the fear, greed, and

violence of the white population. Once the structure of apartheid was firmly established, adjustment could be made without
threatening the essential structure of white supremacy or the
economic system. The process by which apartheid maintains the
interests of capital and national hegemony is explained thusly by
Keith Gottscholk:

> A creeping or sliding color bar is a key technique in maintaining
> inequality between the races. Depending on White unemployment
> or manpower scarcities for entrepreneurs, the color bar is adjusted
> to slide downwards ("civilized [white] labor") or to creep upwards
> ("job reservation exemptions"). By sliding the color bar upwards
> slower than entrepreneurs desire, artificial manpower shortages
> are created in jobs classified "White." Employers are compelled to
> offer high wages to attract white artisans and blue-collar aristoc-
> racy, but enabled to offer low wages to Black and Brown labor
> (suffering unemployment because of the color bar and pass laws).
> Thus, regardless of which jobs are at one moment classified as
> "White" or "Black" the ratio between White and Black pay packets
> remains constant, or becomes more unequal.[49]

What this means is that in appraising South Africa's racial
policies, we must take into account not only the control of the
economy and politics but also the distribution of the national
income; the whole organization of production and exchange—
not only the average quantity of the products consumed by the
owners of capital and workers but also, in particular, the forms
of consumption; not only facts about the enslavement of the
working class but also divergent ideas and concepts or those that
may emerge in the heads of the exploiter or the worker under
the influence of the facts. Obviously, the analysis of South Africa
must take into account a whole series of historical, objective, and
subjective factors.

This, of course, is not to say that ideas are mere iridescence;
on the contrary. The Nationalist Party, having assumed power at
a moment of crisis, was confronted with a number of factors,
some internal and others external, which were hostile to *herren-
volkism* as a way to order human relations—hence the evolution
of apartheid.

The key to apartheid, then, does not lie in any desire to

separate the races, nor in any respect of ethnic differences; at this point in history it lies in the threat to the status quo. What is at stake in South Africa is nothing less than the destruction of capitalism and white supremacy. Within its framework apartheid combines the admission of guilt and ideological absolution. As the social base of white supremacy was narrowed, racist ideology was obliged to change its form and advocate slogans which ran counter to its basic intentions so as to have a semblance of credibility.

The Machiavellis of Apartheid

The spiritual crisis engendered in transitional periods has always been marked by a profusion of conflicting philosophical, sociological, and ethical assumptions, and a multitude of ideological struggles. The era of transition from capitalism to socialism is also marked by an unprecedented diversity of ideological struggles, whose sole purpose is to preserve the old order of things. Under pressure from popular movements, and to outflank the sharpening political crisis, the rulers must often pretend that they agree with some of the moral ideals and political slogans of those they oppress and exploit. Thus, in addition to cynical Machiavellian doctrines, many notions are advanced to give a moral slant to politics. One aspect of apartheid is that it tries to conceal its inhuman political content by playing on the national sentiment of the oppressed.

The elaboration of effective methods of political duplicity is a sequel to the loss of faith in the values and principles that the bourgeoisie preached in the eighteenth and nineteenth centuries. Pure political expediency is nothing new; it springs from the dogma of Machiavellianism. Maybe it is unfair to Machiavelli to describe the exponents of apartheid as Machiavellians. They are too crude to qualify for the title. But it would seem that Machiavelli did his work so well and contrived his generalizations so aptly that since his time would-be tyrants have followed his advice with varying degrees of success. It may not be necessary here to begin where Machiavelli begins, but rather with the logical basis of his theory.

There are two ways of conducting political contests: one is by law, the other by force. According to Machiavelli, the "first method is proper to men, the second to beasts. However, the first method is demonstrably insufficient, so the prince must learn to make use of both. Adopting the beast, then, he ought to choose the lion and the fox. It is necessary to be a fox to discover the snares and a lion to terrify the wolves. In short, the prince has two chief weapons—craft and force."[50]

Since the Nationalist Party came to power, it has created a formidable military armory and has enacted legislation which has created a quasi police state. Realizing that these methods cannot work alone, and that it was making too many enemies inside as well as outside the country, the government opted for the strategy of the fox and decided to create separate communities of blacks and whites. Following Machiavelli, the Nationalists felt that, of all the deceptions which the prince should attempt, the most important is to pass as persons of spectacular virtue. However, there is a difficulty in this, for they do not really possess the virtues they pretend to have. In fact, the policy of separate development carries weights which must drown them in the end. This is the dilemma of the bantustan policy now, since the government has no intention of making the former reserves autonomous states.[51] The "independence" of the Transkei and Bophuthatswana has only been recognized by its creator, South Africa.

The following statements by Dr. Malan reveal that political Machiavellianism can only grow in the poisonous atmosphere of immoral chicanery. Malan stated at the beginning of the 1953 election campaign:

> Apartheid, both in principle and application, is not a specifically South African product, and much less a creation of the Nationalist Party for political ends. Europe itself, the matrix of Christian civilization, is the outstanding example of apartheid. The map resembles a Joseph's coat of some twenty-five sections, each represented by its own nationality and for the most part also its own race, with its own tongue and its own culture. . . . Apartheid is

accepted in Europe and in the rest of the world, as we rightly ask: why then should it be regarded as deadly sin in South Africa?[52]

The prime minister, while acknowledging that all men are equal before God, found it difficult to see what relevance this had to an equal franchise. In any event, that cannot be the end of the matter. Apartheid is also founded in another act of Divine creation—in the natural differences between race and race, color and color, incorporating for the most part differences also in nationality, language, and culture. He concludes with the argument that apartheid is morally justified, since it promotes friendship and cooperation and avoids exploitation.

In 1954, in a reply to a letter by an American clergyman, Malan wrote, among other things:

> The deep-rooted colour consciousness of the white South African . . . rises from the fundamental differences between the two groups white and black. The difference in colour is surely the physical manifestation of the contrast between two irreconcilable ways of life, between barbarism and civilisation, between heathenism and Christianity and *finally between overwhelming numerical odds on the one hand and insignificant numbers on the other*. Such it was in the early beginning and such it largely remains.[53] [Emphasis added]

Dr. Malan's argument combines fear, bigotry, and fraud: it manipulates notoriously false biblical statements, pseudoscientific myths, and irrational convictions to confuse and to suggest that apartheid is autonomous from the economy. Instead of explaining the true reasons for apartheid and its implications, he justifies the abomination of apartheid by declaring that it is rooted in the general and abstract logic of differences. This gives apartheid a semblance of truth and lends it conviction. But in truth, South Africa is nothing but a police-guarded military despotism, embellished with parliamentary forms, alloyed with a feudal admixture. This much was made clear by Malan's director of state information when he wrote:

> We Nationalists believe that we must maintain white supremacy for all time. A policy of partnership must lead to black domination. . . . We want the Bantu peoples back in the reserves where

they come into their own and when they will be given self-government—under white trusteeship. We cannot have independent Bantu States to threaten white South Africa. We must keep some natives in the white areas, for a long time to do the work. I am being quite candid with you, but we are sincere when we say that we want natives to develop in their own areas.[54]

The statements by Malan and his director of information reveal fear and dishonesty, which produce an ugly and sinister self-righteousness that is used to justify the violence, trickery, and fraud that maintains white supremacy. The nationalists play on the ignorance and prejudice of the whites who feel threatened by the challenge of black power. To maintain their insecure privileges, the Nationalists have summoned up among their followers the meanest and most malignant passions of the human breast. Thus, as DeKiewiet points out:

In their statements when they mean them most sincerely, there is both confession and absolution. There is the confession that the natives cannot be indefinitely denied the privileges of modern life. There is the self-administered absolution of guilt in the promise that these privileges can be theirs. They cannot gain them at the expense of the white man by swamping him with the vote or depressing his standard of living by their competition. But they can achieve them in their own separate areas.[55]

Having now gotten hold of the essential doctrine, we need not further explore the wisdom of the prince. We have seen how the Nationalist Party strives in accordance with the character and position of its constituency to freeze the status quo. That the party ignores the present realities of the South African socioeconomic structure by no means puts an end to its existence. The antagonisms cannot but continue to develop, for every growth of capitalism thrives on the surplus value produced by Africans. This exposes the faults of the economic system, and necessarily of the superstructure and, at the same time, makes those who benefit from the system cling more tenaciously to their self-deceptions. Thus, South Africa has become a racial fortress and apartheid justifies extreme reaction, counterrevolution, and fascism—and this has added to the bitterness of the struggle ahead. The dilemma the nationalists face is in perpetuating and enhancing their petty-bourgeois self-aggrandizement within the context of the present world situation.

From what I have said, it is quite clear that apartheid, in its later version which envisages what it calls "independent African homelands," has a psychosociological function. It enables the apartheiders to declare anyone opposed to their schemes and who wants to change the status quo a communist agent or a dupe and therefore a nonperson. They can create "industrial peace" by eliminating African trade unions and can make white workers secure at the expense of the African masses. They can declare Japanese "honorary" whites. By declaring the urban-industrial areas "white areas," they can expel those termed "idle" to poverty-stricken areas, where they will be available as cheap labor for European farms and the mines. Under apartheid the nationalists can create Bantu education to permanently enslave the African mind, and they can create bantustans to permanently deny Africans their political rights in the larger society. In fact, the apartheiders can do one hundred and one other things because they have already performed the rite of self-absolution.

Moreover, apartheid reduces the African population to a state of complete destitution, i.e., the situation of people separated from meaningful objects and works. According to Marx:

> The state of non-having is the extremest form of spiritualism; a state in which man is totally unreal and inhumanity totally real; it is a state of very positive having—the having of hunger, cold, sickness, crime, degradation, stupor, every conceivable inhuman and anti-human natural thing.[56]

This state of African indigency is sanctioned and consecrated by the apartheid morality. If white survival is (as it appears to be) the aim of the Nationalist Party, if racism and oppression of the African are necessary to that survival, and if a false description of history is essential to that survival, then what is chiefly required of apartheid is not correspondence with the facts of the present reality, but persuasiveness to the membership.

Apartheid aims to present to the new revolutionary situation "that stubborn surface which rocks present to the waves, but alas!—waves do wear down rocks, and history wears down ideology, but time with one is geological and the other epochal."[57] This is both the crux and the tragedy of apartheid. Its adherents cherish a pathetic confidence in the perpetual stability of white supremacy, except that, of late, the only permanence which seems to be left is that of permanent crisis. It confirms the old observation that those in power in any situation become so intensively bound to the status quo that they can no longer see certain facts which undermine their domination. Thus, the ideological forms, by which the ruling classes uphold their own special interests, are made to appear to be of universal interest, a belief that is essentially an illusion. Only those who want to be deluded succumb, but a point is reached when those who have duped themselves are given a rude awakening. This period is fast approaching in South Africa.

> What shall the end be? The world—old and fearful things, war and wealth, murder and luxury? Or shall it be a new thing—a new peace and new democracy of all races: a great humanity of equal men?[58]

This is the question posed to South Africa and the world by the current struggles of the African peoples against the inhuman policies of apartheid.

10

The Dynamics of African Opposition to Conquest and Domination

The African National Congress . . . lit the torch of freedom
. . . also for the people of Southern and Central Africa. . . .
Basutoland (now Lesotho), Swaziland, Nyasaland (now Malawi)
and Northern Rhodesia (now Zambia) formed their own Con-
gresses to fight for freedom and independence . . . as a result
of students from these countries who went to Fort Hare University College in South Africa or workers who had gone to
South Africa to seek employment.

—Ethel Khopung

The history of white politics in South Africa cannot be fully
understood unless we take into account Africans' struggles both
to resist colonial conquest, and, after the creation of the Union
of South Africa in 1910, to advance themselves politically and
economically. A study of the basic stages of the national struggle
throws more light on the evolution of what the rulers call their
native policy—viz., the development of administrative machinery to curb and contain African national and working-class aspirations. In pursuit of their political and economic goals,
African leaders have had to work in difficult circumstances of
constant persecution and repression.

The struggle of the African people over the past three
hundred years took shape under unique socioeconomic and
political conditions. As we have seen, various African societies
came under white rule at different times. After the discovery of
diamonds and gold, the incorporation of many Africans as a
wage-earning labor force took place even as other African

societies further inland were being conquered. Thus, the political forms of struggle developed unevenly. There were ebbs and flows, slumps and upsurges in the interaction between national and class struggles. It is important, for example, constantly to ascertain the relationship between national and working-class aspirations in the development of African nationalism.

To get a clear grasp of the dynamics of African struggle, it is important to understand the wars of resistance to white rule. They provide a clue to the nature of the African National Congress (ANC), formed in 1912 as a response to conquest and as a medium to articulate African political aspirations. The developments in the working-class movement, which took definite shape during World War I, must form part of the picture of African resistance.

It must be noted as well that the African struggle grew under the influence not only of domestic conditions but also of developments in the international arena. The impact of historic events, such as World War I, the Bolshevik Revolution, and the Great Depression, stamped the subsequent history of the national and class struggles of the African people.

In this chapter, rather than encumber the exposition of African resistance to conquest and exploitation with details that the reader can find elsewhere—especially in several recent accounts of the "birth" and growth of African nationalism—I have set myself the task of selecting and characterizing those crucial historical factors and circumstances which have defined African resistance in the past and must define the liberation movement in the immediate future.

I shall be talking mainly of African resistance as crystallized in the African National Congress (ANC), and not about the struggles of the coloreds, Indians, and whites who opposed white oppression. These latter have their own lines of development that closely paralleled, and sometimes preceded, those of the African; and they have increasingly converged with the line followed by the ANC.

My analysis will take into account the distribution of power, social classes, economic processes, and other components of what is called social history. To look at African opposition from a historical-structural point of view means to explain it, not in terms of isolated, self-contained events or individual personalities, but as part of a wider structure—the explanation itself being based not so much on the properties of the individual as on the place the individual or individuals occupy in society and the significance their acts have to the general mass of African people.

The first questions are: How did the Africans respond to conquest? How did they cope with the changing historical circumstances, with the loss of national autonomy and economic self-sufficiency? The colonial system of domination and capitalist exploitation closed off any means of independent livelihood for the African people; the subordinated were impressed with the notion that any improvement in their condition could be achieved only on terms set by the oppressors. In the nineteenth century, as we have seen, the agents of the conquering bourgeoisie were so strong that they thought they could rearrange everything and everybody to serve the interests and power of capitalism. At the same time they affirmed certain progressive and democratic ideals which they claimed to be universally applicable.

In the study of subordinate groups and classes, Gramsci points out that it is necessary to examine:

1. The objective formation of the subordinate group as a result of transformations occurring in the sphere of economic production; the qualitative diffusion of new norms and their integration by pre-existing social groups, whose previous mentality, ideology, and aims are conserved for a time.

2. The active and passive affiliation of the new status groups to the dominant political formations in order to press claims of their own, and the consequences of these attempts in determining processes of decomposition, renovation, or neoformation.

3. The birth of new parties among the dominant groups, intended to conserve the assent of the subaltern groups and to maintain control over them.

4. The formation within the subordinate groups themselves of organs that are used to press claims of a limited and partial character.

5. The further growth of these new formations, which assert the autonomy of the subordinate groups, but within the old framework.

6. Those changes in these formations which assert the integral autonomy of the subordinate groups.[1]

Broadly speaking, seven phases can be distinguished in the development of African opposition to white conquest and domination. The first, which lasted for over two hundred years, involved armed resistance against invasion. During this period Africans made a heroic defense of their national sovereignty, and figures arose whose memories have provided future generations with a source of pride. The latter part of the nineteenth century and the first half of the twentieth saw the emergence of a second phase, in which the struggle took a political form as the Africans, whose claim to the new state had been eliminated, searched for tactics and strategies to deal with the situation. Edward Roux, in a classic study of African nationalism, describes the changeover from armed resistance to political struggle:

> The Bambata Rebellion in Natal in 1906 may very well be taken as the turning point between two periods in the history of the black man in South Africa: The early period of tribal wars and fights against white invaders which ended in the loss of country and the reduction of the Bantu to the status of an internal proletariat; and the second period, one of struggle for national liberation and democratic rights within the framework of present-day South Africa, where black and white intermingle in complex economic and political relationships. During the first period the Bantu fought as isolated tribes and on military lines. Though they did not meet the whites on equal terms, but opposed shield and assegai to the rifle and machine gun, at least they met them as members of independent tribes or nations having their own territory and military organization.[2]

The pioneers of the political phase of African struggle faced many problems: they all had been educated in mission schools. For their education they had paid a price—alienation from the masses and loss of their cultural heritage. A gulf existed between them and their "heathen" brethren that took time to bridge. The urgent task they faced was to build unity among people from previously independent communities. The nature of the new states to which they had been sacrificed and their relation to Britain determined the early direction of the political struggle. Furthermore, political opposition to the new states was continually undermined by liberal members from the dominant class. From their precarious position the educated African elite opted for moral persuasion and for "constitutional" methods of "struggle" in the form of petitions. The formal organizations they created were more the expression than the mobilizer of national and class conflict; their political functions were largely indirect, in that organizers were concerned with "leading," guiding, raising new issues, educating, and so on. The ideological attack on the evolving system of white supremacy and oppression was diffuse.

The third phase began during World War I, when large numbers of Africans came to the cities and began to be integrated into the secondary sector of the economy as a full-fledged proletariat. In 1914 the urban black proletariat numbered 243,509; in 1915 it had grown to 260,495; and in 1918 it numbered 268,412. Strike action accompanied the process of incorporation into the economy, both during and after the war. Thirty to forty thousand African mine workers staged an action in 1920.[3]

In response to these developments the Industrial and Commercial Workers' Union (ICU) was formed in 1919, under the leadership of Clements Kadalie, from Nyasaland; and the Communist Party of South Africa (CPSA) was founded in 1921. These two organizations played a central role in the development of the black working-class movement during the 1920s. In 1927 Raymond Buell, after studying the various African organizations of this period, wrote:

> As a result of political organizations such as the African National Congress and the Bantu Union, the independent churches and the I.C.U., the natives are organizing a resistance to the white man. . . . Their leaders, moreover, are too wise to think of starting an armed revolt. But by organizing movements for industrial passive resistance and by promoting a series of strikes tying up the mining and manufacturing industries, these native organizations

may eventually make the position of the white man in South Africa as untenable as would a successful native war. At any rate, the government and public opinion are coming to realize the seriousness of the situation and the necessity of taking steps which will remove the causes of such a conflict.[4]

The fourth phase began during World War II and continued until 1950. As reformist options were cut off with the abolition of the qualified franchise for Africans in the Cape Province and as Africans became increasingly involved in the urban economy, the strike weapon was used more and more. Between 1921 and 1945, the urban African population trebled; the ratio of African women to men rose from under 1:5 in 1921 to 1:3 in 1945. This rise was indicative of the undermining of the migrant-labor system and laissez-faire segregation policies.

The fifth phase began in 1949 with the adoption of the Programme of Action by the ANC and the South African Indian Congress (SAIC). In 1952 the two organizations launched the Defiance Campaign (DC). It was during the 1950s that the ANC became a mass organization dedicated to class action.

The sixth phase began in 1960 with the banning of the ANC and the Pan-African Congress (a splinter group from the ANC). In 1961 *Umkhonto We Sizwe* ("Spear of the Nation") was formed for the purpose of conducting armed struggle. After a series of sabotage attacks on government installations, the armed struggle began in 1967; its initiation meant that white capitalist rule would sink into history as it was born, in blood and violence. By the late 1960s Africans were aware that military confrontation was now possible, given the changes in the world order—in particular, the emergence of socialist and African states.

The Soweto uprising, which constitutes the seventh phase, was brought about by internal as well as external developments. A description of the various phases is necessary to comprehend the complex reality of the evolution of South African society. One important point about this reality is the interconnection of all the different phenomena. A correct approach to the study of African resistance concentrates on that rather than focusing on a series of discrete aspects of the black/white conflict. Separatist churches, political organizations, strikes, and so on must not be thought of in isolation but must be studied within a framework which defines these in relation to each other—that is, as expressions of a complex and total structure.

Obviously, since we are dealing with the total transformation of the African society, this process must be examined dialectically; its contradictory aspects must be grasped, and no absolute and definitive judgments can be made about any phase. We must not consider African responses in isolation from the white rulers. Since their incorporation into the new settler state, black and white exist as two "classes" living inextricably together, even though they have different fundamental interests. This is the only way we can hope to understand the development of South Africa as a society and the behavior of Africans as an oppressed national class. Black and white should not be viewed schematically; they are both elements of a concrete historical process, in which action by either party is strictly conditioned by and related to the actions of the other.

Let me now discuss each of the phases into which I have divided African responses in more detail.

Armed Resistance to Conquest

African resistance to white conquest is almost as old as the first colonial settlement. In 1510 the Portuguese, who had grown accustomed to capturing the herds of the Khoikhoin with impunity, suffered a humiliating defeat, which resulted in DeAlmeida, the Portuguese "viceroy" of India, and seventy-five of his retreating escort being killed by the poisoned arrows of the Khoikhoin on the banks of the Salt River.

A few years later the Portuguese took a bloody revenge for their first defeat. The British general E. D. Napier, in a book published in 1849, gives this account of what happened:

> The Portuguese, extremely mortified at this disgrace, vowed a smart revenge, which yet they seemed not to look for till two or three years after, when the fleet for the Indies anchoring again at the Cape, they found the art of cajoling the Hottentots; and,

knowing their fondness for brass, they carried a large brass cannon ashore, under pretence of making them a present of it. This piece of artillery they had loaded with a number of heavy balls, and fastened to the mouth of it two long ropes. The Hottentots, ravished to receive such a weight of their adored metal, and being jealous of no design, laid hold of the two ropes in great numbers, as they were directed, in order to drag it along; and a great body of them being extended in two files all the length of the ropes, and standing cheek by jowl full in the range of the shot, the cannon was suddenly discharged, and a terrible slaughter made of them. Such as had escaped the shot fled up into the country in the wildest consternation, and left the Portuguese to re-embark at their leisure. And from that day to this, it seems, they have dreaded both the touch and the sight of a firearm.[5]

When the Dutch established the Cape as a victualing station, the Khoikhoin resisted the colonist intrusion of their lands. Already in 1659 the Khoikhoin tribes were engaged in armed resistance against the usurpation of their lands and cattle. In the interior the struggle of the San for survival was even more tenacious and raged throughout the eighteenth century. Leo Katzen, a South African economic historian, writes of the San resistance:

Further north east, [Boer] expansion was halted by increasingly ferocious warfare between trekboers and San hunters. After 1715, trekboers went further into "Bushman Country". By 1770, the conflict was so intense that the trekboer Commandos systematically exterminated the San, while San raids forced trekboers to abandon farms in the Nieuwveld and Sneeuberg regions and endangered trekboer occupation in the Tarka region, in the 1780's.[6]

Above, we saw that the advent of British settlers into the Cape pushed the Boers further into the interior and brought them headlong into conflict with Sotho and Nguni groups, who fought long and valiantly to defend their lands against the invaders. Ultimately, the superior arms and technology of the British overcame the Africans, superior though they were in numbers. However, the Africans' desire to preserve their sovereignty, together with their military capability, was to influence future relations between conqueror and conquered. In discussing the tenacity of the African resistance in defending their land rights, Lord Bryce had this to say:

> The other set of race troubles, those between white settlers and the aborigines of the land, have been graver in South Africa than any which European governments have had to face in any other new country. The Red men of North America, splendidly as they fought, never seriously checked the advance of the whites. The revolts of the aborigines in Peru and Central America were easily suppressed. The once warlike Maoris of New Zealand have, under the better methods of the last twenty-five years, become quiet and tolerably contented. Even the French in Algeria had not so long a strife to maintain with the Moorish and Kabyle tribes as the Dutch and the English had with the natives at the Cape. The Southcoast kaffirs far outnumbered the whites, were full of courage, had a very rough and thickly wooded country to defend. . . . The melancholy chapter of native wars seems now all but closed. . . . These wars, however, did much to retard the progress of South Africa and to give it a bad name. They deterred many an English farmer from emigrating thither in the years between 1810–1870. They annoyed and puzzled the home government, and made it think of the Colony as a worthless possession whence little profit or credit was to be drawn in return for the unending military expenditure.[7]

In their struggle the Africans used typical guerrilla tactics. G. E. Cory, a British historian, writes: "Seldom was the enemy caught in the open. Often after the troops had performed very long and fatiguing marches, Kaffirs had to be followed into mountain fortresses, necessitating the scaling of almost inaccessible heights and then only to find that the enemy had decamped and, in full view, but out of gunshot, was holding other positions attainable only with difficulty."[8]

The Zulu Resistance

In chapter 2 I discussed the armed resistance of the Xhosa against the English's occupation of their country in the first half of the nineteenth century. The example of the Xhosa was followed by the Sotho and the Zulu, who encountered the white colonist later. The trek-Boers, who had been forced by the arrival of the English to move into the interior of the country, met stubborn and heroic resistance from the Sotho and Zulu kingdoms in the interior and from the east of the country.

The Zulus knew of the fate of the Xhosa and were ready to defend their lands. Professor Leonard Thompson relates the story of a Xhosa man who had been captured during fighting on the Cape frontier and taken prisoner to Robben Island in Table Bay and had eventually been trained as an interpreter. In 1830 Jacob (as he was called by Europeans) left his job and visited Dingane, the Zulu king who had succeeded Shaka, and told him that white people were plotting to take his land and destroy his kingdom. Quoting the secretary of the colony of Natal, Thompson writes:

> Jacob had reported to the King that as he was going to the Colony he had met a Frontier Kaffir, who told him he wanted to find a home with the Zulus, as there was no living so near the white people; that at first the white people came and took a part of their land, then they encroached and drove them further back, and have repeatedly taken more land as well as cattle. They then built houses among them, for the purpose of subduing them by witch-craft; that at the present time there was an *umlungu*—and a white man's house, or missionary in every tribe . . . ; that during his stay at Grahamstown the soldiers frequently asked what sort of a coun-try the Zulus had . . . and had said "we shall soon be after you"; that he had heard a few white people had intended to come first and get a grant of land as I, Farewell, King and Dambuza [Isaacs] had done; they would then build a fort, when more would come, and demand land, who would also build houses and subdue the Zulus, and keep driving them further back, as they had driven the Fron-tier tribes.[9]

This report made Dingane and his councillors highly suspi-cious of the motives of the white colonists who had settled in Port Natal. In 1831 Dingane sent a regiment to destroy a white man's property at Port Natal. At the end of 1837 the trek-Boers from the Cape began to cross the Drakensberg passes into upper Natal. To avoid the fate of the Xhosa, Dingane made a preemptive strike on the Boers who, even before he had granted them permission, had established settlements in the areas of northern Natal. Prolonged warfare followed between the Zulu forces on the one hand and the Boers in the north and the British at Durban on the other. The Zulu suffered heavy casualties at the Battle of Ncome River (Blood River). But Dingane's power was only broken when a split occurred between him and his brother Mpande, who took with him 17,000 followers to join the Boers.[10]

The splits in the African ranks at this time were their greatest weakness. The development of a united front among the African kingdoms was a dream of the most far-sighted leaders and the intermittent nightmare of the whites.

For instance, Cetshwayo, who had succeeded to the Zulu throne in the 1870s, was eager to form an alliance with Sekukune, chief of the Bapedi, in his struggle against the Boers. There is evidence that Cetshwayo continually sent emissaries to Sekukune in the guise of tobacco sellers to give him advice and encouragement. To prevent the Boers from giving them both trouble, Cetshwayo even proposed a military alliance, so that the white invaders could be fought on all fronts. The strategy was to push out the weaker Boers first and then to proceed to clear Natal of the British.

Cetshwayo had established a reputation as an arch-conspirator against the white settlers. The Reverend A. Nachtigall, a missionary from Lydenberg in the Transvaal, wrote on January 14, 1878: "Sekukuni has again received a message from Cetshwayo wherein he says that his people have taken one of the laagers of the white people; that the remainder of the white people have escaped and cattle are at the Vaal River and Komati; Sekukuni, therefore, also had better begin at once, then he easily can get the upper hand."[11]

The thought of the Zulus massing on the republic's southern borders, of the rebellious Sekukune and of the Swazis posed for war, and of the indescribable and chaotic state of the republic's finances forced the British to "persuade" the president of the South African Republic to accept annexation. According to DeKiewiet, "the demoralization of the Transvaal enabled Sir Theophilus Shepstone to annex the Republic to the British

Crown on 12 April 1877."[12] When the Transvaal was safely under the British crown, Shepstone, who had negotiated the Boer surrender, returned to Natal, where he began preparations for the 1879 war with Cetshwayo. The latter's plan for uniting the Africans against the whites had to be forestalled to avoid disaster for the settlers. The British concluded that African unity was their most formidable enemy, and it had to be frustrated.

Sekukune's refusal to pay taxes, his open defiance of the Boers, and the humiliating defeat he inflicted on the Boers when they marched on his mountain fortress were all cited as proof of Cetshwayo's machinations against the whites. A dispatch by Sir Bartle Frere, dated November 5, 1878, gave this opinion of Cetshwayo:

> It is not this [Cape] Colony alone, but wherever the Kaffir races are to be found, from the Fish River to the Limpopo, and from the Lower Orange River to Delgoa Bay, that the influence of the Zulu king has been found at work festering and directing this warlike spirit. It is not of late years only that the danger was seen by most competent judges; and every month since has accumulated evidence of the reality of the danger.[13]

It was the incipient threat of African unity that eventually unified the Dutch and the English. In pursuance of the policy to unify Boer and English, the British secretary of state informed the cabinet in 1879:

> There is no question as to the necessity of uniting . . . South Africa under a confederation or union charged with the full responsibility of defense against the natives . . . Unless and until this is done there is clearly no prospect of avoiding the periodical recurrence of wars carried on at great cost to this country and to the Colonies. Confederation therefore is to be kept in view as one object to be attained as speedily and as completely as possible.[14]

Finally the British government decided to destroy Cetshwayo and Sekukune, whom the Boers had feared. An expedition under Sir Garnet Wolseley reduced Sekukuni's stronghold. In 1879 Sir Bartle Frere's war with Cetshwayo destroyed Zulu power, the dread of which, according to Bryce, might have induced the Boers to resign themselves to British supremacy. According to Bryce:

> It was probably necessary to deal with Sikhukhuni [sic], though the British government seems to have forgotten its former doubts as to the right of the Boers to the territory of the chief; but in extinguishing the Zulu kingdom the High Commissioner would seem to have forgotten that he was also extinguishing the strongest motive which the republicans had for remaining British subjects. The British government was doubly unfortunate. It was the annexation of the Transvaal in 1877 that had alarmed Cetshwayo and helped to precipitate the war of 1879. It was now the overthrow of Cetshwayo, their formidable enemy, that helped to precipitate a revolt of the Boers.[15]

In the War of 1879 the Zulus acquitted themselves well, inflicting upon the British at the battle of Isandlwana one of the most humiliating defeats in their history of colonial adventure. Friedrich Engels paid tribute to the prowess of the Zulus:

> [The Zulus] did what no European army can do. Armed only with lances and spears, without firearms, under a hail of bullets from the breechloaders of the English infantry—acknowledged the best in the world at fighting in close order—they advanced right up to the bayonets and more than once threw the lines into disorder and even broke them, in spite of the enormous inequality of weapons and in spite of the fact that they have no military service and know nothing of drill. Their powers of endurance and performance are shown by the complaint of the English that a Kaffir travels farther and faster in 24 hours than a horse. His smallest muscle stands out hard and firm like whipcord, says an English painter.[16]

The defeat of the English army by Cetshwayo aroused a storm of protest in the British Parliament. The British cabinet decided that "to restore British prestige, the Zulu nation was to be defeated." It took many months of fighting and the blood of thousands of brave men to implement that decision.[17]

The Zulu war, according to Professor DeKiewiet, exposed the white settlers' disjointed political framework. While the imperial troops fought these difficult campaigns in Zululand, the Boer leaders of Transvaal sulked in their tents, and the Boers in the English colony of Natal acted as if they were neutral.[18]

Thus, with remarkable heroism the African peoples of South Africa resisted the robbery of their lands by the white invaders. The superiority of arms and technology against spears and knobkerries meant that the struggle was from the beginning unequal. But such was the resistance that the conqueror refused to arm the Africans in World Wars I and II, for fear that the arms and knowledge of the new technology might be turned against the oppressors. The history of armed struggle always informed the political strategy of the settlers.

Early Forms of Political Struggle

The above may seem too schematic; but such a picture of armed resistance is necessary. It puts a different light on the origins of African nationalism and other forms of political resistance. When the Africans became involved in the agricultural and mining economy of the white settlers, they found that they had to develop new methods of resistance to deal with the exploitative conditions. The Africans who came to work in the mines developed a new consciousness based on their common interest as workers. Lionel Foreman writes that

> with the commencement of the diamond diggings in 1870, the way was open for a great change. At Kimberley men were able for the first time to see themselves not only as Zulu, Xhosa or Sotho tribesmen, but also as Africans. Members of the separate tribes came to recognise themselves as drawn into a single fraternity by their common economic interests. . . . The coming into a great single brotherhood was a completely new phenomenon. For many years Africans had worked for the white man on their frontier farms, and since the time of Sir George Grey there had been small groups employed in road making and on the harbours of the Eastern province. But Kimberley was something different. Here was a nucleus of a true African proletariat whose future would be in the cities and whose only way of keeping lawfully alive would be by the sale of their labour. Here was a nucleus of a new class, whose ties with tribal society would become of the slenderest, whose

economic—and inevitably political—weapon would be that of the workers of all the lands, the strike.[19]

Thus, conquest and incorporation of the African peasant into a labor force divorced from the land provided one of the primary requisites for the growth of African nationalism and of African working-class consciousness. In 1875 a magistrate in the Cape Colony complained that black construction workers had "banded together for the purposes of a strike, refusing to work and preventing other labourers from taking their places."[20]

In the late nineteenth century and in response to specific historical developments and particular events and issues, a diversity of latent forces emerged, which would define African resistance in the twentieth century. Besides strike actions, the breakaway church movement began in 1872, and the Native Convention was formed in 1909 to discuss the impending union of the four provinces. The Native Convention provided the first occasion on which the politically minded Africans came together from all corners of South Africa to discuss common problems. However, the life of this organization was short.[21]

Thus, by the first decade of the twentieth century, the entire African population—peasants, city dwellers, and the proletariat—all in their own way were struggling against the yoke of colonial oppression and capitalist exploitation.

The Formation of the African National Congress

The South Africa Act, while retaining the qualified franchise of the African voters in the Cape Colony, excluded Africans from voting in Natal, the Orange Free State, and the Transvaal colonies. At the end of 1911 a movement which aimed at giving African public opinion in South Africa a more permanent form of expression began to gain ground.[22] The leading exponent of the new movement was P. Ka I. Seme, a young African lawyer from Natal, who had returned to South Africa after receiving his B.A. degree at Columbia University in the United States. Addressing African personalities from all over Southern Africa on the subject of the "Native Union," he wrote:

> The demon of racialism, the aberrations of the Xhosa-Fingo feud, the animosity that exists between the Zulus and the Tongas, between the Basutio and every other Native must be buried and forgotten. . . . We are one people. These divisions, these jealousies, are the cause of all our woes and of all our backwardness and ignorance.[23]

Seme advocated the formation of a South African Native Congress and proposed an agenda for an inaugural meeting. Addressing the first meeting of the African National Congress (ANC), which met in Bloemfontein in 1912, Seme spoke on the political situation of the African since the creation of the Union of South Africa in 1910:

> We have discovered that in the land of our birth Africans are treated as hewers of wood and drawers of water. The white people of this country have formed what is known as the Union of South Africa—a union in which we have no voice in the making of laws and no part in their administration. We have called you, therefore, to this Conference so that we can together devise ways and means of forming our national unity and defending our rights and privileges.[24]

The formation of the ANC on January 8, 1912, signified not just the birth of an organization, but also the development of a new national consciousness—the idea of nationhood. From the day of the inauguration of the ANC, Xhosas, Zulus, Sothos, and other African peoples would begin to develop a loyalty of a new type. The nationalism of the African people as expressed in the ANC was an ideological commitment to the pursuit of a new purpose: political emancipation. The ANC expressed the collective interests of the African people who had been subjected to alien rule.

The formation of the ANC confronted the newly formed white state, whose aim was to unite Boer and Briton, with a potentially serious situation; it raised the prospect of Africans constructing a strong popular alliance that transcended ethnic and language differences. The ANC was to coalesce Africans around vital issues raised by their conquest. National struggle, as embodied in the ANC, is more than class conflict: it is a process of popular mobilization, characterized inevitably by the formation of a supraclass organization, and a national movement often crystallized around nonmaterial issues and appeals. Not only intellectuals but also traditional rulers and peasants were to be part of the ANC.

I pointed out in an earlier chapter that after the second British occupation of the Cape Colony in 1814, the British administration began a systematic program of creating among the Africans an elite of teachers, ministers, and civil servants (who were educated in mission schools) as a medium of control and communication, an elite that inhabited a kind of twilight zone between the oppressor and the oppressed. Once this group came into being, some of its members became aware of the contradictory nature of their new position and began to exceed the limits the oppressor had defined for them. They began to speak the language of freedom and equality, using the idiom the conquerors had used to justify their activities. Though the use of a borrowed idiom reflects social and intellectual subordination, the demands themselves were unmistakable, motivated as they were by a refusal to accept subordinate status.

The various tactics adopted by the educated elite—parliamentary and extraparliamentary forms of opposition, deputations to Britain, and so on—were relevant in the historical context out of which, and with reference to which, they evolved. These methods of struggle were not the same thing as reformism, because at the time they were adopted they consciously or unconsciously accentuated those contradictions which were objectively antagonistic to the world of white hegemony. Even individual struggles for excellence were part of an effort to refute the white man's assumption about the black's inferiority. The parliamentary demands of these leaders had, of necessity, a revolutionary dynamic. They were a conscious testimony to the fact that Africans were not accepting their subordinate status. The early struggles of the educated elite signify what Gramsci called the "war of moral positions" that must occur in civil society before the revolutionary struggle can begin. This is the reason why the educated elite were viewed with such suspicion and hostility by the governing classes. When those individuals who had achieved the white man's standards of excellence were scorned, the struggle had of necessity to be elevated to a higher plane, toward self-definition, self-determination, and liberation.

The demand for equality and integration must be understood as a typical response of an educated elite of an oppressed group when it has achieved sufficient political self-awareness to oppose the hypocrisy of the oppressor without having the means to force a real change in its status. Deprived of the instruments of challenging the structure of conquest, the elite among the oppressed demand only admission into the precincts of the oppressor's society. By educational, propagandistic, and various forms of agitational work, the "intellectual" group builds up its moral case against discrimination.

However, there were important weaknesses in the political strategy of "moral" persuasion. Having been defeated militarily, the Africans who initiated the phase of political agitation tended to accept prima facie the postulates of the British sense of justice, which claimed to be dedicated to truth, freedom, and "fair play," in spite of all the many betrayals Africans had experienced. The predisposition in favor of the British by some African intellectuals provides a critical point of departure for an understanding of certain opportunistic political behavior, such as cap-in-hand deputations to London. The elite Africans' greatest intellectual error, if it can be called that, was their failure to realize that the British were actuated by the dictates of purely objective circumstances and not by any subjective good will toward black people.

The programs, ideology, and methods of political persuasion followed by the educated elite at the beginning of the century thus owe as much to agency as to conditioning: they were influenced by the Christian ideology, by the subjective attitude certain African leaders had come to have about their English sponsors, and by the fact that Africans in the Cape Colony could vote (which meant that those who met so-called civilized standards could strive individually for acceptance by the ruling class). The result was an opportunism that acted to alienate the educated few from the mass of the uneducated.

The 1912 constitution of the ANC states, among other things, that its aim is to unite all African organizations within a single "medium of expression of representative opinion" in order to formulate a standard policy of national affairs for the benefit and guidance of the Union government and Parliament. In addition, it aims to educate the Bantu people on their rights, duties, and obligations to the state, to encourage mutual understanding, and to bring together into common action as one political people all the tribes and clans of the various tribes or races. By means of combined effort and united political organization, the ANC intends to defend Africans' freedom, rights, and privileges, to agitate by just means for the removal of the "color bar" in political, educational, and industrial fields, and to work for equitable representation of natives in Parliament.[25]

Today this statement sounds curiously reformist and unrealistic, quite unsuitable as a formulation of the goals toward which an organization of a defeated and oppressed people should work. At base, it embodied a paradoxical attempt to realize humane ideals in a world of power. Yet this is the case with most nationalistic movements, which are at first an expression of a diversity of latent social forces, characterized by a disjunction between an intense consciousness of separate identity and a failure to set even theoretically independent goals for themselves as struggling groups. This is no wonder, since the exploited or oppressed classes are ruled not only by authority but also by intellectual power—they are ruled by the ideas of the ruling class.

An ideology for social change cannot be a mere construct; it has to be discovered, in part or whole, from among current and familiar notions. This means that ideologies themselves are tied to their eras and are capable of nothing absolutely new. National and class consciousness develop in struggle; in the course of struggle they become clearer and sharper, at the same time as they extend to and embrace ever greater sections of the oppressed.

The ANC in 1912 was a living critique, an assertion of the negative power of the Africans in opposition to the existing state, as well as a regenerative force. At first its leaders acted on the assumption that if the British meant what they said, even a qualified voting participation in all the provinces of the Union would enable the Africans, in time, to achieve their goals of political majority and create a just society without resorting to violence. Just as a numerical majority enabled the Boers to become an important factor in the first Union government, so the number of "educated" and "civilized" Africans would one day lead to a situation where Africans would become the majority power in the land of their origin. This hope, which history has proved wrong, was at the time taken seriously.

Furthermore, the important objective of unifying diverse groups into a single national fraternity, encouraged by the recent defeat of individual nationalities, had to be nurtured to maturity. The desire to create a unified people out of a variety of ethnic elements would not be easy, given the divide-and-rule strategy of the rulers, but it had to be done if Africans as such were to meet the new challenges. The desire to build *one nation* was reflected in the newspaper *Abantu-Batho*, the ANC's multilingual organ. Until it was discontinued in 1931, it carried the message of African unity and freedom throughout the length and breadth of the country.

All this was done by individuals who were, as we have seen, mostly professionals, chiefs, and government servants. Even if they entertained dreams of self-determination, they did not believe that it was a matter of practical politics in 1912. Nearly all of those who met in the first congress at Bloemfontein had lived through one phase or another of the turbulence that had toppled South Africa's kingdoms and chiefdoms. They had either known or seen defeat, and their own lives had been affected by that. The use of "constitutional methods" was therefore the most logical at the time, and they called public meetings, made protests, organized demonstrations, passed resolutions, and made deputations. This gave them time to lick the wounds inflicted by defeat and to nurse the unity they were creating that would make the congress an effective force. While moving toward this goal, they were willing to do all they could to agitate for reforms without provoking a head-on collision with white power.[26]

This fact is brought out most eloquently in what Daniel Kunene, a South African literary critic, has called "vernacular political-protest literature." The themes of these novels reflect the dilemma faced by African intellectuals:

> The African had just emerged from a prolonged battle which he had lost. While this battle raged, he had composed heroic lines for the warriors and kings upon whom he placed his trust. . . . This came to pass—the country perished. But the struggle was not over, it had only shifted from physical to intellectual plane. Education was the new weapon, the intellectual the new warrior. A correspondent of the *Isigidimi* . . . commenting on the African's suffering under the white man's rule, suggested that "the spear" was not the solution. "No," he said, "we have tried and failed. The only solution is learning and knowledge. I mean that kind of knowledge that will make us realize that each one lives for all. Nor must this knowledge be confined to the males. Our young women must have it too."[27]

What all this means is that the phenomenon of nationalism is not an abstraction to be neatly tied up in academic definition. It is a changing thing, and its real meaning is apparent only in its history. All we need to assume, to begin with, is that African nationalism in the early phase corresponded to a concrete political reality.

In order to cope with the new situation, Africans not only had to acquire the techniques and skills of the conquerors, but to accept their value system as well. Since there was no possibility at this point of overcoming their oppression, since the correlation of forces on the national and international level was unfavorable, the Africans were compelled to endure, to accommodate themselves, while at the same time testing the ideological arguments and maintaining whatever integrity they could.

There is a strong temptation in certain circles today to denounce the ANC's strategies in the 1912–1930 period as reformist and nonrevolutionary. One is forced to agree with Edward Roux that there was a kind of naive heroism in the spectacle of thousands of black men assembled on Von Brandis Square crying: "Down with the passes!" But then, "no violence" surrendering their sticks, setting about their defiance of injustice with songs of Britannica, with cheers for England's King and for President Wilson, only to have their meetings roughly dispersed by the police.[28]

But for the African in the first twenty-five years of this century it was difficult to grasp fully the meaning and overall intents of their erstwhile rulers, with whom the Africans interacted only on the basis of their own history and social ideology. To comprehend the nature of the new society required a detailed understanding of the economic and social forces operating at the time—it needed an understanding of the nature of liberal democracy. This was impossible for African intellectuals, for whom white hegemony determined what and how much they were to know. Nevertheless, it did not take long for the African to penetrate the mystifying illusions created by the agents of conquest, and to see the difference between word and deed. The typical exploitative devices constantly nullified the professed good intentions of white rulers. Though individual Africans became the victims of white philanthropy and sponsorship, and continued to believe in the good intentions of their rulers, the rest found the injustices unacceptable.

In an antagonistic society the formation of political relations, and of congruent ideological trends, depends on the divergence of interests between ruler and ruled. The history of the ANC reveals this tendency. Though formed with a hesitant revolutionary vision and no clear goals for its nationalism, its shift to radical and revolutionary politics testifies to the antagonistic nature of the society.

The Formation of the Industrial and Commercial Workers' Union (ICU)

At the same time that the national liberation movement was unfolding, economic development based on mining was creating

a new force, the African working class. It did not take long for
the black worker to use the weapon of the strike. Lionel Forman
wrote:

> It is remarkable how soon these men were using the universal
> weapon of the working class—the strike. In December 1881, be-
> fore there is any record of a strike by white workers in South
> Africa, one hundred Africans at a Kimberley mine stopped work
> for two days and brought the mine to a halt, when wages were
> reduced from 25s. to 20s. per week. . . . By 1884 there were at
> Kimberley no fewer than four different Non-European Benefit
> Societies, the predecessors of a trade union movement.[29]

After World War I the Industrial and Commercial Workers'
Union (ICU) began its eventful history with the dockers' strike at
Cape Town in 1919, and also led a historic strike among African
and municipal workers which broke out in 1920. During this
period the white workers, too, were fighting back against their
employers and government, which had responded to the postwar depression by cutting workers' wages. The political impact
of these strikes was immense, given the successes of the Bol-
sheviks in toppling the tsarist regime in Russia. The industrial
strikes in South Africa became even more ideologically iden-
tified with the struggle between classes and the clash between
capitalism and communism. This upsurge by labor brought into
sharper focus the new forces at work in the political economy
and revealed not only the weakness of the ANC but also the
bankruptcy of liberalism in general.

In no time, the ICU spread like a veld fire over the length and
breadth of South Africa, and as far north as Malawi (Nyasaland),
where a member of the ICU was sentenced to three years'
imprisonment for possessing a copy of its official organ, the
Workers Herald. Throughout the 1920s the ICU was the largest
national organization, wielding great influence. Its membership
ran into the thousands, and it reached both urban and rural
workers, provoking a new consciousness among them.[30] According to Professor Martin Legassick, the strength of the ICU "lay
in its loose but appealing amalgam of economic and political
demands, attracting support from the ill-defined groups of dis-

sidents characteristic of early industrialization. Landless peasants, rural squatters, domestic servants, unemployed migrants and other aspirant rural and urban entrepreneurs were its bases, as well as workers per se."[31]

Controlling and taming this new force became a major concern of the white ruling class in the 1920s. African labor was indispensable for the prosperity of the capitalist economy, yet exploitation and conditions in the urban industries were welding this labor into a revolutionary force that could overcome chauvinism and thus threaten capitalist exploitation and oppression. For the exploiters of African labor, these developments posed an insoluble problem indeed. The South African industries needed and drew Africans into the urban areas, but the political consciousness which accompanied their proletarianization increased their power and amalgamation. Given the militancy of white workers, what were the rulers to do?

The ICU, by directly engaging African labor in the act of its own liberation, began the process that has transformed the consciousness and determination of the black workers to what it is today. The followers of Clements Kadalie were rank-and-file workers, with a ruggedness and militancy that would not accept obeisance. Their oppressed life had taught them that pious resolutions make no impression on those determined to exploit. Capitalist exploitation could only be tempered by organization, power, and by an assault on the industries and institutions of the oppressor.

Kadalie aroused the African workers, taught them awareness of their economic bondage, and revealed the power that lay in unity. Against formidable odds, the ICU, according to Roux, "made the voice of the voiceless and disinterested African masses heard. It awakened the revolutionary national and class consciousness among tens of thousands of working people in town and country, and brought them their first lessons in organization and unity. The ICU awakened and mobilized many of the working class cadres of the Congress and trade union movement and the Communist Party for the stern struggles ahead."[32]

The formation and growth of the ICU provide only a partial

answer to the question: What produces class consciousness? Class consciousness is the awareness, first, of the community of interest among workers and their common position as members of a class. As this consciousness becomes more clearly defined, there arises a need for a special organ which will articulate the consciousness of this new force. This new organization can reflect the interest of a class more or less correctly or falsely. During its history, the ICU embraced the false, as well as the correct, consciousness of the workers. Thus, as encouraging as the formation of the ICU was, it eventually faltered because it did not develop ideological clarity.

The founding of the ICU was followed in 1921 by the formation of the South African Communist Party (SACP). Its emergence and its effort to unify in a single party all groups that accepted revolutionary Marxism represented a potentially major step forward in the development of the labor and socialist movements in South Africa. From then on, the aims, character, and outlook of the national liberation and labor movements were informed by a scientific ideology. A new task became that of linking this revolutionary vanguard with the mass of workers, both black and white, and of providing a concrete and systematic program of struggle. The critical question that faced the SACP was how to relate to the ANC. That is, what was to be the role of nationalism in the liberation movement?

The SACP encountered immense problems in quest of these goals. In 1922 a white mine workers' strike was launched, with far-reaching political demands and consequences. The issue of substituting black workers for white workers in the mines, which had precipitated the strike, was the one most certain to split black and white workers and to arouse antagonism on both sides. Thus, the fledgling and as yet untested Communist Party was subjected to a severe test, one it could not pass. If the 1922 white miners' strike was a high-water mark for white labor in South Africa, it also marked its decisive defeat as an independent force. From 1922 onward the "white" labor movement was transformed step by step into an emasculated adjunct of Afrikaner nationalism, exchanging its independence for concessions and privileges.

The SACP committed serious mistakes during the 1922 strike. Ignoring the unique and specific historical conditions and obviously overestimating the revolutionary potential of the white proletariat, it mistakenly supported the chauvinism and racism of the white miners; it alienated the African labor movement, organized in the ICU, and dismissed the ANC as a petty-bourgeois organization. In 1924 the SACP backed what it called the "anti-imperialist front"—the alliance of racist white labor and Afrikaner nationalism that defeated the South African Party, which had ruled South Africa since 1910. Thus, it rejected the African organizations, which, it said, were not engaged in a revolutionary struggle against capitalism.

The inevitable result of such a posture was the isolation of the revolutionary vanguard of the proletariat from the bulk of the workers and a failure to deal with the real problems facing the black population and its labor movement. Yet without the leadership of a Marxist party, the further evolution of the ICU and the ANC was rendered highly difficult. In 1921 the English bourgeoisie launched the Joint Councils of Europeans and non-whites to counter the influence of the SACP. This is why the overcoming of sectarian trends and the establishment of close ties between the SACP, the ICU, and the ANC became in the early 1920s the central task facing the progressive forces in South Africa.

In the 1920s every effort was made to disrupt and undermine the unity that was being forged between the ANC, the ICU, and the SACP. For instance, in December 1924, the third conference of the SACP, at the urging of Sidney Bunting, adopted a policy of mass work among the African proletariat. The party accepted the ICU and worked within it. However, in December 1926, Kadalie, on the advice of white liberal "sympathizers," forced a split with the Communists by sponsoring a resolution excluding SACP members from holding office in the ICU. This policy was disastrous: within a few years the ICU lost its most effective members and was soon reduced to a series of splinter groups, until by the 1930s nothing was left of this once mighty voice of black labor. Rebuffed, the SACP set out to build trade unions on its own. In 1928 the South African Federation of Non-European

Trade Unions was formed, mainly in the laundry, tailoring, engineering, and baking trades.

The Pact government, elected in 1924 as a result of the coalition of white labor and the Nationalist Party, was hostile not only to the SACP but to the ICU and the ANC as well; and it became difficult for those in these organizations to build ties between black and white labor. In 1927 the Pact government passed the Native Administration Act, which made it an offense to disseminate "certain doctrines among natives, to say or write anything intended to promote hostility between the races." The act introduced the penalty of banishment, which was speedily invoked against the leaders of the ICU, the ANC, and the labor movement. In 1930 the government passed the Riotous Assemblies Act, which gave the minister of justice dictatorial powers of banishment and control over public meetings.

These laws caused a great deal of confusion in the various movements that were opposed to the government at this time. In particular, they overawed the ICU, whose ranks split into numerous factions, while the bulk of the membership dissipated. By the 1930s the ICU had faded out as a movement. While it lasted, it had, more than any other movement of the African working class, raised the specter of workers' militancy over the heads of capitalists and put fear into the hearts of the authorities. But persecution, lack of organizational skill, and reliance on the charisma of its leader helped to kill it.

The short history of the ICU illustrates, as do the histories of other mass movements of the oppressed, the tremendous disparity between the urgent desire for change on the part of the downtrodden blacks and the inadequacy of their political leadership. Antonio Gramsci recognized dichotomy between the popular masses and the "intellectuals" in popular movements:

> The popular element "feels" but does not always know or understand; the intellectual element "knows" but does not always understand and in particular does not always feel. The two extremes are therefore pedantry and philistinism on the one hand and blind passion on the other. . . . The intellectual's error consists in believing that one can know without understanding and even more without feeling and being impassioned: in other words that the

intellectual can be an intellectual if distinct and separate from the people-nation, i.e., without feeling the elementary passions of the people. . . . One cannot make politics-history without this passion, without this sentimental connection between intellectuals and people-nation.[33]

The rise and fall of the ICU can be explained in terms of the lack of clarity of what the issues at stake were in the leadership of the ANC and the ICU and in terms of its relations with the liberals on the one hand and white Communists on the other. These weaknesses were underscored in the debate about associating with either group. Between 1918 and 1925, whether as members of the ICU or the ANC, the Africans fought not their enemies, but "the enemies of their enemies." Kadalie, acting on the advice of liberal friends and the British TUC, purged, as we have seen, the ICU executive of Communists, hoping thereby to achieve membership in the International Federation of Trade Union Movements. At the same time, some ANC leaders became associated with liberals, who through the Joint Councils of whites and Africans, urged them to abandon militancy and to rely on education, moderation, and patience. In a recent study of the ICU, Zania writes that

> the Joint Councils and those connected with them represented the interests of British imperialism in South Africa, mainly the mining houses. They influenced Kadalie to adopt what they called "sane, constitutional" trade unionism. This meant deputations to the authorities and the employees, and above all, avoidance of the strike or any mass action by the African people.[34]

Kadalie was not unaware of the dangers of liberalism and warned of the Joint Councils:

> It is there [Johannesburg] where the English capitalists have succeeded to capture men of the African race . . . men with intellectual ability . . . to preach the gospel of cooperation between white exploiters and the exploited blacks. Let the African workers not be deceived, nothing tangible can come out from the "Joint Councils of Europeans and Natives." An exploited race has not to look to the exploiters for emancipation from shackles of slavery.[35]

Yet Kadalie failed to take his own advice. During the 1924 election campaign he allowed himself to become the spokesman for Hertzog's Nationalist Party at the 1923 ANC congress, and again at the meeting of the Cape Native Voters' Convention.

Thus, the whole African opposition in the 1920s was subject to white manipulation of one kind or another. The ruling circles, threatened not only by the specter of the Russian Revolution but also by the rise of the ICU and the SACP, still were able to consolidate their power and launch a counteroffensive without any serious challenge from Africans, whose energies were diverted into safer channels.

In revolutionary politics it is not enough merely to generate a socially radical consciousness among the masses (which Kadalie was able to do); a leader of a social movement must also be able to direct mass radicalism toward politically relevant goals, and Kadalie failed in this respect. He misdirected the popular radicalism he had harnessed. The success of the ICU showed that the African masses could be mobilized against exploitation. Kadalie gave the black masses a new consciousness of themselves and for themselves, which he then diverted away from issues of class exploitation and racial discrimination.

The reverses suffered by Africans in the post–World War I period were the inevitable fate of a class or a people that allows itself without discrimination to be influenced by representatives of the ruling class. The major historical legacy of this period was that the South African labor movement was stamped with a division between white and black workers that it has not yet been able to breach.

The ANC Reemerges

The ANC, which had been eclipsed by the ICU, gradually emerged from the doldrums. The election of the Pact government and the segregation policies it launched in 1925 provoked anger among broad sections of the African community. In February 1926 the ANC called a national convention at Bloemfontein. Among other things, the convention rejected segregation in any form, demanded equal rights for all in the Union constitution, and decided to boycott "native conferences" called by the government. In June of the same year the first united front—in the form of a Non-European Convention—took place at Kimberley, attended by representatives of the ANC, the African People's Organization (APO), and various African welfare, religious, and other bodies, as well as the South African Indian Congress (SAIC).

The mood of the African in this period was summed up in the June 23, 1925, issue of *Imvo Zabantsundu Bamzantsi Afrika:*

> This is certainly the age of white supremacy over all the black communities of the world, not by virtue of any quality of higher moral standard and civilization which the white man, in every part of the globe, arrogates to himself, but because it is the age of the mighty gun power—the demon of white supremacy. Modern democracy . . . is a democracy only of white skinned peoples of the world, and its philosophy is that of brazen spoliation and the violation of human rights of all peoples whose color is black . . . The black peoples wherever they reside, under so-called civilized authority, are not respected in the matter of human rights . . . There is a great unrest in Africa amongst the intelligent black inhabitants through the oppressive laws under which they live . . . Truly! the white man's religion (Christianity) has failed to interpret to us the meaning of life in the world. . . .[36]

It was the former cadres of the disintegrating ICU, now members of the ANC and of the SACP, who set the pace in organizing trade unions for African workers on a sound and militant basis.* At the same time they helped strengthen the ties between the ANC and the international working-class movement. The election of T. S. Gumede as president of the ANC and his attendance at the League Against Imperialism conference in Belgium in February 1927 were important steps in the internationalization of the South African problem.

---

* The members of the ANC could also be members of the SACP and other organizations. The ANC always considered itself a nationalist movement, whose members had more specific interests.

The contact between the advanced leaders of the ANC and the SACP was of immeasurable importance, because it broadened and deepened the political and ideological understanding of the ANC membership. A number of young Africans, who were educated in the SACP's evening school and who became active in the SACP and the ANC, played pivotal roles in the revival of the ANC and in the difficult tasks that faced the liberation movement, especially after World War II.

In sum, the 1920s saw the beginning of important trends in the liberation movement. First, the African working class emerged, under the leadership of the ICU and later the SACP, as an important force. Second, the unification in a single party, the SACP, of all progressive forces which accepted revolutionary Marxism along with nationalism represented a major step forward, even though at this time its success was problematic. F. Meli sums up what developed as follows:

> As the industrialisation of the economy and proletarianisation of the African masses developed, the African workers became increasingly aware of the need to organise on class lines. The rise of the I.C.U. of Kadalie reflected this awareness. Rejecting racialism, national degradation and class exploitation, the African workers fought many a glorious battle. Especially following the C.P.'s "turn to the masses" in 1924, advanced African workers, such as E. J. Khaile, Albert Nzula, Johannes Nkosi, Gana Makabeni, Moses Kotane, E. T. Mofutsanyana, J. B. Marks, Josie Mpama and others, came forward to join the Communist Party.
>
> They became pioneers in the difficult task of combining Leninism with African resistance and helped strengthen the ties between the ANC and the international working class movement. This tendency became more pronounced following the 1927 visit of Gumede, then President-General of the ANC to the Soviet Union, which he referred to on his return as "the new Jerusalem."[37]

In assessing the period between 1925 and 1935, we should not forget the international context. The destructive force of the economic crisis of 1929–1933 was reflected in the sharp decline of political activity on the part of the national liberation movement. In September 1933 the SACP attempted to stage joint demonstrations of black and white unemployed. One of these demonstrations is described in the Communist Party paper *Umsebenzi* (October 7, 1933) as "the most important event of its kind since May Day, 1933." About three thousand unemployed workers demonstrated, of whom about one-third were Europeans and the rest Africans.[38]

The Struggle Against the "Hertzog Bills"

In 1925 General Hertzog formulated the so-called Native Bills. They were then referred to a select committee, and in 1935 they were presented to a joint sitting of both houses of Parliament. The first bill was intended to complete and perpetuate the alienation of the Africans from the land, as envisaged under the 1913 Land Act. The second was to remove the remaining African votes in the Cape from the common electoral roll. To meet this challenge, the ANC met at a special convention, which included Africans from all walks of life. The 1935–1936 All African Convention (AAC) showed a remarkable unity among the more than five hundred delegates who came to Bloemfontein. Indeed, even former opponents—Jabavu, Seme, Kadalie, and Champion—met to discuss their common problems. Yet after the fire of the conference had dissipated, the unity of purpose disintegrated, leaving Africans to face the consciously organized power of the ruling class as separate organizations and individuals. According to Mary Benson:

> Jabavu and his delegation were very anxious to see the best in others, quite unable to argue militancy on behalf of their people. Hertzog, when they saw him, powerfully persuaded them that he had no alternative. Meanwhile the Cape M.P.'s were busy persuading them that they should suggest a compromise—that half a loaf might be better than none.[39]

The bills were passed. The abolition of the Cape franchise made clear the futility of the strategy advocated by liberal friends of the Africans. Another weakness of the African strategy in 1935–1936 was that of timidity and subservience to white paternalism. In one way or another, Africans looked to the liberals, who talked a great deal about the powerless Native Representative Council as being better than no representation. The acceptance of the compromise suggested by the Cape liberal MPs points, therefore, to the dilemma Africans faced each time they were told half a loaf is better than no bread at all. Thriving on the fervor and friendship of white liberals and the crumbs that fell from their political tables, the petty-bourgeois African leaders served a negative role as a buffer between the deprived black masses and the white reactionary ruling interests.

Though the All African Convention was an impressive assembly, it lacked unity of purpose. In the end it could only recommend yet another meeting with the authorities. The "spirit of moderation," and the constant refrain of the conservative elements within the movement, instead of arousing sympathy from the rulers, only evoked indifference and contempt. The struggle against the Hertzog Bills made it very clear to certain sections of African opinion that white liberalism only justified white supremacy, and that as long as Africans took counsel from white liberals they would be forced to renounce militancy in favor of appeals to the nonexistent conscience of the rulers. As a result, the power of the white rulers and the conscience of the blacks became corrupted. White powerholders became contemptuous of moral appeals because they were backed by little meaningful resistance from the African leaders, who lacked a mass base to implement their demands. Powerlessness had reduced Africans to a nation of beggars.

The African leadership that met in the AAC, despite its treatment at the hands of Hertzog, still failed to understand the specific features of their class position and continued to collaborate in their own degradation. Some of the delegates to the convention agreed to vote for white Native Representatives and to participate in the powerless Native Representative Council. Some were not aware that the class exploiters were connected by many threads of political organization, and others opportunistically accepted token gestures in the false hope that the society could still be reformed.

According to the Simonses,

> The conservatives and their white liberal advisers never quite under-
> stood their society or its power structure. They persisted in
> believing against all the evidence that liberation would come to
> them through reasoned argument, appeals to Christian ethics, and
> moderate, constitutional protest. Because of timidity, as Bunting
> alleged, or want of confidence in their people, they refused to
> mobilize them for mass struggle. Yet only by defying constituted
> authority—by "pure active extremism"—could a voteless, frag-
> mented proletariat and peasantry force it to consider their claims
> seriously. The main issues in parliamentary politics arose out of
> conflicts between British and Afrikaner interest groups. Neither
> side was interested in coming to terms with Africans, whose role
> was to supply labour at low cost for mines, farms and factories. All
> whites, apart from a handful of communists and liberals, were
> determined to maintain their supremacy through the ballot box,
> repressive sanctions and brute force.[40]

The necessary, if painful, lesson of the 1935–1943 period
gradually brought many Africans to political maturity. The
faith, which some still cherished, in the good intentions of the
government and the influence of people of good will on the
actions of the government disappeared. The change was not an
easy one, for it was a change which necessitated a major turn in
the African's self-conception and political outlook.

After the exclusion of the Cape African voters from the qualified common voters' roll, there was a qualitative turnaround in
the Africans' conception of their political problems. The change,
however, was slow, in part because the disqualification of the
Cape voters left African leaders dumbfounded. They had tried
to avoid blows aimed at them without asking by whom the blows
were delivered. They were leaders without a base; they had not
yet grasped the fact that individual acts of oppression were but
pieces in a larger plan aimed at reducing them to a state of
complete powerlessness. Although Africans had united as a
political body in the ANC, they did not exist as an independent
force with a combative ideology. The key weakness was that the
Africans were engaged in a moral struggle, an attempt to convince the white society to live by the Christian ethic, by which

European civilization defined itself. Although, in time, a mature political consciousness would develop, Africans paid a high price for their immaturity.

The Aftermath of the AAC:
The Emergence of Radical Nationalism

It fell on the shoulders of the new forces that were developing within the African community to find new ways of thinking and new methods of solving the problems facing the African. From 1935 onward, the younger Africans gradually became conscious of their double oppression, as workers and as members of a despised nation.

Impatient of the association of Africans with liberals, a group of younger ANC members formed a Youth League in 1943, and the era of radical nationalism began. The new consciousness would reach a dramatic height when in 1943 blacks in the urban slums of Johannesburg occupied land and created homes, defying the authority of the city council.

The number of Africans in industry rose from 156,000 in 1939 to 245,000 in 1945. In Johannesburg alone, the African population increased by 57 percent between 1936 and 1946. Yet no additional housing was provided for them, which led to the growth of atrocious slums. In 1944 thousands of families seized unoccupied land and erected their own dwellings out of corrugated iron, packing cases, and whatever makeshift building material they could lay their hands on.

The ANC was unable to respond to the war situation, and the struggle for housing fell on spontaneous community organizations. The birth of the Youth League was a response to these dramatic developments. The Youth League thought it ridiculous for the African to be involved in a war fought to decide which European power would have what sphere of influence, while, on the other hand, squatters' movements gave evidence of the combativeness of an urban proletariat groping for leadership. Strike activity by African workers reached a new peak, with

304 strikes, involving 58,000 Africans, coloreds, and Indians, taking place—all in the teeth of the notorious War Measure 145 of 1942, which outlawed *all* strikes by Africans and imposed severe penalties for participation by blacks in any industrial stoppage. The African proletariat was learning by struggle.

This situation made clear to Youth League leaders the strong connections between "society" and "state." The state was no longer presumed to somehow stand apart from the antagonisms of class and ethnic interests, with its representatives being neutral judges and conciliators between hostile sides. As it became clear that the state was an expression of white-settler interest, there were fewer appeals to the government for redress of grievances—particularly since the government turned a deaf ear to pressing grievances, despite Africans' support of the war effort.

The 1946 African Mine Strike

On the labor front major class conflicts continued to erupt in rapid succession during and after World War II. In 1946 the African proletariat in the mining industry, guided by the African Mine Workers' Union (AMWU), staged its largest strike ever, when seventy-five thousand gold miners on the Witwatersrand went out. In 1922 the Witwatersrand had been the scene of the most protracted and bloody strike in the history of the white workers' movement of South Africa, as we have seen in the previous chapters. In 1946 it was the turn of the most exploited and oppressed section of the mine workers. The black miners had asked the Chamber of Mines for a wage increase of ten shillings, and when the mine owners refused even to discuss the matter with the representatives of the union or to acknowledge their letters, there was no alternative but to strike. On August 4, at a massive open-air conference, the decision was taken to strike. Between August 12 and 19, at least one hundred thousand people, one-third of the African work force in the mines, took part in a stoppage that brought a large proportion of the mining industry to a standstill. The strike was a classic confrontation of class forces, and from the beginning the Chamber of Mines and its agency, the government, decided to meet this expression of working-class solidarity with force and terror. A special cabinet subcommittee was set up to implement the policy of violent suppression. Two thousand armed police were sent to the Witwatersrand and placed at the disposal of the Chamber of Mines to break the strike and force the miners back to work, even at bayonet point. When this show of force failed to intimidate the miners, the police opened fire, killing hundreds (no official figures were ever released).

The brutal suppression of the strike brought to the surface the deep discontent that had been simmering among the African masses since the war. The events of 1946 were, in effect, a series of ruthless object lessons by means of which history drummed into the heads of the working class the character of their oppressor. Michael Harmel observed that the strike was

> one of those great social events which at once illuminate and accelerate history: brilliantly showing up and hastening the main conflicts which determine social development, pitilessly exposing the hypocrisy, cowardice and futility of those who seek to evade those conflicts and stand on the side lines. The strikes destroyed once and for all the myth of the state as a "neutral" body. It spelt the end of the compromising concession-begging tendencies which had hitherto dominated African politics.[41]

The strike ended in disaster, doomed to failure because it was not based on a political will strong enough to carry it through. It was a desperate revolt, produced by desperate conditions, but it was not guided by long-range planning. It showed that isolated sacrifices are useless. The task of the ANC and its allies became that of charting a course of action that would channel energies and resources in such a way that if another revolt became necessary, it would be meaningful in creating a revolutionary situation.

Although the strike was a failure, the readiness of the pseudoliberal Smuts government to use brute force rather than meet the legitimate demands of the African miners angered all sections of the African population and further discredited the liberals, depriving them of the traditional means of lulling the so-called educated African elite to sleep. The strike sealed the fate of the Native Representative Council and the Joint Councils of white liberals and Africans. The ANC thus learned one of the great lessons of liberation: political self-reliance and self-help. It changed from an elite nonaction group to a mass membership action organization. It established new approaches with other oppressed groups and with those within the white community who were prepared to face squarely the problems of political and economic dispossession of the African people.

It was at this time also that new questions were asked: Was the struggle of the oppressed a struggle for national liberation alone or a national and a class struggle? What, therefore, was the role of nationalism to be? Who were friends and who enemies?

In spite of the strong pressures from certain of its members, the ANC chose a nonracial strategy and forged political alliances with those groups it considered friendly in the Indian, colored, and white communities.

The coalescence of progressive forces, made up of the ANC, the SAIC, the Coloured Peoples Organization (CPO), and the SACP, prepared the way for substantial ideological development of the liberation movement. On the basis of common struggles, the leadership and the membership of the various organizations gradually overcame the chauvinistic tendencies of their ethnic-based organizations. This new development laid the basis of the struggles waged by the liberation movement in the late 1940s and the 1950s.

To sum up the era of politics by persuasion, we can say that despite its marginal relevance to the whole issue of power and change in South Africa, it provided a sound basis for later political action of a more revolutionary kind. It was only by going through the hard school of struggle for separate political concessions that Africans could produce a leadership and acquire the persistence, daring, and consciousness necessary for the decisive phase of armed struggle. In the next chapter I analyze the struggles of the 1950s.

11

The South African National Congress: The Politics of Mass Insurgency

The real education of the masses can never be separated from the independent, the political, and particularly from the revolutionary, struggle of the masses themselves. Only the struggle educates the exploited class. Only the struggle discloses to it the magnitude of its own power, widens its horizon, enhances its abilities, clarifies its mind, forges its will; and, therefore, even reactionaries had to admit that the year 1905, the year of struggle, the "mad year," definitely buried patriarchal Russia.

—V. I. Lenin

The end of World War II ushered in a new phase in the struggle of the colonized peoples all over the world. As long as imperialism was unchallenged master, no amount of self-sacrifice or heroism could bring victory to the fighters for freedom in the colonies if they did not possess the military technology to counter that of the oppressor or if they did not unite forces in the struggle against the common enemy. After studying liberation movements, Lenin had concluded that their success would depend on:

The concerted efforts of the huge number of people in the oppressed countries (hundreds of millions in our example of India and China), or in particular favourable conjunctures of international conditions (e.g., the fact that the imperialist powers cannot interfere, being paralysed by exhaustion, by war, by their antagonisms, etc.) or the simultaneous uprising of the proletariat against the bourgeoisie in one of the big powers.[1]

296

With the disintegration of colonialism, there has been a fundamental change in the alignment of forces. Those struggling for national emancipation are no longer alone; they can now rely for material and moral support not only on their compatriots in the former colonies but on the socialist countries as well. The source of power of the political revolution now taking place in Southern Africa lies in the unity that exists between the various national movements and their support by independent African states and the socialist world. The interconnection between the national struggles in Guinea-Bissau, Angola, Mozambique, Namibia, Zimbabwe, the former High Commission Territories of Botswana, Lesotho, and Swaziland and the struggle of the people of South Africa is becoming clearer, just as imperialism's support of South Africa has become an acknowledged fact.

We have seen that white colonial rule was never accepted by its African victims, who lived under it only as long as they saw no chance of overthrowing it. But there is no such thing as a hopeless situation. Spontaneous uprisings have constantly challenged the South African settler state since its creation. Lenin regarded spontaneity as an indication of mass upsurge growing naturally from the contradictions of the social existence of oppressed classes and oppressing groups. Once uprisings occur, however, they pose two crucial questions: "What is to be done? Whither to go?"[2] They generate a need among the conscious elements to understand the forces at work in society and to point to new directions.

The election of the National Party in 1948 signaled to the oppressed that the whites had decided to dig in, if not turn back the clock. The avowed aim of the Nationalist government was to put the Africans back in their place. The Nationalist Party was determined to ignore the "winds of political change" that swept the colonial world immediately after the war. It promised firm control and stringent prevention of any further erosion of white supremacist rule: it was elected on a policy of apartheid which then meant *baaskap,* or "boss-rule."

In 1949 the Nationalists began their counterrevolutionary offensive by passing the Anti-Communist Act, which not only barned the Communist Party but also made any advocacy of

change equivalent to espousing communism and hence subject
to criminal prosecution. The African National Congress (ANC)
quickly realized the import of these oppressive policies and in
1949 adopted a <u>Programme of Action (PA)</u>, which was to lead to
sustained and militant activities by all the sectors of the African
population in conjunction with the South African Indian Congress (SAIC), Coloured Peoples Organization (CPO), and the
Congress of Democrats (CD). Among the demands included in
the PA were

> freedom from white domination and the attainment of political
> independence. This implies the rejection of the conception of
> segregation, apartheid, trusteeship or white leadership which are
> all in one way or another motivated by the idea of white domina-
> tion or domination of Whites over the Blacks. Like all other
> people, the African people claim their right of self-determination.[3]

The right of self-determination by its very logic necessitated
the eventual destruction of white rule through mass revolutionary action. The PA, then, was the first sortie from a politics of
conformity and persuasion to a politics of confrontation, and
thus required both caution and daring. For the first time the
ANC turned consciously to the masses to stimulate political
action and to arouse their fighting spirit. The political machinery to guide the practical search for methods of struggle was
contained in paragraph three of the PA, which envisaged the

> appointment of a council of action whose function should be to
> carry into effect, vigorously and with the utmost determination, the
> programme of action. It should be competent for the council of
> action to implement our resolve to work for: (a) the abolition of all
> differential political institutions, the boycotting of which we accept
> and to undertake a campaign to educate our people in this issue
> and, in addition, to employ the following weapons: immediate and
> active boycott, strike, civil disobedience, non-cooperation and such
> other means as may bring about the accomplishment and realiza-
> tion of our aspirations, (b) preparation and making plans for a
> national stoppage of work for one day as a mark of protest against
> the reactionary policy of the Government.[4]

The PA was based on the simple principle that revolutionary
change is inseparable from the day-to-day political struggles that

must be engaged in by the masses to educate them and raise
their political consciousness. The leadership believed that the
real heroes of the people are made in the field of struggle. Until
then political activity had been limited to the self-interest of the
educated elite. The PA called for putting the great masses in
motion in order to test their will and strengthen their resolve to
act toward their own liberation.

The 1949–1961 Extra-Parliamentary Campaigns

With the government dominated by a clique of fanatical Afrikaner rulers, who made no bones about their willingness to
imprison and torture Africans in order to uphold white rule,
and with the Africans having no legal means to defend their
interests, how were the African masses to be aroused to a full
consciousness of what was at stake? A movement without mass
support, according to Gramsci, is like "vanguards without armies
to back them up or 'commandos' without infantry or artillery."[5]
How to bring the mass of Africans into a revolutionary combativeness, to overcome the enervating lethargy caused by powerlessness: that was the crux of the matter the ANC had to resolve
in 1949.

Among the complicated questions to which the PA was intended to provide answers were these: What was the methodology to create a mass movement, and, once created, how was it to
be transformed into a revolutionary force? How were the various opponents of apartheid to act without prejudicing the specific interests of their constituents? What forms and methods of
struggle were to be used, given the ruthlessness of the government? What were to be the immediate and ultimate goals of the
struggle the various groups were about to launch? How were the
groups to be most effectively organized to win the hard struggles
that lay ahead? There were no ready-made answers to these
questions. They had to be answered by the struggle itself. The
success or failure of the tactic of direct action envisaged in the
PA would provide a partial answer to some of the questions.

common class interests!

In the new phase of the struggle the ANC and its allies continually confronted the oppressor and educated the masses. Through patient teaching the alliance between Africans, coloreds, Indians, and some whites became acceptable. The various struggles convinced the people that they had common class interests which overruled their ethnic and sectional interests. Only in this way were thousands of workers and peasants who participated in the Defiance Campaign welded into a force for liberation.

The first direct political action stemming from the Programme of Action was a demonstration by workers in the Transvaal on May 1, 1950. The "Freedom Day Strike" was called by the Transvaal branch of the ANC, the South African Communist Party (SACP), and the SAIC as a protest against the restrictions placed by the government on the movement of various leaders. In Johannesburg eighteen people died as a result of disturbances which occurred during the demonstrations, and a general strike was called for June 26 to protest the killings: this was the first of the famous "June 26 Campaigns." Thousands of people throughout the country responded to the strike call. From then on, June 26 became a national day of protest, and various other campaigns were launched on that day in later years.

The Defiance Campaign

Conscious of the need for sustained and constant struggle and for attracting growing mass support, the ANC escalated its efforts and in 1951 launched the "Campaign for the Defiance of Unjust Laws" (DC).

The plan of action proposed that the defiance of unjust laws was to take place in three stages: first, selected personnel were to go into certain segregated centers to ask for service and to see what would happen; next, the number of volunteers and centers of operation was to be increased; and finally, the stage of mass action was to be arrived at, where the countrywide struggle was to assume a general mass character involving both urban and rural people.[6]

All the preparations were made under the shadow of the Suppression of Communism Act, which meant that the leadership was constantly subjected to severe repression, banishment, and massive police round-ups. But the leaders were not deterred. Since there was no other means to challenge the status quo, the risk had to be taken. The DC campaign effectively avoided a suicidal insurrection while gaining the confidence of the masses.

On June 26, 1952, volunteers in Johannesburg and Port Elizabeth began the defiance of certain discriminatory laws. They were arrested, duly brought to trial, and sentenced to varying terms of imprisonment. During the months that followed, the campaign spread to all the major urban centers, and a total of 8,500 men and women of all "races" went to jail for their participation in the campaign. Mary Benson, an English writer, summed up the amazing success of the campaign in these words:

> Of the 10,000 volunteers called for, more than 8,500 had gone voluntarily to jail despite the intimidating effects of police action, of dismissal by employers, and the propaganda of the bulk of the press and of the radio; some teachers who had done little before had thrown up their jobs to defy; the United Nations had been inspired to discuss apartheid and the non-white challenge to oppression more seriously than ever before. Even the Government— instead of talking about *Baaskap*—began to talk about Bantustans and self-government for the Bantu. Congress prestige was enhanced; its membership greatly multiplied to more than 10,000. Yet the unjust laws remained intact: indeed, they had been augmented.[7]

The DC jointly launched by the ANC and the SAIC was the most sustained and protracted struggle ever undertaken by the oppressed peoples of South Africa. It acted as a catalyst for the combined involvement of blacks, coloreds, Indians, and whites in later struggles. It represented the growing maturity of the revolutionary movement as it began to transcend the fragmented and often conflicting ethnic demands of particular interest groups. It was carried out under the banner of the ANC to affirm the leadership role of the African masses. A spirit of unity among the oppressed has been an established fact ever since.

In the DC the liberation movement confronted the government with a mass movement of self-conscious African, colored, and Indian masses, which in time was augmented by a few hundred white supporters. The fact that this "Afro-Asian" working solidarity came only four years after the destructive Durban riots, in which Africans directed their frustration against Indians, is indicative of the growing maturity of the ANC and the SAIC.

During this period, the movement for African liberation strengthened its position by becoming allied with the revolutionary working-class movement organized in the South African Congress of Trade Unions (SACTU), formed in 1954. It was SACTU's policy that every trade-union member be a member of the Congress Alliance (CA) and vice versa. This alliance was to prove most effective for both sides; for the campaigns launched by the ANC and SAIC were always supported by SACTU, and vice versa. The labor movement now negotiated from a position of great strength as a result of its alliance with the national movements. For instance, when the Durban committee of SACTU sent its representative to negotiate with a number of employers of African labor for improved wages and when one milling company dismissed eight African employees suspected of SACTU membership, SACTU immediately addressed a letter to the company stating that since all efforts to bring about an amicable relationship between the company and the workers had failed, SACTU was "calling on the African National Congress, the Natal Indian Congress, and its allied organizations to boycott the products of the company so as to bring relief to the workers in your employ."[8] As a result of this threat, the company withdrew its notices of dismissal and promised to increase wages for Africans.

The spectacle of Africans, Indians, coloreds, and the working class voluntarily joining together to advance their political demands split the white society. It prompted some liberal whites to reevaluate their attitude toward Africans' initiative and to disabuse themselves of the "master race" psychology developed under centuries of white hegemony. Now that they had lost their role as brokers between the government and the helpless African, what role liberal whites were to play became the key question.

The emergence of the white opposition in the forms of the Liberal Party, the Congress of Democrats, and the Federal Party, and the continued fragmentation of the White United Party parliamentary opposition illustrate the impact of the African initiatives begun by the Defiance Campaign. The Liberal and Federal parties were attempts by liberal whites to find new roles for themselves, now that they were no longer able to act as the self-appointed spokespeople for the politically voiceless. Both the Liberal Party and the Federal Party advocated a direct, but qualified voting franchise for the African. The former party was not only willing to have face-to-face consultation with African and other movements in the CA but even opened its membership to Africans, some of whom achieved leadership positions. This exposed the fact that whites were not a monolithic structure of oppression, but that the white bloc was stricken by conflicting class interests that could be exploited with correct tactics and strategies.   CLASS WARFARE !

At the opposite extreme, the government panicked and responded to the DC with a repressive armory of laws, including the Criminal Laws Amendment and the Public Safety Act, both passed in 1953. Under the first, a person convicted of breaking a law in protest against any law could be charged a maximum of £300 (£1 = $2.80), imprisoned for three years, and given ten lashes, while leaders who incited others to commit such an offense were liable to a fine of £500, five years imprisonment, and fifteen lashes. The Public Safety Act authorized the government to proclaim a state of emergency, amounting to martial law, for a period of twelve months. The Nationalist Party government believed that it was confronting a real threat from below and that altogether different forms of struggle against this threat were necessary. The dimensions of the repressive laws passed by the government to counter mass demonstrations warrant the label "class warfare" from above.

As a result of these laws, the campaign was suspended in order to provide the leadership a chance to study the implications and to plan further strategies. In sum, the DC was a major landmark in the annals of the liberation movement. According to A. Lerumo, an activist in the liberation movement, the DC

> transformed the character of the African National Congress from what may have seemed to many a body of words to one of deeds. The Defiance Campaign marked the transition of the ANC from a loosely knit body to an effective organization in which men of action counted far more than orators, in which workers of town and country, and young men and women, played an increasingly preponderant role. The temper of the "new congress" found a warm answering chord among the masses, who surged to the ANC in support and membership.[9]

The question that faced the liberation movement after the suspension of the DC was how to capitalize on the revolutionary mood of the masses to forestall the demoralization that may descend as soon as the illusion of immediate success evaporates. Between 1953 and 1954 the ANC and its allies conducted two more mass actions: a national campaign against Bantu education and a local campaign against the Western Areas Removal scheme in Johannesburg. Although these campaigns did not prevent either the enforcement of Bantu education or the removal to Western Areas, they were a further test of the resolve of the mass of Africans even in the face of new punitive measures legislated by the government to stop the Defiance Campaign. The new spirit of unity was also manifested in a program for a future, free, nonracist South Africa, one drawn up on the basis of the genuine needs and aspirations of the oppressed. In 1955 a nationwide call went out from the headquarters of the CA for people to meet in branches, in groups, on farms and in cities, in factories, in townships and towns to discuss their aspirations, put them down on paper, and forward them to the head office of the ANC. After many months of patient work, a national convention, the Congress of the People, comprising 3,000 representatives from all sections of the South African population, met at Kliptown, near Johannesburg; and on June 26, 1955, the delegates adopted the now famous "Freedom Charter," a summary statement of the proposals sent in from all over the country. Joe Matthews, a one-time member of the ANC executive committee, wrote:

> The Charter was a clear and noble expression of the ideas of the Congress Movement regarding the future South Africa. It laid down the basis for a national democracy which would afford all peoples in South Africa the opportunity to live a free and cultured existence. It is the most important single document in South African history.[10]

Following the convention, in December 1956, the government staged midnight raids throughout the country and arrested 156 leaders of the CA on charges of high treason. Thus began the infamous Treason Trials, which were to last more than four years and to result in the acquittal of all the accused. The charge of treason was in effect an acknowledgment by the government that the Freedom Charter was a fundamental challenge to capitalist social relations and to the white supremacist political structure. In court the state charged that the Freedom Charter was a "blueprint" for a communist state.

The developments following the arrest and trial of the 156 leaders followed fast upon one another. Local strikes, boycotts, and demonstrations became a continuing feature of the struggle. In 1957 the people of Alexandra township boycotted the bus service for three months because of a penny increase in the fare, and other townships (Orlando, Moroka, and Jabavu), though not threatened by fare increases, came out in sympathetic boycotts. After extensive negotiating behind the scenes, the fare was reduced. The Africans were learning the power of united action; they were voting with their feet.

In 1957 a campaign to boycott selected Nationalist-owned or -supported businesses was launched "to kick the Nationalist supporters in their pockets" and to vote with "our stomachs," as Chief A. H. Lutuli, the president of the ANC, put it.[11] Then, after press exposure of the treatment of African workers on the potato farms of the Transvaal, the ANC called for a boycott of potatoes. The campaign was so effective that at Pietermaritzburg, for instance, a packet (20 lbs) of potatoes which normally sold for 7/6d ($1) was selling for as little as 1/6d ($.20). In Natal a boycott of beerhalls caught on, and in a number of municipalities women picketed them. Dr. W. W. M. Eiselen, secretary for Bantu administration and development, was forced to tour Natal, consulting officials and magistrates. He declared that the senseless destruction of beerhalls and other symbols of the government could only be understood against the background of the "sustained and exaggerated criticism of everything the State did for the Bantu. . .": he blamed the ANC.[12]

During the mid-1950s African women carried on a stubborn and militant struggle to frustrate the extension of the hated pass laws to themselves. In August 1956, to demonstrate their opposition to the pass system, the South African Women's Federation organized a protest at the Union Building in Pretoria attended by 20,000 women from all corners of South Africa. The protest was extended from the main urban centers to the rural areas of the Transvaal, Orange Free State, Cape, and Natal, where hundreds of women were arrested in the following years. There appeared to be no turning back. The mood was one of optimism, of militancy, of inevitable victory as the movement grew from strength to strength.

As the 1950s drew to a close, the continuing struggles contributed to a revolutionary impatience and a tendency to speed up events. The general slogan was *Action*. At the 1958 ANC Annual Conference, held in Durban to recognize the activities of Natal women, a new factor was the presence of peasant women, who took part in all the conference deliberations. These were women who normally would have been loyal supporters of their husbands and the traditional authorities.

The 1950–1960 period saw even more serious incidents of disorder, mass demonstrations, and bloody clashes between the Africans and the police at the reserve of Witzieshoek, near Basutoland, in 1950 and in the Eastern Pondoland in the Transkei in 1953. The Pondo revolt, not directly organized by the ANC, had its origins in local grievances, but in no time its aims became merged with the basic goals that the ANC was fighting for at a national level. This made it easy for the people of Pondoland to accept ANC leadership and guidelines in struggling over their local grievances. Also in 1958 resistance and violence reached a stage of open revolt in Sekukuneland, where sixteen peasants, including a woman, were sentenced to death and executed for killing government agents; and Zeerust, an African reserve in northern Transvaal, was also up in arms against government regulations.

In its October–December 1960 issue *Africa South* editorialized:

> The prospect of revolution is agitating South Africa as never before. With parliament reduced by the psychosis of Apartheid to the function of the status of a Government Gazette, and all constitutional opposition restricted to the fumbling a race-frenzied electorate will allow, change without revolution has become finally impossible. Government spokesmen make sporadic nostalgic asides on the frontier wars, as though rebellion and repression constitute a series of open battles, where white supremacy will once again shoot its way through assegais [spears] to decisive survival. The non-white political movements meanwhile engage in convulsive campaigns, their leaders for the most part as fluid in the conception of how to accomplish power as their opponents are rigid in their own of how to retain it.

The editorial then quoted the 1957 *Report of the South African Commissioner of Police*, which reflected the pulsating reality of a country under seige. In 1957, for instance, 1,525,612 people, out of a population of 14,500,000, were committed for trial in South Africa—1,448,582 of whom were convicted. An average of 4,200 South Africans were arrested and tried daily. Every year one out of every ten inhabitants—women and children included—was convicted of a crime. Even more significant were the figures for crimes of violence. The same editorial pointed out that, whereas during 1957 metropolitan London had eleven convictions for murder in a population of 8 million, the statistics for South Africa showed an increase of convictions from 396 in 1953 to 798 in 1957. The editorial concluded that "surely this is a society slithering into anarchy."

The 1958 Split of the Pan-Africanist Congress

In seeking the origins of the Pan-Africanist Congress (PAC) within the ANC, we need to glance back to the beginnings of African political opposition. We need to distinguish as well between national and nationalist sentiment. In peoples' experiences, the national psychology, in contrast to the nationalist, is part of the universally human, and it opposes itself to the national-particular of any other nation.

Within the ANC the two strains, national and nationalist, existed side by side and jockeyed for control at various times in the history of the ANC. The *nationalist* sentiment was very strong among those who formed the ANC Youth League in 1943. A look at the experience of Africans working with white liberals is useful in understanding the objective cause of the nationalist. I discussed in the previous chapter the role of the African educated elite, most of whom were sponsored by liberals. In their programs the African elite, in order to continue enjoying liberal support, found that they had to mute their demands and defer to their liberal sponsors. When the issue of the African franchise was being discussed prior to the formation of the Union, African opposition had to be restrained for fear that any radical expression would alienate white liberal opinion. Even in the Joint Councils of Whites and Africans formed in the 1920s, the price of admission for the Africans was moderation. English liberals were satisfied to work with Africans so long as the latter remained "tokens" in white-dominated institutions.

During the debate on the Hertzog Bills, which eventually took away the African franchise in the Cape Province, it was the liberal white members of parliament whose vote for the bills was critical. Their ineffectual political response and eventual support of the bills was yet another in a series of betrayals. The Africans discovered to their grief that liberals were a great liability to their cause and thus became very suspicious of *all* whites of *good* intentions, whether liberal or communist. Hadn't the Communist Party in 1922 supported reactionary white labor as well? In the 1940s and 1950s the crucial question, constantly raised, was whether members of the white community, liberal or communist, could be trusted to work sincerely for Africans' political emancipation. The past betrayals struck deep root in the consciousness of the younger Africans.

The so-called Nationalist wing of the ANC and the Youth League rejected all forms of cooperation with members of other groups for fear of manipulation and deception. After deliberately exaggerating the influence of white Communists, Indians, and coloreds in the ANC in 1950 and 1951, a so-called Nationalist wing of the Congress, the ANC (Nationalist-minded Bloc), broke away under the leadership of R. V. Selope-Thema. The grounds for secession were the ousting of Dr. Xuma from the leadership of the ANC because of his conservatism and the election of Dr. Moroko, who invited the SAIC to join in drafting the PA which eventually launched the DC. When the ANC (National-minded Bloc) met in Pretoria in October 1952, it found itself in an invidious position. Members attacked the Indians and Jews and pledged support of the government. In his presidential address Selope-Thema said it was the aim of his congress to build a nation of law-abiding citizens who were to be loyal to their chiefs and traditions. He emphasized that when the ANC was started in 1912, it had pledged to unify the black people of the Union, with their chiefs included.[13]

The position of the PAC in 1958 had something in common with the ANC (National-minded Bloc). An analysis of the various writings of the PAC leaders and theoreticians show clear overtones of appeals to narrow, chauvinistic sentiments. The PAC claimed a direct link with the Pan-African movement of George Padmore, and it also claimed to be the true heirs of the ANC Youth League. Padmore's book *Pan-Africanism or Communism?* became the PAC's "bible." Padmore wrote in his book:

> The white man in East and Central Africa has forfeited the loyalty and goodwill of the Africans, who no longer have illusions about professions of "trusteeship" and "partnership." These British settlers, to say nothing of the fanatical racialists and rabid defenders of *Apartheid* in South Africa, have made it abundantly clear to the Africans that they regard them merely as hewers of wood and drawers of water in their own countries.[14]

The PAC program started from the premise that people who can trace their origins from continents other than Africa are foreigners and that before they can be granted African citizenship they must declare their loyalty to Africa. Thus the PAC program of principles declared that the aims of the PAC were to unite and to rally the African people into one national front on the basis of African nationalism. To fight for the overthrow of white domination and maintenance of an African-Socialist democracy, recognizing the primacy of the material and spiritual interests of the individual. To advance the concept of the Federation of Southern Africa and Pan Africanism.[15]

This declaration did not contribute to the understanding of the PAC's policy. It was difficult to know what the phrase "recognizing the primacy of the material and spiritual interests of the individual" meant. In the PAC program relatively progressive and anti-imperialist slogans of the Pan-African movement were interwoven in bizarre fashion with reactionary nationalist concepts. Hatred of whites who were Communists became widespread. Professor I. I. Potekhin commented on the PAC split:

When all these organizations formed a common front of struggle against Verwoerd's fascist policies, a small group of ANC members split away, complaining that the ANC had fallen under white influence, and set up their own organization, the Pan Africanist Congress, as a purely racial organization allegedly "free" from white influence. The PAC leadership immediately came out with violently anti-communist statements and soon attracted the support of the white Liberal Party also engaged in vicious anti-communist propaganda. The leader of its Right Wing, Patrick Duncan, a rabid anti-communist, became a particularly enthusiastic champion of the PAC. After having left the ANC for the alleged reason that it cooperated with progressive whites, the PAC fell into company with white reactionaries. This is, of course, quite natural; the main contradiction in bourgeois society is not between races but between antagonistic classes, between the forces of progress fighting for the socialist transformation of society and the forces of imperialist reaction striving to save the outlived decadent capitalist system. The PAC leaders are no exception. There are political figures in other African countries who counterpose black to white, and with the same result: in turning their back on friends, they find themselves bound in a shameful alliance with the enemies of African freedom.[16]

The PAC spoke as if Africans were a homogeneous group, ignoring the deep changes that had occurred in the class content of the African population. The emergence of capitalism and the involvement of the black workers in the new economy meant that the national element in the movement had reached a new stage and had become more complex and influenced by class. But in the PAC's scheme of things, the national element was distorted out of all proportion for egotistical reasons.

There is no doubt that the PAC's demise would have come sooner if the police at Sharpeville and Langa had acted with some caution, instead of unleashing their fury on the peaceful demonstrators. The Sharpeville massacre and the march of 30,000 Africans from Langa to Cape Town made a historical landmark out of what would have passed as a quiet day, and created a legend for the PAC. Commenting on the PAC's strategy prior to Sharpeville, the Non-European Unity Movement wrote:

> Before launching the Anti-Pass Campaign, the PAC had visited a few centres, amongst them Cape Town, where they held well-attended public meetings. They were elated by their "success" and translated this as meaning a following for their organization, according to them they captured Cape Town. . . . It did not occur to the inexperienced young leaders that in a situation as it was, the people responded not to the PAC as such—whose policy they did not even know—but they were ready to attend any meeting that criticized the government. There was not only constantly mounting pressure of oppression, but the people of Langa in particular had been made aware of the present political climate in and outside the Union of South Africa.[17]

It was the Sharpeville massacre that actually made the PAC a "viable" organization. And the reasons are not too hard to find: At Sharpeville, where there was some response to the PAC's call, the atmosphere was extremely charged. The Coalbrook mine disaster a few weeks earlier had shocked everybody, and no doubt some of the victims were known to, or relatives of, the people who answered the PAC's call.

The happenings at Sharpeville and Langa showed that the simplest and most vulgar Nationalist slogans, especially if they are antiwhite, can be effective in rallying the masses. It is easy to fire the struggle of the African masses by drawing attention to some of the external characteristics of capitalist exploitation—

blacks are oppressed, and whites are the common enemy—
rather than to the substance of it. White racism was an objective
reality, for it was in evidence all the time, everywhere, insulting
the national pride and dignity of Africans.

Once the split had been consummated, the ANC redoubled its
energies and seemed to have been instilled with a greater sense
of purpose now that the devisive activists had been purged.
According to Mary Benson:

> Not only had the hiving off of the Africanists jolted Congress
> leaders into a determined unity, but the executive's recent disrupt-
> ing tendency to waste time on the "cold war" issues was replaced by
> concentration on Africa. Congress sponsored the Pan African
> Conference in Accra in December, 1958, where its call for the
> boycott of South African goods found a hot response.[18]

In 1959 the ANC decided to prepare for what Chief Lutuli
and O. R. Tambo called a "long and bitter struggle against the
pass laws—the main pillar of our oppression and exploitation."[19]
The pass laws in South Africa are the cornerstone of the regulations that facilitate oppression of Africans, and such a campaign thus had a momentous significance both for the African
masses and the government.

In December 1959 the annual conference of the ANC met in
Durban to set the date for the campaign. April 1, 1960, was
agreed upon, and demonstrations were scheduled for May and
June. The Pan-Africanist Congress, however, decided to jump
the gun and begin its campaign a week before the date chosen by
the ANC. Sobukwe, the PAC leader, wrote to the chief of police
in Pretoria advising him that he and his followers would present
themselves for arrest on March 21. He expressed the hope that
"you will cooperate to make this a most peaceful and disciplined
campaign." But at the Sharpeville and Langa police stations, the
police opened fire on innocent bystanders and demonstrators,
killing, according to official reports, 68 Africans and wounding
227 at Sharpeville and killing 8 and wounding 48 at Langa. Thus
an ill-conceived and hurriedly organized protest met a kind of
force to which it was not prepared to reply in kind.

The resentment of the pass laws aroused Africans to new
heights of protest and plunged South Africa into the Sharpeville

crisis, so that the name "Sharpeville" has become, like "Amritsar," "Saint Bartholomew," and "Peterloo," a symbol of massacre.[20]

Why did the police act so irresponsibly? Africans had been killed in South Africa before, but in 1960 the police were very much conscious of what had happened at Cato Manor, a shanty town near Durban. On January 24 angry Africans had turned against a party of raiding police, killing nine of them—four whites and five Africans. The second question is: Why did this shooting suddenly become world news? Because the ANC mobilized all its resources, both internal and international, to publicize the massacre. Chief A. J. Lutuli called for a day of mourning on March 28, and there were marches and demonstrations in all the major towns. Between thirty-five and fifty thousand Africans invaded the houses of Parliament in Cape Town. International reaction was overwhelming in its condemnation; the UN Security Council took a stand against the barbarous policy of apartheid.

The government panicked. It declared a state of emergency and arrested two thousand political leaders and ten thousand men and women, members of the ANC and the PAC.

The events following the Sharpeville shootings clearly showed how deep the newly awakening popular movement was. What Lenin called the "spontaneous elements" in the history of mass struggle were clearly demonstrated by the mass involvement in the demonstrations called by the ANC and its allies in the aftermath of Sharpeville.

On March 31 and April 1 Africans staged demonstrations in many centers: Cape Town, Stellenbosch, and Simonstown in the Cape Province; Durban in Natal Province, where three Africans were killed; and Johannesburg and Pretoria in the Transvaal Province. Passes were burnt in Bloemfontein. On April 3 came the police "day of reckoning" in Cape Town. The *Rand Daily Mail* reported on April 4, 1961:

> Shortly after dawn detachments of troops moved in to guard all key points in Cape Town. . . . While the troops stood by, armed with rifles and machine guns and supported by armoured cars, groups of policemen scoured the streets. They stopped and

checked hundreds of Natives and ordered those standing around
to move on. They beat up some with their truncheons and sjam-
boks. Some they put into pick-up vans and took away.

During what a special correspondent of *Africa South in Exile*
called the "nineteen days,"[21] the African masses ran ahead of
their organization. When the ANC called for the day of mourning, the response was beyond anyone's expectation. After the
day of mourning, there was another call for a general strike
throughout the country on March 28, and this too found a warm
response in the masses. The day before, Chief Lutuli, president
general of the ANC, had publicly burned his pass in Pretoria,
the administrative capital, an act that was repeated throughout
the country. A few days later the passes were suddenly suspended, and for a wonderful moment it seemed that the campaign had brought victory, especially when a senior government
minister, Paul Sauer, declared that the "old book of South
African history was closed and the new one must be opened."
F. S. Steyn, a Nationalist MP, declared that African nationalism
had developed a unique quality that had never been seen before:

> The African's instinctive spirit of massing together in a revolution-
> ary tendency was wholly anarchical and destructive, as witnessed
> by the organized marches. The spirit supplied the leaders, who
> shared the language, psychology and mood of the masses, with
> ideal revolutionary material.[22]

Writers on revolution have detailed three situations that often
occur within the dominant classes prior to the outbreak of serious revolutionary violence. The first is the desertion of the
ruling strata's intellectuals, which is in effect a challenge to
the existing modes of thought and the whole perception of the
possible cause of the crisis, as well as to the old remedies for
human suffering. In the 1950s in South Africa the main supporters of the Liberal Party, the Congress of Democrats, and even
the Progressive Party were English intellectuals, whose perception of the possible causes of the South African malaise involved
a different outlook from that of the Afrikaner ruling elite.

The second situation is the appearance of the sharp conflicts
of interest within the dominant classes themselves. The decade

of the 1950s revealed important splits in the ruling white bloc, as illustrated by the post-Sharpeville debates in the House of Assembly, and the flight of capital represented a temporary vote of no confidence in the rulers by international finance. Although the third situation did not apply, i.e., the loss of unified control over the instruments of violence, the army and the police, the loyalty of the African police in a sustained offensive was doubtful.

The debate in the House of Assembly, according to *Africa South in Exile*,

> revealed a deep cleavage, at least in the minds of the Government members, between Afrikaner and English South African. Some Nationalists spoke as though the Afrikaner people were fighting against the world—the Blacks and English in their midst. One might almost suppose that of the three evils, the English were the greatest. Mr. Ben Schoeman, the Minister of Transport, expressed his personal conviction that "the British newspapers in South Africa would rather that the Natives governed than that the Afrikaner Nationalist remained in power." These newspapers . . . had never forgotten that the despicable Boers had taken over the reins of government; they were still fighting the Anglo-Boer War.[23]

In the aftermath of Sharpeville those who ruled quarreled among themselves, and a financial crisis threatened the country; but there was no core revolutionary body, such as the Bolshevik Party in Russia, to lead an armed uprising and create a civil war situation with the aim of taking over state power. The kind of *dynamism* that was achieved by the Bolshevik Party in 1917 was simply out of the question in the South Africa of 1960. Though the events leading to Sharpeville were reminiscent of the events in Russia in 1905, there were also important differences. The ANC was not yet in a position to lead a general insurrection. Nevertheless, one of the greatest mistakes of the period was to allow the post-Sharpeville revolutionary mood to peter out. For two weeks, for instance, the African labor force in Cape Town was on strike. In Durban, Port Elizabeth, Johannesburg, and Cape Town mass marches were held to demand the release of the arrested leaders. What might have been achieved had there been an armed vanguard organized and ready for armed insur-

rection cannot be predicted. But for the first time in the history
of South Africa, all the major towns had trouble on their hands.
To compound the confusion, on April 9 an assassination attempt
was made on Prime Minister Verwoerd, who was addressing the
opening of the Union Exposition at the showgrounds in Johannesburg. An article in the April 11, 1960, edition of *Die Burger,*
an Afrikaans newspaper, reflected the mood of the time: "In this
miraculous escape all the faithful will see the hand of God and
thank him that our country, which is already passing through
troubled times, has been spared the greater horror of assassination of its head of state."

In 1961, following the turmoil of 1960, the people of Pondoland, in the Transkei, began an uprising. Eight chiefs and their
councillors, all of whom supported the government, were mur-
dered. In one of the police attacks on an angry gathering, eleven
Africans were shot. L. Legwa, a freelance writer, commented:

> The whole district of Bizana fell into the hands of the *mountain
> men*—the freedom fighters. They set up people's courts and levied
> taxes on black and white in the area. The Government resorted to
> extensive military actions. A state of emergency—which has still
> not been lifted—was declared over the whole area of the Trans-
> keian territory. More than 5,000 peasants and leaders were ar-
> rested and detained. Hundreds were sentenced to long terms of
> imprisonment. Thirty-two leaders were sentenced to death.[24]

We can sum up this period as follows: in the struggle of the
1950s and early 1960s there was a dialectical process of action
and reaction in an escalating conflict, as African initiatives produced government counteraction. The African masses responded to Sharpeville by burning passes, marching on police
stations, and causing a state of economic chaos when foreign
investors began to withdraw their capital. The CA heightened
the conflict by calling for a "stay at home," which was massively
supported, and the government, in turn, banned the ANC and
the PAC and called out the army and the police, arresting many
of the activists under a state of emergency. The ANC countered
immediately with the Pietermaritzburg Emergency Conference
of March 1961, followed by a strike in June, both organized by

its underground machinery. We will turn to these in the next section.

The post–World War II activities of the ANC reveal that the problem it faced was an old one: how to fight at all levels without capitulating to opportunism on the one hand or being immobilized in "infantile disorder" and verbal "revolutionism" on the other. What guided the Congress movement's policy was the awareness that the fundamental political processes of the revolution consist in the masses gradually comprehending the nature of their situation. The various campaigns launched in the 1950s accentuated the social crisis of white rule through the active orientation of the masses by successive struggles that, above all, gave the people confidence in themselves and enabled them to confront their rulers.

If the CA had accepted the liberal standpoint, renounced the use of violence, and pledged to the African people not to diverge from the path of bourgeois legalism, then its extra-parliamentary activities would, after Sharpeville, have collapsed miserably and left the African people to untrammeled reactionary violence. Instead, the CA escalated the struggle, refusing to throw in the towel. Every legal structure created to frustrate the movement was challenged at an ever higher level. In the process, the Africans gained in strength, grew, and learned their power—the strength of numbers, the strength of the masses, "the strength of the inexhaustible springs of self-sacrifice and of the idealistic and honest reserves of the energy and talent of the so-called common people, the workers and peasants, awakened and eager (to shake the yoke of oppression) and to build up a new order."[25]

The Pietermaritzburg Conference

Even though the ANC had been banned, its underground leadership convened an All-in-African Conference at Pietermaritzburg in 1961. Nelson Mandela emerged from hiding to make an address. He called on the government to convene a

national convention. The All-in-African Conference also called
for a work stoppage on May 29 if the government refused the
demand. On the day of the strike, however, an apprehensive
government called out the army and the police, who surrounded
all the major African residential areas in the cities, and the
African response was thus difficult to measure.

After the strike, the leaders of the CA concluded that the time
had come to depart from the "nonviolent" technique as the sole
method of struggle. Reactionary violence had to be met with
revolutionary force. Lenin had warned that

> an oppressed class which does not strive to learn to use arms, to
> acquire arms, only deserves to be treated like slaves. We cannot
> forget, unless we become bourgeois pacifists or opportunists, that
> we are living in a class society, that there is no way out of this
> society, and there can be none, except by means of the class
> struggle. In every class society, whether it is based on slavery,
> serfdom, or as at present, on wage labour, the oppressing class is
> armed.[26]

The ANC's response to the government's use of force was thus
an inevitable historical development. It was an acknowledgment
on the part of the ANC that the class violence of the rulers could
not be countered except by revolutionary violence. The Pietermaritzburg Conference thus marked a climax in the history of
the resistance movement. On June 26, 1961, *Umkhonto We Sizwe*
("Spear of the Nation") was born. On Dingane's Day, December
16, 1961, it issued a manifesto which declared:

> The time comes in the life of any Nation when there remains only
> two choices—submit or fight. That time has come now to South
> Africa. We shall not submit, and we have no choice but to hit back
> by all the means within our power in defense of our people, our
> future and our freedom.

To prepare for the new phase of armed struggle, Nelson
Mandela was sent on a tour of independent African states to
mobilize support. In 1962 he addressed the Pan-African Movement conference in Addis Ababa, Ethiopia, and visited the Alge-
rian National Liberation Front base in Morocco, where he observed
firsthand the methods of waging armed struggle against an

intransigent white settler state. He returned to South Africa to direct the underground activities of Umkhonto We Sizwe, which had begun a campaign of sabotage in all the major urban centers. The government reacted by passing the ninety-day detention law—enabling massive police raids, arrest without trial, torture of suspected prisoners. Thus, the government stepped up its campaign of terror against all suspected enemies.

Faced with this brutal reaction in which many Umkhonto cadres were tortured to death, the movement decided to move on to guerrilla warfare. Guerrillas would have to be trained outside the country. Just as preparations were being made, the police discovered the headquarters of the Congress movement at Rivonia and rounded up the CA leaders, including Walter Sisulu, Govan Mbeki, and Bram Fischer, among others, with Nelson Mandela having been arrested earlier on charges of leaving the country illegally.

The arrests revealed serious weakness in the organizational structure of the alliance and its methods of work. Thus, the decision to adopt armed struggle as a strategy for liberation had given rise to a new set of unfamiliar problems. It was necessary for the movement, on the pain of its own destruction, to make a qualitative leap in its forms of organization. This was not to be an easy task. From 1963 to 1967 the government managed to impose a pall of quiescence on the whole country.

In the summer of 1967 the ANC and ZAPU (Zimbabwe African Peoples Union) joined forces and entered Rhodesia. In the area of the Wankie game reserve, heated clashes were fought against a joint contigent of Rhodesian and South African counterinsurgency forces. The young fighters of ANC and ZAPU displayed remarkable courage in the face of severe odds, but the attempt to infiltrate small groups of insurgents into the south through hostile territory proved to be costly.

The discovery and capture of the high command of the CA at Rivonia in 1963 had damaged the internal structure of the underground movements. And political work by the exile movement suffered from the lack of contact with internal developments. The movement had to devise other ways of rebuilding its internal structure. Patiently and with great fortitude,

individuals were sent into the country to study the situation
firsthand. The CA leadership understood that in a revolutionary
era a revolutionary situation can break out at any moment. A
movement must therefore study the various tendencies leading
toward the revolutionary situation. It must encourage developments that accentuate the contradictions in society. The CA
embarked on a number of activities, including building underground cells and distributing leaflets carrying the CA's mes-
sages.

At the same time other voices opposed to the status quo began
to emerge in South Africa. In December 1968 a group of black
students met to discuss the formation of an all-black student
organization. The outcome was SASO (the South African Student Organization), which embraced Africans, coloreds, and
Indians. From the beginning SASO was audacious and ener-
getic. The slogan, "Unity of all the oppressed classes, unity first,"
articulated in the CA during the DC, was its guiding principle.
Implementation of this slogan made it possible for SASO to
achieve success in building up the "black consciousness" movement. The response of the government was savage and, by all
accounts, unparalleled even by South African standards.

The significance of the black consciousness movement, which
sought to build up among blacks in South Africa pride in their
identity and their value system, as well as to build black unity,
was based on the realization that "the most potent weapon in the
hands of the oppressor is the mind of the oppressed" and that
"not only have [the whites] kicked the black but they have also
told him how to react to the kick . . . he is now beginning to
show signs that it is his right and duty to respond to the kick in
the way he sees fit."[27]

While the spirit of black consciousness was ripening, the ANC
and its underground were increasing their propaganda activities. During August 1970 leaflets telling people about armed
struggle were distributed in all the major cities. The campaign-
ing was so extensive and effective that it made the headlines of
every major newspaper in South Africa, as well as receiving
attention abroad. "ANC Shows Its Teeth Again—Bombs in Five

Large Cities—State Threatened in Leaflet" were the front page headlines in the Afrikaans *Die Transvaler* of August 14.

The ANC's ability to spread its message was recognized by the London *Guardian* of August 15, 1970, which commented in an editorial:

> The ANC has now reminded the South African authorities that . . . in spite of being banned the organization can still mount a well-coordinated and sophisticated publicity coup. In a wider sense, the pamphlets are a general reminder not just to the police but to South Africans as a whole that the nationalists still function. They will encourage Africans and alarm whites . . . Once a movement is underground, no white can be sure what the Africans are doing. Are they really passive or are they waiting and growing stronger? Yesterday's propaganda leaflets are meant to develop this psychological waiting game.

The first half of the 1970s saw so many developments that one can only highlight the most significant. The simmering discontent among black, colored, and Indian workers over the burdens they bore for the phenomenal growth of the South African economy after Sharpeville broke into open revolt. First came the great Ovambo strike in South-West Africa (Namibia). By 1973 strikes by black workers—illegal acts—had become a serious issue in all the major cities of South Africa. Toward the end of 1972 Durban became the experimental field for the heroic deeds of the masses: a wave of strikes began in the city and spread to most industries in the province. Nearly a hundred thousand workers in various occupations downed their tools in an effort to increase their starvation wages and ameliorate their appallingly poor working conditions. The militancy of the workers fitted the developing mold of black consciousness and the gathering momentum of a generalized upsurge that was evident throughout the country. The Africans' strikes exposed the low level of wages paid not only by South African capitalists but by foreigners as well. As a result of these strikes, international and local capitalists began to argue the need for higher wages to increase the Africans' spending power and to stem discontent.[28]

As a result of worldwide inflation, the South African economy was bogging down in a quagmire of recession; low industrial productivity was causing concern. In 1971, for instance, the volume of industrial production index showed virtually no increase over that of 1970, although total hours worked by production workers increased by 2 percent, fixed investment by the private manufacturing sector advanced 34 percent, and the average level of salaries and wages rose by 10.1 percent. This classic recipe for inflation produced its expected result: unemployment among white males more than doubled between May 1971 and May 1972; while that among colored and Asian workers increased by 46.5 percent and 20.5 percent, respectively.[29]

The spiral of inflation ensured a continuing incidence of strikes—by the end of 1974 there had been over three hundred illegal strikes since the start of the strike wave in 1972. But as unemployment mounted, the scale of industrial action fell sharply; in 1974 only half as many work hours were lost to strikes as in 1973, and in 1975 the number fell to under a tenth of the 1973 total.

The strike wave revealed more than just economic conditions. If anything, the short-term and partial satisfaction of economic demands merely focused workers' resentment on the wider conditions of life. This was particularly true in the gold mines, which had been free of strikes since 1946.[30] In September 1973 twelve miners were shot and killed after a brief strike. Despite wage concessions and strong repressive measures, more than two hundred strikes were registered in the next three years. The mining compounds were increasingly engulfed in a wave of diffuse violence and unrest, wildcat strikes, and "tribal fighting." The *Johannesburg Star* of January 18, 1973, stated: "The grim totals for the past five months read like an indictment: 37,000 striking miners, 22 fatalities and more than 160 other casualties in 16 strikes and disturbances." This comment was occasioned by the strike at the Val Reefs, one of the largest gold mines in the world, of twelve thousand African miners. This action was quickly followed by a strike of over five hundred coal miners at the Belsbok and New Largo collieries.

The upsurge of "spontaneous" strikes was a potent development in a country where the proletariat had absolutely no political rights and extremely weak organizations, where the masses of the people had a low standard of education, where extreme brutality on the part of the regime was the accepted norm, and where the population was fragmented along language, color, and ethnic lines. The idea of the mass strike had become a reality in the 1970s.

Soweto and After

The sudden end in April 1974 to four centuries of Portuguese colonialism in Africa opened a remarkable chapter in Southern Africa's history. It threw into complete disarray the alliance of repression formed against African people by the white regimes and their imperialist supporters. The stage was thus set for one of the greatest confrontations against the last vestiges of colonial and white rule. The significance of the defeats suffered by Portugal and its allies was not lost to the policymakers in South Africa. To stabilize the situation in its favor, the South African regime of B. J. Vorster began an initiative to settle the Rhodesian and Namibian issues by negotiation and also launched a pre-emptive strike on Angola, where its forces suffered ignominious defeat. Mozambique and Angola, which under Portuguese rule had acted as buffers, protecting South Africa from guerrilla incursions, became bases from which armed struggle for the liberation of Namibia and Zimbabwe have been launched.

While the world was still trying to digest the long-range implications of the triumph of FRELIMO and MPLA, the student rebellion began in Soweto on June 16, 1976. The Soweto uprising heralded a new phase in the African struggle in South Africa. Not an isolated event, it marked the start of new popular upsurge.

What happened at Soweto? The uprising began with a student protest against being taught in Afrikaans, and led eventually to the closing of all schools. Within a few weeks the student struggle had escalated into the largest resistance movement in South

Africa since Sharpeville. By August the struggle had assumed the proportions of a national crisis through simultaneous uprisings by colored and Indian students, large sectors of black workers, and sympathetic demonstrations by white students in English universities. This sudden general rising of the oppressed masses under the powerful impetus of the Soweto events became a political act and a general declaration of war on white rule.

From the beginning, the ANC underground and its allies vigorously supported the students' struggles. To diffuse the escalating uprising, the government first unleashed savage carnage and then offered concessions to the students, including dropping Afrikaans as a medium of instruction and giving urban Africans a thirty-year lease on their homes, a term that has since been extended to ninety-nine years. Coming from a regime as intransigent as Vorster's, these concessions showed the disarray in the governing circles. But the students rejected the government's offer. Abolition of apartheid and equality in all areas of life had become the slogan that mobilized the students and the African working class.

The uprising spread quickly to all the major urban areas of South Africa. On August 11 it broke out in townships around Cape Town, and on August 17 in Port Elizabeth, with devastating results. On August 30 students battled the police in the center of Cape Town, and tear gas fumes sent crying shoppers scrambling for safety. On September 23 students, following the Cape coloreds, staged a demonstration in the center of Johannesburg.

The wave of arson, sabotage, and shooting continued into 1977, with the press reporting bombings of white-owned property, the shooting of police in cities, the ambushing of police vehicles in the country, the arrests of black guerrillas with arms, the alleged discovery of weapons caches, and the shooting of informers. Meanwhile, hundreds, perhaps thousands, of students, realizing that they lacked arms and training to carry on and deepen the struggle, began to cross the borders to Swaziland, Mozambique, and Botswana, where ANC reception stations had been set up to receive them for training. When the first anniversary of the Soweto uprising was celebrated, the under-

ground movement escalated the systematic campaign of sabotage.

The continuing revolutionary upsurge and the deepening
economic crisis compelled the government in September 1977 to
ban *World*, a newspaper, and eighteen African organizations
associated with the black consciousness movement. It arrested
hundreds of Africans, and Steve Biko, the founder of the black
consciousness movement, died in police custody. He was the
twenty-third political detainee to die in the apartheid regime's
jails since March 1976.

The news of Biko's death evoked shock and indignation
throughout the world. The *New York Times* correspondent
wrote from Johannesburg on September 18:

> A week after the event, it is clear that the death of Steven Biko has
> shaken South Africa more than any single event since the police
> opened fire at Sharpeville in 1960 killing seventy-two black dem-
> onstrators.

Meanwhile, in the midst of the worst political crisis the country
had seen since Sharpeville, the crisis in Namibia was worsening.
More than fifty thousand South African troops were waging a
war which was taking an increasingly heavy toll. At the same
time news of a kind of guerrilla war inside South Africa was
slowly beginning to appear in the local press. The police, according to reports, were engaged in running gun battles with members of the ANC in the eastern Transvaal near Mozambique and
in northern Zululand. On May 4, 1978, the London *Times* reported:

> The prospect that SA may be experiencing the first throes of a
> Rhodesian-style guerrilla campaign has been raised by a wave of
> arrests of heavily-armed infiltrators and the discovery of some
> large arms caches. The Durban security police said yesterday that
> they had captured an unspecified number of terrorists, some of
> whom were armed with Soviet-made AK47 rifles and explosives.
> They had also discovered quantities of ammunition, arms and
> explosives hidden in suburban areas of Durban and other parts of
> Natal . . . the insurgents are said to belong to the military wing of
> the banned ANC, known as Umkhonto We Sizwe. . . . The police

326 BernardBernard Magubane

have deployed anti-insurgency units along vast stretches of the country's borders with Swaziland, Mozambique and Botswana.

The Economic Crisis

The outbreak of the student rebellion, coming on top of the labor strikes, deepened the economic crisis. The London *Financial Times* of June 19, 1976, lamented: "The wave of strikes which has swept through the South African township of Soweto . . . is a sorry event . . . it has come at a time when the London market in South African shares was showing signs that it had almost recovered from the severe body blow it was dealt earlier this year by the events in Angola."

Between May 1976 and May 1977, according to the Bureau for Economic Research at the University of South Africa, South Africa's factories slashed their labor force by more than 136,000 workers—a cutback of one in every ten jobs through shutdowns and redundancies. This cutback meant that total employment in the manufacturing industries dropped from 1.37 million to 1.25 million. In the same period more than 22 percent of the production capacity was idle. In addition, employers were forced to cut back working hours an average of 7 percent. The drop in jobs by racial categories was as follows: blacks 59,700, or 7.9 percent; whites 27,000, or 9.3 percent; coloreds 19,700, or 8.7 percent; Indians 11,400, or 13.5 percent (*Johannesburg Star*, May 7, 1977).

Between April 1975 and June 1976, government spending was up $725 million over the preceding year. Twenty-four percent of the increase was due to defense expenditures and 23 percent went to service the normal debt. The decline in the price of gold, from a high of $180 million to around $137 million, meant a tremendous loss of revenues. With unemployment among Africans running at over two million, the situation looked bleak indeed. Chase Manhattan Bank analyst Joel Stein commented, "These debts have placed unusual pressure on the government to resolve the crisis of deficit spending. The result is a stagnating economy that grew seven percent in 1974, two percent in 1975 and none at all last year [1976]."

Another indication of Southern Africa's economic problems is that it was declared a credit risk. The University of Delaware downgraded South Africa to nineteenth place, behind Iran and just ahead of Venezuela and Brazil, in its 1976 worldwide Business Environmental Risk Index. According to *Business Week* of February 14, 1977:

> What worries businessmen is a faltering South African economy and, more disturbing still, the potential for continuing racial conflict in a country where 4 million control over 18 million non-whites. Rioting last year in Soweto—the segregated city of 1 million blacks near Johannesburg—and other urban areas may be only the beginning of a prolonged period of racial tensions. The outburst virtually halted new investments by U.S. companies which already have a $1.5 billion stake in 300 corporate affiliates in South Africa.
>
> The result has been to deepen and prolong South Africa's first recession in 30 years. Gross national product, which increased at an average of 6.4 percent annually from 1959 through 1973, grew less than 2 percent last year as the government of Prime Minister Vorster squeezed the economy to get inflation and a $2 billion balance-of-payments deficit under control. Among the casualties of the slump, which slashed into sales, is Chrysler Corporation, which merged its ailing South African operation last year with a subsidy of the Anglo-American Corporation of South Africa.

The 1977–1978 budget showed even more dramatically Southern Africa's economic plight. For the first time in recent years the government recognized it cannot count on inflows of foreign capital. To meet the 21 percent rise in the defense budget it was necessary to introduce a lottery on "defense" bonds, which outraged Afrikaner churchmen. There were many other indications of the economic crisis faced by the South African regime. Suffice to say, with falling gold prices and heightened black resistance, South Africa is under tremendous pressure. It is hard to imagine where it would be right now without borrowed funds and diplomatic and moral support from its imperialist backers. The *Financial Mail* of July 2, 1976, put it very well:

> The economic implications of the recent riots are going to depend chiefly on the reaction of overseas investors. Without substantial

foreign money—at least R1,000 million a year—South Africa cannot finance its traditional current account deficits. . . .

If the Soweto events had as their cause the worsening plight of the South African economy, the events themselves were a major influence on its downward drift. The continuing revolutionary upsurge and the economic crisis has posed the greatest threat South Africa has faced since Sharpeville. The question is being raised about South Africa's future political stability. The problem facing South Africa was put starkly in the London *Financial Times* of January 24, 1978:

> There is still money to be made [in South Africa]: but the really tempting opportunities are few and far between, and the medium-term outlook is heavily clouded . . . It follows that a prudent British Government would even now be thinking about how to encourage the orderly disengagement of our economy from theirs. . . .
>
> That South Africa has become a poor political risk should be plain to all who take even the slightest notice of events out there. The outlook over the next few years must surely be for an increase in civil disturbances, a gradual increment in the number of acts of violence against the State and a continuation of the policy of repression. . . . The stability that has attracted some investors to the Republic in the past is undoubtedly being eroded, and the pace of that erosion must surely increase . . . for the medium term, we need a special study of officials of the advantages and disadvantages of a policy of deliberate switching of British investments out of the Republic. It is not a simple subject, and a serious study would take both time and the services of people of rare ability. But the more one considers the facts, the more it becomes apparent that it is in our own best self-interest that such a process be started as soon as possible. The bad risk is likely to grow worse, not better.

Quite obviously the present economic situation in South Africa is so unique that it can without doubt be called unprecedented. It displays many novel features—like the coexistence of severe unemployment and inflation. This situation is a reflection of the continuing economic recession in the capitalist world. Retarded growth, rising unemployment, increasing amount of idle productive capacity, reduced investor confidence, South

Africa's continued involvement in the Namibian war, and increased guerrilla activity inside the country—all these developments acting in concert will cause further effects and enhance revolutionary possibilities.

In the previous pages we have studied the contradictions that plague the South African political economy. In recent years these economic and political contradictions have acquired an appropriate political expression and are refracted in relations between classes and in their political demands. Though the Africans, coloreds, and Indians do not represent a homogeneous class, the interests and goals of the various groupings since the 1950s, and in particular since Soweto, have merged on the basis of a common lack of political and economic rights in opposition to white supremacist rule and capitalist exploitation. Neither Africans, coloreds, nor Indians are prepared to remain reconciled to exploitation, white rule, and racially defined patterns of life. The existing political and social structure is incompatible with the interests of large sections of the country's population and is also a hindrance to the full utilization of the country's economic potential.

For more than eighty years South Africa was able to link the whole of Southern Africa south of the twenty-second parallel into a single economic subsystem. The independence struggles in these areas extended the social basis of the struggle against white capitalist rule. Thus, the struggle against South Africa involves a whole series of class and national struggles. As one country after another achieved independence and dropped out of South Africa's hegemonic economic and political dominance, conditions were being created which facilitated the struggle within South Africa itself. The victory of the peoples of Mozambique and Angola and the impending victory of the people of Zimbabwe and Namibia have produced a general crisis of monumental proportions in the South African political economy.

All these developments continue to favor the revolutionary forces within South Africa. An acute contradiction has been developing between the expansionist aspirations of the monopoly bourgeoisie, which spring from the very nature of the capitalist economy, and the possibilities of sabotaging these aspirations with the emergence of socialist states on South Africa's periphery.

The struggle against oppression and exploitation in South Africa is a long, continuous social process. It is a struggle that has many fronts. Thus, the strike period that began in 1972 became a prologue to an endless series of ever spreading economic struggles. The political agitation of the late 1960s and early 1970s was a counterpart to the economic struggles, and external events complemented the internal developments in a classic fashion. Soweto and its aftermath destroyed the illusion of stability in South Africa. The imperialist backers of the regime no longer see it as a formidable and granite-like fortress that can endure. The social, economic, and political forces that helped to entrench a white supremacist capitalist structure have placed the South African ruling class and its imperialist allies in a straitjacket from which they cannot extricate themselves. Since the struggles of the African people arise from the vices of white capitalist rule, and since these vices in turn arise from the incurable defects in the social structure, no reform will do. The struggle, wrote Marx of the Paris Commune in one of the greatest of political eulogies, "cannot be stamped out with any amount of carnage. To stamp it out, governments would have to stamp out the despotism of capital over labor—the condition of their own parasitical existence."[31]

Notes

Notes to Chapter 1

1. United Nations Unit on Apartheid, *Facts and Figures on South Africa,* Publication No. 16/72 (August 1972), p. 29.
2. Cited in Julian R. Friedman, "Basic Facts on the Republic of South Africa and the Policy of Apartheid," *Objective: Justice* (United Nations Office of Public Information), Winter 1977–78, p. 33.
3. See Gail Omvedt, "Towards a Theory of Colonialism," *Insurgent Sociologist* 3, no. 3 (Spring 1973): 1.
4. Harry Magdoff, "Imperialism Without Colonies," in *Studies in the Theory of Imperialism,* ed. Roger Owen and Bob Sutcliffe (London: Longman, 1972), p. 145.
5. Louis Ruchames, *Racial Thought in America: From the Puritans to Abraham Lincoln* (New York: Grosset and Dunlap, 1970), p. 3.
6. Ibid., p. 4.
7. Quoted in H. J. M. Hubbard, *Race and Guyana: The Anatomy of a Colonial Enterprise* (Georgetown, Guyana, 1968), p. 7.
8. Ruchames, *Racial Thought in America,* p. 4.
9. W. E. B. DuBois, *The Negro* (New York: Oxford University Press, 1970), pp. 139–40.
10. W. E. B. DuBois, *Black Reconstruction in America* (New York: World Publishing, 1962), pp. 15–16.
11. C. Wright Mills, *The Sociological Imagination* (New York: Oxford University Press, 1959), p. 146.
12. Karl Marx, *The Grundrisse* (New York: Harper & Row, 1971), p. 29.
13. J. A. Hobson, *Imperialism* (Ann Arbor: University of Michigan Press, 1965), p. 258.

14. E. J. Hobsbawm, *Industry and Empire: The Making of English Society* (New York: Random House, 1966), p. 112.

15. Cited in J. A. Hobson, *The War in South Africa: Its Causes and Effects* (New York: Macmillan, 1900), p. 234.

16. J. C. Smuts, *Selections from the Smuts Papers,* 4 vols., ed. W. K. Hancock and Jean Van Der Poel (Cambridge: The University Press, 1966), 2:337.

17. Perry Anderson, "The Origins of the Present Crisis," *New Left Review* (January-February 1964): 40.

18. The speech was published in full in the *Cape Times* of March 3, 1909.

19. V. I. Lenin, *Imperialism: The Highest Stage of Capitalism* (Moscow: Foreign Languages Press, 1969), pp. 93–94.

20. Karl Liebknecht, *Militarism and Anti-Militarism* (New York: Dover Publications, 1972), pp. 2–3; emphasis added.

21. J. C. Smuts, *Jan Christian Smuts* (London: Cassel & Co., 1952), p. 303.

22. Kwame Nkrumah, *Class Struggle in Africa* (New York: International Publishers, 1975), p. 27.

23. W. E. B. DuBois, *The World and Africa* (New York: International Publishers, 1965), p. 56.

Notes to Chapter 2

1. Ernest Mandel, *Marxist Economic Theory,* 2 vols. (New York: Monthly Review Press, 1968), 2:433.

2. Monica Wilson and Leonard Thompson, eds., *The Oxford History of South Africa* (New York: Oxford University Press), vol. 1, *South Africa to 1870* (1969), p. 49.

3. Ibid., p. 68.

4. Walter Rodney, *How Europe Underdeveloped Africa* (London: Bogle L'Ouverture Publications, 1972), p. 141.

5. See Amilcar Cabral, *Revolution in Guinea: An African People's Struggle* (New York: Monthly Review Press, 1969), p. 80.

6. Quoted in Leonard Thompson, "The South African Dilemma," in *The Founding of New Societies,* ed. Louis Hartz (New York: Harcourt Brace Jovanovich, 1964), p. 182.

7. Ibid.

8. Jan Van Riebeeck, *Journal of Jan Van Riebeeck,* 3 vols., ed. H. B. Thom (Cape Town: A. A. Balkana, 1952–1958), vol. 1, *1651–1655* (1952), p. 112.

9. Cf. Thomas Farrell Buxton, *Memoirs of Sir Thomas Farrell Buxton,* ed. Charles Buxton (London: John Murray, 1866), p. 217.

10. Van Riebeeck, *Journal,* vol. 3, *1659–1661* (1958), p. 196.

11. Ibid.

12. Ibid.

13. Sir John Barrow, *Travels in the Interior of South Africa,* 2 vols. (London: T. Cadell and W. Davis, 1801), 1:17.

14. Buxton, *Memoirs,* pp. 218–19.

15. Raymond Williams, *The Country and the City* (New York: Oxford University Press, 1973), p. 37.

16. Barrow, *Travels,* pp. 94–95.

17. Quoted in H. Lawson, "Cape Society in the Eighteenth Century," *Liberation,* no. 17 (March 1956): 16.

18. See Wilson and Thompson, eds., *Oxford History,* p. 196.

19. Ibid., pp. 196–97.

20. James Bryce, *Impressions of South Africa* (1897; reprint ed., New York: New American Library, 1969), pp. 104–5.

21. C. W. DeKiewiet, *A History of South Africa: Social and Economic* (Cape Town: Oxford University Press, 1966), p. 58.

22. Darcy Ribeiro, "The Cultural-Historical Configurations of the American Peoples," *Current Anthropology* 4–5 (October–December 1970): 402–34.

23. H. Lawson, "Cape Society," p. 16.

24. Karl Marx and Frederick Engels, *On Britain* (Moscow: Foreign Languages Publishing House, 1962), pp. 387–88.

25. Oscar Handlin, *Race and Nationality in American Life* (Garden City, N.Y.: Doubleday & Co., 1957), pp. 4–5.

26. William and Lily Ries, *The Life and Times of Sir George Grey* (London: Hutchinson & Co., 1892), 1:356.

27. Quoted in Sir George E. Cory, *The Rise of South Africa: A History of the Origin of South African Colonization and of its Development Toward the East from the Earliest Times to 1857* (New York: Longman's, Green & Co., 1930), p. 3.

28. Ibid., p. 4.

29. Ibid.

30. Ibid., p. 108.

31. Ibid., pp. 388–89.

32. W. M. McMillan, *Bantu, Boer and Briton: The Making of the South African Native Problem* (Oxford: Clarendon Press, 1963), pp. 300–1.

33. Ibid., p. 337.

34. Quoted in J. Rutherford, *Sir George Grey: A Study in Colonial Government* (London: Cassell, 1961), p. 384.

35. Ibid.

36. Ibid.

37. Ibid., p. 385.

38. Ibid.

39. Further Papers Relative to the Cape of Good Hope, vol. 10, no. 6 (session 2202): 187.

40. Ibid., 42:185–86.

41. Wilson and Thompson, eds., *Oxford History,* 1:252.

42. Ibid., p. 11.

43. DeKiewiet, *South Africa: Social and Economic,* pp. 53–54.

44. Bryce, *Impressions,* p. 124.

45. Quoted in McMillan, *Bantu, Boer and Briton,* p. 41.

46. See Sheila T. Van der Horst, *Native Labour in South Africa* (London: Frank Cass and Co., 1971), p. 20.

47. A. Lerumo, *Fifty Fighting Years: The Communist Party of South Africa, 1921–1971* (London: Inkululeko Publications, 1971), pp. 24–26.

48. Quoted in G. B. Pyrah, *Imperial Policy and South Africa, 1902–1910* (London: Oxford University Press, 1955), pp. 38–39.

49. H. J. and Ray Simons, *Class and Colour in South Africa, 1850–1950* (Baltimore: Penguin Books, 1969), p. 65.

50. George M. Theal, *History of South Africa,* 11 vols. (Cape Town: G. Struik, 1964), 10:347–56.

51. Rodney, *How Europe Underdeveloped Africa,* p. 235.

52. Quoted in Theal, *History of South Africa,* 10:347–50.

53. Quoted in Pyrah, *Imperial Policy,* p. 79.

54. Karl Marx, *Grundrisse* (New York: Harper & Row, 1971), p. 31.

55. Karl Marx, *Selected Works* (Moscow: Progress Publishers, 1969), 2:288.

56. J. C. Smuts, Jr., *Jan Christian Smuts: A Biography* (New York: Morrow Publishing Co., 1952), p. 306.

57. See Barrington Moore, *Social Origins of Dictatorship and Democracy* (Boston: Beacon Press, 1966), p. 437.

58. Wilson and Thompson, eds., *Oxford History,* 2:364.

Notes to Chapter 3

1. See Bernard Magubane, "A Critical Look at Indices Used in the Study of Social Change in Colonial Africa," *Current Anthropology* (1971):422.
2. W. M. McMillan, *Bantu, Boer and Briton: The Making of the South African Native Problem* (Oxford: Clarendon Press, 1963), pp. 300–1.
3. Louis B. Wright, *Religion and Empire, The Alliance Between Piety and Commerce in English Expansion 1558–1625* (New York: Octagon Books, 1965), p. 151.
4. Perry Anderson, "Portugal and the End of Ultra Colonialism," part 2. *New Left Review* 16 (1962): 102–3.
5. John Philips, *Researches in South Africa,* 2 vols. (London: J. Duncan, 1828), 2:227.
6. Frantz Fanon, *The Wretched of the Earth* (New York: Grove Press, 1968), p. 42.
7. Ibid., p. 53.
8. See Sheila T. Van der Horst, *Native Labour in South Africa* (London: Frank Cass and Co., 1971), p. 20.
9. George M. Theal, ed., *Records of the Cape Colony,* 36 vols. (London: Public Records Office, 1898), 3:113–14.
10. Quoted in H. Lawson, "The Role of Capitalism in South African History: The Destruction of Tribal Society," *Liberation,* no. 21 (September 1956): 19.
11. Quoted in ibid., p. 21.
12. Quoted in H. J. Simons, *African Women: Their Legal Status in South Africa* (Evanston, Ill.: Northwestern University Press, 1968), p. 22.
13. Both quoted in ibid., p. 23.
14. Quoted in Van der Horst, *Native Labour,* p. 17.
15. Norman Etherington, "African Economic Experiments in Colonial Natal, 1845–1880," *African Economic History* (Spring 1978): 1.
16. J. C. Smuts, *Selections from the Smuts Papers,* 4 vols., ed. W. K. Hancock and Jean Van Der Poel (Cambridge: The University Press, 1966), 2:338.
17. Thomas Farrell Buxton, *The African Slave Trade and Its Remedy* (London: John Murray, 1840), p. 323.
18. Ibid., p. 164.
19. Thomas Farrell Buxton, *Memoirs of Thomas Farrell Buxton,* ed. Charles Buxton (London: John Murray, 1866), p. 462.
20. Ibid., p. 223.

21. Ibid.
22. Darcy Ribeiro, *The Americas and Civilization* (New York: E. P. Dutton, 1972), p. 38.
23. Fanon, *Wretched of the Earth,* pp. 41–42.
24. Ribeiro, *The Americas and Civilization,* p. 74.
25. Jean-Paul Sartre, "On Genocide," *Ramparts* 6 (1968):38.
26. See Renate Zahar, *Frantz Fanon: Colonialism and Alienation* (New York: Monthly Review Press, 1974), p. 43.
27. Daniel P. Kunene, "Deculturation—The African Writer's Response," *Africa Today* 15, no. 4 (August–September 1968).
28. F. Meli, "A Nation Is Born: Foundation of the African National Congress: 8 January 1912," *African Communist,* no. 48 (first quarter 1972): 19.
29. Max Horkheimer, quoted in Zahar, *Frantz Fanon.*
30. Frantz Fanon, *Toward an African Revolution* (New York: Monthly Review Press, 1967), p. 34.
31. Ibid.

Notes to Chapter 4

1. Karl Marx, *Capital* (London: Everyman's Edition, 1957), 1: 850.
2. Ibid., pp. 848–49.
3. Sheila T. Van der Horst, *Native Labour in South Africa* (London: Frank Cass and Co., 1971), p. 16.
4. Ibid., p. 17.
5. Ibid., p. 25.
6. Quoted in P. S. Joshi, *The Tyranny of Colour: A Study of the Indian Problem in South Africa* (1942; reprint ed., Port Washington, N.Y.: Kennikat Press, 1973), p. 100.
7. District of Natal, *Report of the Natal Native Commission 1852–1853,* part 1, p. 55.
8. Ibid., part 5, p. 75.
9. Ibid.
10. Ibid., p. 18.
11. James Bryce, *Impressions of South Africa* (1897; reprint ed., New York: New American Library, 1969), p. 23.
12. Van der Horst, *Native Labour,* p. 61.
13. Ibid., p. 118.
14. Quoted in A. Hepple, *South Africa: A Political and Economic History* (New York: Frederick A. Praeger, 1966), p. 197.

15. H. J. and Ray Simons, *Class and Colour in South Africa, 1850–1950* (Baltimore: Penguin Books, 1969), p. 81.
16. Van der Horst, *Native Labour,* p. 168.
17. Ibid.
18. Basil Davidson, *Report on South Africa* (London: Jonathan Cape, 1952), p. 93.
19. Cape Province, *Report of the South African Native Affairs Commission 1903–1905* (Cape Town: Cape Printers), p. iii.
20. Solomon Plaatje, *Native Life in South Africa: Before and Since the European War and the Boer Rebellion* (London: King, 1916), p. 17.
21. Quoted in Monica Wilson and Leonard Thompson, eds., *The Oxford History of South Africa,* vol. 1 (New York: Oxford University Press, 1971), pp. 130–31.
22. C. W. DeKiewiet, *A History of South Africa: Social and Economic* (Cape Town: Oxford University Press, 1966), pp. 180–81.
23. South Africa, *Report of the Transvaal Local Government Commission 1922* (Stallard Commission) (T.P.T.), p. 22.
24. Edgar M. Brookes, *The History of Native Policy in South Africa* (Pretoria: J. L. Schack, 1927), pp. 137–38.
25. DeKiewiet, *South Africa: Social and Economic,* pp. 239–40.
26. See R. W. Johnson, *How Long Will South Africa Survive?* (London: Macmillan, 1977), p. 176.
27. Ibid., p. 27.
28. Stephen Castles and Godula Kosack, "Common Market Migrants," *New Left Review,* no. 73 (May–June 1972): 3–22.
29. D. Hobart Houghton, "Economic Development, 1865–1965," in Wilson and Thompson, *Oxford History,* vol. 2, p. 13.
30. Johnson, *How Long?,* p. 182.
31. Rosa Luxemburg, *The Accumulation of Capital* (New York: Monthly Review Press, 1965), p. 363.
32. Karl Marx, *Precapitalist Economic Formations* (New York: International Publishers, 1965), p. 105.
33. V. I. Lenin, *The Development of Capitalism in Russia* (Moscow: Progress Publishers, 1960), p. 176.
34. Frederick Engels, *The Housing Question* (New York: International Publishers, 1960), pp. 13–17.
35. Maurice Dobb, *Studies in the Development of Capitalism* (New York: International Publishers, 1963), p. 275.
36. Ibid., p. 233.
37. A. Hepple, *South Africa,* pp. 204–5.
38. See Jack Woodis, *Africa: Roots of Revolt* (London: Lawrence and Wishart, 1960), p. 82.

39. Charles Bettelheim, "Theoretical Comment," in A. Emmanuel, *Unequal Exchange: A Study of the Imperialism of Trade* (London: New Left Books, 1972), p. 301.
40. Quoted in Martin Legassick, "Ideology and Social Structure in Twentieth-Century South Africa" (M.S. thesis, University of London, 1972).
41. S. Trapido, "South Africa in a Comparative Study in Industrialization" in *Collected Seminar Papers on the Societies of Southern Africa in the Nineteenth and Twentieth Centuries* (London: University of London, Institute of Commonwealth Studies, October 1970–June 1971), 2:59–60.
42. Johnson, *How Long?*, p. 182.
43. Ibid., p. 68.

Notes to Chapter 5

1. Karl Marx, *The German Ideology*, ed. C. J. Arthur (New York: International Publishers, 1970), p. 146.
2. Quoted in D. Hobart Houghton, *The South African Economy* (Capetown: Oxford University Press, 1967), p. 136.
3. "Editorial," *Africa Today* 17, no. 5 (1970): 5.
4. See Theodore Gregory, *Ernest Oppenheimer and the Economic Development of Southern Africa* (New York: Oxford University Press, 1962), p. 77.
5. Timothy Green, *The World of Gold* (New York: Walker and Co., 1968), p. 58.
6. John A. Hobson, *The Evolution of Modern Capitalism*, 4th ed. (1894; reprint ed. London: George Allen and Unwin, 1926), p. 267.
7. Gregory, *Ernest Oppenheimer*, p. 496.
8. Quoted in Michael Williams, "An Analysis of South African Capitalism—Neo-Ricardianism or Marxism," *Bulletin of the Conference of Socialist Economists* 4, no. 1 (1975): 9.
9. Ralph Horwitz, *The Political Economy of South Africa* (New York: Frederick A. Praeger, 1967), pp. 8–9.
10. Quoted in ibid., p. 238.
11. Quoted in Williams, "South African Capitalism," p. 10.
12. Basil Davidson, *Report on South Africa* (London: Jonathan Cape, 1952), p. 95.
13. G. Fasulo, "Net Capitalism and the South African Mining Industry," *Liberation*, no. 39 (December 1959): 19.

14. Quoted in ibid., p. 38.
15. Green, *World of Gold,* p. 58.
16. R. W. Johnson, *How Long Will South Africa Survive?* (London: Macmillan, 1977), p. 183.
17. Green, *World of Gold,* p. 48.
18. Houghton, *South African Economy,* pp. 104–5.
19. A. Bakaya, "World Capitalism, Gold and South Africa," *The African Communist,* no. 50 (1972): 86.
20. John Burger, *The Black Man's Burden* (London: Victor Gollancz, 1943), p. 28.
21. Orlando Patterson, *The Sociology of Slavery: An Analysis of the Origins, Development and Structure of Negro Slave Society in Jamaica* (London: MacGibbon and Kee, 1967), p. 9.
22. Quoted in Frederick Engels, *On Capital* (New York: International Publishers, 1937), p. 27.
23. Quoted in the *New York Times,* October 23, 1973.
24. Francis Wilson, *Labour in the South African Gold Mines 1936–1969* (Cambridge: The University Press, 1972), p. 13.
25. V. I. Lenin, *Selected Works* (Moscow: Foreign Languages Publishing House, 1968), pp. 656–57.

Notes to Chapter 6

1. Karl Marx and Frederick Engels, *Selected Works* (Moscow: Progress Publishers, 1969), 1:9.
2. A. Lerumo, *Fifty Years of Fighting: The Communist Party of South Africa, 1921–1971* (London: Inkululeko Publications, 1971), p. 55.
3. Quoted in David Welsh, "The Growth of Towns," in *The Oxford History of South Africa,* eds., Monica Wilson and Leonard Thompson (New York: Oxford University Press, 1971), vol. 2, *South Africa 1870–1966,* p. 186.
4. Martin Legassick and David Hemson, "Foreign Investment and the Reproduction of Racial Capitalism in South Africa," *Foreign Investment in South Africa: A Discussion Series,* Anti-Apartheid Movement, no. 2 (London, September 1976), p. 4.
5. Cf. H. J. and R. E. Simons, *Class and Colour in South Africa, 1850–1950* (Baltimore: Penguin Books, 1969), p. 220.
6. J. Merriman to Bryce, May 10, 1917, *Merriman Papers IV,* British Museum, p. 295.

7. See also Simons and Simons, *Class and Colour,* p. 220; and Ralph Horwitz, *The Political Economy of South Africa* (New York: Frederick A. Praeger, 1967), p. 92.

8. South Africa, *Report of the Transvaal Local Government Commission 1922* (Stallard Commission) (T.P.T.), p. 22.

9. H. J. Simons, *African Women: Their Legal Status* (Evanston, Ill.: Northwestern University Press, 1968), p. 281.

10. South Africa, *Report of the Native Laws Commission 1946–1948 (The Fagan Report)* (U.G. no. 28), 1948, p. 4.

11. Quoted in Martin Legassick, "Ideology and Social Structure in Twentieth-Century South Africa" (M.S. thesis, University of London, 1972).

12. Quoted in Welsh, "Growth of Towns," p. 205.

13. See also Simons and Simons, *Class and Colour,* p. 547.

14. Colin Bundy, quoted in Bernard Magubane, *The Continuing Class Struggle in South Africa,* University of Denver Studies in Race and Nations, no. 6 (Denver, 1976), p. 27.

15. South Africa, Social and Economic Planning Council, *Native Reserves and Their Place in the South African Economy* (U.G. no. 32), 1946.

16. South Africa, *First Interim Report of the Board of Trade and Industries* (B6116/215/45), 1945, p. 139.

17. South Africa, *The Fagan Report,* p. 125.

18. Ibid., p. 13.

19. Ibid., p. 17.

20. Ibid., p. 19.

21. Ibid.

22. Ibid., p. 20.

23. Quoted in Robert Davis, et al., "Class Struggle and the Periodization of the State in South Africa," *Review of Political Economy,* no. 7 (September–December 1976): 26.

24. See Simons and Simons, *Class and Colour,* pp. 564–65.

25. Quoted in United Nations, Department of Political and Security Council Affairs, Center Against Apartheid, *Land Tenure Conditions in South Africa,* no. 37 (December 1976), p. 44.

26. Walter Sisulu, "The Extension of the Pass Laws," *Liberation,* no. 17 (March 1956): 12.

27. See H. J. Simons, "Passes and Police," *Africa South* 1, no. 1 (October–December 1956): 61–62.

28. Alpheus Hunton, *Decision in Africa* (New York: New World Paperbacks, 1956), p. 56.

29. See John Burger, *The Black Man's Burden* (London: Victor Gollancz, 1943), p. 79.
30. South Africa, *A Summary of the Report of the Commission for the Socio-economic Development of the Bantu Areas Within the Union of South Africa* (Pretoria, U.G.: The Government Printer, 1955), p. xviii.
31. Ibid., p. 102.
32. Ibid., p. 103.
33. Ibid., p. 104.
34. Ibid.
35. Ibid.
36. Ibid.
37. Quoted in Simons, "Passes and Police," p. 62.
38. Karl Marx and Frederick Engels, *On Britain* (Moscow: Foreign Languages Publishing House, 1962), pp. 155–56.
39. Karl Marx, *Capital* (New York: International Publishers, 1967), 1:593.
40. This section owes a great deal to U.N., Center Against Apartheid, *Land Tenure Conditions in South Africa,* pp. 46–51.
41. *Africa News: A Weekly Digest of African Affairs,* June 13, 1977, pp. 9–10.
42. Quoted in S. Osipov, *Sociology: The Problems of Theory and Method* (Moscow: Progress Publishers, 1969), p. 18.
43. Karl Marx and Frederick Engels, *On the Paris Commune* (Moscow: Progress Publishers, 1972), p. 160.
44. Cf. Kenneth A. Jordaan, "The Black Workers' Struggle in South Africa," *International Socialist Review* 35, no. 5 (May 1974): 28.
45. Quoted in Alex Hepple, *South Africa: Workers Under Apartheid* (London: A Defense Aid Pamphlet, 1969), p. 13.
46. Otto Rühle, *Karl Marx: His Life Work* (New York: The New Library, 1928), p. 327.
47. Albert Memmi, *The Colonizer and the Colonized* (Boston: Beacon Press, 1965), p. 54.

Notes to Chapter 7

1. See Nicholas Mensargh, *South Africa 1906–1961: The Price of Magnanimity* (New York: Frederick A. Praeger, 1962), p. 27.
2. Oliver C. Cox, *Caste, Class and Race: A Study in Social Dynamics* (New York: Doubleday and Co., 1948), pp. 154–55.

3. H. J. and R. E. Simons, *Class and Colour in South Africa, 1850–1950* (Baltimore: Penguin Books, 1969), p. 612.

4. See Amelia Marriot, "The Position of Women in South African Industry 1920–1970" (Ph.D. diss., University of Connecticut, Storrs, 1979).

5. Ibid.

6. Ibid.

7. H. Lawson, "The Economic Basis of Afrikaans Nationalism," *Liberation*, no. 27 (September 1957): 19.

8. Simons and Simons, *Class and Colour*, p. 612.

9. Quoted in T. Dunbar Moodie, *The Rise of Afrikanerdom: Power, Apartheid, and the Afrikaner Civil Religion* (Berkeley: University of California Press, 1975), pp. 131–32.

10. Simons and Simons, *Class and Colour*, pp. 517–18.

11. Ibid., p. 518.

12. Quoted in David Welsh, "The Growth of Towns," in *The Oxford History of South Africa*, eds. Monica Wilson and Leonard Thompson (New York: Oxford University Press, 1971), vol. 2, *South Africa, 1870–1966*, p. 184.

13. Herbert Tingsten, *The Problem of South Africa* (London: Victor Gollancz, 1953), p. 23.

14. See Robert Davies *et al.*, "Class Struggle and the Periodization of the State in South Africa," *Review of African Political Economy*, no. 7 (September–December 1976): 15.

15. See Brian Bunting, *The Rise of the South African Reich* (Baltimore: Penguin Books, 1969), p. 370.

16. Ibid., p. 374.

17. Quoted in ibid., p. 377.

18. Davies *et al.*, "Periodization of the State," p. 11.

19. E. P. Thompson, "An Open Letter to Leszek Kolakowski," *Socialist Register 1973* (London: The Merlin Press, 1974), p. 72.

20. Quoted in Moodie, *Rise of Afrikanerdom*, p. 203.

21. Quoted in Bunting, *South African Reich*, p. 378.

22. Ibid.

23. Ibid.

24. Ibid.

25. Ibid., p. 379.

26. Ibid., p. 381.

27. Quoted in ibid., pp. 383–84.

28. Quoted in ibid., p. 380.

29. Quoted in ibid., p. 389.

30. Ibid., pp. 389–90.
31. Quoted in ibid., p. 380.
32. Ibid., p. 391.
33. Quoted in ibid.
34. Quoted in ibid., p. 392.
35. Quoted in ibid.
36. Robert Davies, "The White Working Class in South Africa," *New Left Review* 82 (November–December 1973): 43–44.
37. Simons and Simons, *Class and Colour,* p. 32.
38. See Dan O'Meara, "Analysing Afrikaner Nationalism: The 'Christian-National' Assault on White Trade Unionism in South Africa, 1934–1948," *African Affairs* 77, no. 306 (January 1978): 50.
39. Simons and Simons, *Class and Colour,* p. 455.
40. Carnegie Commission, *Report on Poor Whites* (Stellenbosch: Pro Ecclesia, 1932), par. 1, pp. 99–100.
41. Ibid., par. 5, pp. 73–74.
42. See Edward Roux, *Time Longer Than Rope: A History of the Black Man's Struggle for Freedom in South Africa* (Madison: University of Wisconsin Press, 1966), pp. 272–73.
43. Quoted in Moodie, *Rise of Afrikanerdom,* p. 169.
44. Davies *et al.*, "Periodization of the State," p. 44.
45. Ibid., p. 156.
46. Simons and Simons, *Class and Colour,* p. 613.
47. Ralph Horwitz, *The Political Economy of South Africa* (New York: Frederick A. Praeger, 1967), p. 410.

Notes to Chapter 8

1. Eric J. Hobsbawm, *Industry and Empire: The Making of Modern English Society* (New York: Pantheon Books, 1968), vol. 2, *1750 to the Present Day,* p. 112.
2. See Ronald Robinson and John Gallagher, with Alice Denny, *Africa and the Victorians: The Climax of Imperialism* (Garden City, N.Y.: Doubleday and Co., 1968), p. 210.
3. Quoted in ibid., p. 432.
4. Theodore Gregory, *Ernest Oppenheimer and the Economic Development of South Africa* (New York: Oxford University Press, 1962), p. 85.
5. Ibid., pp. 86 and 89.
6. Ibid., p. 33.
7. Ibid., p. 84.

8. Ibid., p. 96.
9. Ibid., p. 97.
10. A. Stadnichenko, *Monetary Crisis of Capitalism* (Moscow: Progress Publishers, 1975), pp. 70–75.
11. Quoted in R. Pahne Dult, *The Crisis of Britain and the British Empire* (New York: International Publishers, 1953), p. 174.
12. *Time,* February 5, 1951.
13. Gregory, *Ernest Oppenheimer,* p. 37.
14. See United Nations, Department of Political and Security Council Affairs, Center Against Apartheid, *Activities of Transnational Corporations and their Collaboration with the Regime in South Africa* (72-13750), July 1977, pp. 10–11.
15. Quoted in *Muhammed Speaks,* August 11, 1972.
16. F. J. C. Cronje, "The Textile Industry in the Union of South Africa," *South African Journal of Economics* 20 (1952): 23–30.
17. *Business Week,* November 29, 1947.
18. Quoted in Martin Legassick and David Hemson, *Foreign Investment and the Reproduction of Racial Capitalism in South Africa* (London: The Anti-Apartheid Movement, 1976), p. 5.
19. The source of tables 1 to 5 is U.N., Department of Political and Security Council Affairs, Center Against Apartheid, *Activities of Transnational Corporations.*
20. D. Hobart Houghton, *The South African Economy* (Cape Town: Oxford University Press, 1963), p. 212.
21. Hartford *Courant,* October 27, 1977.
22. Ralph Horwitz, *The Political Economy of South Africa* (New York: Frederick A. Praeger, 1967), p. 328.
23. U.N., Department of Political and Security Council Affairs, Center Against Apartheid, *Activities of Transnational Corporations,* p. 5.
24. Ruth First, Jonathan Steele, and Christabel Gurney, *The South African Connection* (Middlesex, Eng.: Penguin Books, 1972), pp. 26–27.
25. U.N., Department of Political and Security Council Affairs, Center Against Apartheid, *Activities of Transnational Corporations,* p. 10.
26. Ibid.
27. Quoted in B. Magubane, "Apartheid, Kissinger and the Rebellion in South Africa," *African Youth* 1, nos. 5–6 (1976).
28. *New York Times,* October 23, 1977.
29. *The Wall Street Journal,* October 28, 1976.
30. Martin Legassick and William Burnett, "The United States and South Africa," mimeographed (Santa Barbara, Cal.: University of California, 1970).

31. Dult, *Crisis of Britain,* p. 174.
32. Peter Janke, "Southern Africa: New Horizons," *Conflict Studies* (August 1976): 16.
33. Reed Kramer, "In Hock to U.S. Banks," *The Nation,* December 11, 1976.
34. Hartford *Courant,* October 27, 1977.

Notes to Chapter 9

1. Raymond Williams, "Base and Superstructure," *New Left Review,* no. 82 (November–December 1973): 6.
2. Aristotle, *The Politics of Aristotle,* ed. and trans. Ernest Barker (New York: Oxford University Press, 1962), pp. 13–14.
3. Edward Gibbon, *The Decline and Fall of the Roman Empire* (New York: Dell Publishing Co., 1972), p. 44.
4. Raymond Betts, *Europe Overseas: Phases of Imperialism* (New York: Basic Books, 1968), p. 43.
5. C. L. R. James, "Colonialism and National Liberation in Africa: The Gold Coast Revolution," in *National Liberation,* ed. Norman Miller and Roderick Aya (New York: The Free Press, 1971), p. 104.
6. See Bernard Crick, *In Defence of Politics* (Chicago: University of Chicago Press, 1962), p. 84.
7. Quoted in Lorene Bennett, Jr., *The Shaping of Black America* (Chicago: Johnson Publications, 1975), p. 207.
8. Quoted in Vitalii Vygodoskii, *A Book for All Time: Centenary of Karl Marx's "Capital"* (Moscow: Novesti Press Agency, n.d.), p. 169.
9. See Frantz Fanon, *Towards an African Revolution* (New York: Monthly Review Press, 1957), p. 35.
10. Rosa Luxemburg, *The Accumulation of Capital* (New York: Monthly Review Press, 1951), p. 413.
11. Herbert Velakazi, "History, Racism, and Liberation," manuscript, 1974.
12. Luxemburg, *Accumulation of Capital,* p. 413.
13. Hannah Arendt, *The Origins of Totalitarianism* (New York: Meridian Books, 1962), pp. 199–200.
14. James Bryce, *Impressions of South Africa* (1897; reprint ed., New York: New American Library, 1969), p. 402.
15. Quoted in George Padmore, *Pan-Africanism or Communism?* (London: Dennis Dobson, 1956), p. 85.
16. Ibid.

17. Quoted in W. K. Hancock, *Smuts: The Field of Force* (Cambridge: The University Press, 1968), p. 475.
18. Paul A. Baran, "On the Nature of Marxism," *Monthly Review* 10, no. 7 (November 1958): 262.
19. Leo Kuper, *Passive Resistance in South Africa* (New Haven, Conn.: Yale University Press, 1960), p. 31.
20. Robert C. Tucker, ed., *The Marx-Engels Reader* (New York: W. W. Norton and Co., 1972), p. 15.
21. Louis Althusser, *Reading "Capital,"* trans. Ben Brewster (London: New Left Books, 1970), p. 142.
22. Keith Gottscholk, "Race and Economics in South Africa," *U-Fahamu* 1, no. 2 (Fall 1971): 17.
23. For a good discussion of this point, see Herbert Johnstone, "White Prosperity and White Supremacy in South Africa," *African Affairs* (April 1970).
24. V. I. Lenin, *Collected Works* (Moscow: Foreign Languages Publishing House, 1968), 1:45.
25. S. Pienar and Anthony Simpson, *South Africa: Two Views of Separate Development* (London: Oxford University Press, 1960), p. 25.
26. Karl Marx and Frederick Engels, *Selected Works* (Moscow: Progress Publishers, 1969), 1:397.
27. C. W. DeKiewiet, *The Anatomy of South African Misery* (London: Oxford University Press, 1956), p. 25.
28. Jan C. Smuts, Jr., *Jan Christian Smuts: A Biography* (London: Cassell and Co., 1952), pp. 305–6.
29. Christopher Caudwell, *Studies and Further Studies in a Dying Culture* (New York: Dodd, Mead and Co., 1948), p. 151.
30. Quoted in Hancock, *Smuts: Field of Force,* p. 473.
31. DeKiewiet, *South African Misery,* p. 47.
32. Pienar and Simpson, *Separate Development,* p. 25.
33. Ibid., p. 36.
34. Ibid., p. 21.
35. See Maurice Cornforth, *The Theory of Knowledge* (New York: Little New World Paper Books, 1955), p. 100.
36. DeKiewiet, *South African Misery,* p. 32.
37. Aimé Cèsaire, *Discourse on Colonialism* (New York: Monthly Review Press, 1972), p. 9.
38. Quoted in Vitalli Vygodoskii, *Book For All Time,* p. 150.
39. Victor Alba, *Nationalists Without Nations: The Oligarchy Versus the People—Latin America* (New York: Frederick A. Praeger, 1968), pp. 6–7.

40. Paul Q. Hirst, *Problems and Advances in the Theory of Ideology* (Cambridge: Cambridge University Communist Party, 1976), p. 7.

41. Harold Wolpe, "Capitalism and Cheap Labour Power in South Africa: From Segregation to Apartheid" (M.S. thesis, Polytechnic of North London, 1973), p. 23.

42. H. J. and Ray Simons, *Class and Colour in South Africa: 1850–1950* (Baltimore: Penguin Books, 1969), p. 328.

43. Ibid., p. 623.

44. Stanley Trapido, "Political Institutions and Afrikaner Social Structure in the Republic of South Africa," in *African Politics and Society,* ed. Irving Leonard Markovitz (New York: The Free Press, 1970), p. 369.

45. Quoted in H. L. Lawson, "The Economic Basis of Afrikaner Nationalism," *Liberation,* no. 27 (September 1957): 18.

46. South Africa, *Assembly Debates,* col. 4246, May 13, 1954.

47. South Africa, *Assembly Debates,* col. 1047, February 6, 1956.

48. Quoted in Basil Davidson, *Report on Southern Africa* (London: Jonathan Cape, 1952), p. 26.

49. Gottscholk, "Race and Economics," p. 13.

50. Niccole Machiavelli, *The Prince* (London: Fontana, 1972), pp. 122–43.

51. Ibid., p. 216.

52. Quoted in Kuper, *Passive Resistance,* pp. 32–33.

53. Ibid., p. 33.

54. Ibid.

55. DeKiewiet, *South African Misery,* p. 48.

56. Quoted in Henri Lefebvre, *The Sociology of Marx* (New York: Random House, Vintage Books, 1969), p. 84.

57. Burrows Dunham, *Heroes and Heretics: A Social History of Dissent* (New York: Alfred A. Knopf, 1964), p. 304.

58. W. E. B. Du Bois, "African Roots of War," *Monthly Review* 24, no. 11 (April 1973): 40.

Notes to Chapter 10

1. Antonio Gramsci, *Selections from the Prison Notebooks of Antonio Gramsci,* ed. Quintin Hoare and Geoffrey Nowell Smith (London: Lawrence and Wischart, 1971), pp. 3–23, 123–205, 378–472.

2. Edward Roux, *Time Longer Than Rope: A History of The Black Man's*

Struggle for Freedom in South Africa (Madison: University of Wisconsin Press, 1965), p. 87.

3. See Ralph Horwitz, *The Political Economy of South Africa* (New York: Frederick A. Praeger, 1967), p. 92.

4. Raymond L. Buell, *The Native Problem in Africa* (New York: Macmillan Co., 1928), 1:130.

5. E. D. Napier, *Excursions in Southern Africa,* 2 vols. (London: W. Shoberl, 1849), 1:9–10.

6. Monica Wilson and Leonard Thompson, eds. *The Oxford History of South Africa* (New York: Oxford University Press), vol. 1, *South Africa to 1870* (1969), p. 212.

7. James Bryce, *Impressions of South Africa* (1897; reprint ed., New York: New American Library, 1969), p. 477.

8. G. E. Cory, *The Rise of South Africa,* 6 vols. (Cape Town: Struik), vol. 5, *From 1846 to 1853* (1965), p. 365.

9. Wilson and Thompson, eds., *The Oxford History,* 1:353.

10. Ibid., p. 355.

11. Quoted in Jordan Ngubane, *An African Looks at Apartheid* (New York: Frederick A. Praeger, 1963), p. 43.

12. C. W. DeKiewiet, *A History of South Africa: Social and Economic* (London: Oxford University Press, 1957), p. 104.

13. Quoted in Ngubane, *African Looks at Apartheid,* p. 45.

14. Great Britain, *Cabinet Papers,* Sir Robert Herbert, "Future Policy in Zululand and South Africa Generally" 1 (March 10, 1879), c.o. 806/123.

15. Bryce, *Impressions,* p. 162.

16. Friedrich Engels, *The Origin of the Family, Private Property and the State* (New York: International Publishers, 1972), p. 351.

17. See A. Lerumo, *Fifty Fighting Years: The Communist Party of South Africa, 1921–1971* (London: Inkululeko Publishers, 1971), p. 15.

18. DeKiewiet, *History of South Africa,* p. 104.

19. Lionel Forman, "Chapters in the History of the March to Freedom," *New Age,* Cape Town, 1959.

20. See Colin Bundy, "Vorster's Restless Slaves," *New Statesman,* February 16, 1973, p. 228.

21. See Roux, *Time Longer Than Rope,* p. 108.

22. Ibid., p. 110.

23. Quoted in ibid.

24. Quoted in Peter Welsh, *The Rise of African Nationalism in South Africa: The African National Congress 1912–1952* (Los Angeles: University of California Press, 1971), p. 34.

25. See Buell, *Native Problem,* p. 121.

26. See Ngubane, *African Looks at Apartheid*, p. 80.
27. Daniel Kunene, "Deculturation—The African Writer's Response," *Africa Today* 15, no. 4 (1968): 23–24.
28. Roux, *Time Longer Than Rope*, p. 129.
29. Forman, "March to Freedom," p. 6.
30. H. J. and Ray Simons, *Class and Colour in South Africa: 1850–1950* (Baltimore: Penguin Books, 1969), p. 364.
31. Martin Legassick, "Class and Nationalism in South Africa Protest," *East African Studies* 15 (1973): 6–7.
32. Roux, *Time Longer Than Rope,* p. 196.
33. Gramsci, *Prison Notebooks*, p. 417.
34. Teresa Zania, "The I.C.U.," *The African Communist,* 38 (third quarter 1969): 72.
35. *The Workers Herald*, January 9, 1925.
36. Quoted in Buell, *Native Problem*, p. 124.
37. F. Meli, "A Nation Is Born," *The African Communist*, no. 48 (first quarter 1972): 25.
38. Roux, *Time Longer Than Rope*, p. 272.
39. Mary Benson, *The Struggle for a Birthright* (London: Penguin Books, 1966), p. 67.
40. Simons and Simons, *Class and Colour*, p. 425.
41. Quoted in Duma Nokive, "The Struggle for National Liberation in South Africa," in *Against Racism and Neo-Colonialism: For the Liberation of South Africa* (Berlin: Afro-Asian Solidarity Committee, 1968), p. 24.

Notes to Chapter 11

1. V. I. Lenin, *Collected Works* (Moscow: Foreign Languages Publishing House, 1968), 22:312.
2. See Y. Krasin, *The Dialectics of Revolutionary Process: Problems of Methodology* (Moscow: Novosti Press Agency Publishing House, 1972), p. 105.
3. Quoted in Ben Turok, "South Africa: The Violent Alternative," in *The Socialist Register 1972*, ed. Ralph Miliband and John Savile (London: The Merlin Press, 1972), p. 263.
4. Ibid., p. 265.
5. Antonio Gramsci, *The Modern Prince and Other Writings* (New York: International Publishers, 1954), pp. 204–5.
6. See Turok, "The Violent Alternative," p. 271.

7. Mary Benson, *The Struggle for a Birthright* (London: Penguin Books, 1966), p. 160.
8. *New Age* (Johannesburg), December 12, 1959.
9. A. Lerumo, *Fifty Fighting Years: The Communist Party of South Africa, 1921–1971* (London: Inkululeko Publications, 1971), p. 90.
10. Joe Matthews, "On the History of the African National Congress," *Fighting Talk* 15, no. 5 (1961): 5.
11. *New Age* (Johannesburg), December 26, 1954.
12. Benson, *Struggle for a Birthright,* p. 208.
13. See *Bantu World*, November 15, 1952.
14. George Padmore, *Pan-Africanism or Communism? The Struggle for Africa* (London: Dennis Dobson, 1956), p. 21.
15. *Africa South* 3, no. 4 (1958): 31.
16. I. I. Potekhin, *African Problems* (Moscow: Nauka Publishing House, 1968), p. 117.
17. *The Pan-Africanist Venture in Retrospect* (Non-European Unity Movement, September 1960).
18. Benson, *Struggle for a Birthright*, p. 208.
19. Ibid.
20. Eddie Roux, *Time Longer Than Rope: A History of the Black Man's Struggle for Freedom in South Africa* (Madison: University of Wisconsin Press, 1966), p. 405.
21. *Africa South in Exile* (July-September 1960): 12–13.
22. Ibid., p. 15.
23. Ibid.
24. Quoted in Lerumo, *Fifty Fighting Years*, p. 103.
25. Rosa Luxemburg, *Social Reform or Revolution* (New York: Pathfinder Press, 1971), p. 25.
26. V. I. Lenin, *"Left"-Wing Communism: An Infantile Disorder* (New York: International Publishers, 1940), pp. 76–77.
27. United Nations, Department of Political and Security Council Affairs, Center Against Apartheid, "Steve Biko (1948–1977), Fighter Against Apartheid and Apostle of Black Consciousness," October 1977, p. 2.
28. See United Nations, Unit on Apartheid, *African Workers Strike Against Apartheid,* by Frere Ginwala, June 1973.
29. Colin Legum, *A Republic in Trouble: South Africa 1972–73* (London: Rex Collings, 1973), p. 53.
30. R. A. Johnson, *How Long Can South Africa Survive?* (London: Macmillan, 1977), p. 188.
31. Karl Marx and Frederick Engels, *Selected Works* (Moscow: Foreign Languages Publishing House, 1962), p. 541.

Index

Aborigines Protection Society, 59
African children: pass system for, 134; as superfluous appendages, 144
African elite: early struggles of, 261–63, 274–78; purpose of developing, 148; after 1946 mine strike, 295; in urban industrial areas, 69
African Mine Workers' Union (AMWU), 293
African National Congress, see South African National Congress
African nationalism: apartheid to destroy, 241 (see also Apartheid); emergence of radical, 292–93; Pan-African Congress and, 307–9; see also Opposition; South African National Congress
African peasants: becoming wage laborers, 59, 60; see also Cattle confiscation; Land confiscation
African People's Organization (APO), 297
African proletariat: distinguishing characteristics of, 53; growth of, 262; pass system and, see Pass system; peasants deprived of their means of subsistence becoming members of, 59, 60; in public works, 42, 60, 134; reduced to commodity, 159–60; relative quantitative deployment of, on labor market, 150–62; wages of, 157–159; see also Apartheid; Migrant-labor system; Rural proletariat

African societies, 22–43; destruction of, 36–43; effects of British conquest on, 33–36; impact of Dutch conquest on, 25–33; see also Cultural domination; *and specific African societies*
African subsistence economy, 100; destruction of, 71, 73–76; legislation to destroy, 84–87; purpose served by destruction of, 59, 123; see also Cattle confiscation; Land confiscation
African trade unions, see Trade unions
African urban settlements, 129–31
African women: barred from cities, 125, 141; British attack inferior status of, 76–77; in labor force, 128; pass system for, 134; in struggle against pass laws, 306; as superfluous appendages, 144
Afrikaner agriculture: apartheid to meet labor demands of, 142–43; border industries, 99–100, 134–36; development of, 172–74; effects of industrialization on rural bourgeoisie, 182; labor shortages in (1960s), 143, 145, 146; legislation to ensure labor supply for, 134–35 (see also Pass system); urban growth and, 133
Afrikaner bourgeoisie: alliance between Afrikaner working class and, 174, 182–89; consolidation of power by, 169–72; cornerstone of

Selected Modern Reader Paperbacks